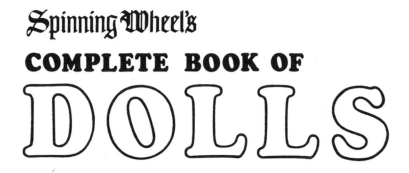

Spinning Wheel's
COMPLETE BOOK OF
DOLLS

Spinning Wheel's

COMPLETE BOOK OF

DOLLS

edited by Albert Christian Revi

Galahad Books, New York

Table of Contents

Foreword

Why do people collect dolls? The late Genevieve Angione, herself an avid doll collector and author of several articles and a book about dolls, once said that people collect dolls to replace their children who have grown up and moved away, or to compensate for the children they never had. Right or wrong, collecting dolls has become one of the most popular fields in the world of antiques, growing by leaps and bounds within the last twenty-five years or more. And believe it or not, men also collect dolls — it's not the exclusive province of women you might think it to be.

Aware of this growing interest in dolls, the Editors of *Spinning Wheel* have been offering their readers the most informative and factual articles available about dolls. Many of the authors of articles in this book eventually wrote books about dolls and doll collecting. Besides Mrs. Angione, the late Luella Hart, Flora Gill Jacobs, and the Colemans — Dorothy, Elizabeth, and Evelyn, have all written excellent monographs on dolls, incorporating much of the material that appeared in their *Spinning Wheel* articles. We've selected the best of these articles and compiled them into one volume which we feel certain will be both informative and helpful to beginner as well as seasoned collectors of dolls.

Covered here are dolls that are rare and dolls that are not-so-rare; dolls made of porcelain, bisque, rubber, composition, wax, plastic, wood, paper, apples, nuts, corn

Back row: large Kestner doll; large Jumeau doll. Middle row: Handwerk doll; Gladie Boy doll; Kestner boy doll; S.F.B.J. "Twerp" doll. In front: Armand Marseille black baby doll. All dolls from the collection of Mrs. John Elicker.

husks, metal, and even rags. What endears them to collectors is that they represent, for the most part, children of various ages, or some favorite movie star or comic strip character. It would seem that nostalgia, rather than an awareness for finely wrought details, is what makes a doll collectible. Some dolls made of mundane materials have exquisitely detailed features, while many dolls made of porcelain or bisque — considered high grade materials, are rather crudely fashioned.

Costumes for dolls range from superbly made dresses and costumes of silk, satin, velvet and lace, to simple printed cotton fabrics. Extravagant or inexpensive, knowledgeble collectors all agree that the costume should be original to the doll. Replacement costumes of the period are tolerated, but not recommended. Dresses lovingly made by the original owner or her mother, and contemporary to the doll, are also acceptable to collectors. Dolls that have had limbs, heads, bodies or other parts replaced for one reason or another are permissible only if the replacements are exact replicas of the originals.

Most of the dolls discussed in this book are still available to collectors at reasonable prices. Fine French and German fashion dolls are not within the reach of collectors of modest means, of course. But the later composition dolls and others contemporary to them are all relatively inexpensive and readily available from people who buy and sell dolls. New collectors are urged to join local chapters of the United Federation of Doll Clubs, Inc. The address of a chapter near you can often be gotten from a dealer in your area who sells dolls. Chances are he or she is a member, too.

While this book has been broken down into chapters dealing with American, English, French and German dolls, plus other categories of specialized interest, it isn't meant to imply that collectors should limit themselves to just one of these areas. On the contrary, there are many good reasons for buying dolls made in various countries, including Japan. Comparison studies of dolls made in all parts of the world will broaden your knowledge and appreciation.

For several years now, members of the National Institute of American Doll Artists, Inc., have been producing superbly hand-crafted dolls which collectors all over the country are buying with enthusiasm. Highly skilled in their trade, their work must pass the judgment of their peers before they are accepted as members of this auspicious group. Many of these artists are covered in this book. Their works vary from tiny one-inch tall dolls to life-size mannequins; in some cases they are portraits of real children and adults. Some of these doll artists will be introduced to the reader by R. Lane Herron, himself a distinguished member of the N.I.A.D.A

Spinning Wheel's Complete Book of Dolls covers all facets of doll collecting. It isn't just all-encompassing — it's fact-filled.

Albert Christian Revi, Editor
Spinning Wheel Magazine
Hanover, PA 17331

American Dolls

The first dolls played with by colonial American children were, of course, imported from England. The American doll industry didn't really begin in earnest until rather late in the 19th century. One of the earliest and most prominent American doll manufacturers was Philip Goldsmith, about whom Dorothy S. Coleman wrote: "In Cincinnati, Ohio, and across the Ohio River in Covington, Kentucky, there was a sizeable settlement of manufacturers and distributors of dolls, toys, and games during the last half of the 19th century. One of the most famous of these was Philip Goldsmith who both made and distributed dolls and dolls' bodies." Later, Louis Amberg, another well-known 19th century doll manufacturer, opened his factory at a location formerly occupied by Goldsmith. In more recent times, Joseph Kallus, manufacturer of the famous Kewpie dolls designed by Rose O'Neill, made his mark in the doll industry. Others, like Madame Alexander, have also made collectible dolls. These are among the best-known names in the world of dolls; but of late, members of the National Institute of American Doll Artists, Inc. have been keeping alive the high quality of American dolls handed down to them by their predecessors.

"Tommy Bangs," an all-composition doll made in America by **Madame Alexander,** about 1950. Collection Dorothy S. Coleman. D'Aquilla photo.

INTRODUCTION

Dolls made by Philip Goldsmith are considered rare by collectors, but a large number must have been produced. They were made over a period of about 25 years, 1870–1894, and the size of the factories suggests a fairly large output. Most of these dolls have perished, but there still must remain some that have not been identified as Goldsmith dolls due to lack of information about them.

It is hoped that the information given in this article will enable collectors to identify many more Goldsmith dolls and to have a greater appreciation of them.

The excerpts from Mrs. Goldsmith's autobiography, the obituary, and notebook material, all were made available through the kindness of her son, Mr. Emil Goldsmith of Cincinnati.

PHILIP GOLDSMITH (1844-1894)

An American Dollmaker

by DOROTHY S. COLEMAN

This doll belongs to one of the great granddaughters of Philip Goldsmith. It has a red corset and red leather boots. The stockings are white with circular stripes of red. This type may be earlier than the bodies with all red stockings or it may be only a variation. The head is of untinted bisque with an unusual hairdo.
Courtesy of Minette Goldsmith Hoffheimer.

IN CINCINNATI, OHIO, and across the Ohio River in Covington, Kentucky, there was a sizeable settlement of manufacturers and distributors of dolls, toys, and games during the last half of the 19th century. One of the most famous of these was Philip Goldsmith who both made and distributed dolls and dolls' bodies. He was in this business for well over a decade before 1885 when he patented a doll's body with a corset on it.

Philip was born in 1844 in Prague, Bohemia, and come to America in 1861. He settled in Milwaukee and married Sophia Heller, a talented young lady who helped him in his business. It is thanks to her autobiography, begun in 1904, and concluded on Armistice Day, 1918, that we know so much about Philip Goldsmith, his family and their contributions to the doll world. Sophia Goldsmith always referred to Philip as "Papa" in her autobiography. Mrs. Goldsmith tells of the Goldsmith's arrival in Cincinnati, "Papa and his brother left (Chicago) for Cincinnati. One week later I received a letter to come to Cincinnati. . . . After inexperienced traveling in a sleeper I arrived at Cincinnati March 25th, 1869. . . . In the afternoon Papa took me to the store which they had rented 242 (246 W.) Fifth Street. . . . The past few years the number has been changed to 312 West Fifth Street. He and his brother Henry were partners. $500.00 they invested together, only half of a store, about 15 feet long. It was to be a 25¢ store, no more and no less were the articles to sell. . . .

"Christmas came and we had a fine business. I must mention a marked occurence. Papa bought for cash now. There was a sale of a double wheel with a wooden man in the center, with a handle attached. It represented Weston the first pedestrian,* ("Pedestrian" was the name of an early bicycle.) as a try out in this country.

"Papa bought a few cases with a good profit for us and same was made to sell for $2.00 apiece and we sold them for 25¢. Our store could have been five times the size it was and it would not have held all the people who came to buy the toy. Finally Papa bought the entire lot about thirty-two dozen after consulting me. The bargain was so great that policemen had to be put at the entrance. A half square down the street people stood and it was just like a mob. One man became so furious because he could not get a toy he threw over the red hot stove. We thought we would all be burned to death. At 3:30 in the morning we closed our doors, with fourteen clerks behind the counters, we could not get hands enough.

First building occupied by Philip Goldsmith.

AMERICAN

Goldsmith was employed as a clerk at 145 Walnut Street, an address made famous a few years later by Louis Amberg, a well-known doll manufacturer. Across the street at 144 Walnut Street, Strobel & Wilken carried on a toy and doll business for years. Charles Goldsmith was employed by Fechheimer who from 1881–1889 was a partner of Louis Amberg. The relationship, if any, of these other Goldsmiths to Philip is not known.

In 1875 Philip Goldsmith had a display at the Cincinnati Exhibition. Soon after that, business grew poor. About 1878 Goldsmith severed his partnership with Flechter and each of

"During that time (1869–1870) a Mr. (Wolf) Flechter, manufactured doll bodies which were much purchased for dolls' heads. Later the man manufactured baseballs. We bought from this man for years. I think all he could manufacture. Business was very satisfactory. . . . (ca. 1874) The manufacturer Flechter from Covington tried to induce Papa to become a partner in manufacturing of dolls' bodies and baseballs which he finally did."

Flechter's shop was located at 714 Madison Avenue, Covington. He made and repaired dolls for the Fall and Christmas season and made baseballs for the Spring and Summer season. The Cincinnati City Directories tell us that Philip Goldsmith kept his store at 246 West Fifth Street at least through 1875. At that time Harry

Right: All of the limbs on this doll are made in the same manner as those found on the Goldsmith corset body dolls but it does **not** have a corset. It should be noted that the laces and tassels on the boots are replacements made some time ago. The brown leather hands have the customary round sticks in each finger. The leather boots are blue and the stockings have blue circular stripes. The stockings end a short distance below the knee joint and have a simulated garter band at the top which is also a Goldsmith doll characteristic. This type of bisque head is most frequently found on lady type kid bodies and it is rarely certain that bodies and heads have always been together. However, a similar body and head have been found together in the Children's Museum of Indianapolis. Since Goldsmith dolls are rare, it probably is more than a coincidence to find the same type of head on more than one of these bodies. This type of head also is found on several of the Lacmann bodies which were patented in 1871 and 1874 and made in Philadelphia. (See illustrations 1052 and 1053 in the Coleman **Collector's Encyclopedia of Dolls**) It seems to be a logical conclusion that the doll pictured above is a Goldsmith doll made prior to his patent for a corset body. These heads all have closed mouths, applied ears and cork pates, which characterize dolls made in France. A similar type body in the Children's Museum of Indianapolis has a marked "F. G." French bisque head. Height of Doll 23 inches.
Courtesy of the Western Reserve Historical Society. Photograph by Elroy Sanford.

Building occupied by Philip Goldsmith 1880–1891.

the men had their own factory where both baseballs and dolls were made.

Mrs. Goldsmith recollects these difficult times. "Business was poor, expenses large. . . . He (Papa) finally traveled for the dolls' bodies and baseball factory in Covington of which he became a partner. The factory was situated at the corner of 7th and Madison Avenue upstairs. . . . If I would be willing to help him he thought by moving to Covington we could live cheaper and I could assist him in the factory while he was on the road.

"February 15, 1878 we moved to Covington. . . . Papa had to borrow $1,000.00. . . . There was no other way of getting assistance. Papa had saved a few sewing machines which was all he had left to (re) start the business with."

Their struggles were rewarded and Mrs. Goldsmith wrote that by 1879 "Business was fine. It seemed as if all were coming our way again once more. Dear Papa worked hard and he showed it. I still kept going to the factory when I was able to do so. I had learnt to sew baseballs so as to be able to instruct the girls. After a while we dressed dolls. I made patterns for them and assisted in dressing them. . . ." (Mrs. Goldsmith had been a dressmaker at one time.)

"By this time patent dolls' heads and wax heads with hair were manufactured. Business was getting larger. . . . Dear good Papa. . . . Business was very good with him. At this time he was contemplating to rent the Alison (Elliston) House, an old hotel on Russell Street near Pike. It contained fifty two rooms. It was remodeled and the factory moved."

The Elliston Hotel, located on the northwest corner of Russell and Harvey Streets, in its day was one of the most fashionable southern hotels. It consisted of two large buildings which in 1880 were converted into the P. Goldsmith & Co. factory. A picture of the buildings shows the larger one

the corner to be five stories high. The words "P. Goldsmith & Co. Toy Manufacturers, Baseballs, Dolls Bodies & Doll Heads" were written in large letters on the building. A flag flying from the roof bore the legend, "American Toy Co."

An article published in *Playthings* Magazine in December 1908 describes the manufacturing process used in this factory as follows:

"The first doll manufactured in this Covington factory was what was styled the patent-head doll. It was a composition of flour, glue and pulp ground up. The mixture was put into a tub and worked with the feet in a truly primitive way until a dough resembling that of a pie crust, was produced. The dough was rolled out to a desired thickness and then put in a mold made of sulphur. This mold

Corset body made by Philip Goldsmith. The patent date is stamped on the upper part of the body, under the head. The corset, shoes and stockings are in red. There are two tassels, each lace which crisscrosses up the boot, ends in a tassel. There are crisscross lacings up the front of the corset and rickrack around the top of the corset. The two diagonal pieces of tape do not belong on the body. The Height of doll 18 inches. Coleman Collection.

was made in three parts; one for the back of the head and two for the face, which was cut in halves. After trimming off the dough clinging to the molds, the molds were placed on shelves in a hot room where the composition was dried.

"When the sulphur molds were removed from the hot room the now half doll heads were edged with the same composition as above described by means of a stick resembling a drumstick, and was used to stuff in the dough around the half edges, and thus connect the two halves after the stick was made wet. The heads, being connected, were thoroughly hardened again in the drying room. The rough edges were then trimmed off with a sharp knife and sandpapered. The heads were then ready for the painting.

"The first step in the process of painting was to dip the head in flesh-colored paint and then set it down to drip off. Following this, the eyes were painted in, then the hair, and finally the eyelashes and the eyebrows. A piece of cotton, dipped in a red powder, gave color to the cheeks. After the head dried it was then ready for the finishing process, which consisted of two coats of varnish to prevent the colors from wiping off.

"The doll bodics were made of muslin, which was stuffed with hair and sawdust. The upper part of the arm was made of muslin, while the lower part was made of two pieces of leather, stitched together to represent fingers. The finger stitching was guided by small sticks about the size of match sticks, which were inserted in the leather. The arms were stuffed with sawdust, and at the shoulder joints some cattle hair was used to keep the sawdust from coming out. The shoes for the doll were made of red and blue cambric."

Mrs. Goldsmith continues her story:

"At this time (ca. 1880) Uncle Adolph (Goldsmith) was with Papa in business. All went well and business increased. Dolls' heads with hair, wax figures, toys, etc. were quite extensively manufactured especially show figures. Many workmen were imported from Nurnberg, business was spreading and dear Papa was looked upon as a very rich merchant. . . . He had his team of fine horses. Uncle Adolph at this time was foreman in the doll body department. . . ."

In 1882 Philip Goldsmith advertised that his company made "baseballs, doll bodies, doll heads, indestructible dolls, and novelty toys." At that time the term "indestructible" was generally applied to certain types of composition of which dolls were made.

Competition with imported European dolls was growing more and more keen. In 1880 Charles Dotter of Bawo & Dotter, an international company, had patented in the U.S. a dolls' body with corsets simulated by a printed section. The china heads for these dolls were imported from Europe and it is not known whether the bodies themselves were also made in Europe. Being a resourceful man, Philip Goldsmith patented an improved type of doll's body with a corset as an integral part of the body. The article in *Playthings* of December 1908 describes his invention:

"In 1885 Mr. Goldsmith invented the corset body doll, which was the same as the ordinary stuffed doll. A piece of red or blue cambric, with rickrack on the edge, was sewed on the body. This doll became an instantaneous success, and the demand became so great that the factory was compelled to work a night turn. These dolls were shipped loose in the cases, as boxes could not be secured fast enough to meet the orders. In 1885 experiments were made in the Cincinnati potteries with bisque doll heads, but the clay continually cracked and the experiments were finally abandoned. As side line, Mr. Goldsmith began the manufacture of wax figures for window display purposes and secured skilled help from Sonneberg, Europe, for working up this branch of the business. The business grew and all kinds of show forms were manufactured."

A Montgomery Ward & Co. catalog of 1887 lists, "Patent Corset Bodies (no head), entirely new, with seat, kid arms, colored stockings, shoes with tassels, and adjustable lace corsets (105)—

Length	Each	Doz.
10 in.	$0.24	$2.50
13½ in.	.32	3.50
16½ in.	.48	5.00

The picture of this doll's body is almost the same as that shown on the 1885 patent papers.

As the business increased so did the need for leather and by 1888 Philip Goldsmith had an interest in a local tannery where his son Oscar was employed. Competition was growing at home as well as abroad. Arnoldt began to manufacture dolls in 1880 and the Klein doll factory began in 1885, both in Cincinnati. Though there were several large toy distributors in Cincinnati at this time, notably among them Strobel & Wilken and Fechheimer & Amberg, Goldsmith decided to branch out to other cities. We return to Mrs. Goldsmith's autobiography for details about this period:

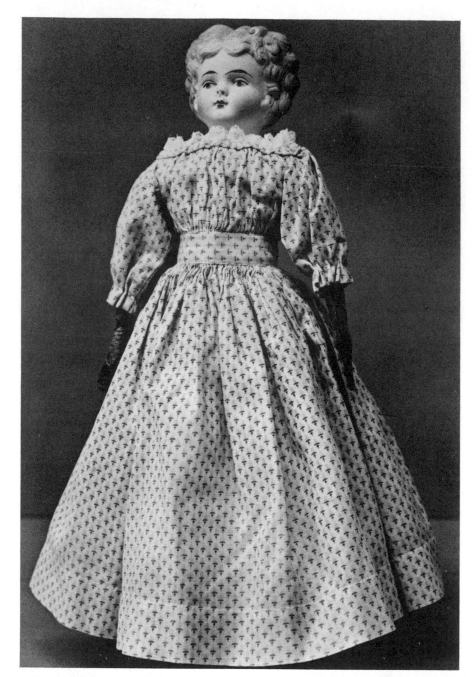

Goldsmith corset bodied doll has brown leather hands with round sticks in each finger. The boots are red leather and the stockings are red cloth to a little below the knee joint. These corsets appear to always be made in either red or blue cloth and the boots and stockings have matching colors. Sometimes the boots were made of imitation leather instead of real leather. This head is of untinted bisque. The doll wears an old blue and white cotton print dress. The lace at the neck is not old. Height of doll 14 inches. Courtesy of the Western Reserve Historical Society. Photograph by Elroy Sanford.

"Several years previous (to 1890) dear Papa brought to our home a Mr. Hensel from Pittsburgh with whom he did business. . . . Another, his name was Shueck. . . . Hensel and Shueck became partners in a toy house in Chicago. Papa was to import goods for this firm for a certain percent profit. All went well for a time. Goods were imported and shipped for this firm in Chicago. . . . Shueck would come occasionally to Cincinnati." In the 1890 Chicago Directory Schueck & Recht were located at 79 Wabash while Strobel & Wilken were located at 50–51 State Street. Both firms were described as "manufacturers" and "wholesale toy" dealers.

Mrs. Goldsmith continues, "Papa was interested at that time in Steinharter's tannery and gradually he bought it out. . . . November 26th 1890 dear Papa and Mr. Cairo left for Nurnberg, Europe. After three months trip they returned well satisfied with their enterprise. The trip was a business one. . . . Papa had bought several other business properties. Business went along successfully and we enjoyed prosperity." Philip Goldsmith's son, Emil, says that his father brought back from Nurnberg, two men who were trained in ceramic manufacturing.

The *Playthings* article of December 1908 tells us: "In 1890 Mr. Goldsmith brought a machine from Europe for making a kid leather body doll, but could not compete with the foreign trade in this line, although protected by a duty of 35 percent. The demand for the kid leather and the bisque head doll gradually began to cut into the product of P. Goldsmith Co., these foreign dolls being sold as cheap in 1891 as the cambric body with patent head made in this country.

"To maintain his ground, Mr. Goldsmith then began to make a better head. He put a coating of wax on the patent head doll, used imitation hair and put in glass eyes imported from Europe. He also commenced the manufacture of an imitation bisque head doll, which was made by the same process as the patent head, but instead of using a finish of varnish, ether was used to give a dull finish."

In 1890 Philip Goldsmith was assigned by Julius Wolf one half the right in his patent for attaching arms on a body, preferably made of papiermache.

Tragedy descended and Mrs. Goldsmith tells of the horror of a night in April 1891:

"Our baby Emil was five weeks old, I remember the fire bells rang. From our window we could see the flames. On awakening our first thought was our factory, at the same time the doorbell rang. The private policeman was there to tell us it was our factory. How well I remember that it took less time than to explain. Edgar (one of her sons) was dressed and out of the house. Poor Papa was so stunned from it all arrangements were made to remove the factory to Hemingray's glass house which had been put into good condition for manufacturing purposes. Our building was packed for a large shipment for the next morning. It was a sad blow and an enormous loss.

"Four hours later Papa and the boys came home. Alfred and Edgar were all worn out. Our dear Papa, I can see him as if yesterday, haggard and an altered man for he well knew what loss it meant for him. He always thought it was one of the discharged foremen who took to drink and set the building on fire.

"Business in the new building was increasing yet I noticed Papa had a good many cares and many irons in the fire brought him many sleepless hours."

At this time several of his sons were working in the business of P. Goldsmith & Co. Alfred was a clerk and Oscar Goldsmith was bookkeeper. By 1892 Alfred had become manager

Fig.1.

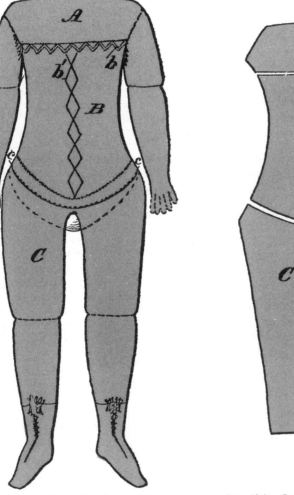

Fig.2.

Fig.3.

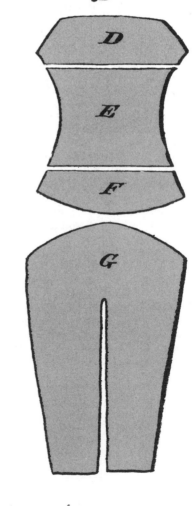

Illustrations from patent papers issued to Philip Goldsmith in 1885. At that time two years of grace were permitted before an application was made for a patent. Thus, Goldsmith could not have made corset bodied dolls earlier than 1883 and his patent would have expired in 1902. In this document, Goldsmith's given name was misspelled "Philipp." This was the fault of his attorney, for the name is spelled with only one "p" in his obituaries, and elsewhere. The patent date, "PATD. DEC.15,1885" is found on doll's bodies stamped in red or blue ink on the top of the chest where "A" is located on Fig. I in the diagram.

and Oscar was a traveling salesman for the Goldsmith Company. The new location for the factory was on the northwest corner of 2nd and Madison Streets, formerly occupied by the Hemingray glass factory.

The preceding selections from the autobiography were written in 1904 while the following excerpt was written in 1918:

"July 1894 they (Papa and two of his sons) left for Cedar Lake. . . . No room was to be had in the hotel at Cedar Lake so they lived across the lake from Cousin Ida Heller at Zimmerman's. . . . His untimely death came at Cedar Lake, Wisconsin through a terrible storm, as he could not swim."

His obituary from *The Post*, Covington, July 12, 1894 is as follows:

"DROWNED"

Fate of P. Goldsmith, the Doll Manufacturer,

While Enjoying an Outing at Cedar Lake.

He meets his death beneath the Waves.

"The family of P. Goldsmith, the toy manufacturer of Covington, was plunged into grief by a telegram received yesterday announcing his death by drowning at Cedar Lake, Wisconsin.

"Mr. Goldsmith was enjoying an outing there in company with his two youngest sons and his brother, A. Goldsmith, of the Cincinnati Freie Presse, and had been at the lakes about a week.

"The first telegram simply announced the fact without giving details. Late last night a second wire was received stating that the body had been recovered and was on its way to Covington, where it will arrive this evening.

"Mr. Goldsmith was 50 years old, and was senior partner in the firm of P. Goldsmith & Sons, manufacturers of toys and show goods at Second and Madison Avenue. He was a native of Austria, and came to this country when 17 years of age, with only a few cents in his pocket. With a letter of introduction which he brought to a

Building occupied by Philip Goldsmith after the 1891 fire.

gentleman in New York he borrowed $100 and set out for the West. He got as far as Milwaukee, where he settled down to peddling notions. In about four years Mr. Goldsmith had accumulated $1500. He married and moved to Chicago, where he went into the dry goods business.

"A few years later he came to Covington and opened the first 25-cent store in the city, and soon branched into the manufacture of baseballs, toys and wax show figures.

"Mr. Goldsmith was noted for his kindness to the poor, and performed many acts of charity in a quiet, unostentatious way. Last Christmas he furnished many of the dolls which were distributed by The Post, in Cincinnati, to the poor children of that city and Covington."

After Philip Goldsmith's death a small notebook was found among his personal belongings. This notebook contains many names and various notes, the full meaning of which elude us unfortunately. However, there are some names and notations of great interest to doll collectors. The name Amberg or L. Amberg, no doubt Louis Amberg, appears no less than thirteen times, once "stock and cases"

follows the name Amberg. The names Fechheimer, Amberg's partner, and Fahlbusch of the Cincinnati Doll Manufactory, also appear. The name Wolf appears several times and once it is next to L. W. & Co., which suggests that it could refer to Louis Wolf & Co., a famous contemporary doll manufacturer and distributor. The name Steiner appears frequently but there is no way of knowing whether this Steiner was related to any of the European Steiners who made dolls. "Bisque arms, Sample Dolls" are noted as well as just "Arms." "Red and Blue Thread" appear several times, once it is "Thread 40–." "Drill, 6 yds." and "Muslin" are noted. On a page under the heading "Corset Bodies" are found the following cryptic notations:

```
0/3  1/4  2/4  3/4  4/3  5/2
4 gro L 6–
1–20 dz H 125
3–12 - - 175
4–12 - - 2 –
5–12 - - 250
7–8 - - 375
1–4 gr A 350
2–2 - 550
432 -2- D 15 –
675 -2- 1350
```

Some of these notes are probably coded numbers and may refer to size or price or style. The first column seems to indicate quantity and the last column price.

Goldsmith's sons continued part of the business left by their father but they moved to Cincinnati and confined their products to "Baseballs, Sporting Goods" and "Show Figures and Forms" according to the signs on their factory building located at 207–211 West Pearl Street, Cincinnati. The sons did not continue the manufacture of dolls. Wolf Flechter disappeared from the Directories at about the same time that Philip Goldsmith did. A few years later, Amberg and Strobel & Wilken moved to New York City and thus ended an era of doll manufacturing and distribution in the Cincinnati area.

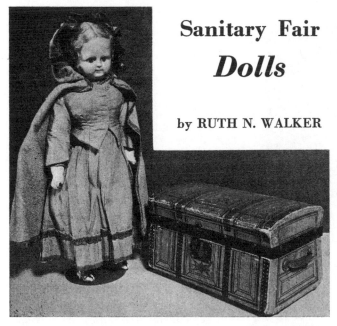

Sanitary Fair
Dolls

by RUTH N. WALKER

Left: *This wax-head doll with composition body, now in the Chicago Historical Museum, was dressed for the Great Western Fair in Chicago in gray wool trimmed with light blue ribbon. Pressed paper trunk holds additional clothing.* Above: *"Flora McFlimsey," Montanari-type wax doll, described in text.*

IN THE early days of the Civil War, a Commission was organized to cooperate with the Government in supplying comforts as well as necessities to the soldiers. This organization was called the Sanitary Commission, and the "Sanitary Fairs," which were held, in cities and villages, to raise money for its work produced more than four million dollars.

Dolls played a part in contributing to this sum. Reports from these Fairs, as given in the histories of the work of the Commission, invariably mention, and sometimes describe, dolls offered for sale or raffle.

An account in the Boston *Journal* of the Grand Fair held in Boston in December 1863 writes of a "live" doll which "cries quite naturally." A partial list of dolls sold there adds up to $700. "The History of the Great Southern Fair," held in Cincinnati, reports remarkable dolls on sale, but gives no word of the money realized from them. At both the Brooklyn and Manhattan, New York, Fairs, a great Shoe held a little girl dressed as The Old Woman who lived in it, surrounded by dolls for sale. Five of these dolls are now at the Brooklyn Museum. The Museum of the City of New York owns two china heads, dressed as bride and groom, contributed to the Poughkeepsie Sanitary Fair. A tailor costumed the groom.

Famous among the Sanitary Fair dolls is the wax "Rose Percy," named for the little girl who became her owner. She was chanced at the Great Metropolitan Fair in Manhattan in 1864, bringing the amazing sum of $1200. Her elaborate wardrobe of stylish silk and velvet gowns and dainty undergarments was made by the girls of Mrs. Hoffman's fashion-able boarding school from materials donated by Arnold & Constable. Gunther, the furrier, gave an ermine muff and tippet; Tiffany, a lovely coral necklace and monogrammed stationery. Doll and finery are now displayed in the foyer of the American Red Cross Headquarters in Washington.

Equally well known is "Flora McFlimsey," who took her name from the then popular verses concerning Miss Flora back from Paris with laden trunks but "nothing to wear." She was dressed by Philadelphia merchants for the Great Central Fair of Philadelphia. Corsetmakers, shoemakers, dressmakers, milliners, and jewelers contributed to a wardrobe estimated worth $500. She was chanced and brought in $250. She may now be seen, with her wardrobe, at the Philadelphia Historical Museum.

Above: *China doll with real hair wig, kid body, white muslin with pink silk overdress, and Saratoga trunk filled with pretties, was chanced at the Boston Fair, 1863; is now in author's collection.* Left: *"Rose Percy."*

Wax miniature and flowers, New Hampshire, ca. 1840-50. White silk dress on brown eyed figure; fruits include peaches, nuts, lemons, barberries, red cherries, leaves; very crude box covered with paper.

Shadow-Boxed Waxed Figures

By AMELIA E. MacSWIGGAN

Photographs Courtesy of Essex Museum.

THE proper young miss of the 1800s was offered many opportunities to learn the arts and crafts of her period. Accomplishment in embroidery, painting, sewing and writing were expected of all young ladies of culture and means. These were the "basics"—but instruction in all current fads and foibles was available, too.

Among "ladies' work taught by appointment" in most of the larger cities, wax work was often advertised. In the mid 1800s, Mrs. Abigail Hill, a popular teacher of the crafts in Boston, Massachusetts, listed wax work in her curriculum, along with painting on glass, needlework, and bead work.

For those to whom classes were not available, a number of publications dedicated to "Ladies' Fancy Work" appeared in the 1850s, filled with directions and suggestions for wax work. Godey's Magazines devoted chapter after chapter to the art, and gave full directions for making molds of plaster-of-paris for all sorts of fruits, berries, and flowers. Arrangements of wax fruits and flowers in combination with shells, leaves, dried grasses, even feathers, were suggested.

Shops sold wax in sheets to be tinted as desired by the addition of colored pigments while the wax was soft. Wax was also available in stick form of various widths and lengths with accompanying directions for use.

Such fruits as lemons, limes, oranges and berries were suggested for beginners, flowers and dolls for more advanced workers.

Most wax arrangements were assembled as table ornaments to be placed under glass domes, but occasionally pictures were made in this fashion and placed in so-called shadow boxes for hanging.

These wax pictures are interesting and unusual finds today. Those containing doll-like figures are often called "grave-yard dolls" by collectors who feel these quaint Victorian figures, surrounded by wax fruits and flowers were surely made as memorials.

The accompanying photographs present two specimens of this type. Very little is known of them. Whether they were made in memory of some child to be placed upon a little grave or hung in a saddened parlor, or were made simply as pictures for the enjoyment of the family, is anyone's guess.

These two dolls are very crudely fashioned. One rests in a bower of lace, surrounded by wax fruits, while the other, in a silk dress, stands in a bower of fruits and berries, flowers and leaves. Their small beady eyes, painted lips, hair, and eyebrows, show the unsophisticated touch, as do the frames and glass which cover them. The glass on the boxes is crude, greenish in color and full of bubbles, attesting to an early period. Frames and glass are put together with paste, thread and colored paper. The outside edges of one box are covered with gilt paper edging, the other has colored paper edging sewed on with thread.

Bright orange-red peaches about 2" in diameter, 2 lemons the same size overhang wax bust and hands held down with lace and ribbon bow in lace nest. Face is very crude, with red cheeks, brown hair. Wooden box covered with all sorts of colored paper.

The Kewpie collection, above, once Mrs. McDowell's, now dispersed among her married daughters, includes Kewpie decorated cereal dish and ashtray, along with Kewpie dolls in various poses. One of the lying-down Kewpies is on the cover to a stamp box; the other is on a pin tray.

Rose O'Neill's Kewpies

by KATHLEEN McDOWELL

ROSE O'Neill (1874–1944), author of several novels, and member of the Paris Beaux Art Salon, won lasting remembrance as the creator of Kewpie, an appealing little dream creature with wispy topknot, cherubic face, tiny wings, and fat little tummy, who went about doing good deeds.

Kewpie first appeared on paper. As O'Neill Latham (she was then using her own and her first husband's surnames), Rose O'Neill had drawn decorative angel heads for *Puck Magazine.* Edward Bok, editor of *Ladies Home Journal* suggested she complete the figures and have verses written to accompany her drawings. Her first page of Kewpies—she elected to write her own verse—appeared in *Ladies Home Journal* in 1909. In

1910, *Woman's Home Companion* used a series of "Dottie and the Kewpies," and the following year her book, *The Kewpies and Dolly Darling,* was published. In 1911–12, Kewpies appeared in *Pictorial Review,* and in 1915, in *Good Housekeeping.* (They showed up in *Good Housekeeping* in December 1961, too, along with a modern Kewpie doll, complete with wardrobe, put out by Cameo Doll Products Co.)

Almost as soon as Kewpie drawings appeared, children clamored for a "Kewpie to hold." The bisque Kewpie doll was Rose O'Neill's answer. She registered her Kewpie trademark for dolls on July 15, 1913, under her own name, Rose O'Neill Wilson. (Her second husband was author-playwright Harry Leon Wilson.) The earliest

bisque Kewpies were made in Germany by both the J. D. Kestner firm and by George Borgfeldt & Company of New York whose factory was there. Borgfeldt trademarked the Kewpies in Germany in 1913, afterward in France, England, and the United States. Soon other companies, authorized and unauthorized, in this country and abroad, were turning out Kewpies. Many were made in celluloid.

A popular series in bisque was the Kewpie Band, straight from the magazine pages with Wag, the Chief, a flag in his topknot, The Army, in soldier hat, The Cook, wearing an apron, The Gardener, The Carpenter, "Careful-of-his voice," in wrap-around head scarf, "Always-wears-his-over-shoes," The Life Preserver, The Instructor, with book of Useful Knowledge, "Careful-of-his-complexion," in sunbonnet, and clumsy little Blunderboo. Scootles, a real baby tourist to Kewpieville, was another so appealing that as a doll he was made in several sizes.

Kewpie motifs adorned all manner of novelties from children's desk sets to soap, rattles, and toy pianos. Manufacturers printed cloth with Kewpie designs for children's dresses, and with Kewpie dolls to be cut out and stuffed. Royal Rudolstadt, in Prussia, produced beautiful china play dishes, Kewpie decorated.

Kewpie never seems to age though his original little wings have disappeared with time. In 1928, he turned up as a soft cuddle toy for babies; in 1939, George Borgfeldt and Company registered the trademark again; recently Kewpie has appeared in plastic as a squeeze toy, as well as in the Cameo doll creation.

Most doll collections include examples of these cherubic diminutives, and Kewpie collectors seek the whole range of Kewpie decorated items as well as the doll itself.

After the Kewpies . . .

The Happifats

by GENEVIEVE ANGIONE

IN THE midst of the Kewpie madness which has been upon the land since Rose O'Neill's little figures first orbited, doll collectors have suddenly found something else to absorb attention—the little Happifats.

The Kewpie was patented in 1913; the Happifats, following in its wake, were on the scene by 1915-16. They were made of hollow bisque of widely varying quality, in two sizes and three types. The boy and girl illustrated here, quite possibly for the first time anywhere outside of trade catalog

drawings, came in both 3½-and 4½-inch sizes. There was also a Happifat Baby in the 3½-inch size in a "white painted chemise."

Only the arms move, and while they are sufficiently balanced by the ballooning clothes to stand alone, the breakage rate must have been phenomenal. This undoubtedly endeared the little creatures to their manufacturers, but parents evidently had other ideas about them for they do not now seem to exist in the quantities Kewpies still enjoy.

The little girl's dress is light blue shading into deep blue in the gathers. Her sash and shoes are pink. The boy's jacket and shoes are a pretty Hunter green and his pants are a lively brown which also deepens in the creases. The "Mohawk" hair-dos are painted a reddish brown and divided into two back whisps on both.

The soft-bodied models with composition heads and hands, approximately 16 inches tall, seem not to have survived young mothering — or were not too popular. The same type hair-do is a sure sign of the breed, however.

Photos by the Author

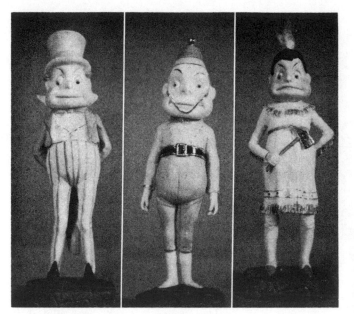

Uncle Sam   Bellhop   Indian

In the doll world, where the names of Rose O'Neill and her Kewpies or Grace Storey Putnam and her Bye-Lo Babies are instantly recognized by everybody, Palmer Cox and his Brownies enjoy a lesser fame. Yet they have a magic of their own both in and out of dolldom among oldsters and those who were children in the first quarter of this century.

The Dude   Chinaman   Bobbie

BROWNIES DELUXE

by Genevieve Angione

THE BROWNIES were born in 1883 in the twinkling imagination of bachelor Palmer Cox for a story which appeared in *St. Nicholas*, an "Illustrated Magazine for Young Folks." They were gentle, comical, little do-gooders who never sought praise, and were apparently based on some Cox combination of good fairies and gnomes. From 1887 on, Brownies, roamed through all kinds of hilarious, worldwide adventures in a steady flow of books which children loved and grownups loved to read to them.

Born of Scotch immigrant parents in 1840 in Granby, Quebec, not far from the Vermont state line, Palmer Cox died in 1924 at 84, a shining example of "build a better mousetrap." He and his Brownies were known the world around.

Not many of the Brownie books survived the enthralled children for whom they were written but paper cut-outs, figurines, small printed rag dolls, souvenir cups and spoons, framed pictures, and such treasures are still to be found in those wonderful inventions of a by-gone era—attics.

The Brownies illustrated here are exceptional because they are beautifully molded of the finest bisque, unmarked but unquestionably German. The trim appears to be the 14-karat gold used on fine china; the colors are bright pastels; and the decorating is expertly done. They fairly scream "quality."

They, vary from 7½ to 8 inches over-all. Each stands on a gold-flecked flagstone platform 2½ by 1½ inches, about ½ inch high. All have blue eyes and gray-blonde hair except the Indian; he has pitch black hair and brown eyes.

Individual Descriptions

Uncle Sam: blue-banded white topper with brush marks in the texture to indicate fur felt; blue swallowtail coat and white vest with gold bands; rose bow tie; rose-striped white pants and black shoes.

Bellhop: rose cap with yellow, gold-striped band, gold topknot and chinstrap; pink jacket with rose collar, gold buttons, gold trimmed black belt; blue pants with gold banding; white socks; black slippers.

Indian: yellow feathers, rose- and blue-tipped, with gold flecking; blue-belted yellow suit, rose and gold fringe; molded jacket decoration outlined in gold; yellow leggings, rose and gold fringe; brown handled gold hatchet; rose moccasins.

The Dude (said to be one of the most popular c h a r a c t e r s): blue-banded white topper with gold edge; gold monocle; blue tailcoat with gold band, pink rose in lapel; white shirt, yellow bow tie; white vest, gold banded and buttoned, yellow lapels; yellow-handled brown cane; yellow gloves; pale blue g o l d - b a n d e d trousers; white spats; black shoes.

Chinaman: yellow-banded rose cap, gold knob and trim; blue smock with gold braid closures, gold-banded collar, cuffs, and edge; white undersmock; blue gold-banded pants; white socks; yellow "Dutch wooden" shoes.

London Bobbie: blue helmet, gold knob, emblem and banding; blue coat, black belt, gold buttons and all-around banding; yellow nightstick with gold bands; blue trousers with gold bands; turned-up black shoes.

As in all quality figurines, these little fellows are as perfectly detailed and decorated in back as they are in front. The paints are exactly the same shades in every one, proof that at least these six were made as a set.

Sizes and Markings on Bisque
FULPER DOLL HEADS

by RUTH RICKER

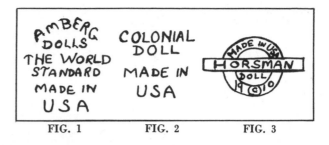

AMBERG DOLLS THE WORLD STANDARD MADE IN USA   COLONIAL DOLL MADE IN USA   MADE IN USA HORSMAN DOLL 19 C 10

FIG. 1   FIG. 2   FIG. 3

FULPER MADE IN USA 2B

FOR a short period, from 1918 to 1921, when war conditions prohibited the importation of doll heads from abroad, the Fulper Pottery Company of Flemington, New Jersey, undertook to meet the demands of American doll manufacturers by producing a line of bisque doll heads, utilizing American clays. These doll heads were subsequently mounted on doll bodies by the doll manufacturers who purchased them.

Such doll heads were impressed with the Fulper trademark, pictured here; the factory number 2B sometimes appears above "Made in U.S.A." The doll heads made to order for Amberg dolls, Colonial dolls, and Horsman dolls carried, in addition to the Fulper mark, the impressed trademark of the specific company for which they were made. (See Figs. 1, 2, 3.)

From the additional letters and numerals which appear on Fulper doll heads can be determined the head size, style, and in specific instances, the doll manufacturer who ordered them. When doll heads are of the same circumference but facial contours differ, identifying symbols indicate a difference. For example, 11" circumference swivel-type Fulper boy heads were made in three styles, each

bearing its identifying mark—16B indicates a baby boy head; 9, an older boy head, and 13, another older boy head differing in facial contour and expression from that marked 9, but all are 11" head circumference.

The following listing of Fulper doll head sizes and corresponding markings is compiled from actual specimens of Fulper doll heads. The head circumference in inches is given first, followed by incidental information, if any, then the number always to be found on that size and type head. All markings are impressed and appear below the Fulper mark, except where noted. The eight sizes and types photographically illustrated on this page are indicated. All doll heads pictured are from the author's collection and have been mounted on bodies.

Swivel Fulper Girl Heads: head circumference 8½", closed mouth, number on head 4; 9"—1 (*illus*); 10"—2C; 10½"—7; 11"—2B; 12"—2A; 13½"—2AA; 14"—2 (*illus*).
Shoulder Bust Fulper Girl Heads: head circumference 8½", closed mouth, number on head S-8½; 8½"—SS-8½; 9"—No. 1 (above Fulper mark); 9"—S-9; 9½"—S-9½; 10"—S-10; 10"—H-3 (no Fulper mark); 11½"—S-11½; 13"—S-13; 14"—S-14.
Swivel Fulper Boy Heads: head circumference 10½", baby, number on head 16C; 11", baby, 16B; 11"—9; 11"—13; 11½"—A-11; 11½"—11; 12½"—10; 13"—8 (*illus*); 13½", baby—16A; 14"—A 8 (*illus*); 16"—16.
Swivel Amberg Fulper Girl Heads (see Fig. 1 for mark): head circumference 8½", number on head 40; 10½"—35; 15"—70-A (*illus*); 20", stamped *Amberg Dolls The World's Standard*—20 (*illus*).
Swivel Colonial Fulper Baby Boy Heads (see Fig. 2 for mark): head circumference 10", number on head A-15-C (*illus*); 11"—A-15-B; 14"—14"—A-8 (*illus*); 16"—16.
Swivel Horsman Fulper Girl Heads (see Fig. 3 for mark): head circumference 10", number on head H-1 (*illus*); 11"—H-2; 12"—H-3; 13"—H-4.

Colonial boy head marked A-15-C, 10" size; Horsman girl head marked H-1, 10" circumference.

Fulper swivel girl head marked 1, 9" size.

Beautiful Amberg Fulper doll head marked 70-A, 15" circumference. Largest Amberg doll head, human size, marked 20, 20" circumference, shown with Fulper swivel doll heads: girl marked 2, 14" circumference, baby boy marked 8, 13" circumference.

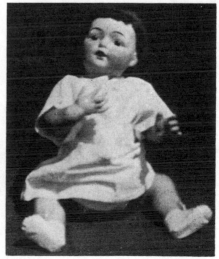

Fulper baby boy head marked A8, 14" size.

Madame Alexander Dolls

by LUELLA HART

BEATRICE Behrman, whose Austrian-born parents came to America in 1890 and opened a doll hospital in New York City, was born above their shop, and literally grew up with dolls. Her parents had retired by 1913 when she married Philip Berhman, but in the dynamic, beauty-loving Beatrice, dollmaking was ingrained. In 1915, for her own pleasure, she made a portrait doll of her baby daughter, Mildred. This won so much approval, she began to think of making dolls commercially. The Alexander Doll Company — and Madame Alexander — came into being at the time World War I had halted German doll imports. Her first commercial doll, cut from muslin, stitched on a sewing machine, and stuffed with excelsior, represented a Red Cross nurse. Thousands of Madame Alexander dolls have been made since. Their creator strives to make each doll lifelike, yet with the touch of fantasy children love. She models from clay, and a die is cast in steel or bronze. It takes nearly a year from the time she originates a model until it is in volume production.

Madame Alexander with the "Queen Mother," one of 36 dolls depicting the Coronation of Elizabeth II in 1953. Exact in every detail, this $25,000 collection was donated to the Brooklyn (N. Y.) Children's Museum where it is frequently on display. Madame Alexander's exquisite creations have won many of the coveted Fashion Academy Gold Medal Awards, in the doll costuming division.

Photographs of past and contemporary Madame Alexander dolls shown here, as an aid in identifying those whose labels have been lost, come through the courtesy of Madame Alexander and Laura D. White of the Alexander Doll Company, and members of the Madame Alexander Fan Club, of which Margaret Winson is president. Dolls are listed by year as they appeared on the market, though not all are pictured.

1925—*Blue Boy*, inspired by Gainsborough's painting.
   —*Pinky*, based on Sir Joshua Reynold's "Pinky."

1933—*Little Women*, Meg, Jo, Amy, Beth, with Marmee, from Alcott's classic. Trademark #334,080, Nov. 24, 1933; made in plastic in 1951, 1955, and 1957.

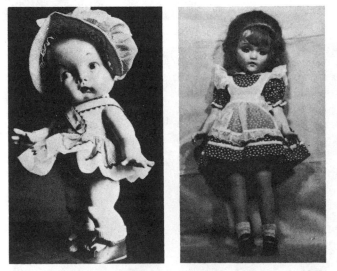

1927—An early Madame Alexander, above left, ca. 1927.
1933—*Alice in Wonderland*, right, inspired by Teniell's illustrations; trademark #335,763, March 17, 1933. In 1951, Alice, in plastic, appeared in the Gold Medal Collection. (Kathryn de Fillipo Collection.)

1935—*The Little Colonel*, of Annie F. Johnston's book series. Trademark #362,009, March 1, 1935, shown in three costumings. Often mistaken for Shirley Temple who played in the movie. Madame Alexander did not patent a Shirley Temple doll.

Jane Withers DOLLS

1936—*Jane Withers,* child movie star doll, came in four sizes, with variety of costumes.

1936—*Susie Q. and Bobby Q.,* left, from comic strip.
—*Pitty Pat* and *Tippie Toe,* also called *Country Cousins,* right, inspired by a Eugene Field poem. Semi-hard cloth, hand painted face, all cloth body; made in 10″, 26″, and 30″ sizes. Also listed in the Madame Alexander "Album of Dolls," 1942–43.

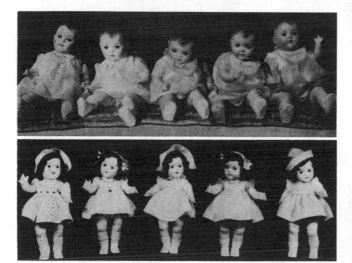

1936—*Quintuplets,* Annette, Emelie, Yvonne, Cecile, and Marie Dionne, born May 28, 1934, in Callender, Ontario, were represented as they progressed in age. *The Five Babies,* #374,273, top, above; 2-year old *Quints,* #374,274, below; other trademarks were *Quinties,* #374,271, and *Quins,* #374,269; all trademarks registered January 30, 1936.
—*Five Little Peppers,* from the book, trademark #374,268, Jan. 30, 1936.
—*The Little Genius*
—*Little Lord Fauntleroy,* from the book, trademark #374,270, Jan. 30, 1936.
—*Doris Keanne,* in "Romance."

1936—*Carmen,* representing Geraldine Farrar in the opera "Carmen." Also listed in 1942–43 catalog.

1937—*Princess Elizabeth* at her father's coronation, left, was made in 3 sizes.
—*Scarlet O'Hara,* right, from Margaret Mitchell's *Gone with the Wind,* trademark #392,003, April 29, 1937. (Kathryn De Fillipo collection.)

1937—*Margaret O'Brien,* child movie actress, left.
—*Princess Alexandria,* right, trademark #392,004, April 29, 1937. (Thelma Fisher collection.)
—*Neva Wet,* trademark #321,942, April 29.
—*Tweeny Winkle,* trademark #392,002, April 29.

1937—*Little Shaver,* in cloth, from painting by Elsie Shaver, who sold Madame Alexander the patent trademark #125,515, Dec. 2, 1919. (Esther Drath collection.)

More Madame Alexander Dolls

1937—*Baby McGuffey,* left above, composition head, soft body, 14", 18", 20" with voice, 11" without.
—*McGuffey Ana;* right, patent #393,886, Jan. 10, 1937. Reissued, 1942, 1943, 1953, 1955. Below, left, is McGuffey Ana of 1953.

1937—*Snow White,* right. Trademark #363,240, Nov. 9.
—*Annie Laurie,* Trademark #401,099, Dec. 21.

1938—*Dickens' Character Dolls.* Tiny Tim in cap, David Copperfield, and Little Nell (in two outfits.)
—*Mother and Me,* 2 dolls in a box, 15" and 9", fully jointed composition, with moving eyes. First made in 1938, but trademarked #431,899, May 14, 1940.

1937—*Madelaine du Bain,* small composition doll, costumed in French style of 1880s, above; made exclusively for F.A.O. Schwarz toy store; reissued 1938 and 1939.

1938—*Sonja Henie,* portrait, above left, in 15½", 18", and 22" size dolls, fully jointed, composition, moving eyes, lashes; elaborate skating costumes in assorted styles, skates attached to high skate shoes; 1951 model in plastic.

1939—*Madelaine,* above right, advanced issue of the Madelaine trademarked #431,900, May 14, 1940; this is not the same doll as Schwarz' Madelaine du Bain.

1938—*Flora McFlimsey,* in various sizes, represented a doll in books by Mariana; reissued in 1952.

1939—*Jennie Walker*, fine walking doll, first of its kind in the U. S.; worked by pulley and levers. Patent #2,328,704, granted R. E. Burnbaum and assigned to Bertha Behrman, was not registered until Sept. 7, 1943. Composition, fully jointed, able to sit, doll came in 14″ and 18″ sizes. Listed also in Madame Alexander's "Album of Dolls" for 1942–43.

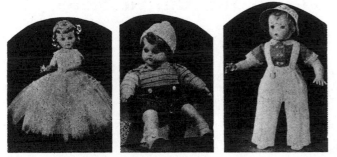

1940—*Madelaine*, above left, in 1940 is a blonde.
—*Butch McGuffey*, center, one of the few boy dolls of the period; trademark #431,898, May 14; 14″ and 18″ had voice, 11″ size did not. No date is given for later Butch, shown right.

1941—*Love-Le Tex*, trademark #444,850, June 26.

1942–43—*Fairy Princess*, slim type, jointed, composition, shoulder length blond wig, long satin gown, gold necklace and tiara, 11″, 15″, 18″, and 22″.
—*Southern Girl*, fully jointed, composition, black hair, full dress, pantalets, 11″, 15″, 18″, 22″.
—*Kate Greenaway*, composition, arm length mitts, ¾ length coats, various costumes, 15″, 16″, 20″, 24″.

1942–43—*Carmen*, fully jointed composition, in Pan-American or Bahaan costume, headdress of fruits, flowers, etc. 7″, 9″, 11″, 15″, 18″, and 22″.

1942–43—*Bride Doll*, fully jointed, composition; **blonde** ringlet wig; 7″, 9″, 15″, 18″, and 22″.

1942–43—*Baby Genius*, soft body, composition head, arms, and legs; voice; 11″, 14″, 18″, 20″, and 24″; same with wig in 18″, 20″, and 24″.
—*So-Lite Dolls*, soft cuddly cloth body, semi-hard cloth hand-painted face, yarn wig, 10″, 12″, 18″, 20″, and 24″; in white organdy, with bonnet.
—*Special Girl*, soft body, "mama" voice, 24″.—*1942–43 Repeats:* Sonja Henie, McGuffey Ana, Mother and Me, Jennie Walker, Butch McGuffey, Baby McGuffey, Country Cousins.

1949—*Mary Martin* as Nellie Forbush in *South Pacific*, left; repeated in 1950. Thelma Fisher collection.

1951—*Clarabelle the Clown* of the Howdy Doody Show.
—*Portrait Group*, 2 dolls in formal gowns, **chair**.
—*Slumbermate*, baby doll in blanket, soft body.
—*Maggie*, teenager, 15″, 18″, 23″, pleated skirt and sweater; 13″ and 15″ with trousseaus.
—*Violet*, first American fully jointed hard plastic doll, made also in 1952, 1953, 1954.
—*Penney*, comic strip teenager; soft floppy body, 34″, newtex hair to be combed and curled.
—*Christening Baby*, long christening robe; 11″, dressed 22″; 16″, dressed 30″; 19″, dressed 34″.
—*Sunbeam*, newborn infant; soft molded plastic head; diaper, shirt, bootees, shawl; 16″, 19″, 25″.
—*Bonnie*, toddler-type outfit; durable plastic head, soft body, soft plastic arms and legs, 11″, 16″, 19″.
—*Bitsey*, newtex wig can be combed and curled; with box of curlers and comb; 11″, 16″, 19″, 23″, 26″.
—*Honey-Bun*, baby doll; soft molded plastic head, sleep eyes, ringlet wig of newtex; 19″, 23″, 26″; same doll dressed in white organdie, coat, bonnet.
—*Kathy*, little girl doll; pedal pushers, roller skates, comb and curlers; 15″, 18″, 23″; same with dress, velvet beret, patent leather slippers.
—*Nina Ballerina*, 15″, 18″, 23″, jointed plastic body, newtex wig, red only; white ballerina dress.
—*Wendy Bride*, 15″, 18″, 23″; plastic body, fully jointed, newtex wig; bridal gown and veil.
—*Rosamund-Bridesmaid*, 15″, 18″, 23″; plastic body; newtex wig; frothy net gown, straw lace headdress.

1952—*Tommy Bangs and Stuffy*, above right, won Fashion Academy Award; (Margaret Winson collection.)

1952 — New version of Flora McFlimsey, right. In 1953, the highlight of production was a diarama of newly-crowned Queen Elizabeth with 6 attendants leaving Westminster Abbey; she in embroidered gown, Imperial State crown, real ermine, jewels; ladies in silver gowns and tiaras. Also produced in 1953 were Binnie Walker, the Glamour Girl set, Snow Baby, Flower Girl, Mary Ellen, and Bonnie, with vinyl body, rooted hair.

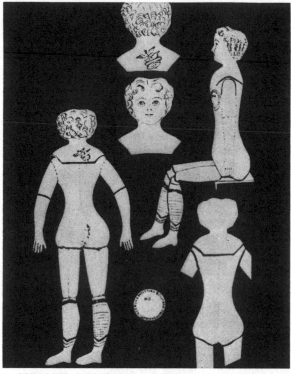

GIBSON'S CINDERELLA SITTING DOLL BODY

The Rag Doll
Made in the United States

by LUELLA HART

BEFORE 1860, most play dolls for American children were made by mothers. Some of these early cloth dolls have personalities; many of them are in museums (see *Spinning Wheel*, May 1961). The lineage of the rag or cloth doll goes back into antiquity; linen dolls stuffed with papyrus were found in tombs of ancient Egypt; rag dolls from old Rome still survive.

In the United States, the cloth doll was the folk toy. Colonists used materials at hand—cloth, corncobs, or sticks wrapped in cloth—to serve as dolls for their children. Toy manufacturers were slow in realizing the commercial value of the cloth doll. Though a handful of patents were issued in the 1860s and 1870s, it was not until after the mid-1880s that patented and perfected rag dolls appeared in any quantity in the United States.

As far as it is known, Irene Gibson, of Marlboro, New Hampshire, sometime before 1860, designed and supervised the making of the bodies of the "Cinderella Sitting Dolls." These bodies have kid arms and red kid boots. Composition heads, similar to the "Superior," were used on them. One example is known of a Cinderella Sitting Doll whose head is stamped with the German "Holz Masse" trademark.

Several men patented cloth doll heads in the 1880s. These heads were made to be used on homemade bodies. Earlier, G. H. Hawkins, of New York City, on September 8, 1868, was granted patent #81,999, for a doll head of textile fabric, stiffened with glutinous stuff pressed by heated dies.

Carl Wiegand, also of New York City, patented a doll head of two or more layers of textile fabric with intermediate layers of paper, on May 23, 1876 (Patent #177,777).

The Izannah Walker cloth dolls, although not pretty, are greatly treasured by collectors. Mr. Walker of Central Falls, Rhode Island, patented the complete doll on November 4, 1873 (Patent #144,373).

HAWKINS

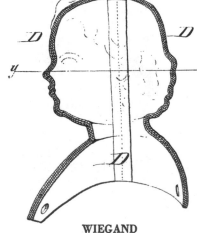

WIEGAND

Fig. 4.

C

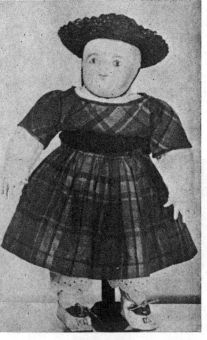

WALKER

Patent drawing, left; actual doll, above.

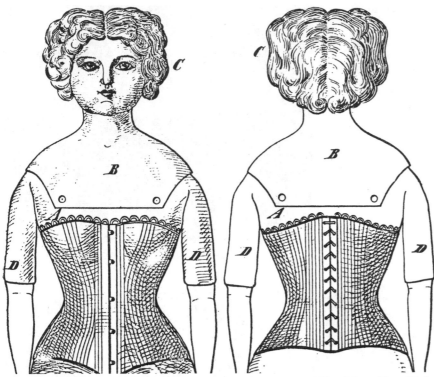

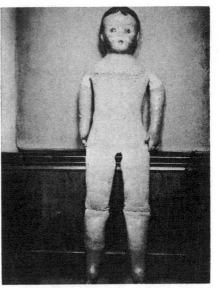

PHILADELPHIA DOLL

DOTTER. On December 7, 1880, Charles T. Dotter, of Brooklyn, New York, patented a cloth doll body featuring a printed corset (Patent #235,218). German heads were used on these dolls. Patent drawing shows that corset is stamped on both front and back of the doll.

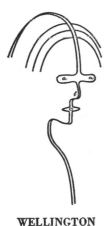

WELLINGTON
(above)

ROBINSON
(far right)

Martha Wellington, of Brookline, Massachusetts, took out a patent September 25, 1883 for a doll built over a wire framework outlining the features. Stockinette was the material used over the padded wire; features were painted. (This was patent #285,448).

Another patented jointed doll body was the creation of Sarah Robinson of Chicago, Illinois. Patent specifications call for either cloth or leather, stuffed with bran or hair. Joints are held together by cords or wires, passing through the sections of the joints and fastened by buttons or washers to prevent cutting the fabric when doll is seated. Imported china or Parian heads are used on these bodies. The patent, #283,513, is dated August 21, 1883.

No patent is known for the much disputed so-called "Philadelphia doll." A picture of the doll above, from the collection of Mrs. Wilbur Jones, Dublin, Georgia, was sent, in 1946, to Mr. Sheldon, at that time manager of the Chase Doll Factory, for identification. Indicating this as a Philadelphia doll, he stated: "The eyes of the Philadelphia doll are apt to be starey and protrude a little. Although the Wellington dolls were made about the same time and are somewhat similar, there is a difference in that the Wellington doll has a very short neck and looks as though the head were resting on the shoulders, whereas the picture of the doll you sent me, shows a neck. The Philadelphia doll came after the Izannah Walker doll, but before the Chase doll."

BEECHER MISSIONARY BABIES

In 1885, Julia Jones Beecher of Elmira, New York, with other ladies made rag dolls to sell for their church missions. Known as "Beecher Missionary Babies," they were made both as negro and white infants. They were never advertised. Pink stockinette was used for the white babies. Features were flat and painted; hair of soft yarn was sewn into the heads. Dolls were from 16 to 21 inches tall, priced from $2 to $8, according to size. (Mrs. Beecher was a granddaughter of Noah Webster; her husband, a brother of Henry Ward Beecher and Harriet Beecher Stowe.)

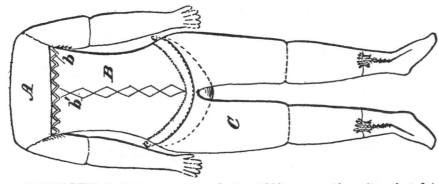

GOLDSMITH. Doll factories, rare before 1860, were active after that date in New York, New Hampshire, Boston, Philadelphia, and Kentucky. One, the Goldsmith Company of Covington, Kentucky, set up by Wolf Fletcher, manufactured cloth doll bodies with corset stamped on front. Porcelain heads from Germany, completed the doll. (Patent #332,248, December 15, 1885).

By the Mid-1880s, rag dolls were more and more popular with doll and toy makers. Some were being printed on cloth, which could be cut out, sewed, and stuffed at home, so that every child in the country could have one. Eventually a great many of this type came to be used as advertising premiums. On December 20, 1886, E. S. Peck, of Brooklyn, New York, patented a Santa Claus doll (Design #17042) which was printed on cloth, to be stuffed at home.

PECK'S "SANTA CLAUS" Courtesy Mary Kramar

REBECCA JOHNSON

The July 19, 1887, patent by Rebecca Johnson, of New York City, called for a cloth doll waxed on the outside and supported internally by a shell filling. (Patent #366,730).

CHASE DOLLS

Chase play doll (1891-1900) Courtesy Sue Godding Ruggles. Chase Hospital Infant, Author's Collection

Over seventy years ago, Martha Chase, of Pawtucket, Rhode Island, wife of a prominent physician, created her now famous stockinette doll. She made it for her own children; however, when she took it to a store to be fitted with shoes, an enthusiastic salesgirl seized on it and gave it to the world. Since then Martha Chase dolls have gone into every corner of the globe. They have become museum pieces and collector finds. The Chase doll, from the first cut of the shears to the last painted eyelash was entirely hand-made by skilled craftsmen. Of woven stockinette, stuffed with white cotton batting, it approximates the lifelike responsive body of a young child. Only the purest and best paint is used; as it is completely waterproofed, it may be bathed, and kept sanitary. Until World War II, dolls to be played with by children were produced. After the war, the factory created the Chase Hospital Dolls. These include the new-born infant, a 2-months old baby, a 4-months old baby, a year old and a 4-year old child, and adult female and male dolls. They come with internal tanks for nasal, oral, and rectal care, and are used in nurses training in all leading hospitals. They are also considered standard basic equipment by the American Red Cross, various State Health Departments, and Home Economics classes in schools.

In 1892, Miss Emma Adams of Oswego Centre, New York, started to make rag dolls for pleasure with the help of her sister Marietta. Their hobby developed into a thriving business. In 1893 at the Chicago World's Fair, these dolls won a Diploma of Merit and received the name "Columbian Dolls." Soon after, Mrs. E. R. Horton of Boston, decided that a fine specimen of this doll should be sent around the world to be exhibited for benefit of children's charities. The Adams Express Company sent the doll free on a tour which circled the globe. When the little traveler returned, her clothing was covered with souvenirs of her trip. She is now on permanent display at the Doll Museum, Wenham, Massachusetts, and is shown here by their courtesy. Before 1900, the dolls bore the stamp "Columbian Doll, Emma Adams, Oswego Centre, New York." There were a dozen dolls, numbered from 1 to 12, according to size, which ranged from 15 to 29 inches. After Miss Adams' death in 1900, the label was changed to "The Columbian Doll, manufactured by Marietta Adams Rutlan, Oswego, New York."

COLUMBIAN DOLL

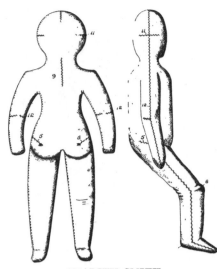

CHARITY SMITH

ARNOLD PRINT WORKS
"Pickaninny" and "Kitten"
Courtesy Carolyn Abbott

BERTHA TRUFANT

In the late 1890s, artists created rag doll patterns which they patented and sold to the Arnold Print Works, of North Adams, Massachusetts, manufacturers of dress goods and printed fabrics. Among these artists were Charity Smith, of Ithaca, New York, and Mr. Palmer Cox. Charity Smith's patent was for a *jointed* rag doll, Patent #505,679, dated September 26, 1893. Mrs. Smith specialized in dolls and animals.

Mr. Palmer Cox's stories and drawings of Brownies, appearing in the *St. Nicholas Magazine*, were already well known when he patented, on January 15, 1892, twelve of his Brownie characters which he sold to the Arnold Print Works. This company printed the twelve little figures, each seven inches tall, on a yard of muslin. They are shown on the cover: Uncle Sam; Dude; Policeman; Irishman; Indian; Soldier; Sailor; German; Chinaman; John Bull; Highlander; and Captain. (Pictures courtesy Mary Kramar, Ruth Larson, and Mrs. Earle Andrews.)

Other figures printed by the Arnold Print Works were Tabby Cat; Little Tabbies; Tatters (a Skye terrier) and Little Tatters; Red Riding Hood; Pickaninny and Topsy; Rooster; Owl; Hen and Chicks; Jocko and Little Jocko; Pitti-song; Our Soldier Boys; Bow-wow and little Bow-wows; Bunny and Floss. These were not sold at retail by the Arnold Works, but were distributed through dry goods stores throughout the country, where patterns could be purchased by the yard and the half yard at 20 cents and 10 cents. In the popular Tabby pattern, for instance, Tabby appeared alone on a half yard of cloth; four kittens on a half yard, or eight kittens on one yard.

Other rag doll patents of the 1890s were those by Bertha Trufant (#537,791, dated April 16, 1895); Ida Gutsell (Patent #503,316, August 15, 1893); and Louise Bowden (Patent #511,111, December 19, 1893). All of these printed cloth dolls to be cut out and made up were popular and are still found in many collections.

Between the years 1890 and 1942, with the rapid increase in advertising, there appeared an avalanche of play dolls, printed in color on cloth, marked to be cut out, ready for sewing and stuffing. Aunt Jemima and her Pickannies were the products of the advertising of the R. T. Davis Mill Company of St. Joseph, Missouri. They were obtained by sending one box top from an Aunt Jemima flour package and 24 cents in stamps. The design of the dolls changed as printing methods improved. The mill itself changed its name to the Aunt Jemima Mills Company. Aunt Jemima, Wade Davis (on cover, from the collection of Ruth Larson) and Diana Jemima and Moses were among the earlier of the cloth dolls. In 1924 the Grinnell Lithograph Company of New York City offered the services of a commercial

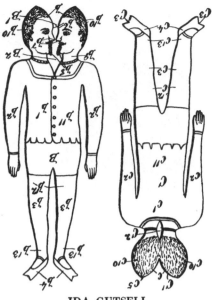

IDA GUTSELL

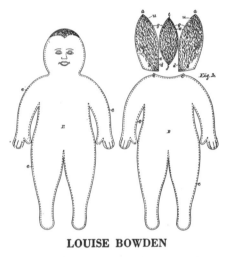

LOUISE BOWDEN

ART FABRIC MILLS
"Dorothy Monroe"
Courtesy Carolyn Abbott

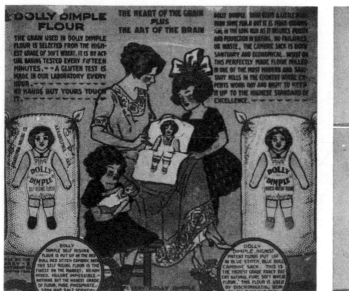

Left to right: ART FABRIC MILLS, Courtesy Helen McInstry; ARKADELPHIA MILLING COMPANY, "Dolly Dimple"; KNICKERBACKER SPECIALTY COMPANY, Foxy Grandpa, Buster Brown and Tige, Courtesy Ruth Larson.

artist to re-design this doll family. An advertisement in the *Ladies Home Journal* of December 1925 announced his new Aunt Jemima dolls for the purchasers of flour. Later, in 1950, this company issued other cloth figures such as Mary Muslin, Ver Meulin, Clarabel, Raggedy Ann, and Raggedy Andy.

Other milling companies stamped dolls upon the sacks in which they packed their flour. Among these was the Dolly Dimple doll of the Arkadelphia Milling Co., of Memphis, Tennessee. The name Dolly Dimple was stamped across her underclothing.

The Art Fabric Mills of New York printed sheets of rag dolls from 1900 to 1910. The name of the mill and the date, February 13, 1900, appear on the seams of these dolls. They came in many sizes. This company also printed a "Life Size French Doll" stamped on heavy sateen with golden hair and red stockings and black shoes. This doll was advertised in the November 1907 *Designer*. The same company sold a sheet of six small dolls: Diana, Bridget, Uncle, Baby, Billy, and Newly Wed Kid.

The successor to the Art Fabric Company was Silchow and Richter. This company patented a life-size doll stamped on cloth. The date stamped on the sheet of Merrie Marie (pictured below uncut) is February 13, 1900. It is quite possible that Silchow and Richter bought the patent which Edgar Newell had taken out on the same date. His patent drawing (Patent #643,385) closely resembles the stamped doll.

Madge Mead of Philadelphia, Pennsylvania, patented a rag doll, so constructed that the doll was jointed (Patent #661,185, November 6, 1900).

In the 1900s, artist and designer R. F. Outcault, creator of the comic strip characters Foxy Grandpa, Buster Brown and Tige, sold these designs to the Knickerbacher Specialty Company. Children could now play with the figures they had come to love through the comics.

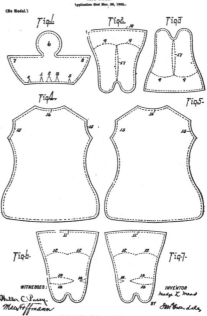

MADGE MEAD

SILCHOW AND RICHTER
"Merrie Marie"
Courtesy Mary Kramar

Right: E. G. NEWELL patent drawings.

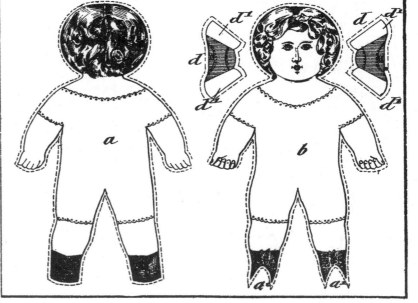

SAALFIELD PUBLISHING CO.
"Baby Blue Eyes"

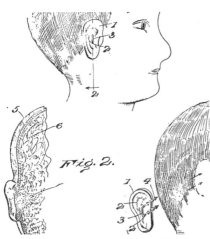

ELLA SMITH (Attachable Ear)

ELLA SMITH
Courtesy Cecil Perry

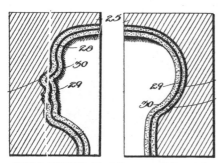

ELLA SMITH (2nd Improved Patent)

One of the most treasured rag dolls of modern times is Ella Smith's "Alabama Indestructible" doll. Her first patent was taken out September 26, 1905 (Patent #800,-333). Over the years she applied for and received three more patents, one for improvement in construction, (Patent #1,321,135 on November 11, 1919); one for "an attachable ear," (Patent #1,292,113 on January 21, 1919); and the last for complete and improved doll, (Patent #1,308,816 on July 8, 1919). Ella Smith employed widows and orphans of Alabama in the making of her dolls, and all materials used were from that State. Some dolls were as tall as 36 inches, with beautiful long curls of real hair.

The negro dolls created by Mrs. Ida Chubb, author of a book of negro rhymes, came out sometime in the 1900s, the exact date undetermined.

In the February 1908 *Delineator,* the Butterick Publishing Company ran an advertisement of an 18 inch rag doll, printed flat on durable cloth in eight colors, with a series of doll dress patterns, offering the doll and two patterns for 25¢.

One year later, in 1909, the Saalfield Publishing Company of Akron, Ohio, printed a 12 inch rag doll named "Baby Blue Eyes." (Collectors who loaned examples for photographing: Mrs. Lloyd Brown, Mrs. Mary Kramer, Miss Ruth Larson, and Mrs. Bernard Ruggles.)

ELLA SMITH (4th Patent)
Complete Doll Improved

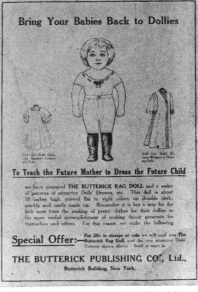

BUTTERICK PUBLISHING CO.

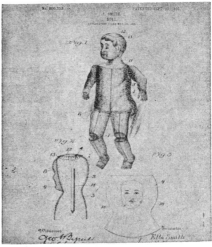

ELLA SMITH (First Patent)

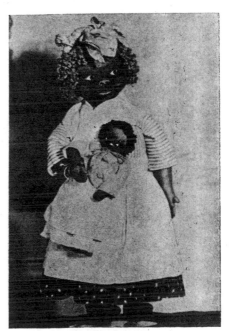

IDA CHUBB

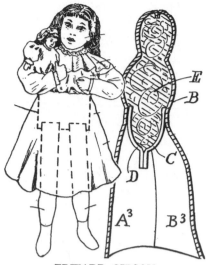

EDWARD GIBSON

CHARLES SACKMAN

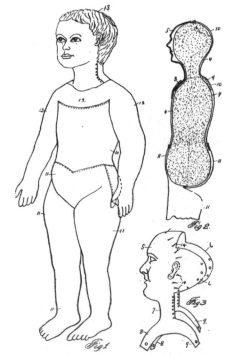

MARIE BAKER

Edward Gibson's patent for a rather unusual cloth doll was granted on March 22, 1910—Patent #952,731. The patent drawing shows this sittable doll holding a small replica of herself.

A rough and tumble doll which looked as if it would take a hard beating was patented by Charles Sackman of Brooklyn, New York, on January 31, 1911—Patent #982,880.

Marie Baker of Houston, Texas, patented a stuffed rag doll on May 7, 1912—Patent #1,025,234.

In 1913, Alice Butler took out a patent for a doll body on February 18—Patent #1,053,902, and on August 19, Annie Stevens of Fresno, California, patented a rag doll—Patent #1,070,553. Also in 1913, the Empire Art Company of Chicago, Illinois, patented a doll stamped on cloth called the American Beauty Doll; and the Cruver Manufacturing Company of Chicago, Illinois, printed Berney B. Borg's "Betsy and Bill" cloth dolls, and the "Ding-A-Ling Circus," which consisted of animals, two clowns, and tickets for entrance to the various animal exhibits.

In 1915, Anne Maxwell patented a rag doll with plaitable hair—Patent #1,127,661; Leon Rees patented a sailor rag doll—Patent #1,139,997; and Clifford Switzler patented cloth dolls which he sold to the Ruly Trooly Toy Company of Boston, Massachusetts—Patent #1,150,792. "Quaddy" was the trademark for a cloth doll put out by Thornton W. Burgess of Springfield, Massachusetts, patented on April 15—Patent #85,960.

The last six dolls are not illustrated here, nor is the knitted Fabric doll with Kapoc filling and colored fea-

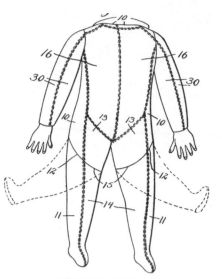

ARTHUR BUTLER

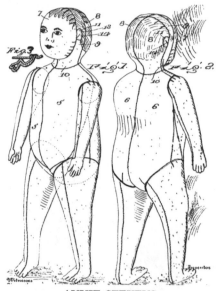

ANNIE STEVENS

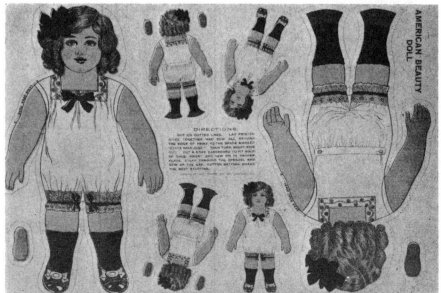

AMERICAN BEAUTY DOLL

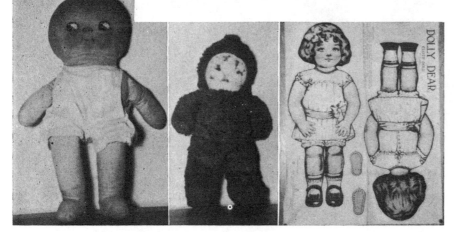

RAGGEDY ANN

tures which Jane Sokes of New York patented in 1916—and sold the patent, #1,206,483, to the Jane Gray Company of New York.

The war years between 1914 and 1920 meant sacrifices for everyone. Toys were limited to those not made of essential war materials; consequently rag dolls were made in some quantity. In 1916 the Bentley Franklin Manufacturing Company put out Grace Drayton's stuffed dolls. This artist is known among collectors particularly for her "Dolly Dingle" paper dolls which were featured in women's magazines between 1915 and 1930. The Cuddle Kewpie, a stuffed Kewpie, came onto the market about 1921. "Dolly Dear," a product of the Saalfield Company of Akron, Ohio, was copyrighted in 1918.

Everyone knows the Raggedy Ann and Raggedy Andy characters created by Johnny Gruelle, whose stories and pictures were inspired by an old rag doll his mother had made. The Georgene Novelty Company made the first of the manufactured Raggedy Ann dolls in 1918. When Mr. Gruelle died in 1930, his wife formed a new partnership, and since then many companies have made these dolls. At present a mill in Greenfield, Massachusetts, is stamping them on cloth to be made up at home.

Georgene Averill, who headed the Georgene Novelty Company of New York, patented a doll body on June 11, 1918 — Patent #1,269,363. This body was used with heads imported from Germany. There has been much controversy over these dolls as they were advertised as "all American made." Germany and the United States were then at war, and anything made in Germany was taboo. The German marking on the heads did not show as the body casing covered the mark.

Other rag dolls patented in the war years were Jennie Allen's stuffed rag doll—Patent #1,261,994, dated April 9, 1918, and the water proof rag doll, finished with shellac which Lenora Price of Davenport, Oklahoma, patented on July 30, 1918—Patent #1,274,328.

Lita and Bessie Shinn patented a hand painted rag doll on January 13, 1920—Patent #1,327,884; and Charlotte Glossbrenner of York, Pennsylvania, patented a fabric doll on March 2, 1920—Patent #1,332,825.

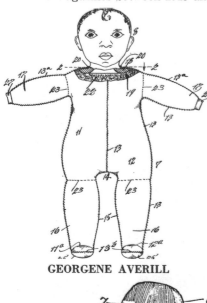

GEORGENE AVERILL

LENORA PRICE

JENNIE ALLEN

Fig. 11.

LITA and BETTY SHINN

CHARLOTTE GLOSSBRENNER

KOOKIE—*Courtesy Caroline Abbott*   PUFFY, *Abbott Collection*; GOLDILOCKS, THREE BEARS, *Courtesy Mary Kramar.*

The advertising rag doll began to be popular as early as 1900. Aunt Jemima and her Pickaninnies have already been pictured (August 1962), as have Buster Brown and Tige, and the Palmer Cox Brownies. The last two sets are considered advertising figures to the extent that they put into the hands of children tangible forms of characters they had learned to love in books, magazines, and comics.

Sunny Jim, well known through Minny Hanff's jingles and drawings, advertising the breakfast cereal Force, came to rag doll form in 18-inch size, printed on cloth by the Niagra Lithographing Company of New York. He was used as a premium.

Rastus the Chef, a rag doll 16-inches tall, with red jacket, blue trousers and cap, appeared in 1930 as a premium for Cream of Wheat Corporation; Puffy was a cloth premium for Quaker Puffed Wheat and Puffed Rice. The rag doll, Kookie, designed by Spence Wildey, advertised an automatic range.

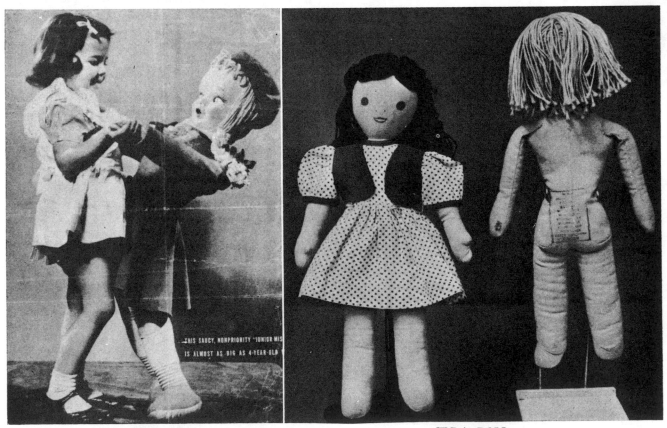

JUNIOR MISS   W.P.A. DOLL

Hundreds of other rag dolls were used in advertising. Uncle Sam was stamped on large size sugar sacks of the Western Sugar Refinery, San Francisco, California, under copyright taken out in 1935. Other dolls on Sea Island 10-pound sugar bags were Gobo, Minka, Scotty, and Uluk. Kellogg's cereals created little Goldilocks and the Three Bears. Collectors will find many others to add to this list.

In the depression year of 1930, dolls were made as W.P.A. projects. Mrs. Guilia Cuthbert, Charleston, West Virginia, owns one with this label: "Works Progress Administration Handicraft Project/Milwaukee, Wisconsin/Sponsored by Milwaukee County and Milwaukee State Teachers' College." This doll is 11-inches tall, of peach colored cotton, with painted features and string hair. A well-made dress and panties complete the doll; she wore no shoes.

Most collectors know the work of Lewis Sorensen. In 1930, while working for the Z.C.M.I. in Salt Lake City as designer of children's and ladies' wash dresses, he started making rag sailor boy dolls in the evenings. These sold as fast as he could turn them out. About 1935, in Los Angeles, he made a lady doll, dressed in rayon pajamas, with a bust, painted features, and yarn hair. Later he created a lavish lady doll in Colonial costume, with a profile instead of flat features. He refers to this type as "cloth sculpture." Just before composition dolls came on the market, he was making 12-inch cloth little girls with braids and roller skates. From these he went to rag dolls with pressed faces, even creating wrinkled old lady dolls. These sold for $25. He considers his Flapper his finest cloth creation. It was 12 inches tall when seated. College girls bought hundreds.

Bernard Ravca, of New York City, was another gentleman who worked in cloth sculpture, being best known for his stockinette dolls. His ability to catch likenesses of old folk won him fame.

PUPULE (crazy) KIDS, felt over wire. Lanakila Craft, Inc. *Morse Collection.*

BEACH BOY and HATTIE. Lanakila Craft, Inc. *Morse Collection.*

Life magazine, November 29, 1943, hailed the floppy rag doll as the newest Christmas gift. Faced again with wartime shortages, the doll industry developed the floppy rag type stuffed with cotton, with painted eyes and yarn hair, requiring neither metal nor elastic. Among them were Junior Miss, a life-size child of four, by the Ideal Novelty and Toy Company; a bride, by Madame Alexander Doll Company; a little girl with yellow yarn pigtails holding a baby doll, and a Jack and Jill, dressed-alike brother and sister pair, by the Effanbee Doll Company.

A call by the writer in June 1961 on Mrs. Marion Backus of Lanakila Craft Inc. in Honolulu, Hawaii, and a guided tour of the plant brought to light cloth dolls which, though intended for children, are already considered treasures by adult doll collectors. This firm employs only handicapped people, sells wholesale, and is self-supporting.

Talking rag dolls, in keeping with the times, appeared on the 1961 Christmas market. Sister Belle, the talking girl, Matty, the talking boy, and Casper, the talking ghost, who can each say several sentences when the magic ring at the back of the neck is pulled, were created by Mattel Inc., Hawthorne, California.

Many fine old cloth figures made by Indian tribes are to be found in fortunate collections. Some of these dolls wear real silver belts, bracelets, and trimming. The old women of the tribes were responsible for these treasures. Now they are gone, it is difficult to find present-day Indian dolls worthy to be collector items.

Appreciation is expressed to the Doll Collectors of America, Inc. for permission to use in this series several photographic illustrations which have appeared in their publications, *American Made Dolls and Figurines, Doll Collectors' Manual,* and the drawing of the Cinderella Sitting Doll, by Mrs. Henry Johnson, which was used in the *Supplement to American Made Dolls and Figurines,* 1942. Thanks go also to Mrs. Gordon Bennett for the picture of her Ida Chubb mammy doll.

Full patent papers of dolls discussed here may be obtained at 25¢ each from the U. S. Patent Office, Washington 25, D. C. Give patent number, date, and patentee when ordering.

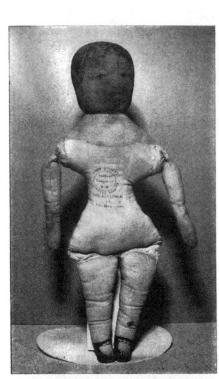

Mothers' Congress Doll

Head of Mothers' Congress Doll

PHILADELPHIA'S OWN
Rag Dolls

by Genevieve Angione

Patent Detail, Mothers' Congress

*Photographed by the author
from the collection of
MRS. HOMER STRONG, Rochester, N. Y.*

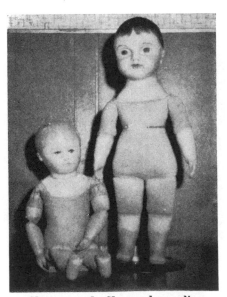

Chase, seated; Sheppard, standing

NOT TOO many dolls can pinpoint their birthplace to one city with any degree of certainty but two dolls proudly hail from The City of Brotherly Love. The better known is the Sheppard or "Philadelphia Baby"; the other is the "Mothers' Congress Doll . . . Baby Stuart . . . Childrens' Favorite."

Technically both dolls classify as *cloth,* but almost without exception the old name "rag dolls," is used by both the public and collectors. Until fairly recently rag dolls did not enjoy the place in fine collections which they now hold, and always there have been comparatively few for sale.

Many battered, bursting dolls were, of course, thrown out by those apostles of neatness who settle estates, but the most surprising reason for their scarcity has always been the reluctance of families to part with existing rag dolls for the prices offered. Many rag dolls are fondly remembered by several generations, and the sentiment accumulated around these over-loved bundles of cloth and cotton is beyond price. They take no special care, cannot be further damaged, and they are just not for sale.

The Sheppard and the Chase

The Sheppard, or "Philadelphia Baby," somewhat resembles the better known Chase Stockinet Doll, and a Sheppard is pictured here with a seated Chase so that the differences can be pointed out for easier identification. Because the Sheppard seems never to have any printed trademark or evidence of a pasted label, it apparently was sold without markings or with a string-held tag which was removed. This specimen is 18 inches tall.

The picture clearly shows the funnel-like neck always found on a Sheppard, whereas the Chase neck is sufficiently play-worn to show the juncture of the neck and the shoulder. Both dolls are well painted where the body is not covered.

The two most salient differences are unmistakable. While the Chase is called "stockinet doll," it is generally covered with pink sateen, which is cleverly folded and sewed in such a way that it fits quite snugly around the shoulder plate with no evidence of any attachment. The Sheppard is actually made of a fairly coarse grade of knitted, off-white underwear material with vertical ribs like purled knitting. At the base of the neck, the heavy, painted muslin is always overcast to the body, apparently by hand.

The illustration also shows clearly the arm formations. The Sheppard has no elbow hinge because the stockinet is sewed to the painted forearm and sheathes the upperarm construction. The Chase has an elbow hinge and the painted portion extends into the upperarm.

Other differences are: Sheppards usually look like boys because their features are more rugged, their cheeks more prominent, and the ears, sometimes referred to as "bubble gum," are not as accurately formed as those of most Chases.

Clearly visible in the picture are the common stained feet of the Sheppard. Many of these dolls are found with what must be their original buttoned boots where the dyes used on the leather has bled through to the painted feet. Boots from one doll will exactly match the stains on a barefoot specimen.

The "Philadelphia Baby" is generally believed to have been made about 1900 for the J. B. Sheppard Company, a Philadelphia department store. The first identified specimens must have been the same size, 22 inches, for it was thought only one size was made. This 18-inch doll would question that conclusion.

The Mother's Congress Doll

The Mothers' Congress Doll, infinitely poorer in material and construction, is not so shy about its origin. Even the patent date, Nov. 6, 1900, is clearly visible in the center panel of the body.

Instead of being hand-painted over cloth, the head, shoulders, arms, and legs of this doll are printed on a thin but sturdy grade of muslin. The shoulders, arms, and legs are stippled with red to give the flesh tone. The close-up picture shows part of the seam which almost encircles the head so that it could be flattened like the Sheppard, the Chase, and others. There is also a back seam through the printed hair which leaves the face unmarred except for three darts below the mouth; these give some illusion of a chin—the only concession of any kind to sculptured features.

Although the doll is crude compared to many of the well known rag dolls, it nevertheless is factory-made. There is hand-stitching where the arms attach to the shoulder stumps, and bastings show at the leg attachment; all the rest of the sewing is machine-done with a surprisingly small stitch.

No attempt was made to indicate fingers except for printed red lines; thumbs were simply ignored. The tiny, printed Mary Jane slippers are black with white bows.

We are indebted for these pictures to the outstanding collection of Mrs. Homer Strong of Rochester, N. Y. Although she has over 11,000 dolls, including several Sheppards, she has only one Mothers' Congress Doll. Love, lime, countless spring cleanings and attic thrower-outers have decimated their ranks. If you find one, don't pass it up as "that dirty old thing." Rather, cherish it for the rare old doll it is, prominently displayed in Mrs. Strong's all-embracing collection.

*From the collection of water color renderings of dolls in the Index
of American Design, National Gallery of Art, Washington, D. C. come these . . .*

Early American Rag Dolls

by HELEN BULLARD

(1) (2) (3) (4)

(5) (6) (7) (8)

(1) "Aggie," the sturdy doll Mrs. Martha Reed of Kalamazoo, Michigan made in 1851, has withstood four generations of little Reeds.

(2 and 3) Lively little Mollie Bentley and her older sister, Maggie, who lived in Lancaster County, Pennsylvania, in the 1880s, each made herself a cloth doll from a single pattern. So different were the sisters that the dolls they made were highly individual, too. Doll 2 is "Mollie Bentley"; Doll 3 is "Maggie."

(4) From a little muslin, some cotton fluff, and scraps of wood, a Mrs. Tread-well, about 1800, contrived this charming doll, now displayed at the Cooper Union Museum, New York City.

(5) Said to have been made in San Miguel in 1795, this rag doll, fashioned by a California Indian woman for Señora Villa, may be considered an Indian's interpretation of the women of the conquerors.

(6) Displayed at the Pennsylvania Museum, Memorial Hall, Philadelphia, is this simply made rag doll. Her nose, a twist of cloth, was an inspiration of her creator, and the lacy pantalettes above

black leather shoes suit her country clothes of the 1830s.

(7) "Susie," made in Santa Cruz, California, by the mother of the original owner (Mrs. Frank Taylor), dates from 1860.

(8) Boy dolls have never been common and are seldom as well-proportioned as "Johnie" in his blue "Chalais" suit and finely hand-tucked linens. He dates from the early 1800s, and is made of heavy cotton cloth with hair and features embroidered in yarn. His expression suggests his maker had a special little boy in mind.

A Pictorial Selection of American Handmade *Wooden* Dolls

by HELEN BULLARD

From the collection of water color renderings of dolls in the Index of American Design, National Gallery of Art, Washington, D. C.

(1)   (2)

(3)   (4)   (5)   (6)   (7)

(8)

HAND-CARVED WOODEN DOLLS LAST LONGER THAN OTHER TYPES; MAY BE ANYTHING FROM A LIGHTLY CUT PIECE OF WOOD TO A CONVINCING PORTRAIT FROM LIFE.

(1) A doll so small (1¼") she can be mounted in an old daguerreotype frame is lucky to have knee joints even if her arms are missing. "Phoebe," whose original owner was Phoebe Phelps, dates from about 1865.

(2) Negro doll with carved wooden head and stuffed body, ca. 1870, is now in the Museum of Folk Arts, Riverdale-on-Hudson, New York City.

(3) One of the oldest dolls shown here has wooden head, kid arms and hands, and soft stuffed body. She is believed to have been made in the mountains of West Virginia about 1755.

(4) Carved from a block of walnut for a little girl named Elsey Bentley, about 1805, this doll found its way eventually to the Milwaukee (Wis.) Public Museum.

(5) This painted wooden doll with jointed wooden arms and legs was carved in New England for a girl named Caroline Broad, ca. 1818. She is now owned by the Society for the Preservation of New England Antiquities, Boston.

(6) A contemporary of the preceding doll, this man doll, carved about 1815-30, was found in Maine.

(7) A fine Quaker lady of the 18th century, with head, arms and legs of carved and painted wood.

(8) "Sadie Berman", carved in Massachusetts, date unknown, appears to be a portrait doll.

Unusual American Handmade Dolls

From the collection of water color renderings of dolls in the Index of American Design, National Gallery of Art, Washington, D. C.

by HELEN BULLARD

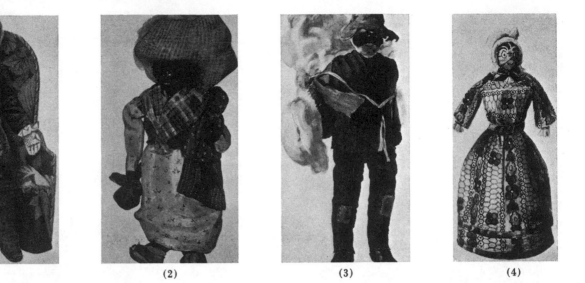

(1) (2) (3) (4)

Nuthead Dolls

NUTHEADS, like cloth dolls, were usually the most expendable sort of toy. Made of the simplest materials, always at hand, they could be pitched in the fire or even cracked and eaten, as soon as the children began to tire of them. To survive, as did the Colonial gentleman (1), a nuthead must have earned his survival by some outstanding characteristics. This nuthead's fine clothes and his face, so like that of a Daumier judge, doubtless helped to preserve him for over two hundred years. He is owned now by the Milwaukee (Wisc.) Public Museum. Although (2) and (3), a pair of cotton-picking nutheads and their soon-to-be-picking baby are quite different from the Colonial gentleman, they, too, are a lesson in making much from little. Representing field hands of the late 19th century when they were made, this group is now at the Essex Institute, Salem, Massachusetts. (4) A nuthead with a cornhusk body adds up to a real country-type doll, but the gay print frock and white crocheted bonnet of this little 6½" woman are not usual country doll clothes of the late 19th century.

Dolls of Odd Materials

ALL sorts of materials were utilized for dolls. These applehead ladies (5) with a gentleman friend, not shown, were designed and made in North Carolina by Mrs. Almira Smith about 1892. Although the appleheads have long since decayed, the group still ably represents hill people of the period at the Wenham Historical Society. (6) This "General Grant" doll, with papier-mache head and kid body, was made in the 1860s for an aunt of Mrs. Irene Welsh of Cressy, Michigan; is now in a private collection. (7) Doorstop doll is made of a glass bottle filled with shot and given a stuffed cloth head. Before 1890 a number of these were made by the ladies of the Episcopal Church of Hampton, Virginia. (8) Mary Schwartz of Point Pleasant, Bucks County, Pennsylvania, made this unusual doll by coating the muslin head with wax, then painting over it with white oil paint. The black painted features are built up with beeswax; the eyes are shoe buttons; the hair, candlewick. The body is muslin, stuffed with cotton. She has remained in the Schwartz family ever since she was made in 1876.

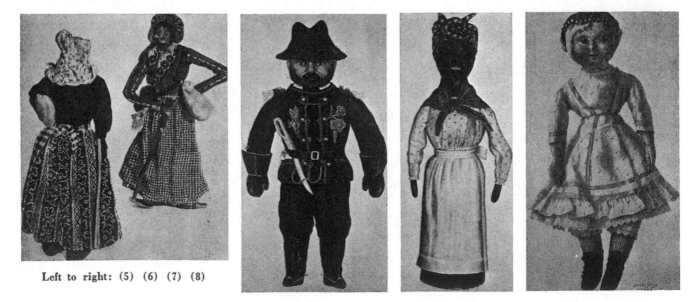

Left to right: (5) (6) (7) (8)

(9)

(10)

(11)

(12)

Cornhusk Dolls

WHAT could be harder to save for posterity than a cornshuck doll? She must never be stored where the mice can get her; she must not be left in a house which is about to catch fire; she must be kept from the baby who can end her simple or elegant personality by peeling off, strip by strip, her entire self. Yet here is one (9), some eighty years after she was made, with not a puff or ribbon looking disturbed. (10) An old lady in Essex County, Massachusetts, her name now unknown, made this cornhusk doll in 1895. It is now at the Essex Institute. (11) This elegant cornhusk lady, studded with pins, dates from the late 19th century; is now in the New York Historical Society Collection. (12) This cornhusk head doll with cloth body is said to have been the favorite doll of Henry DuPont when he and she were young, about the time of the Civil War.

(13)

(14)

(15)

(16)

Indian Dolls

EARLY American Indian dolls show startling variations in the handling of simple materials like wood, cloth, leather, and clay. Those made before tourists created a market show greater creative freedom in design and execution than do later-day productions. (13) This pair has carved wooden heads and stuffed bodies. They are Crees, designed and made by Marie Rose of the Montana Cree Reservation, and now at the Wenham (Mass.) Historical Society. (14) These two Apache squaws in voluminous bright cotton dresses were made about 1899 in Arizona. From Anna Kittare of San Carlos, Arizona, the original owner, they were passed along until they, too, found a permanent home at the Wenham Historical Society. (15) "The Frontiersman" in buckskin clothes is a cloth doll, made about 1850 by Plains Indians. (16) More than forty years ago an old man in northern Michigan carved this Indian from pine. (17) Chief, squaw and tiny papoose of the Winnebagos were made about 1898 by Winnebago Indians for Capt. W. A. Mercer, U. S. Army. Cloth was used for faces and bodies, human hair for wigs. These, also, are at the Wenham Historical Society Museum.

(17)

Late Bye-los
And Bisques

by
LUCY CUNNINGHAM

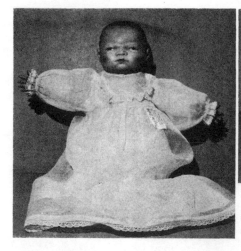

At left: 15" vinyl Bye-lo doll, 1951; original dress with label; painted eyes and hair. *Above:* Box the 15" vinyl Bye-lo came in.

In 1951 a quantity of Bye-lo dolls with vinyl heads was sold through the George Borgfeldt Co. of New York. As this is the company which handled the original Bye-lo Baby in 1923, there is no doubt that the dolls are authentic. They do resemble rubber in a way, but the early vinyl dolls became very sticky when stored, whereas rubber becomes hard and is apt to crack with age.

These dolls came in individual boxes labeled, "Bye-lo Baby — THE ALMOST HUMAN DOLL—Modeled and copyright in 1923 by Grace Storey Putnam. Geo. Borgfeldt Corporation, New York, N. Y."

The vinyl heads are marked "C Grace Storey Putnam." They have painted hair and eyes. The head circumference is 12", and the complete doll 15" tall. The cloth body is apparently cut by the original body pattern, although the hands are composition rather than celluloid. The baby wears diaper, bootees, slip, and organdy long dress and bonnet. The dress has a label of blue silk which says "Bye-lo Baby."

These dolls did not sell well because, at that time, vinyl was not considered collectible, and children did not like the faces. When I gave one to my little granddaughter, she said, "I think he looks kinda mad," and I had to replace the head before she would play with the doll.

At the same time, 1951, a factory in East Germany, not far from Bonn, was making bisque Bye-lo heads with sleeping eyes from the original molds. These dolls did not last long because production was shut down after about six months. According to Jack Fixit, who operated a doll hospital supply house in Washington, D. C. for many years, "The elderly lady who was making these dolls had to leave in the night when she learned she was going to be jailed for some reason. She has since died in Berlin."

These bisque Bye-lo heads came in five sizes and were sold without bodies. Some were of a fine, smooth

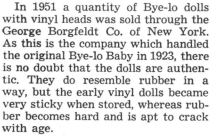

At right: 1951 all-bisque jointed doll, 7" tall, marked on head, "83 over 125." *Above:* 6" bisque Kewpie made in Germany, 1951.

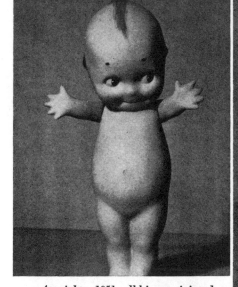

bisque which compares favorably with the early dolls; others were not of high quality. The poorest were of a bright pink color which resembles a composition finish, caused by spraying the paint on after the head was fired. In time, these heads flaked, showing the uncolored bisque underneath.

All-Bisques

This short-lived factory also produced five sizes of all-bisque jointed dolls, from 5½ to 7½ inches in height. They had sleeping glass eyes and painted socks and slippers. The bisque was inferior but acceptable, and the hair was of bright synthetic material.

These all-bisques were numbered in the catalog as: #25, 5½", set eyes. #50, 5¼", slp. eyes. #100, 5¾". #125, 7". #150, 7¼". The 7-inch doll pictured here is marked on the head 83 over 125, and below that 16 0/2. The box she came in is marked "No. 83— 100 125." All these dolls were stamped

"Germany" on the back in ink, which faded.

This same factory also made a line of bisque Kewpies with the little blue wings. These came in three sizes and were stamped "Germany" on the body. This marking rubbed off almost immediately, and as the bisque was of excellent quality, it is impossible to distinguish them from the original dolls.

Composition Bye-los

The composition Bye-lo dolls seem to have been made about 1926. They are shown in an old Montgomery Ward catalog, undated, but alongside a picture of a "Bubbles" doll (patented 1926), and some early composition dolls of that period. This composition doll is dressed much as the early bisque Bye-los, and the advertisement describes it as "The Genuine Bye-lo Baby Doll with hard-to-break composition head."

Whence comes "Becky"?

By GENEVIEVE ANGIONE

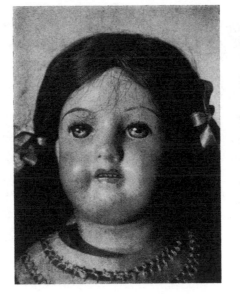

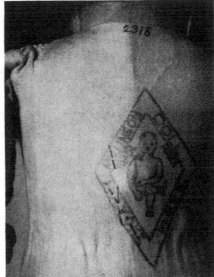

ASIDE FROM the fact that she is American made, information about Becky is strangely lacking. Many people have examined her through the years but not one has ever had or seen a duplicate. There must have been others, however, because she is factory-made. The question is: Where are they now?

"Brunson Doll, Holyoke, Mass." is quite readable in the border of the stamped trademark on her body. There is no patent number or warning of patent pending, and long hours at the Patent Office have yielded nothing. Inquiries have also been fruitless.

Unless the doll is taken apart (and badly damaged or even destroyed), any description of her is inadequate. Consequently, words like "seems to be" must crop up with annoying frequency in writing of her.

Becky is 17½ inches tall, with molded, painted features, and blue eyes which are painted in the old manner, i.e., with the pupils disappearing into the upper lid. Her mouth is open-closed with painted upper teeth; her wig is made of rather coarse blonde hair on a gauze cap.

Stitch-jointed at shoulders, elbows and hips, her construction seems to be closely patterned after the Chase Stockinette Doll. The body is sateen-covered, but the to-elbow arms and above-knee legs appear to be molded of the same light weight composition as the head. Arms and legs have a hollow sound when tapped, so they may be coreless.

Every knowing doller comments on her hands and feet. They appear to have been molded from Chase parts; even the stitch marks of the superimposed Chase thumb, for instance, were picked up in the molding process. Two questions always arise from this obvious likeness.

One: Could she be an experiment by the Chase Hospital Doll firm in the competitive doll market after World War I, perhaps in the 1920s when the quite expensive Kathie Kruse unbreakable play dolls first appeared in U. S. toy stores? One very poor clue is that she may have her original

clothing which includes "bloomers" such as those Kruse used so often to eliminate petticoats and to make dolls easier for a child to dress and undress.

Two: Could she be the product of a lease arrangement with the Chase firm? The figure "2318," which appears to be hand-written at the top of her sateen body in the back, could have been a royalty numbering system. (Kruse dolls were also hand numbered but generally on the bottom of the left foot.) Such a leasing system would account for the complete lack of patent references in the trademark. Royalty leases grant temporary use of patent rights to the lessee, and all advertising promotion centers on

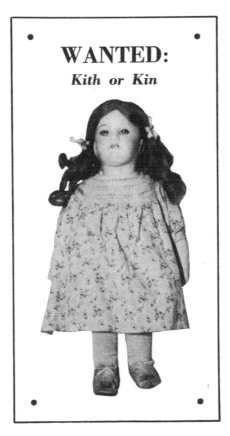

WANTED:

Kith or Kin

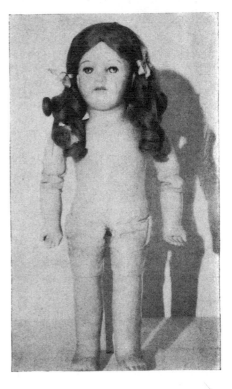

the identifying trademark. (Kruse similarly licensed her dolls for a time to Schildkrote but she permitted the use of the Kruse name as well.)

Doll nomenclature has been so lax, Becky can serve as a classification model for her type. Like Chase, Sheppard Philadelphia Baby, Kruse, etc. she is *cloth*. But while the others have "painted heads and limbs," hers should be listed as "painted composition w/wig." This distinguishes them from *cloth bodied* dolls with heads and limbs of any one or several kinds of materials whose bodies can be replaced without difficulty.

Technically none of these is a *rag* doll. The word *rag* should be reserved for soft cloth dolls with printed. painted, embroidered or needle-molded features.

The Compo Craze is for Real!

by R. LANE HERRON

THIS CENTURY'S composition doll, long ignored by advanced doll fanciers, is now attracting a vast amount of collector interest. Most popular are dolls dating from World War I to the mid-1950s. Their age often corresponds to that of the collector, who perhaps unconsciously finds in them a reminder of happy childhood days.

As a practical consideration, especially appealing to the beginning collector, the average price of composition dolls, with the exception of a few movie personality dolls of the 1930s, is not prohibitive. Best of all, there are still many fine composition dolls to be found. The bisque doll and her china sister broke easily; the wax doll melted; the rubber doll rotted. But the "late" and lowly composition doll has proved sturdy and durable.

When World War I halted imports, drastically affecting the toy business, American dollmakers, long backseat drivers, seized the opportunity to market their wares without foreign competition. Several major doll firms emerged in this hectic period; hundreds of lesser firms began and ended.

Today the dolls made by those companies which came and went so quickly are the ones collectors seek most avidly. On the long list of companies known to have produced dolls, though their dolls are elusive, are the Bijou Doll Company (1915-17), Arcy Toy Mfg. Co. (1912-25), Alisto Mfg. Co. (1920), Progressive Toy Co. (1917-23), Baker and Bennett Co. (1902-25), Moran Doll Mfg. Co. (1919-21), and American Bisque Doll Co. (1919).

Successful pioneer doll firms like Ideal, Horsman, Alexander, and Effanbee are still providing superior dolls, though not all are as interesting to collectors as those from the golden years between 1920 and 1940. Mme. Alexander's dolls seem to improve annually; her current crop of character babies and tots are more appealing than ever.

Whether the soft vinyl used today will stand the ravages of time and wear remains to be seen. Children like the realistic skin texture of vinyl, and it is almost unbreakable, but so far few vinyl dolls are in the cabinets of collectors, who find them lacking in warmth and appeal.

Grace Drayton *Campbell Kids* past and present.

Dolls of the 1930s rate high with collectors. Mme. Alexander at this time gave little girls such memorable treasures as Baby Jane, Little Colonel, Jane Withers, the Dionne Quints, Doris Kranne (in the movie *Romance)*, Geraldine Farrar (in *Carmen)*, Princess Elizabeth, Annie Laurie, Scarlet O'Hara, Wendy-Ann, and Sonja Henie.

The Ideal Toy Company, dating from the Teddy Bear in 1902, produced in that same 1930 period their famous Shirley Temple, Deanna Durbin, Judy Garland, Fanny Brice. Later came favorites like Miss Curity, Bonnie Braids, Joan Palooka, Sparkle Plenty, the Toni doll, and Saucy Walker, all highly desirable dolls to the collector. Ideal's productions of earlier days, though many, are hard to find today. Particularly appealing are Artic Boy (1913), Baby Betty (1917), Baby Talc (1915), Baseball Boy (1913), Flossie Flirt (1924), and Buster Brown (1915).

Noted Effenbees—the trademark used by Fleischaker and Baum of New York—are the Patsys, Baby Grumpy and his relatives, Bubbles, the Dewees Cochran line, Skippy, Marilee, Rosemary, and their 30 historical dolls (1917).

Horsman is the oldest of all; E. I. Horsman began in 1865. At first he assembled dolls, then in 1901 began to make his own, starting with his "Babyland" rag dolls. Best remembered Horsman composition dolls are his Billiken, the Cambell Kids, Ella Cinders, Jackie Coogan Kid, and a great array of "Can't Break 'Ums." Though Mr. Horsman died in 1927, dolls with the Horsman label are still being made.

These continuing doll firms with their constant, abundant, and always creative output helped edge the minor, less inventive, or perhaps less financially able doll companies into oblivion. Yet some of the short-lived companies made fascinating dolls. High on the list are

the dolls of Jessie McCutcheon Raleigh (1916-20), Mme. Gerogine Hendren, K & K Toy Co., Borgfeldt, Amberg, Fulper, Jane Gray and Margaret Vale, Art Fabric Mills, and Aetna.

Of all the composition, fabric, rubber, and vinyl dolls made in America since 1900, none have remained as popular as the "portrait" or celebrity doll. Margaret Vale's early celebrity doll line is rare and seemingly unprocurable. Easier to find are the celebrity dolls made by Ideal, Effanbee, Alexander, Horsman, Lenci, and Norah Wellings.

Perhaps Ideal's Shirley Temple leads the race for composition doll supremacy, closely followed in desirability by Judy Garland, Jeannette McDonald, Deanna Durbin, and Margaret O'Brien. Collectors also seek Signora Lenci's creations in felt—Mary Pickford, Raquel Miller, Valentino, Marlene Dietrich, and Shirley Temple.

Fig. 1: Contemporary composition doll dressed and sculpted by R. Lane Herron depicts *Queen Marie Antoinette*, ca. 1775. **Fig. 2:** Effanbee's *Ann Shirley* and Alexander's *McGuffey Anna*; both 21'' tall (1930s). **Fig. 3:** Ball-jointed, composition flapper doll, puffing on cigarette, advertised a popular brand of cigarettes in the 1920s. **Fig. 4:** *World War II WAAC* composition doll. **Fig. 5:** *Bubbles* doll by Effanbee with cloth feet and flange neck; larger baby made by Uneeda Doll Co. in 1917. **Fig. 6:** All original Mary Hoyer compositon from the late 1930s. **Fig. 7:** Three all-time favorites in miniature . . . *Terri Lee*, 13'', *Shirley Temple,* and Mme. Alexander's *Sonja Henie.* **Fig. 8:** *Rosemary*, by Effanbee, 1925. Labeled "Effanbee's Durable Doll''. . ."Walks, Talks, Sleeps." **Fig. 9:** Mme. Hendren *Victrola Doll,* early 1920s. **Fig. 10:** Ideal's rare *Deanna Durbin*, 15'' tall. A "posing" doll, her breast plate swivels on a wooden center section, enabling her to bend at the hips. Originally she wore a "name pin" on her gown. **Fig. 11:** Harry Coleman's *Dolly Walker* walking doll, ca. 1917; composition head, wood jointed body.

1

2

3

4

5

6

7

8

9

10

11

DOLLS created by Joseph L. Kallus

by DOROTHY S. COLEMAN

Fig. 1: Mr. Joseph Kallus surrounded by Kewpies®. Courtesy of Joseph Kallus.

DOLL COLLECTORS are becoming more and more interested in the dolls that were produced between the two great wars. These are the dolls that were played with by a large portion of our present population, either as their own dolls or as their mothers' dolls. The dolls that were manufactured from 1918 through 1925 have been covered in the Coleman book, *The Collector's Encyclopedia of Dolls,* but the dolls made from 1926 through 1941 remain to be studied.

One of the outstanding doll creators of this later period was Joseph Kallus of Brooklyn, N.Y. *(Fig. 1),* President of the Cameo Doll Company of Port Allegany, Pa. He, himself, designed and made the models for many popular dolls. He also obtained numerous patents for their construction. Many of the Joseph Kallus dolls bear a decal or paper sticker with his name on it. He put his initials behind or below the ears on some of his later vinyl dolls.

The dolls of Joseph Kallus are avidly sought by knowledgeable collectors, and with a few exceptions are obtainable in good condition at two digit figures. However, they are not easy to find and this may be partially due to the fact that they are not always recognized. It is hoped that this series of articles will rectify this situation.

While not having the appeal of some of the European bisque dolls, they do have a definite charm and are among the top quality American dolls of the 20th century, both in artistry and construction. Mr. Kallus had years of training in art and the character faces which he designed and modeled have great appeal. These dolls give evidence why the American composition dolls won out in competition with the cheaply made German bisque dolls of the postwar period. *Figure 2* shows that "Margie," made by Mr. Kallus, with a wooden body and a character face, originally cost only 98 cents retail and included a one piece garment and a hair ribbon.

In the 1920s Madame Alexander made suggestions for some of the dresses worn by the Joseph Kallus dolls. It is not known which ones these were.

Joseph Kallus is most famous for working with Rose O'Neill in the modeling of the dolls which she created, especially *Kewpies®.* After Mr. Kallus assisted in this work, he became sole maker of woodpulp (composition) *Kewpies* in the U.S.A. All of the composition *Kewpies* manufactured by Mr. Kallus, doing business as the Cameo Doll Co., were distributed by Geo. Borgfeldt & Co. Joseph Kallus has continued to make Kewpies from 1916 to the present time. The changes in material and techniques during this period were consistent with the advances in technology.

Kewpies are probably one of the most popular 20th century dolls among collectors today. More want ads appear for *Kewpies* than any other type of dolls. With such a tremendous demand and a limited supply of antique Kewpies, naturally there have been many reproductions and imitations. Joseph Kallus has all of the *Kewpie* copyrights, trademarks, design and common law rights. Only firms which he licensed could produce *Kewpie* items in any form. This applies not only to graphic representations of *Kewpies* and to *Kewpie* dolls but also to *Kewpie* clothes, *Kewpie* books, *Kewpie* games etc. Through the years there have been innumerable law-suits about infringements on these *Kewpie* rights.

The *Kewpie* doll is revered in Missouri, the birthplace of Rose O'Neill, to such an extent that it was pictured in a 1963 history textbook for high schools entitled *The Heritage of Missouri*. Annually a celebration called "Kewpiesta" takes place in Missouri to honor the memory of Rose O'Neill. (See *Memo From Marcia* jun and sep '71.)

Some of the dolls made by Joseph Kallus prior to 1926 include *Babie Bundie, Bo-Fair, Dollie, Vanitie Doll, Baby Bo Kaye* and *Little Annie Rooney*.

The following is a chronological summary of most of the dolls produced by Joseph Kallus from 1926 through 1929. Some of these dolls continued in production long after 1929 and even into the Vinyl era of the 1950s and later. Other installments will describe dolls from 1930-1941.

1926

BABY BO KAYE and LITTLE ANNIE ROONEY

Some of the records on both *Baby*

Fig. 3: MARGIE undressed, showing her joints and ability to stand in a particular pose. Height 10 inches.© Coleman collection.

Bo Kaye and *Little Annie Rooney* are dated 1926 but the information on these two dolls is given in *The Collector's Encyclopedia of Dolls*.

1927

BABY BLOSSOM (Copyrighted)

This doll has the "character face of a small child," according to the copyright papers. It resembles a baby's head with eyes glancing to the side, a tiny pug nose and dimples in each fat cheek. The molded hair is short with a lock coming down over the forehead. There are composition versions and fabric versions with embossed buckram backed faces. After World War II a 16-inch composition *Baby Blossom* was made in a version with a flock spray finish. It had stencil finish decorations and shading spray for a portrait effect.

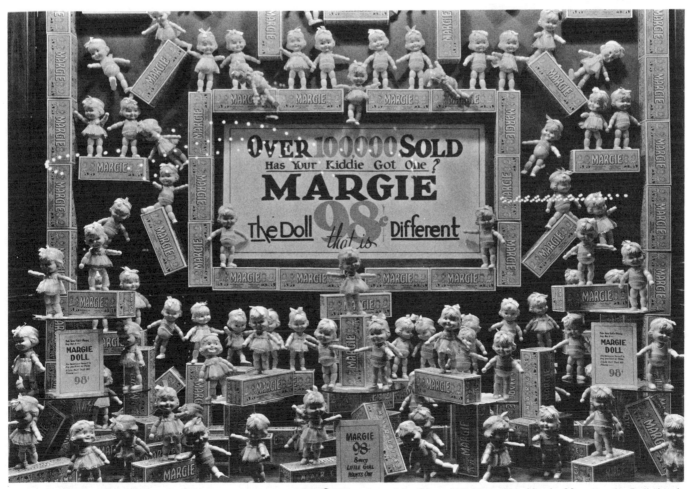

Fig. 2: MARGIE dolls in store window, New York City, 1929.© The print reads, "Over 100,000 sold— Margie 98 cents, the Doll that is Different—She balances herself in any position or poise." This picture shows two types of this doll's original clothes. A third type of original commercial clothes has been found and no doubt others exist. Courtesy of Joseph Kallus.

CANYON KIDDIES
(Copyrighted)

These *Kiddies* from Canyon Country were taken from drawings by James Swinnerton, Palo Alto, California. The children, probably a boy and a girl, had bands around their heads which held down their thick bobbed hair and bangs.

KEWPIE
(Regular patent for a cloth doll resembling a Kewpie.)

The patent for a cloth doll resembling a *Kewpie* was filed by Rose O'Neill Wilson and her sister, Calista O'Neill Schuler, of Saugatuck, Connecticut. It was later produced by Joseph Kallus. The entire doll was made of fabric and came in two versions. One had a hand-painted face with features put on with an air spray. The other version had a face that was done by a lithographic printing process. Various materials were used for the face, chief among them was sateen. This was mounted on embossed buckram or canvas to provide the contours of the features. The earliest bodies were cut in four pieces, but a 1929 improvement in this patent reduced the number of pieces in the body to two.

1928
BOZO
(Copyrighted)

This toy is in the form of a humanized dog.

SISSIE
(Copyrighted)

This doll has the head of a smiling child.

Fig. 4: MARGIE, a close-up showing the detail of her features.© Coleman collection.

1929
MARGIE
(Copyrighted and patented)

A regular patent was applied for in this year for making a doll with a separate neck piece which was a feature of *Margie*. The object of this patent is described as, "Constructing the doll necks as separate units or elements, independent of the heads or bodies, and then combining such separate necks with the heads and bodies in predetermined ways to form the completed dolls." The patent drawings show either a spring wire or a hook connecting the elements. The neck is held rigid in the body recees. The patent also states, "Up to the present time the necks of dolls . . . have always been constructed as integral parts

Fig. 5: MARGIE, an advertisement for the vinyl model.© Courtesy of Joseph Kallus.

either of the heads or bodies thereof and dolls constructed in this manner with adjustable heads are old and well known . . .

"By constructing the neck member as a separate member independently of the body or head of the doll . . . it is possible in the case of dolls having molded heads to simultaneously cast more heads per given die than has heretofore been possible; experience has shown that the number of heads which may be molded with the present construction is as much as double that which is possible under existing conditions . . . The novel construction applies with equal advantage to either soft or hard dolls, thus overcoming a disadvantage existing heretofore, which required one type of head for soft dolls and another for hard or wood turned dolls.

" . . . If the doll should be dropped either accidentally or intentionally the yielding action of the head and neck

Fig. 6: Paper tag used on dolls. This is similar but not the same as the trademark which was registered in 1930.® Courtesy of Joseph Kallus.

member within the body absorbs the impacts and thus reduces the possibility of breaking the doll to a minimum."

A soft doll has a cloth body and a hard doll has either a composition or a wooden body. Margie has a woodpulp composition head with molded hair and headband. The body is entirely of turned wood, and is composed of 18 pieces. It is articulated at the neck, shoulders, elbows, hips, knees and ankles with elastic stringing. It is the first segmented wooden doll created by Joseph Kallus. The balance is such that it will stand erect. The composition head is made in a 2-part mold. In each section of the head "an undercut recess is formed at the free edges thereof during the molding." Note the fact that the undercut was made during the molding.

The eyes are painted with large black pupils surrounded by a small circle of blue for the iris. Some glance to the right side and some to the left side. There is usually a white highlight on the left upper side of the iris. Upper eyelashes are painted on but no lower ones. *Pinkie, Joy* and other Kallus dolls have their eyes painted in the same manner. *Margie* has her mouth painted as if smiling and open with four teeth showing.

On the upper part of the torso (front or back) is a triangular heart shaped label with "MARGIE" in white letters including the quotation marks *(See Figs. 4 & 5.)* This is over two lines of smaller black letters which read, "DES. & COPYRIGHT BY JOSEPH KALLUS." It appears to be a decal label.

Margie was made in several forms of construction. The segmented wooden version was distributed all over America and England. Several hundred thousands were produced. It was made also as a soft body doll with an embossed buckram face. Recently another doll named *Margie* was made of vinyl plastic which was combined with some wooden segments *(Fig. 5)*. All of these dolls were made by Cameo. Another company which copied the wooden bodied *Margie* was eventually stopped by court order. The imitation *Margies* do not carry the label described above.

THE DOLLS created by Joseph Kallus from 1926 through 1929 were discussed in a previous issue. The dolls that Mr. Kallus and the Cameo Doll Company produced from 1930 through 1932, the depression years, are summarized here.

It should be remembered that the composition *Kewpies* and *Scootles* of Rose O'Neill and the composition *Bye-Lo Babies* of Grace Storey Putnam as well as many other dolls were produced throughout all of these periods (1926-1941) by Mr. Kallus, doing business as the Cameo Doll Company. Borgfeldt tried to get their subsidiary, K & K Toy Company, to make wood-pulp composition dolls but they were unsuccessful in their efforts and soon after 1925 Cameo took over the products formerly made by K & K Toy Company.

Fig. 7: PINKIE, composition head, hands and legs, wooden torso and arms. Height 10½ inches.© Coleman collection.

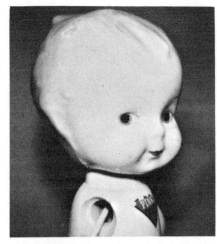

Fig. 8: PINKIE, a close-up showing the elastic stringing and the label.© Coleman collection.

1930

ADVERTISING DOLL
(Design patent)

This is an advertising doll designed by Mr. Kallus and manufactured by Cameo Doll Company. It is a R.C.A. trade figure for radiotrons, and is marked "R.C.A. Radiotrons" on its hat and on a band across its chest. (See "Who Knows," jul-aug '67, page 34 for query and pictures, and mar '68 page 37 for the answer.) It is fully jointed with complete lifelike articulation so that it can stand and hold practically any desired position. The doll has molded boots and a high hat that simulates a radio tube. It came also in a black skin version to represent Amos and Andy, a favorite radio team of the era. About 200,000 of these dolls were produced.

BABY ADELE
(Copyrighted)

This doll has a character head that represents a two-year old child.

CAMEO DOLL COMPANY
(Trademark registered)

Joseph Kallus, New York, N.Y., doing business as the Cameo Doll Co., registered a trademark bearing the profile of a child's head, with the words, "Art Quality" over the head and "Cameo Toys" under it.

KEWPIE
(patent granted)

The 1927 patent was granted for the cloth doll which resembles a *Kewpie*. Actually this patent had been superseded by a later improvement for which a patent application had been filed in 1929.

MARGIE
(Design patent)

The design patent pictures *Margie* with her smiling face, four teeth

showing in an open-closed mouth and around her head a ribbon is tied in a large bow over her right eye.

Regular patent application relating to limbs for dolls.

This patent was designed for a doll with a composition and wood body to enable a section of turned or carved wood to be joined to a section of plaster, papier-mache or other type of molded composition to produce a doll's limb.

PINKIE
(Copyrighted)

This is the head of a child with baby features *(Figs. 7 and 8)*. It has composition head, legs and hands. The arms, torso, and neck are wood. The same type of red triangular heart-shaped label is used as found on *Margie*, except the word *PINKIE* in white does not have quotation marks around it. *Pinkie* was made in several versions with various types of construction. It was made of segmented turned wood and/or composition parts. The eyes on *Pinkie* resemble those on *Margie* but the mouth is painted as if it were closed. *Pinkie* was also made as a fabric doll with an embossed buckram backed face. Recently another doll also named *Pinkie* was produced in vinyl *(Fig. 9)*.

1931

Regular patent application for a "Limb for a Toy Figure"

The leg as shown and described in

Fig. 9: PINKIE, vinyl version. Height 27 inches.© Courtesy of Joseph Kallus.

Fig. 10: BETTY BOOP, store display. Fleischer Studios created the movie cartoon but Mr. Kallus created the dolls.© Courtesy of Joseph Kallus.

the outside of the label is a gold frame with scalloped edges and on this are the words, "Des. & Copy" at the top and "J. L. Kallus" at the bottom. The lower wood extremities of the doll are shaped like shoes and painted pink or blue. It has the eyes painted like those on *Margie* and *Pinkie*. The smiling mouth is simply a curved line similar to ones found on *Kewpies*. *Joy* was made in two sizes, 11 and 15 inches, and several hundred thousand were produced.

Regular patent granted for a "Limb for a Toy Figure."

Patent application for "Jointed Toy Figures."

Mr. Kallus applied for a regular patent pertaining to "jointed toy figures having hollow bodies and other members made of collapsible material such as soft rubber." The invention provided for the construction of the rubber doll "in a manner to simulate naturally the relatively rigid and yielding parts of the original which the toy figure is intended to represent." It goes on to state, "special means is provided to prevent collapse of the doll under tension" by reinforcement with a rigid device located inside the body and vulcanized to the body. The rigid device in the body includes recesses for contact with ball joints in the rigid devices in the neck and limbs to enable the doll to have articulation. This appears to be one of the early patents for producing articulated soft skin dolls of latex. Joseph Kallus used the name "Beauty Skin" for his dolls made of latex.

POPEYE

Mr. Kallus was licensed by King Features Syndicate to make a *Popeye*

this patent is the same as one of the types used on *Pinkie*. Previously the nail or brad which held the elastic to the limb after it had hardened and become brittle which resulted in frequent breakage and loss. This was a popular method of production, although there had been others.

The patent proposes to mold the nail or metal device into the composition so that it is already there in place when the composition hardens thus eliminating possible breakage.

1932
BETTY BOOP
(Doll copyrighted by Joseph Kallus)

This doll was designed to resemble the famous movie cartoon character of the day, created by Fleischer Studios for Paramount Pictures. The head, hands, upper torso, and skirt are composition while the arms, legs, and lower torso are made of turned wood. It is fully articulated. The legs terminate in high-heeled shoes. These shoes, made from turned wood, are a masterpiece of clever designing by Joseph Kallus so that they could be made very simply but give the desired effect. *(Figs. 10 and 11)*

Betty Boop was a landmark case in the copyright office because it established the fact that a copyright on a

three-dimensional object covered a two-dimensional figure as well. This involved a lawsuit which was won by Joseph Kallus.

Betty Boop came in several versions, among them a soft body version and a version with composition legs which was dressed as a little girl *(Fig. 10)*. One of the composition and wooden versions is 12½ inches tall and has the dress, drawers, and shoes painted green. It has black eyes and long black upper eyelashes.

JOY
(Copyrighted)

This character doll represents a child. One version is fully jointed at neck, shoulders, elbows, wrists, hips, knees, and ankles. The arms, legs, and feet are wooden while the head, torso and hands are composition. Another version has composition lower legs and is not articulated at the ankles. There are still other versions. The wispy molded hair has one curl in the front on the forehead and two curls in back. *(Figs. 12, 13, and 14)* Some of the *Joy* dolls have a loop of hair on top through which a ribbon can be placed and tied into a bow. On other *Joy* dolls there is just an indentation in the curl on top of the head. The first version described above has on the upper part of the torso a red circular label with the word *"JOY"* on it. Around

Fig. 11: BETTY BOOP close-up showing black hair and eyes. The doll wears a green dress. Height 12½ inches.© Courtesy of Dorothy Annunziato.

doll based on the Segar cartoons. After Mr. Kallus had successful experiences with *Popeye* dolls, he arranged with the King Features to license Fleischer studios and Paramount Pictures to make animated moving pictures of *Popeye*. When the moving picture cartoons were created the *Popeye* dolls were put in different poses to provide models for the Fleischer artists. The early segmented wooden *Popeye* dolls had "©//King Features//Syn. Inc.//1932" on one of their feet. Later vinyl versions were marked "Cameo K. F. S. ©" and were advertised by Sears, Roebuck & Co. in 1957-1959.

1933
MARCIA

Marcia is an all-composition doll representing a young girl *(Fig. 16)*. It is jointed at the neck, shoulders, and hips. It has molded hair and painted eyes with a wide staring look to the side. The shoes and socks are painted on the legs and feet. The doll comes in a range of sizes and wears a French-type outfit. Blanche Cromien, the chief dress designer for Mr. Kallus, designed the outfit by copying some French clothes displayed at Lord & Taylor's store.

Regular patent granted for constructing dolls like Joy.

Mr. Kallus obtained a patent which was used in the production of *Joy (Fig. 17)*. The doll shown in the patent diagram resembles the *Joy* doll shown

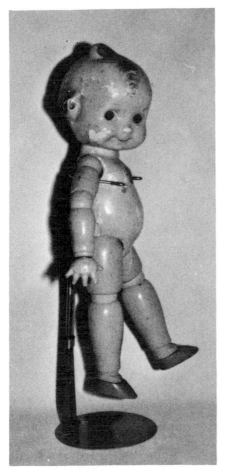

Fig. 13: JOY undressed; another version of Joy undressed will appear in the next installment. Height 15 inches.© Courtesy of Dorothy Annunziato.

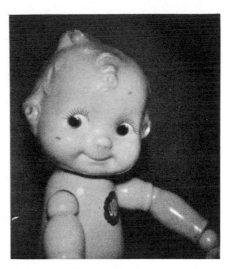

Fig. 14: JOY close-up showing detail of features and label.© Height 11 inches. Courtesy of Dorothy Annunziato.

in *Fig. 17*. This was a later version than the dolls with all-wooden legs. The molded wood-pulp legs had a hollow wooden core which was used for stability in stringing. The labeled *Joy* dolls shown in the previous article *(Figs. 13 and 14)* also appear to have been made in accordance with this 1933 patent.

The patent papers state: "The object of the invention is to improve the construction of the limbs or other members of the toy figure with a view to increasing the efficiency thereof and to materially reduce the cost of

Fig. 12: JOY in store display about 1932.© Joy is shown in two types of commercial outfits and a bow on its head. It is priced at 98 cents. Courtesy of Joseph Kallus.

production." In essence the invention provided for a turned wooden upper leg with "an inclined end surface" and a body that "is tapered at its lower portion having downwardly and inwardly converging external surfaces." The joint itself was produced by taking a turned wooden ball, cutting it in two and nailing the hemisphere to the "inclined end surface" of the leg to obtain a smooth rounded joint which enabled the doll to be seated without spreading its legs apart.

Regular patent for the articulated rubber doll granted.

1935
BANDMASTER (See Drum Major.)
DRUM MAJOR (Copyrighted.)

This doll was named *Drum Major* on the copyright but was later named "Bandmaster" which was soon shortened to *Bandy*. It was an advertising doll or trade figure for General Electric Company and was manufactured by Cameo Co. with the turned wooden parts made by Holgate Co. for Cameo according to the design and specifications of Joseph Kallus. Hol-

Fig. 15: KEWPIE-GAL, designed by Joseph Kallus and made in the vinyl era. It came in two sizes.© Courtesy of Joseph Kallus.

gate had the intricate wood-turning machinery which this doll required.

Printer's Ink described this doll: "He is a salesman eighteen inches tall, with a humorously cheerful painted face, a smart red and white drum major's uniform and legs and arms so limber that he assumes almost any human attitude. He was intended to be put into window displays. . . . He stopped so many doll lovers that radio shops are now going into the doll trade. They sell *Bandy* . . . to women who make doll collections, to mothers and fathers who see in him the ideal Christmas present for little Isobel, . . . And so General Electric, somewhat astonished, is in the Christmas doll business."

The body and head is of wood pulp composition and all other parts are of segmented wood. There are about 20 segments of wood which are assembled with coil springs. On the head is a high molded shako and the doll carries a baton. A molded medal around its neck bears the familiar "G. E." trademark initials.

Other trade figures designed by Mr. Kallus and made by Cameo include "Koppers Coke" and "Hotpoint." In addition Mr. Kallus designed several trade figures which Ideal Novelty and Toy Company produced. These include: Planter's, *Mr. Peanut; Conmar Major* of the Conmar Zipper Co. and a *Santa* for Shaeffer Pen Co. All of these were used as dolls and for display purposes.

Fig. 16: MARCIA, all composition doll of 1933. It wears an outfit copied from a French design.© Courtesy of Joseph Kallus.

1936-1938

No information found.

1939
BABY SNOOKS

The head for the *Baby Snooks* doll was designed by Joseph Kallus and produced by Ideal Novelty and Toy Company. From 1939-1941 Mr. Kallus designed several dolls for Ideal. *Baby Snooks* is a flexible doll which resembles Fanny Brice in her role as Baby Snooks. The head is of composition with molded hair having a loop of molded hair through which a bow or ribbon can be tied.

PINOCCHIO

Mr. Kallus designed the authentic Walt Disney *Pinocchio* doll produced by Ideal Novelty and Toy Company. This doll is 11 inches tall and has segmented wooden parts so that it can stand in any position. A colored picture of the doll shows it with a red suit trimmed with three yellow buttons and a yellow hat with a red feather. The large bow tie under its chin is white. The smiling mouth is open with lower teeth showing. In 1940 *Pinocchio* was made in three sizes, 8 inches, 11 inches, and 20 inches.

1940
CROWNIE (Copyrighted.)

This is a caricature of a king and is one of the many segmented dolls that were designed by Mr. Kallus. Note the poses which the jointed construction makes possible *(Fig. 18)*. The round ball for a hand is typical of this type of doll. Similar hands are found on *R.C.A. Radiotron, Bandy, Koppers Coke, Hotpoint,* and *Pinocchio.*

1941
COOKIE (Trademark for dolls registered by Joseph Kallus.)
Regular patent for a Toy Figure.

Application was made by Mr. Kallus for a patent relating to the joints of a doll with a body of soft rubber fabric or the like. The ball joints fit into rigid concave sleeve sections which provide stability as well as movement.

It is hoped that doll collectors have learned many things from this series of articles on the dolls created by Mr. Kallus. First of all that a doll with a given name can be found in several versions, even of the same material. *(See Figs. 13, 14 and 17 in Part Two)* If your doll has legs that differ from those on another doll with a similar named head, it does not necessarily

mean that there have been replacements, both types can be original. Sometimes a doll may come with molded loops in its hair and at other times it may have only an indentation in the hair. But both types are authentic and original.

The extensive use of wood in the bodies of dolls made during the late 1920s and 1930s may come as a surprise to some collectors. As collectors study composition and wooden dolls further, the patent information becomes of great importance in the dating of their construction. It must

be remembered that patent applications could not be made on products that had been on the market longer than one or two years. Thus if your doll has joints or other parts that resemble these patents, you can probably date it within a few years. However, just because the construction is similar to one of these dolls, do not jump to the conclusion that it was created by Mr. Kallus. Alas, he had many imitators. We can only be certain of a doll if it is marked or, in some cases, if it is absolutely identical with one that is marked.

Fig. 18-A: CROWNIE, front view of a fully jointed character doll with a composition head and wooden body. © Courtesy of Joseph Kallus.

Fig. 18-B: Side view of Fig. 18-A.

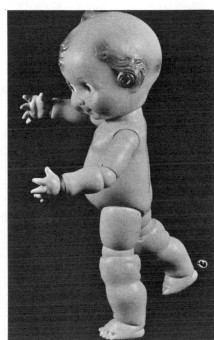

Fig. 17: JOY, front and side views showing patented hip joint. See previous installment for other pictures of Joy. © Courtesy Joseph Kallus.

GRACE DRAYTON'S
ROLY-POLY "KIDS"

Campbell Kid poster with dressed and undressed dolls. Age and makers of these dolls unknown. Doll collectors have classified them as Campbell Kids and believe them to be made of vinyl. Heads are large, bodies chubby.

The Composition O'Neill Kewpie posed before the Campbell Kid poster shows a marked resemblance in body type and facial structure. (Kewpie here is jointed at shoulders and hips, head swivels.)

by JULIE MASTERSON CHILD AND LINDA MASTERSON

BY A STRANGE quirk of fate, the life paths of two unrelated baby girls, born in Pennsylvania in the 1870s within three years of each other, were destined to be surprisingly similar. Both were to become successful authors, yet would win greater fame as artists. Even their private lives paralleled. Both entered into two unsuccessful and childless marriages which ended in divorce. Both loved children and had a keen understanding of their ways. What is even more coincidental is that despite their many talents, neither would probably be remembered today had it not been for their appealing drawings of impish creatures with roguish eyes and the many dolls created in their image.

Although a number of books and articles have been written about Rose O'Neill and her famous Kewpies, relatively little has appeared about Grace Gebbie Wiederseim Drayton, the artist who created Dolly Dingle and many other memorable "Kids"—among them, most famous of all, The Campbell Kids.

Born in Philadelphia on October 14, 1877, Grace was blessed with many of the same talents and abilities so generously bestowed upon her Scottish father, George Gebbie, and her good-natured Irish mother, Mary Fitzgerald Gebbie. Grace was educated in private schools within the state. She was 22 when on April 18, 1900, she married Theodore E. Wiederseim, Jr. of the Ketterilinus Lithographic Manufacturing Company of Philadelphia.

According to one well-known authority in the field of registered trademarks, Grace amused herself during the early years of her first marriage—and at the same time received a modest income—with drawing roly-poly twins to be used for party favors and decorations. Representatives of the Joseph Campbell Company saw her delightful drawings and asked that she adapt the activities of her frolicking kiddies to some suitable for streetcar advertisements. He further claims that these advertising posters first appeared in 1904, though statements by present representatives of the Campbell Company place the date four years earlier.

In another version of the tale, Grace's work was brought to the attention of the Campbell Company when Theodore Wiederseim, Jr. persuaded his wife to do a few sketches to aid him in his efforts to solicit their business for his lithographic firm. Despite these differences of opinion, all sources seem to agree that the now-famous Campbell Kids made their national advertising appearance in the *Ladies Home Journal* during 1905.

Contrary to popular belief, the Campbell Kids did not make their debut as one specific set of twins nor were they presented as one particular brother or sister team. Because these impressions have persisted through the years, many present-day collectors still believe that early unsigned drawings of similar Campbell Kids must be attributed to other artists. This is not the case, though it is true that other artists did draw the Campbell Kids at a later date.

Unsigned post cards drawn by Grace and issued by the Campbell Company during the first decade of this century serve as proof of the many different types of Kids that were once featured in their early advertising matter. Grace used blondes, as well as Kids with various shades of red and brown hair. Some of her boys had short cropped hair while others wore it relatively long or in a "Dutch-Cut" with bangs. She frequently included at least one boy with unruly hair or a cowlick; he was often shown in a Buster Brown suit. Her little girls were pictured with bobbed straight hair, as well as with curls; invariably they wore huge hair-ribbons, flowers, or even both at the same time.

Another widespread misconception is that Grace never permitted ears to show in any of her drawings of the Campbell Kids and that pictures of Kids with exposed ears must be attributed to other artists. On post card No. 1 of the little-known "Campbell's Kids" postcard series, (No. 2 is pictured here), the ears of two infants are clearly visible, as well as those of one of the older boys. In addition, a youngster in a sailor suit cooperatively points to his right ear.

Although the post cards in this series do not bear the G. G. Wiederseim signature that Grace was using at that time for her other work, identification presents no problem provided the collector is aware that they were originally issued in pairs. While they contain no copyright data or other printed matter on the reverse side, they are recognizable even when separated, since each card has three straight sides and one perforated edge. They were printed in various shades of red, yellow, blue, green, brown, and black.

No advertising gimmick ever proved more effective or more enduring than the roly-poly Campbell Kids, who soon became known as "The Goodwill Ambassadors of the Advertising World." They also proved to be trend-setters, for Grace was one of the first artists to use the round wide-eyed

Although unsigned, the drawings for this 1908 "Campbell Menu Book" were done by Grace Drayton who was then known as G. G. Wiederseim. Many of her drawings were copyrighted by the Joseph Campbell Company.

Because it is so difficult to decipher, many collectors overlook Grace Drayton's earlier signature, "G. G. Wiederseim."

Card No. 2 (right) in "Campbell Kids" postcard series, shows 7 kids, between them wearing 22 bows, in hair, on sashes and shoes. The card is undated, but a message on the reverse suggests 1908. Card No. 17 (left) in the "Campbell Kids" series No. 3, copyrighted in 1913. Printed matter on back states that a series of six cards would be mailed to any address upon receipt of six cents in stamps sent to the Joseph Campbell Co. By 1913, Grace Drayton's drawings had become highly stylized and there was less contrast between the different types of children used.

look—often with eyes glancing sideward. Known then as "roguish eyes," they are now called "googly eyes" or "goo-goo eyes." Grace used curved variations of the letter "H" to indicate cheeks and mouth, and an abbreviated line, hardly more than a dot, suggested eyebrows. The tiny pug nose that she favored made it relatively difficult to show them with turned heads.

While other artists measured bodies in terms of the number of heads contained therein, Grace ignored the usual rules and did not hesitate to use one-third or more of the total figure height for the head alone. The width of the face was often as great, or even broader, than the width of the shoulders. Their fat little hands with chubby fingers, known to present-day collectors as "starfish hands," may be seen on Kewpies and other dolls. Although children were still wearing long stockings at that time, Grace preferred short socks. Awareness of these characteristics aids in the identification of her work.

The lovable Campbell Kids—part imp, part angel, and part child—smiled and scampered through the pages of leading women's magazines, attracting the attention of millions of housewives, then found their way into the scrapbooks of children everywhere.

Rose O'Neill's rosy-cheeked youngsters were appearing in Jell-O advertisements about this same time. Both the Campbell and Jell-O companies advertised extensively and issued many menu and recipe books. While the Jell-O Company allowed Rose O'Neill to use her name, Grace's artwork for the Campbell Company was neither signed nor credited. Today, collectors eagerly seek the advertising pages, as well as the booklets of both firms.

The paths of Rose O'Neill, originator of the Kewpies, and Grace Gebbie Wiederseim Drayton crossed many times but never more interestingly than in 1909, when the Kewpies made their first appearance in the *Ladies Home Journal* and one of Grace's attractive illustrations appeared on its cover.

Although the Kewpies proved to be overwhelmingly popular, interest in the Campbell Kids continued and they were brought out in doll form in 1910. They were an immediate success. Because the Campbell advertisements in magazines had always featured both boys and girls, most children demanded a pair of dolls, so sales volume was twice as high as it might otherwise have been. The dolls sold for $1 each and were available in a variety of costumes. Jointed at the shoulders and hips, they were made with sturdy cork-stuffed bodies.

Although the patent office in Washington, D.C. claims to have no record of this doll made by the E. I. Horsman Co. of New York City, under license of the Joseph Campbell Company, many collectors of advertising art, as well as doll collectors, own dolls marked, "E. I. H.© 1910," which they claim were the first Campbell Kids ever made.

In Great Britain in 1911, "The Campbell Kids" trademark was registered and the dolls were available in three sizes. In 1912, the E. I. Horsman Co. obtained American patents for matching boy and girl outfits made of cotton, featuring yokes with a distinctive doll print. Dolls are still being found wearing these easily recognizable garments. Horsman dolls were made with the highly advertised "Can't Break 'Em" heads, free-swinging limbs, and bodies covered in pink cotton sateen. They were advertised as being dressed in a variety of garments and special attention was given to a Campbell baby recently added to the line.

The popularity of the Campbell Kids continued, and in 1913, "Kids with Wigs" were introduced. Post cards issued by the Campbell Company that same year show the Kids playing with dolls who wear wigs in natural life-like shades. The following year, dolls with hair painted green, red, and blue appeared on the market; post cards recording this unhappy event have yet to be found.

Collectors fortunate enough to own mail-order catalogs often have a wealth of information available that may be shared with other collectors.

Decal-decorated Campbell Kid feeding dish was produced in bright colors by the Buffalo Pottery. The boy wears blue overalls, the girl a white dress decorated with roses; she has bows in her hair.

In one mail-order catalog published in 1914, 12½-inch Campbell Kids in Dutch costumes were advertised for $.89 each. They were described as: "Charming little dolls with roguish eyes. Costumes are attractive in bright contrasting colors. Unbreakable composition heads and hands in rosy natural tints. Full cloth bodies, well-stuffed, jointed at hips and shoulders. Cloth slippers are made in the shape of wooden shoes."

The "Campbell Kids at Home" recipe and story book, written by Alma S. Lach, the artwork by George Schling Studios, published by Rand McNally & Co. in 1954. Unsigned Campbell Kid poster. Campbell Kid spoon (4⅝" long) and fork (5⅛") bears the legend "M-m-m Good" on the front. Reverse shows mark of "Wm. Rogers Oneida Ltd." Curly-haired girl with hair band is represented on the spoon; boy in chef's cap is on the fork.

Illustration from an unknown (juvenile) book. The G. G. Wiederseim signature (upper left corner) was the one Grace Drayton used before her second marriage in June 1911.

Another advertisement, titled "The Great Campbell Kids," offered 14-inch dolls in shoulder-head styles. It stated: "The newest designs of these unbreakable world famous dolls—heads as well as the bare arms and exposed necks are made of an unbreakable composition which has been wonderfully tinted in natural flesh color. Cork stuffed bodies, jointed at hips, knees, and shoulders. Boy with checkered rompers; girl with pretty striped dress and neat underwear. Socks and felt slippers on both. $.98 each." "Junior Campbell Kids," were available in smaller sizes at $.48 each.

A catalog entry also eliminates any uncertainty in regard to the Campbell Baby introduced in 1911, which many collectors have never seen. They are pictured with the same heads as those used for the regular Campbell Kids; all had roguish eyes and painted bobbed hair. They were listed as being 10 inches long, and available in either long or short baby dresses, though only the ones in long dresses had curved baby legs.

Advertising pictures and posters with jingles, post cards, and dolls are by no means the only Campbell Kids items available to collectors, though many disagree as to which items should be specifically designated as Campbell Kids items and which should be classified as Drayton collectibles. There have probably been more disagreements about feeding dishes than about any other item, though many collectors feel the question was finally resolved when *The Book of Buffalo Pottery* was published in 1969. In it, Violet and Seymour Altman classified these semi-vitreous china dishes as a Campbell Kids item. They claim that feeding dishes with various multicolored pictures of the Campbell Kids appeared in catalogs from 1913 through 1918.

Another point of disagreement between collectors centers upon the belief that Grace never showed the Campbell Kids in profile and positioned the heads so that no portion of the neck ever showed. If these feeding dishes are to be accepted as Campbell Kids items, the one pictured here serves as proof that they were occasionally shown in profile and that the neck was visible.

According to Violet and Seymour Altman, these feeding plates were not premiums of the Larkin Company, but were items to be sold. They further stated, "The purchase of one entitled the buyer to fifty cents' credit towards premiums; or, if he purchased one outright without a premium credit, the cost was half the catalog price or twenty-five cents." The backs of these feeding dishes bear the Buffalo Pottery mark but are undated.

Another plate which also bears the Buffalo Pottery mark shows the same two children but as the boy is not shown in profile, it is regarded as less desirable by some collectors. On this plate the doll is on the ground and the boy is consoling the little girl; the letters of the alphabet appear around the rim.

Various promotional efforts on the part of the Campbell Company have been responsible for other collectibles, including metal or silver-plated cups, mugs, and flatware.

It is not certain just how long Grace actually continued drawing the Campbell Kids, though it is believed her associa-

Cover illustration for the 1909 edition of "The Ladies Home Journal" was drawn by Grace Drayton.

tion with the Campbell company ceased after about 1915 or 1916. Subsequent artists listed by the Joseph Campbell Company include Roy Williams, Corrine Pauli, Dorothy Jones, the Paul Fennell Studios on the West Coast, Johnstone and Cushing of New York, and Mel Richman of Philadelphia.

The Kids have always kept pace with the times and their appearances have changed from time to time. At the beginning of the century the adventuresome Kids drove early sports cars before they graduated to primitive planes. During World War I they enthusiastically sold Liberty Bonds, and in the 1940s they did their bit as air-raid wardens. Since then they have become world travelers and are recognized all the way from Haiti in the Caribbean to Hong Kong in the Orient.

Their image has appeared on paper, glass, china, and metal. Though they have changed with the times, a recent vinyl doll, manufactured by Ideal and marked "Campbell Kid," indicates they have not lost their appeal.

COLLECTING DRAYTON

*by JULIE MASTERSON CHILD
& LINDA MASTERSON*

MOTHER-LOVE

Your face is all washed off, dear,
  'Cause you's lef' out in the rain;
An' you hasn't any mouf to kiss,
  But I'll kiss you jus' the same.
You can't cry—poor Dolly—
  'Cause you hasn't any eyes,
But I love you—twice-t as much,
   Dear,
  Now you look so sad an' wise.

THE PET SQUIRREL

I'm glad I'm coming home from
  school
  'An not jus' on my way,
'Cause 'en I'd have no time to
  stop
  To pet you an' to play.

PUSSY REBELS

My naughty little missie,
  She teased me so, to-day!
She pulled, an' squeezed, an'
  pinched me,
  An' stroked me the wrong way!
Until I couldn't stand it
  Another minute, so
I gave her one big awful scratch,
  An' then she let me go.

THE SUFFRAGETTE

When I grow up—I 'spect to be
A Drug Store Man, 'cause 'n, you see,
I'll have lots of candy an' "lick-
  rish" sweet,
An' Ice Cream Sodas an' Fudge to
  eat.
I'll have stamps in a drawer, an'
  postcards gay—
An' packs of moneys 'at peoples pay,
I'll give little boys powders bad 's
  I can,
I'se a girl— But I'll grow—
  To a Drug Store Man!

AN OLD SONG

"Gavver ye 'rose-bugs' while ye
  may,"
  I heard my Muvver sing,
But—when I gavvered one to-day,
  It stinged like anyfing!

AFTER MOTHER

I fink I'll call him Tommy,
I'd like to call him 'at,
Count o' his muvver bein'
The next-door Folk's—Tom-Cat.

Drayton pages, such as these, are difficult to trace once they have
been removed from a book.

Because Grace Drayton's name has always been so closely linked with the highly collectible Campbell Kids items, some collectors are unaware that she was one of the most prolific artists of her time and was associated with a variety of items which ranged from delicate jewelry to heavy iron doorstops and bookends. She designed all-bisque dolls, rag dolls, dolls with composition heads, and paper dolls. Her artistic projects included designs for commercial illustrations, posters, prints, and post cards. Grace also wrote jingles, poetry, and prose, and illustrated her own work, as well as some of her sister's, Margaret G. Hays.

During an interview in the mid-1920s, Grace was asked if her artwork for the Campbell Company had made her famous. She stated she attributed her success to several newspaper contracts which stipulated her work would be signed or credited. She mentioned having been on the staff of the *New York Journal* and that she had switched to the *Press,* before returning to the *Journal.* In 1906 or 1907, she originated the "Bobby Blake and Dolly Drake" series which eventually led to a long line of books after it had run for two years in the *Sunday Philadelphia Press.* In 1908 her series of "Undiscovered Beauties" appeared in the *New York Herald* and provided the idea for a series of prints suitable for framing.

Books written and illustrated by Grace G. Wiederseim Drayton listed with date, title, publisher, original price, and her current name, include:

1907 *Mother Goose Calendar: Annual,* Scribners, $2.50, Wiederseim.

1907 *Nursery Rhymes from Mother Goose,* Scribners, $1.50, Wiederseim.

1909 *Dolly Drake,* Stokes, $.50, Wiederseim.

1907 *Mother Goose Calendar: Annual,* Scribners, $2.50, Wiederseim.

1907 *Nursery Rhymes from Mother Goose,* Scribners, $1.50, Wiederseim.

1909 *Dolly Drake,* Stokes, $.50, Wiederseim.

1909 *Bobby Blake,* Stokes, $.50, Wiederseim.

1909 *Tiny Tots, Their Adventures,* Stokes, $.60, Wiederseim.

1910 *Baby's Day,* Stokes, $.60, Wiederseim.

1910 *Fido,* Stokes, $.50, Wiederseim.

1910 *Kitty Puss,* Stokes, $.50, Wiederseim.

1911 *Ducky Daddles,* Stokes, $.50, Wiederseim.

1913 *Bunnykins,* Stokes, $.50, Drayton.

1913 *Peek-A-Boo,* Duffield, $1, Drayton.

1914 *Teddykins,* Stokes, $.50, Drayton.

1914 *The Baby Bears and Their Wishing Rings,* Century, $1, Drayton. (Some references list the date as 1915 and 1916).

1914 *Let's Go To The Zoo,* Duffield, $1, Drayton.

1915 *Chicky Cheep,* Duffield, (price unknown), Drayton. (Also listed as *Chickie Cheep* and as *Chickie Cheepie*).

1916 *The Jumble Book,* Hurst, $.35, Drayton.

1916 *Bunny's Birthday,* Kiddie Series, Hurst $.35, Drayton.

1916 *Bettina's Bonnet,* Kiddie Series, Hurst, $.35, Drayton.

1922 *Bunny's Birthday,* Kiddie Book Series, Dodge, $.50, Drayton.

1922 *Bettina's Bonnet,* Kiddie Book Series, Dodge, $.50, Drayton.

1922 *The Jumble Book,* Kiddie Book Series, Dodge $.50, Drayton.

1931 *Dolly Dimples and Baby Bounce,* Cupples & Leon, (price unknown), Drayton.

(Date unknown) *Dolly, Bobby and Cumfy Too,* publisher and price unknown, Drayton.

Books illustrated by Grace Dayton, but which were give-a-ways, rather than sold, include:

Ca. 1920 *The Baby Bears* (Vol. No. 1-12), John H. Eggers Co. On back cover: "A Different story book every day will be wrapped with each loaf of Butter-nut milk bread. 40 different stories."

Grace also submitted work for inclusion in children's books which featured collections of stories and illustrations by various artists and writers. Some of these included special hardbacks to attract the holiday trade during the Christmas season. Although such submissions usually consisted of more than one page, often only the full page drawings were signed, as in the case of the illustration on page 15 of the January-February 1974 issue of *Spinning Wheel,* and its accompanying page which is pictured here. Sources such as these are

especially difficult to trace once they have been removed from the book in which they appeared.

Story series written and illustrated by Grace Drayton may be found in the following issues of *St. Nicholas Magazine:*

1913 *Baby Bear's First Adventure*—November. Vol. 41, pages 73-5.

1913 *Baby Bear's Second Adventure*—December. Vol. 41, pages 173-5.

1914 *Baby Bear's Third Adventure*—January. Vol. 41, pages 265-7.

1914 *Baby Bear's Fourth Adventure*—February. Vol. 41, pages 361-3.

1914 *Baby Bear's Fifth Adventure*—March. Vol. 41, pages 457-9.

1914 *Baby Bear's Sixth Adventure*—April. Vol. 41, pages 553-5.

Story series written and illustrated for *Cosmopolitan* magazine by Grace Drayton were:

1911 *Missionary*—April, pages 718-9.

1911 *My Dog Nero*—October, pages 714-5.

Series Grace illustrated for her sister, Margaret Hays, include:

Ca. 1905 *Mother Goose Rhymes*—a series of verses which ran for about five years in the *Associated Sunday Magazine.*

1909 *The Terrible Tales of Captain Kiddo*—a series which ran in *Sunday North America.*

Books written by Margaret G. Hays and illustrated by Grace Drayton include:

1910 *The Turr'ble Tales of Kaptin Kiddo,* Stern, $.35.

1910 *Kiddie Land,* Jacobs, $1.25.

1911 *Kiddie Rhymes,* Jacobs, $1.25.

1911 *Vegetable Verselets: With Quaint Pictures by G. G. Wiederseim,* Lippincott, $1.

1911 *Kaptain Kiddo and Puppo,* Stokes, $.60.

1913 *Kaptin Kiddo's 'Speriences,* Stokes, $.60.

1914 *Babykins Bedtime Book,* Hurst, $.25.

1914 *Happyland Book,* Hurst, $.25.

1914 *Little Pets Book,* Hurst, $.25.

1914 *Rosy Childhood,* Hurst, $.25.

1914 *Kiddie Rhymes* (listed but publisher and price not known.)

1914 *Kiddie Land* (listed but publisher and price not known).

Ca. 1915 *Pussy Cinderella* (published in Philadelphia, publisher and price unknown).

Post card series No. 357 was copyrighted in 1914 by A. H. Davis Co. All contain Easter verses as well as drawings. The "Drayton-look" proved to be so popular that it was still being used for dolls years later.

"Them As Has, Gits." Grace Drayton's style was widely copied by other artists of the period. This is not a Drayton print. (See December 1973 issue of *Spinning Wheel,* and this issue, for her signatures.)

In 1908, Scribner's Sons published "Blow" and a number of other prints; they appeared in post card form the same year.

Books written by others and illustrated by Grace Drayton:

1913 *The Spartan Primer,* by Mrs. Key Cammack, Duffield, (price unknown).

Some of the comic strips credited to Grace Drayton were:

(Date unknown) "Toodles and Pussy Pumpkins."

Ca. 1913 "Dimples."

1931 "Dolly Dimples and Baby Bounce."

1935 "The Pussycat Princess."

On March 8, 1931, the New York *American* introduced "Dolly Dimples and Baby Bounce." According to Odin Waugh, author of *The Comics,* Grace Drayton addressed the strip to the more roly-poly readers. While attention was at first focused upon the juvenile characters in the strip, they were soon upstaged by "Cumfy," a fluffy pussycat.

The following year, the strip was eliminated from the color pages of the newspaper but the Cumfy characterization and personality reappeared on May 12, 1935 as "The Pussycat Princess," a page revolving around appealing animals. While Odin Waugh claims that as late as 1947, the page distributed by King Features was still being drawn by Grace G. Drayton, though written by Edward Anthony, this would not have been possible, since Grace died in her home, after a brief illness, on January 31, 1936. While the fairy-like loveable and cuddly animal characters remained unchanged, Ruth Carroll was the artist who continued the page.

Prints made from drawings by Grace Drayton, all published by Charles Scribner's Sons include:

1908 "Blow"
1908 "Skiddooo"
1908 "Stung"
1908 "Happy Days"
1908 "Everybody Loves Me."

Since it is known that far more prints were published in this series and in other series, too, as well as individual prints not issued in series, many still remain to be discovered and reported. The Scribner series proved to be so popular that the same drawings soon appeared on colored post cards. These black and white prints all bear the Scribner copyright line, so identification presents no problem even though the Wiederseim style was widely copied by other artists of the period.

Some of the post card series designed by Grace include:

Series No. 99—Copyrighted in 1908 by Charles Scribner's Sons.

Series No. 357—Copyrighted in 1914 by A. H. Davis Co. of Boston.

Series No. 99 was manufactured by Reinthal & Newman, Publishers, N.Y. and was patterned after the popular prints (see list above), but Grace's bold and distinctive signature appears on a different area of the cards than it does on the prints. The desirable No. 357 series was beautifully printed in delicate colors and gave the impression of being in water color. In addition to the drawings, the cards contain Easter verses, and instead of the unusual black ink, the signature was printed in colors which complemented the drawings. When scanning assortments of unclassified post cards, knowledgeable collectors are able to spot them at once because of their size. The unusually narrow 3" cards

were edged in bands of color.

Cards in good condition are difficult to obtain and command a top price. Because printed matter on the reverse side consumed so much space, messages were often scrawled on the face of the card, thereby obscuring the design. For the Drayton collector fortunate enough to find one, they are as precious as gold!

GG Drayton

Signature used by Grace Drayton after her second marriage in June 1911.

WHILE MOST doll collections contain at least one of Rose O'Neill's Kewpies, relatively few dolls designed by the talented Grace Drayton appear. Many collectors believe a legion of Drayton dolls may still remain undiscovered because not enough information has yet been made available to facilitate positive identification; others believe only a token number of these dolls have shown up in collections because so many of Grace's dolls were rag dolls, so well-loved by their young owners that they failed to survive.

SOME DRAYTON DOLLS:

Dolly Dollykins & Bobby Bobbykins: During 1909, Grace collaborated with her brother-in-law, Frank Allison Hays, then operating under the name of Children's Novelty Co. He registered a trademark for "Dolly Dollykins" and for "Bobby Bobbykins," and applied for patents for what doll collectors now believe may have been the first rag dolls designed by Grace Wiederseim (later Grace Drayton). Their theory would appear to be correct, since in 1910, the firm of Strawbridge & Clothier was listed as the wholesale distributor, and in 1911 the Dolly Co. advertised that they had been designed and patented by the author of the well-known Bobby and Dolly books. The dolls were available in three sizes and sold for 25¢, 50¢ and $1 each.

Kaptin Kiddo: In 1909, Grace illustrated *The Terrible Tales of Captain Kiddo,* a series written by her sister, Margaret G. Hays, which ran in *Sunday North America.* She also illustrated Mrs. Hays' book, *The Turr'ble Tales of Kaptain Kiddo,* which followed in 1910. The "Kaptin Kiddo" doll was on the market by 1911 and resembled the character who appeared in the series and book. Like "Dolly Dollykins" and "Bobby Bobbykins," "Kaptin Kiddo" had a flat circular face with printed features. Roguish eyes glanced to the side and his abbreviated eyebrows were hardly more than a dot; he had the typical pug nose and H-shaped mouth which characterized Grace's drawings.

Gee Gee Dolly: For many years a cloak of mystery seemed to surround this doll. Collectors could not agree as to whether it was a rag doll or a composition-headed doll, or whether more than one type had been manufactured. In *The Collector's Encyclopedia of Dolls,* the comprehensive reference book written by the Coleman family, the authors stated that the "Gee Gee Dolly" first appeared in 1912, had a "Can't Break 'Em" head, was manufactured in two sizes, that both boy and girl dolls were available, and sold for $1 and $2 each. They further stated that in 1913, E. T. Horsman changed their name to "Peek-A-Boo" in America, though the "Gee Gee Dolly" name was retained for the German trademark registration.

A report about the "Gee Gee Dolly" appearing in the February 1973 issue of *Doll News,* a quarterly bulletin published by, and restricted to members of the United Federation of Doll Clubs, Inc., stated that a rag "Gee Gee Dolly" in pristine condition had been found in its original box still wearing its original identification tag and clothing. Their accompanying photograph of the Drayton drawing which appeared on the cover of the box showed a chubby little girl wearing a huge hair ribbon, carrying an equally chubby rag doll under her arm.

A label affixed to one end of the box listed the name of the doll. Printed information under it stated, "By license from the artist, Grace G. Drayton. Manufactured by E. T. Horsman, New York. Product of Aetna Doll and Toy Co. Made in U.S.A." The face was reported to be exactly like the ones which later appeared on a two-faced baby and on "Chocolate Drop," as well as on the "Dolly Dingle" rag dolls. The dress and bonnet were pink, and since this color had been noted on the box, it was assumed the doll must also have been available dressed in other colors. A huge white bow decorated the top of the bonnet and there was another under her chin.

Bunnykins: In the 1914-15 edition of *Who's Who in America,* Grace Drayton was listed as the designer of "Bunnykins." Efforts to trace this elusive doll have been unsuccessful, though it appears possible her 1913 *Bunnykins* book may have served as inspiration. Many doll collectors now believe that, as in the case of the "Gee Gee Dolly," "Bunnykins" may prove to be a rag doll, if and when found and properly identified.

Hug-Me-Tights: Between 1915 and 1917, Grace Drayton designed an unconfirmed number of rag dolls. The "Hug-Me-Tight" line of "Mother Goose" dolls advertised by Colonial Toy Manufacturing Co. and by Bently-Franklin & Co. included "Little Red Riding Hood," "Mary and her Little Lamb," "Curly Locks," "Little Bo-Peep," and others. Printed in gay colors, the soft cotton-stuffed dolls were 11 inches tall, had flat circular heads, and sold for 50¢ each. Although Grace's "Uncle Sam" and "Dolly Darling" dolls were not in the group of nursery rhyme characters, they were advertised as being part of the "Hug-Me-Tight" line and appeared during 1916.

Chocolate Drop: In 1923, the Averill Manufacturing Co. registered a trademark in America for "Chocolate Drop." This proved to be one of Grace Drayton's most appealing rag dolls. As the name suggests, the doll was chocolate colored. Her pigtails were tied with ribbons and her printed facial features were the same as those which characterized Grace's drawings. This was one of several dolls she designed for Averill's Madame Hendren Line, and it is therefore assumed it sold for $1 upward.

Dolly Dingle: Patterned after the paper doll cut-outs featured in *Pictorial Review* magazine, "Dolly Dingle" appeared during 1923. The 11-inch rag doll made by Averill Manufacturing Co. was part of its Madame Hendren line and sold for $1 upward. By 1928, Averill was advertising that for 10¢ in stamps or coin, they would send a Dolly Dingle Cut-Out of cloth so that a cuddly doll could be made at home. The coupon showed a typical Dolly Dingle-type boy holding a Teddy Bear and stated that a golden good luck coin, as well as pictures of the newest Madame Hendren Dollies, would be included with each order. (A Dolly Dingle doll was pictured in SW, oct '62, p. 28).

Mah-Jongg & Mah-Jongg Kid: During 1923, the Mah-Jongg Sales Co. of San Francisco registered "Mah-Jongg" as a U.S. trademark for dolls. They registered their "Mah-Jongg Kid" trademark the following year. The firm was under the control of Averill and the dolls were advertised as part of the Madame Hendren line designed by Grace G. Drayton. They were priced at $1 upward. Doll collectors consulted about these elusive dolls assume they were rag dolls but that this was conjecture only.

"Peek-A-Boo" doll with composition head, arms, and lower torso on firmly stuffed body—a doll many collectors have seen.

Left: Dolly Dingle boy paper doll from the February 1931 issue of "Pictorial Review." Right: Dolly Dingle Girl paper doll from the June 1930 issue of "Pictorial Review." The Dolly Dingle paper dolls were always shown with dolls, pets or toys. Since they were seldom shown in profile, and are therefore scarcer, they often command a higher price.

Sis: In 1924, Averill Manufacturing Company registered "Sis" as a trademark. The doll was advertised as being designed by Grace Drayton for their Madame Hendren line and was priced at $1 upward. Doll collectors believe it was probably a rag doll.

Happy Cry: Advertised by Averill in 1924 as part of their Madame Hendren line designed by Grace Drayton, many doll collectors believe this was a two-faced rag doll with one side of the face appearing happy, and the reverse side crying. It sold for $1 upward.

Comfy and Friends: Statements by Grace Dryaton during 1928 suggest that "Comfy" and at least two rag dolls appeared as additions this year. "Comfy" was a stuffed cloth replica of Grace's pet dog.

SOME DRAYTON DOLLS WITH COMPOSITION HEADS

Dolly and Bobby: In 1910 Louis Amberg & Son obtained patents for two dolls named "Dolly" and "Bobby." While the artist was not named, she is assumed to have been Grace Wiederseim. Since "Dolly" is known to have had a molded composition head, it is assumed "Bobby" did too. Some writers have theorized these same dolls were later marketed as "Bobby Blake" and "Dolly Drake."

Dolly Drake and Bobby Blake: These dolls were brought out by Louis Amberg & Son in 1911. Both had composition heads and cork-stuffed bodies covered in pink sateen. Some had tongues placed at the corner of the mouth; all were available with or without composition hands. "Dolly Drake's" head was pierced so that she could wear a hair ribbon. Prices began at $1 each.

Baby Beautiful: In 1911 Amberg introduced more than 50 new models for their "Baby Beautiful" line of dolls. They advertised that they were the world's most productive manufacturers of baby dolls and that this line had been designed by America's finest sculptors and artists. Grace Drayton's name was included among those listed.

Peek-A-Boo: For years confusion has existed about this doll; many collectors had heard of "Peek-A-Boo," but had never seen the doll and did not know if "Gee Gee Dolly" and "Peek-A-Boo" were actually one and the same doll. According to a Sears 1914 catalog, "Peek-A-Boo" dolls were available in two different sizes, with two different heads, and with two different costumes. According to *The Collector's Encyclopedia of Dolls*, the doll was available in an all-composition model, as well as one with a composition head and stuffed body, but was made in only one size, though available in three different costumes.

Sears catalog stated: "Charming little character babies with the cutest most lovable expressions. The heads, arms and legs are made of beautifully tinted unbreakable material and the body is of strong cloth, well stuffed. The arms swing from the shoulders. They have painted eyes and hair. Larger size dolls have twisted top knots." The advertisement listed 7½ inch dolls at 49¢ each, and 11-inch dolls at 98¢ each. The barefoot dolls were pictured in wide striped cotton swim suits with belts, and in lace-trimmed dotted dresses with ribbon sashes.

The Coleman's stated: "Peek-a-Boo. 1913-15. All-composition dolls of 'Can't Break 'em' material made by Horsman; designed by Grace G. Drayton. These dolls had been called 'Gee Gee' when they first came out. 1913: came in three styles of boys and girls; boys wore one-piece striped suit or summer suit and were barefoot; girls were in polka dot dresses and barefoot. The eyes glanced sideward. Head, limbs and lower torso were of composition; upper torso of cloth; legs and lower torso in one piece. Doll was 7½" tall. 1915: Dolls were clad in ribbon instead of bathing suits."

Baby Dingle: Averill Manufacturing Corp. introduced this doll in 1924. It had a composition head with painted hair and was available with movable eyes or with painted roguish eyes. It was dressed as a baby, and as the name implies, was based upon the popular Dolly Dingle paper dolls.

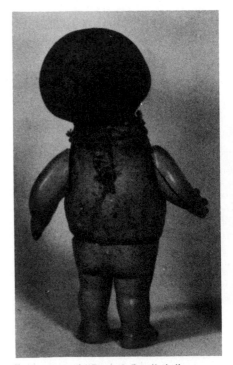

Back view of "Peek-A-Boo" doll.

BISQUES

Grace Drayton's name was also associated with bisque items and included:

September Morn: The 1914-15 edition of *Who's Who in America* listed Grace Drayton as the originator of "September Morn with Apologies" and also listed a September Morn statuette. During 1914, George Borgfeldt & Company registered "September Morn" as a U.S. trademark for an all-bisque doll. Jointed at shoulders and hips, the doll is believed to have been patterned after the drawing.

SOME DRAYTON PAPER DOLLS

Fictional Characters: In *Paper Dolls, A Guide for Collectors,* Clara Fawcett stated, "Grace Drayton illustrated in paper doll form, the old fairy tales for *Pictorial Review.*"

Dolly Dingle: The first Dolly Dingle appeared in the March 1913 issue of *Pictorial Review.* Recent advertisements for Dolly Dingle pages from *Pictorial Review* have listed ones which appeared as late as 1933.

All pages of Dolly Dingle paper doll cut-outs which appeared during the 1920s and into the 1930s bear Grace Drayton's signature as well as the copyright notation. Even when cut, identification seldom presents a problem, since paper dolls with print on the reverse side may be traced to the magazine. The Dolly Dingle paper dolls printed in full color on heavy paper or cardboard were available through the magazine, as well as through firms authorized by Grace Drayton. *Pictorial Review* sent them upon request, provided a two-cent stamp was enclosed for return postage.

In 1928, Laidlaw Bros. in Chicago, advertised: "the World's Best Cutouts by Grace G. Drayton—All about Dolly Dingle and her Friends, beautifully printed in colors on heavy cardboard; four 3-leaf folders, size 10 × 14½"; containing in all, 12 series of cutouts; fifteen dolls with costumes, etc., 120 pieces to cut out and play with; tied with handsome ribbon and packed in glassine envelope with the loveliest Christmas book on which you write your Christmas Greeting; a wonderful gift. All for $.50." The advertisement used one of the sheets for illustrative purposes.

It is heart-warming to know that the spirit of Grace Drayton shall remain with us always, personified in Peek-A-Boo, the Campbell Kids, Chocolate Drop and a legion of other memorable roly-poly kids with roguish eyes.

The first Dolly Dingle paper doll cut-outs appeared in the March 1913 issue of "Pictorial Review" with "Dolly Dingle of Dingle Dell" verses by Margaret G. Hays. The Hays' verses appeared again in April 1913, but were then dropped from the pages of the magazine. It is regarded as a scarce item by Drayton collectors, since few of the verse pages from these issues survived.

DURING THE PAST year or two, some dealers have been puzzled by an increasing number of requests for juvenile books written by a Margaret G. Hays. Only the more knowledgeable were aware that, in most cases, such books were being purchased for the illustrations which were done by her sister, Grace Gebbie Wiederseim Drayton, rather than for the work of the author.

Margaret Parker Gebbie was born in Pennsylvania, on July 31, 1874, and had the good fortune to be born into an artistic family. Her father was George Gebbie, once described by the New York Times as being "Philadelphia's first art publisher." He gave Margaret her first box of paints before she could read or write and instructed her governess to encourage her artistic efforts. Within

a few years, it became obvious that while Margaret was gifted, it was her sister Grace who had the greater talent.

Margaret attended boarding school and the Convent of Notre Dame in Philadelphia. On October 11, 1893, when she was 19, she married Frank Allison Hays of Philadelphia. Little then did she realize that one day she and her sister would be collaborating on juvenile books, and that her husband and Grace would enter into a business relationship which would eventually lead to a life-long interest in designing dolls and many related items.

In 1900, when Grace married her first husband, Theodore Wiederseim, Jr., she moved to Overbrook to be near her sister. Although Margaret did some illustrating she must have

Print of dolls' tea party, 9½ x 11½'', by Margaret Hays is the same as the 4¾ x 5¾'' picture that appears in ''The Mary Frances Cook Book,'' except that it has the copyright symbol in lower left corner, and is printed in several colors. Margaret Hays' Drayton-like doll drawings appeal to collectors.

realized that she would always walk in Grace's shadow, for she began spending more time writing advertising jingles and verses.

Series by Margaret Hays, illustrated by Grace Drayton include:

ca. 1905—''Mother Goose Rhymes''—a series of verses which ran for about five years in the *Associated Sunday Magazine.*

1909—''The Terrible Tales of Captain Kiddo''—a series which ran in *Sunday North America.*

Some books by Margaret G. Hays, illustrated by Grace Drayton:

1910—*The Turr'ble Tales of Kaptin Kiddo,* Stern, $.35.

1910—*Kiddle Land,* Jacobs, $1.25.

1911—*Kiddie Rhymes,* Jacobs, $1.25.

1911—*Vegetable Verselets:* With Quaint Pictures by G. B. Weiderseim, Lippincott, $1.

1911—*Kaptin Kiddo and Puppo,* Stokes, $.60.

1913—*Kaptin Kiddo's 'Speriences,* Stokes, $.60.

1914—*Babykins Bedtime Book,* Hurst, $.25.

1914—*Happyland Book,* Hurst, $.25.

1914—*Little Pets Book,* Hurst, $.25.

1914—*Rosy Childhood,* Hurst, $.25.

1914—*Kiddie Rhymes* (listed but publisher and price not known).

1914—*Kiddle Land* (listed but publisher and price not known).

ca. 1915—*Pussy Cinderella* (published in Philadelphia, but publisher & price unknown).

Although an amazing number of pictures by Margaret Hays appear in the scrap-books or on the walls of doll collectors' homes, they are difficult to locate since many sources list the writer but not the illustrator. Her work appeared in 1912 in *The Mary Frances Cook Book,* one of the Jane Eayre Fryer series of books popular in an earlier time. Unfortunately, most of her work lacks the charm and appeal found in that of Grace Drayton, except when she is drawing Drayton-type dolls. The latter are to be found in ''Doll Daze,'' an attractive series of four prints featuring doll activities.

She had many poems published in *Munsey's, All Story Weekly,* and in other publications. In 1914 when some of Grace's most attractive Campbell Kid advertisements were appearing in *Youth's Companion,* Margaret's poems appeared in the same issues, but instead of being illustrated by Grace, they were done by Mary A. Hays.

Grace Drayton's first Dolly Dingle paper doll appeared in the March 1913 issue of *Pictorial Review,* and the accompanying page of verses, ''Dolly Dingle of Dingle-Dell,'' was written by Margaret Hays. She also wrote the verses for the second Dolly Dingle paper which featured Billy Bumps in the April issue. Her verses were dropped the following month. Since few of these pages survived, they are now difficult and expensive

to obtain. Both pages of verse were illustrated by Grace Drayton.

Although Margaret Hays' name never became as well-known as that of her sister, Grace was always quick to credit Margaret for the many ideas for which she had been responsible. While 1925 was artistically and financially a successful year for Grace, it was also a traumatic one, for the pleasure of her success was dimmed by Margaret's death in September of that year.

Above: Illustration from ''The Mary Frances Cook Book.'' Margaret Hays' drawings lacked the charm and appeal found in those done by her sister, Grace Drayton. Critics said her children were drawn with adult faces and that she never mastered an understanding of perspective (note floor), therefore could never have become as famous as her sister, Grace. **Below:** Cover illustration from ''The Mary Frances Cook Book'' done by Margaret Hays.

While Grace Drayton's signature was almost always done in the same manner, Margaret G. Hays seldom signed her work in exactly the same way. She used only initials for her first and middle name for drawings, but preferred using her full name for her verses.

Fig. 1

Some Early Campbell Kids Collectibles

by MILDRED VELEY HARDCASTLE

THE CAMPBELL KIDS that Grace Drayton originated for Campbell's advertising cards in 1909 became so immediately and intensely popular with the young fry that within a year dolls were being manufactured, not as premiums, but for over-the-counter sale. Since the Campbell company held the copyright to them, these dolls were presumably made with Campbell permission.

The Campbell Kid dolls produced by E. K. Horsman were clearly marked "© 1910." They had Can't Break 'Em composition heads and pink sateen bodies stuffed with cork, jointed at shoulder and hip. In 1912, Horsman obtained patents for the designs for clothes for the Kids. *(Figs. 1, 2.)*

Butler Bros. in their 1915 wholesale catalog, *Our Drummer,* offered "the original Campbell Kids, unbreakable composition heads and hands, painted features and hair, cork stuffed bodies, jointed shoulders and hips. The boy 12", asst. color rompers, solid color trim, attached shoes. Doz. $3.85. The girl 12", asst. color gingham and percale baby dresses, attached shoes, same price."

Undated Campbell Kids dolls appearing in various collections include an important 16-inch Campbell boy in same design as the original, with a cloth tag on one arm reading, "The Campbell Kids—trademark. Lic'd by Joseph Campbell Co.," dressed in red jacket, white shirt, plaid tie, stockings, and

Fig. 2

brown felt shoes, *(Fig. 3)*; a rare all bisque Campbell Kid, "Made in Germany," with molded blonde hair, roguish eyes, blue rompers, and brown shoes *(Fig. 4)*; and an early soft vinyl 8-inch doll with jointed head and arms, marked at lower back of head, "Camp-

bell Kid made by Ideal Toy Corp." *(Fig. 5)*.

The Ideal Toy Corp. in their 1955 catalog announced "A New Item—Campbell Kids Twin Dolls . . . Two cuddly dolls that are perfect three-dimensional copies of the world famous trademarks of the Campbell Soup Company. The Campbell Kid boy is dressed in a white chef's hat, a bright romper suit with white apron, a pair of panties, a pair of booties. The Campbell Kid girl dolls wears the chef's hat, removable dress, a pair of panties, apron, and booties. The twins are washable from their cherubic, rosy red cheeks to their dimpled toes. Squeeze their soft stuffed bodies and they coo."

In the 1920s, foundries such as A. C. Williams Corp. and Wing Mfg. Co. turned out Campbell Kid cast iron banks, and someone made a Campbell Kid cast iron doorstop and painted it *(Fig. 6)*.

Over the years, quantities of Campbell Kid items have appeared, and they still keep coming.

(See "Grace Drayton's Roly-Poly Kids," *SW* jan-feb. 74).

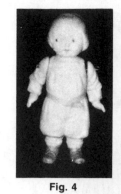

Fig. 4   **Fig. 5**

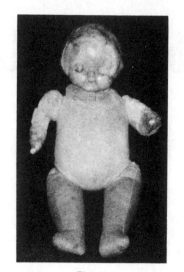

Fig. 3

Fig. 6

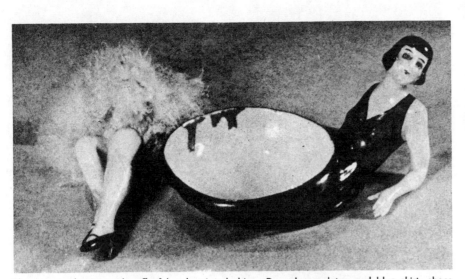

Flapper powder jar and puff of hand painted china. Dress has red top and blue skirt; shoes are painted blue. Jar 3 x 3"; legs (without feather puff) 4¾". Marked on base "D.R.G.M. 6295," indicating the design for this boudoir accessory was registered in Germany.

Bed Dolls, all with sateen bodies in pink or flesh color and composition heads. Left to right: Painted black hair and skull cap; black silk hair; brown mohair wig. The dolls measure from 26 to 30 inches tall.

FLAPPER DOLLS

by JUNE KRESSLEY

BECAUSE MOST of our early doll books were written within the short 10 or 20 years after the flapper period in our history, there is very little to be found in them about the Flapper Doll. She was too recent to be of interest then.

The Flapper herself had only a short span of life if we date her from the knee-high skirt style—1924-1929. This hardly allowed time for a factory to design, mold, retool, then market a new line of Flapper play dolls. Besides, this was a time when children preferred smiling curly-topped baby dolls.

However, there were people in Europe creating contemporary flapper dolls. These were the ultra-modern dolls of the post-war period, intended for grown people rather than for children. One of the best known makers was Lotte Pritzel. Her dolls had wire frames, wax heads, little slips of silk or chiffon, and some glass beads or spangles. Some makers used cloth or felt on a wire frame. These dolls were more for decorative purposes than playthings. Small ones could sit nicely on a gramaphone.

Europe was also making an Art Doll, which looks similar to our Boudoir, Bed, or Pillow Dolls. These dolls were meant to be posed in a corner, on a divan or cushioned chair, or draped on a mandolin against the wall. Parisian women made a fashion of carrying them draped over one arm when they took their afternoon strolls along the boulevards.

In 1922 the United States was commercially making what we know as a Boudoir or Flapper doll. She was long legged, had a starched cloth face, real hair, usually red or white, parted in the center with braids over each ear. Sometimes she wore a black skull cap and three painted spit curls, one in the center of the forehead, one in front of each ear. These might be won as prizes at carnivals and on punchboards, or they could be purchased at stores or from mail order houses. Both Butterick and McCall's offered patterns for those who wished to make their own; three costume changes were included. Probably more ladies made them for themselves than for children.

Armand Marseille made a flapper girl in the 1920s with a bisque head, #323, and slim waist, representing a grown-up. Arms and legs were of

Composition Flapper Doll head on a stick. Reddish-orange silk hair, white and pink cellophane streamers. Height, including streamers, 18".

composition, as was the body, and beautifully modeled. The feet slant downward; there are no joints at wrist and ankles. This doll has a lovely oval face with closed mouth, sleeping eyes, and short natural hair. A medium size was also made, #401 5/0.

At the time women were beginning to win more social freedom, advertising played up the trend. To promote their menthol cigarettes—the first of its kind — Cubeb had a doll made, smoking one. Of composition, she had a long neck, long legs, slanted feet with high heeled shoes, and was jointed at elbows and knees. When, in her short flapper dress, she is made to sit with legs dangling and head tilted upward, cigarette in mouth, she looks the picture of new found independence.

Another type of these dolls occasionally to be found, is just a head, with white silk hair parted down the center, braids over each ear, and a ten-inch fringe of colored cellophane around the neck. A small hole in the center of the neck suggests it was at some time attached to a cane such as might be given away or won at carnivals, fairs, or block parties.

The manufacturer of pincushion dolls could make the change from classic head to flapper head more

Pincushion Flapper Dolls. Clockwise from the far left: Blond china head, 3¾" high; china torso with pincushion dress of gray silk trimmed with silver lace, 4½" high; china torso in typical Flapper pose and wearing a cloche hat, 4½" high; round red velvet pincushion, molded felt face, green hat, 6" in diameter; china torso wearing a tall-crowned hat, 2¾" high; china head with black skull cap and spit curls, 1¾" high; china torso without a hat, 3" high; pincushion dress trimmed with ruffled net, china torso and legs, and wearing a cloche hat, 3½" high.

easily and faster than the maker of full bodied dolls. All he needed to do was to make a model, a mold, pour, fire, and paint—just what he had been doing all along. Both Germany and Japan made flapper-head pincushion dolls; some were excellent, some very poor.

Both countries at this time also

made a head for dresser puffs. These heads were to be sewn onto a velour powder puff and set in a fancy bowl or on a stand on the dressing table. The heads were sold separately for completion of the puff at home, or the whole thing came made up. Two were advertised in the Sears and Roebuck winter catalog, 1927.

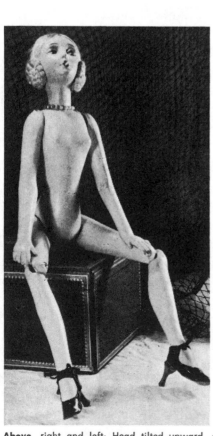

Above, right and left: Head tilted upward, cigarette in mouth, the Flapper Doll declared her prototype's newly-acquired independence. Composition body jointed at the knees, blond silk hair, wearing red high-heel shoes. 25 inches tall.

W. P. A. DOLLS & PUPPETS

by JUDITH WHORTON

Figure 1. George Washington is dressed in velvet, felt, lace and cotton. He wears a black velvet coat lined and trimmed in yellow. Placed inside the hip pockets are smooth pebbles, either to create the effect of full pockets or give the coat weight to hang properly. The 14 brass buttons have a tiny acorn design. The vest, also yellow, has pearlized buttons; the shirt has lace at the neck and cuffs; the white breeches have yellow rosettes at the knees. The tri-cornered hat which is sewed to the "powdered" wig has a matching rosette. The blue gray eyes have large pupils and pronounced highlights. Red dots at the corners of the eyes are reminiscent of antique dolls. There is much shading around the eye socket, nose and chin.

Figure 2. The brown-eyed Martha Washington is dressed in blue and white. Her petticoat is starched to give the pannier or overskirt more body. Unlike the other dolls, she has extra cotton stuffing to create the effect of a mature figure. She has satin bows on her sleeves and on her oil cloth shoes.

Figure 3. This Chinese girl has a different style of painting. The eyes are more almond-shaped and lack eyelashes. The nose is broader and there is very little shading on the skin tones, which are golden brown. The top of her outfit is peach, the coat is blue, and the pants are black. Her black yarn hair with bangs is parted in the middle and has a braided bun at the nape of her neck. The shoes are pointed, a style found only on the oriental dolls.

AMERICAN-MADE dolls are more and more attracting collector interest. Greiner, Schoenhut, and Amberg are names highly respected. Even products of obscure dollmakers are collectible. Yet one manufacturer, possessing almost unlimited resources, is often overlooked—the United States Government.

In the late 1930s, the Works Progress Administration, a federal agency included in F.D.R.'s New Deal to make work for those hard hit by the Depression, set up a project under which artists and seamstresses were hired to make cloth dolls representing different countries. Most of them portrayed Americans or north Europeans, though all popular countries were included. Of the oriental dolls produced, none were Japanese, perhaps because of the then worsening relations between Japan and the United States.

In the Birmingham, Alabama area, clothes and dolls were designed by local people. Hattie Hayes Whorton, now in her nineties, who was in charge of the artists has an excellent memory of the operation. Mrs. Lindstrom, designer of the costumes, is deceased. At the time of the project, few of the workers knew how the dolls would be used, although one artist remembers seeing some of them being created for shipment to other sections of the country.

Eventually the dolls were placed in department store displays or distributed to elementary schools to be used as visual aids in social study classes.

All of the dolls were approximately 12 inches tall and had cotton-stuffed bodies. Each torso was made with four pieces of material. Three of the seams ran the entire length of the body; the front seam stopped at the neck. The separate arms were hand-sewn to the body, but the legs were part of the body; the cotton stuffing made them flexible so the dolls could sit. The hands were mitten-shaped with no indication for fingers.

Portrait painting techniques gave the flat faces an illusion of depth. The heads, necks, and arms were first covered with a complexion coat and allowed a minimum of 24 hours to dry so that the features, painted later, would not blend with the base coat. Legs and feet were left untouched since socks and shoes were always used. All wigs were made of yarn, but each type had a different style.

The dolls were made in assembly line fashion with each worker having an assigned task. Both faces and clothes were made with careful attention to detail. Fewer artists were employed than seamstresses.

The examples pictured are in good condition although there are a few minor scratches on the faces and two of the costumes are slightly faded.

Figure 4. Her Chinese companion is dressed in all blue cotton and has the same square buttons and pointed shoes. The peasants who worked in the fields traditionally wore blue. The yarn queue is an authentic style of old China.

Figure 5. The most colorful of all is a Polish girl. She has an orange blouse, black vest, and purple skirt trimmed with black. Her traditional apron is painted with stripes of green, orange and red. Her face is decorated in the typical style except for the absence of cheek color. Her hair is brown. She wears oil cloth boots which are beginning to flake.

Figure 6. An English lad appears to be from Victorian times. His tailored costume includes a red hat, black jacket, gray vest and black and gray striped trousers, which have a pocket on the left side. He is the only doll to have a mouth painted open revealing teeth. Two highlights to each eye make his large eyes unusually attractive.

Figure 7. The Irish colleen has black curly hair and lively blue eyes. Her black cape, a popular style of southern Ireland, is lined with red; the red plaid apron has fringe trim; the yellow dress with a full gathered skirt is hemmed with heavy black thread. The tiny green bow pinned to the dress is the only trim on any doll that is not permanently attached. Her pink underwear is a departure from the white of the other examples. The black shoes are ties.

Because interest in the 1930s, reflected by current movies and books, continues to grow, it is not surprising that the Smithsonian Institution and National Park Service are currently conducting research on several of the arts projects of the Works Progress Administration. Among these was the Federal Theatre Project which lasted from October 1935 to June 1939, with a total expenditure of $46 million.

Despite this project's short life span—four years—it produced an impressive volume and variety of theatrical activities. These ranged from live productions of Ibsen plays to puppet shows. Hand puppets and marionettes were produced to provide employment for out-of-work artisans; they also provided entertainment, served educational purposes in the schools, and as therapeutic aid for crippled children in hospitals.

The Buffalo Historical Marionettes of New York, in existence before W.P.A., acted as the basis for the W.P.A. project. The program was so popular that the city of Buffalo donated a workshop.

Becoming part of a nation-wide program, the puppets and marionettes performed in at least 19 states, including Maine, Florida, California, Washington, Michigan, and Oklahoma. They not only appeared in schools and hospitals, but also in such diverse places as Civilian Conservation Corps Camps, city parks, theaters, and the 1939 New York World's Fair. Among the plays were adaptations of Shakespeare's *Twelfth Night,* Mark Twain's *Tom Sawyer,* Eugene O'Neill's *The Emperor Jones,* and Gilbert and Sullivan's *The*

Mikado. Occasionally a small admission—10 to 25 cents—was charged, which in some areas decreased attendance.

Additionally, an effort was made to recruit a variety of established artisans.

The Federal Theatre Project employed a number of researchers, directors, stage and costumes designers in New York City. However, the attempt to recruit well-known professionals was not always successful. Tony Sarg, the prominent puppeteer and author of children's books, declined a position in the program. Instead, he designed marionettes for the commercial firm of Madam Alexander.

The W.P.A. puppets pictured here are typical of those made for the Federal Theatre Project; they were donated by a retired schoolteacher and are on display in the Childhood Memories Doll Museum owned by Janet and John Clendeniem of Wormleysburg, Pennsylvania. (At the time of the depression, such puppets could be ordered by teachers in the Harrisburg, Pennsylvania, area by paying the postage.)

These were originally packed in a blue duffel bag stamped with the words, ''Little Red Riding Hood—W.P.A.'' The set of four, ranging from 15½ inches to 19½ inches, may be manipulated by hand or by string. Thus they could be classified as combination puppet and marionette.

The heads are made of sturdy papier-mâché, the limbs of wood, and the clothing of bright cotton, which would appeal to children. The eyes are of varying color, but all have pupils and white highlights and are outlined in black.

Little Red Riding Hood, with blond pigtails of yarn, has blue eyes and rosy cheeks. She wears a yellow print dress, white apron with red flowers, and a red

cape and hood lined with white. She has black shoes and blue and white striped socks.

The gray wolf has an open mouth with two celluloid teeth and a cloth tongue hanging out the left side. The slanted eyes have green iris and yellow background, surrounded by gray shading. The face is accented with black brush strokes. Black ears trimmed with pink, brown paws decorated with white and pink nails, and a tail made of brush bris-

tles fastened by a wire complete the wolfish look. He wears a purple shirt, orange trousers with maroon belt, a lavender scarf and matching night cap.

Grandma has painted gray hair, matching multi-stroke eyebrows, and small gray eyes. To illustrate age, the face has wrinkles, prominent cheek bones contrasted by deep hollows. The chin is shaped as if Grandma is missing some teeth. She is dressed in a white nightgown, trimmed with lavender and covered by a patchwork quilt. Her

ruffled nightcap is identical to the wolf's.

The woodcutter has painted white hair; his thick eyebrows and a handlebar mustache, decorated with gray brush strokes. He is the only puppet to have painted eyelashes. His eyes are brown with lavender shading on the upper lids. His coat is green trimmed with lighter green collar and cuffs; his trousers are tan, his socks red. Sewn on the back of his blue checked shirt is a blue duffel bag. Painted details on the upturned

shoes include laces and stitched soles.

Although the puppets did succeed in providing jobs and entertainment, the project was severely criticized as being in competition with commercial enterprise. Former officials of W.P.A. joined in the protest.

While some of the plays produced for the first time by the W.P.A. continue to be performed on the stage, the puppets' and marionettes' public appearances are now limited to display in museums.

American Wax Dolls

by ELSIE WALKER BUTTERWORTH

Photos courtesy Philadelphia Museum of Art

Above: American Doll dressed for exhibit at "The Sanitary Fair" held in Logan Square, Philadelphia 1864. Wax head, arms and legs, stuffed body. Left: Wax head doll, stuffed body, kid hands, circa 1870.

THE lovely waxen ladies of grandmother's day are highly prized by collectors, some of them of graceful proportion and dress and others produced by people who were not so skilled in their art. Wax dolls go back into the remote ages of history as wax was used as early as known civilization. The Greeks are reputed to have made dolls of wax.

But to speak of dolls which are available to the average collector of today, not a few have been unearthed from old attics, Aunt Mary's old trunk and bandboxes of earlier days. That any have been preserved is a miracle, considering how fragile a wax doll is, but apparently they were brought out for special occasions such as birthdays and holidays, when Sarah Jane was fixed up with a new

dress for her wardrobe, as a birthday celebration.

Some of these wax dolls were made with stuffed bodies and wax hands, arms, legs and heads. Others were made with the wax poured over composition or paper mache, which is the type most usually found. And some of the earlier ones were made by pouring the wax into a mold, forming a shell of the wax. Not a few had glass eyes and the shoes painted on the wax.

Of course, the most highly prized of all wax dolls were those made by Montanari, who made his dolls of poured wax with the hair embedded in the wax. These first made their appearance about 1849. Any collector who possesses one of these dolls has a rare gem for her collection. But other

doll makers followed and also embedded the hair in the wax, and so all such dolls are not Montanari's.

The age of a wax doll can usually be determined by the type of hair-do or the style of shoes painted on. The bonnet-doll with the bonnet and hair fashioned in the wax and painted is a rare doll and was made during the 1860's. Some wax dolls have the heads only, with leather hands and stuffed bodies. These dolls also date around the 1860's.

The author has an early wax doll in her collection which was poured into a mold forming the body and head like a shell. Holding it up to the light shows the hollow part inside. The face is painted over the wax, with beautiful light blue china eyes. It is a wax baby and the body is somewhat depressed or out of shape, due to the fact that there is no base for the wax shell, and the feet are bare showing the baby's foot and toes. The head also has embedded hair and has flattened some, due to the fact that it has been kept in a box for so many years. The arms are movable at the shoulders and are of solid wax. It was originally wrapped in wool.

Wax dolls which have been kept under cover retain their fresh appearance, but those which have been exposed to the light present a darker shade in the wax, probably due to the effects of exposure to air and dust.

Most of these fine dolls were brought from Europe — Germany, France and England (Germany was making them in the 17th Century), and some recent ones have been brought in from Mexico.

In the 1850's dolls were made with the large "pompadour" hair-do, and many of these were made of wax over paper mache, having wooden arms and legs, with stuffed bodies.

Wax dolls are also found with sleeping eyes, although it is difficult to determine the exact date of sleeping eyes. They are known to have been made as early as 1825 but some authorities state them as being earlier. The first sleeping eyes were the so-called wire eyes, the eyes being operated with a wire. After these came the weights for opening and closing the eyes.

Right, 1918 *Fulper doll. Fulper Pottery Co., Flemington, N.J., cast them in the molds of Armand Marseille Co., of Germany. Discontinued after World War I when German dolls were again available. Illustration courtesy Doll Collectors of America, Inc.*

United States Doll Trademarks 1913-1950

By Luella Hart

1913-1934, Rose O'Neill Wilson "Kewpie" dolls. Collection Josephine Jones, Dublin, Georgia.

AMERICAN

Five thousand would be a conservative estimate of the number of doll collectors in the United States alone. Those well experienced ones are already aware of the innumerable types of specialized collections that exist among the members of their cherished fraternity. There are collectors of certain periods, of certain countries, of characters, of wax and endless others concentrated around one particular theme. Not among the least, are those who love dolls of any category and it is their collections which depict, not only the evolution of dolls but that of the tastes, habits, fashions, etc., of our nation. They are among the group of collectors who draw the line at no particular point of time in their pursuit. A doll made in 1930 perhaps, is as desirable an acquisition to these devotees as one made a hundred or so years earlier.

While all patents were recorded and protected by the United States Patent Office, they were, in some instances issued to foreign manufacturers. This was particularly the case prior to 1918 when foreign manufacturers, and especially those in Germany, were considered leaders in the field of doll manufacturing. At the same time, certain importers in the United States, upon purchasing the exclusive sales rights for marketing a particular doll in America, would design their own trademark and apply for patent rights as a protection against other importers.

Occasionally when a doll manufacturer had developed a doll with painstaking care under great expense, and felt assured that his competitors could neither afford, nor were capable of copying it, he felt patent protection unnecessary. One such case is Rheinische Gummu-Und-Celluloid Fabrik Company of Mannheim-Neckarau, Germany who have produced celluloid dolls since 1876.

Henceforth, in using this series of marks, the reader should bear in mind that the designated "patentee" was not necessarily the manufacturer.

Patent Date	Patent Serial No.	Patentee	Trademark	
1913, April 29	91,346	E. I. Horseman Co., New York, N.Y.	"Gee Gee Dolly"	
1913, June 10	91,997	Parson Jackson Co., Cleveland, O.	"Stork" picture of, for dolls	
1913, July 8	92,455	Northport Novelty Co., Northport, N.Y........	"Flintex" for dolls	
1913, July 15	92,611	Rose O'Neill Wilson, New York, N.Y.	"Kewpie" for dolls	
1913, Nov. 18	94,237	H. B. Claffin Co., New York, N.Y.	"Koinigskinder" for dolls & toys	
1914, Nov. 1	59,188	Carson Pirie Scott & Co., Chicago, Ill.	"Dolly Mine" for dolls	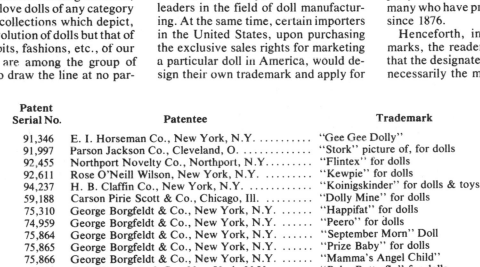
1914, Jan. 20	75,310	George Borgfeldt & Co., New York, N.Y.	"Happifat" for dolls	
1914, Jan. 3	74,959	George Borgfeldt & Co., New York, N.Y.	"Peero" for dolls	
1914, Feb. 12	75,864	George Borgfeldt & Co., New York, N.Y.	"September Morn" Doll	
1914, Feb. 12	75,865	George Borgfeldt & Co., New York, N.Y.	"Prize Baby" for dolls	
1914, Feb. 12	75,866	George Borgfeldt & Co., New York, N.Y.	"Mamma's Angel Child"	1 *(see 1915)*
1914, Dec. 20	74,702	E. I. Horseman & Co., New York, N.Y........	"Baby Butterfly" for dolls	
1914, Jan. 31	75,590	Strobel & Wilken Co., Cincinnati, O.	"Brighto" for dolls	
1914, Nov. 19	74,081	Etta Lyon, Montclair, N.J.	"Tottie" for dolls & doll clothes	
1914, Sept. 10	72,758	George Borgfeldt & Co., New York, N.Y.	"Cubist" for dolls, toys & metal figures	
1914, June 23	97,813	George Borgfeldt & Co., New York, N.Y.	"Prize Baby" for dolls, used since Jan. 1914. Renewed	
1914, Oct.20	100,255	George Borgfeldt & Co., New York, N.Y.	"Juno" for dolls, used since Feb. 1904	
1914, Oct. 30	82,280	J. B. Rowland Mfg. Co., Yonkers, N.Y.	"Dolly Deary" for a doll form	
1914, Nov. 13	82,556	Fair & Carnival Trading Co. Inc., New York, N.Y.	"Innovation" for dolls	
1914, Dec. 1	82,999	German Novelty Co., New York, N.Y.	"Tipperary Tommy" for dolls	
1914, Dec. 1	83,000	German Novelty Co., New York, N.Y.	"Tipperary Mary" for dolls	
1914, Dec. 4	83,072	Japan Import & Export Commission Co., New York, N.Y.	"Dimple" for stuffed dolls, plaster and composition and mechanical toy soldiers	2 *(see 1915)*
1914, Dec. 5	83,111	Elektra Toy & Novelty Co., New York, N.Y. ...	"Favorite" for dolls	
1914, Dec. 5	83,112	Elektra Toy & Novelty Co., New York, N.Y. ...	"Suffragina" for dolls	
1914, Dec. 28	83,563	United Drug Co., Boston, Mass.	"Rexall" for dolls & other toy figures	
1914, Dec. 30	83,594	Anna C. Renwick, Flushing, N.Y..............	"Corker" for dolls	
1915, Jan. 4	83,663	Montgomery Ward & Co. Inc., N.Y. & Brooklyn; N.Y. & Chicago; Fort Worth, Texas; Kansas City, Mo.; Portland, Oregon	*See illus. 1*—for doll bodies, doll heads, cloth dolls & cut-outs	NockWooD
1915, Jan. 11	83,782	Politzer Toy Mfg. Co. Inc., New York, N.Y.	*See illus. 2*	3 *(see 1915)*

	Patent Date	Patent Serial No.	Patentee	Trademark
4 *(see 1915)*	1915, Jan. 15	83,883	Leo Potter assignor to Emil Potter, New York, N.Y.	*See illus. 3*—for dolls
	1915, Feb. 8	84,359	John W. Dick, New York, N.Y.	"Tipperary Kid" for dolls
	1915, Feb. 11	84,441	George Borgfeldt & Co., New York, N.Y.	*See illus. 4*—for dolls
	1915, April 12	85,894	Elektra Toy & Novelty Co., New York, N.Y.	"Boogybear" for dolls
	1915, Aug. 3	85,958	George Borgfeldt & Co., New York, N.Y.	"Flossie Fisher's Funnies" for dolls, etc.
	1915, April 15	85,960	Thornton W. Burgess, Springfield, Mass.	"Quaddy" for paper & cloth doll cut-outs
	1915, April 23	86,149	New Toy Mfg. Co., New York, N.Y.	*See illus. 5*—for dolls
	1915, April 23	86,140	Indestructo Specialties Co., New York, N.Y.	*See illus. 6*
	1915, April 24	86,191	State Charities Aid Assn., New York, N.Y.	"Daddy Long Legs Doll." Dolls manufactured and sold for benefit of Children's Dept. of Said organization
Sunshine Kids **5** *(see 1915)*	1915, May 5	86,403	The New Era Novelty Co. Inc., New York, N.Y.	*See illus. 7*
	1915, May 8	86,472	George Borgfeldt & Co., New York, N.Y.	*See illus. 8*—for dolls & other toys
	1915, July 24	88,167	The New Era Novelty Co. Inc., New York, N.Y.	*See illus. 9*—for dolls & toy vehicles
	1915, July 27	88,240	Katherine Silverman, Chicago, Ill.	*See illus. 10*
	1915, July 31	88,328	George Borgfeldt & Co., New York, N.Y.	*See illus. 11*—for dolls & toy figures
	1915, Aug. 3	86,346	Thomas Hindle, Jr., New York, N.Y.	"Wot-Zat" for dolls
	1915, Aug. 4	88,419	Non Breakable Co., Pawtucket, R.I.	*See illus. 12*—for dolls & stuffed toys
	1915, Aug. 26	88,814	George Borgfeldt & Co., New York, N.Y.	*See illus. 13*—for dolls & stuffed animals
	1915, Sept. 4	89,023	Nellie S. Day, Springfield, Mass.	"Kutie" for dolls & toy figures
	1915, Sept. 27	89,493	Bessie Simmons, Oklahoma City, Okla.	"Grosmutter" for dolls
	1915, Oct. 21	89,977	George Borgfeldt & Co., New York, N.Y.	"Skating Charlotte" for dolls
	1915, Feb. 25	90,445	Kammer & Reinhardt, Waltershausen, Germany	"K & R with star." Used on dolls, heads, arms, legs, and bodies
	1915, Nov. 10	90,553	George Borgfeldt & Co., New York, N.Y.	"Continental Army" for dolls & toys
	1915, Nov. 10	90,565	Norimura Bros., New York, N.Y.	*See illus. 14*—for dolls
	1915, Dec. 22	91,697	J. Henry Smythe, Jr., Philadelphia, Pa.	Victor "His Masters Voice" for dolls & stuffed toys
	1915, Dec. 22	91,696	J. Henry Smythe, Jr., Philadelphia, Pa.	Victrola Vic "The Phonograph Dog" for dolls & stuffed toys
6 *(see 1915)*	1916, Feb. 23	93,051	Anne Maxwell, Bayside, N.Y.	"Little Sister" for rag dolls
	1916, April 18	94,517	Smelzer Arms Co., Kansas City, Mo.	"Schmebrer's" dolls & other toys
	1916, April 20	94,569	J. Alan Fletcher, New York, N.Y.	"J. Alan Fletcher" (applicants signature) for dolls & other toys
	1916, May 4	94,887	George Borgfeldt & Co., New York, N.Y.	*See illus. 15*—for dolls & toys
	1916, May 11	95,070	George Borgfeldt & Co., New York, N.Y.	*See illus. 16*—for dolls & toys
	1916, June 1	95,572	Joseph Cronan, Portland, Ore.	*See illus. 17*—(a novelty doll)
	1916, July 3	96,290	Pearl J. Elliott, Los Angeles, Calif.	"Peter Rabbit" dolls
	1916, Aug. 5	97,112	George Borgfeldt & Co., New York, N.Y.	Word "Hopsies" for dolls & toys
	1916, Aug. 21	97,520	Margaret Philips, Port Allegany, Pa.	*See illus. 18*—for dolls
	1916, Sept. 20	98,109	George Borgfeldt & Co., New York, N.Y.	Words "Pollyanna" for dolls
	1916, Oct. 27	98,927	Robert Lindsay, New York, N.Y.	Words "Buddy Bud" for dolls
	1916, Nov. 13	99,279	Mary Mason, Chicago, Ill.	Words "Once Upon a Time" for dolls, marionettes & toy figures
	1916, Nov. 29	99,618	The Beaver Co., Buffalo & Beaver Falls, N.Y.; Roanoke Rapids, N.C.; Thorold, Ont. Canada; London, England	*See illus. 19*—for dolls & toys
	1916, Dec. 11	99,844	Jane Gray Co., New York, N.Y.	Word "Kuddles" for dolls
	1916, Dec. 27	100,210	Rite Specialty Co., New York, N.Y.	Words "Happy Rite Family" for dolls
	1917, Jan. 4	100,352	Saml. Gabriel Sons & Co., New York, N.Y.	Words "Mother Goose" for dolls
	1917, Jan. 9	100,466	The Beaver Co., Buffalo, N.Y.	Word "Beaverbeasts" for toy figures & dolls
YAMAYAMA DOLL **7** *(see 1915)*	1917, Jan. 19	100,735	George Borgfeldt & Co., New York, N.Y.	Word "Cheerup" for dolls & toys
	1917, Feb. 6	101,195	Henry Sieben, Kansas City, Mo.	Words "Snow White" for dolls
	1917, Feb. 19	101,521	The Utley Co., Holyoke, Mass.	Word "Sanigenic" for dolls
	1917, Mar. 12	102,102	Robins & Herbert, Lakewood, O.	Words "Buffalo Bill" for dolls
	1917, April 3	102,688	The Mechanical Rubber Co., New York; Chicago & Cleveland	Word "Shield" for doll trademark
	1917, April 3	102,689	The Mechanical Rubber Co., New York; Chicago & Cleveland	*See illus. 20*—for dolls of rubber & toys
	1917, April 7	102,798	George Borgfeldt & Co., New York, N.Y.	Words "Betsy Ross" for dolls & toys
	1917, April 7	102,799	George Borgfeldt & Co., New York, N.Y.	Word "Active" for dolls & toys
	1917, April 19	103,121	Mary McAboy, Denver, Colo.	Word "Skookum" for dolls
	1917, May 2	103,465	George Borgfeldt & Co., New York, N.Y.	Word "Em-Boss-O" for dolls & toys
	1917, May 9	103,679	Sig Swartz Co. Inc., New York, N.Y.	"Tynie Tots" for dolls, manikins & toy figures
	1917, May 15	103,834	Etta Mansfield, New York, N.Y.	Word "Gollywog" for dolls
	1917, June 29	104,758	National Joint Limb Doll Co., New York, N.Y.	*See illus. 21*—for dolls & doll novelties
	1917, July 11	104,994	The Toy Tinkers, Evanston, Ill.	Words "Miss Tilly Tinker" for a wooden toy
BV KNOCKABOUT BIG VALUE **8** *(see 1915)*	1917, Oct. 25	106,935	George Borgfeldt & Co., New York, N.Y.	Word "Hollikid" for dolls & toy figures
	1917, Nov. 24	107,583	George Borgfeldt & Co., New York, N.Y.	Word "Preshus" for toy dolls & animals
	1917, Nov. 22	107,525	Sophia E. Delevan, Chicago, Ill.	Words "War Orphan" for dolls

Patent Date	Patent Serial No.	Patentee	Trademark
1917, Nov. 22	107,526	Sophia E. Delevan, Chicago, Ill.	Words "War Nurse" for dolls
1917, Nov. 30	107,682	Hawkins & Stublefield, Rogers, Ark.	See illus. 22—for toy dolls
1917, Dec. 8	107,833	Fleischaker & Baum, New York, N.Y.	See illus. 23—for dolls & doll dresses
1917, Dec. 19	108,059	Elektra Toy & Novelty Co., New York, N.Y. ...	See illus. 24—for dolls
1917, Dec. 27	108,179	Ideal Novelty & Toy Co., Brooklyn, N.Y.	Words "Liberty Boy" for dolls
1918		The Fulper Pottery Co., Flemington, N.J.	Word "Fulper" used molds of Armand-Marseille Co., of Germany. Sold through E. I. Horseman Co. of New York
1918, Mar. 14	109,558	Jean L. Friedman, New York, N.Y.	Words "Liberty Belle" for dolls
1918, Mar. 14	109,559	Jean L. Friedman, New York, N.Y.	See illus. 25—for dolls
1918, April 9	110,083	Martha St. Clair Wingert, Whittier, Calif.	Words "War Baby" for dolls
1918, April 11	110,121	Kellow & Brown, Los Angeles, Calif.	See illus. 26
1918, Nov. 12	114,142	The Faultless Rubber Co., Ashland, O.	Word "Sweetie" for dolls
1918, Nov. 26	114,410	Boulden & Mulligan, Seattle, Wash.	Word "Sammy" for dolls
1918, Dec. 30	114,891	Martha St. Clair Wingert, Los Angeles, Calif. ...	Letters "PAXIE" in double oval
1919, Jan. 2	114,962	Thos. R. Thompson, New Haven, Conn.	See illus. 27—for wooden dolls & animals
1919, Feb. 11	115,756	Dorothy M. Crosbie, Duluth, Minn.	Words "Dolly Winkle" for dolls
1919, Feb. 17	115,943	Zadek Feldstein Co. Inc., New York, N.Y.	Word "Impie" for rubber, Pyroxylin, bisque, plaster, composition, wood pulp & other material dolls
1919, Mar. 8	116,412	Charles A. Goldsmith, New York, N.Y.	"Jonnie Jingles" for dolls
1919, Mar. 25	116,911	Abbie B. Stevens, Atlanta, Ga.	See illus. 28—for dolls
1919, April 8	125,072	Mary A. McAboy, Denver, Colo.	Word "Skookum" for dolls. Used since 1913
1919, April 10	117,316	George Borgfeldt & Co., New York, N.Y.	Words "Kiss-Me" for dolls
1919, April 14	117,444	Dallwig Distributing Co., Chicago, Ill.	See illus. 29—Dolls with detachable and interchangeable wigs
1919, April 29	117,985-117,986	Oxford Print, Boston, Mass.	Words "Joy Toy" for paper, pasteboard dolls & toy soldiers
1919, May 16	118,550	Giebeler Falk Doll Corp., New York, N.Y.	See illus. 30—for dolls, doll outfits & doll parts
1919, June 25	119,961	Republic Doll & Toy Corp., New York, N.Y. ...	Word "Kweenie" for dolls
1919, July 5	120,285	New Toy Co. Inc., New York, N.Y.	See illus. 31—for dolls
1919, July 25	120,944	U. S. Toy & Novelty Co., New York, N.Y.	Word "Wauketoi" for dolls & toy animals
1919, Aug. 9	121,483	New Toy Co. Inc., New York, N.Y.	See illus. 32—for dolls
1919, Aug. 27	122,051	Pacific Novelty Co., New York, N.Y.	Words "Little Miss Muffit" for dolls
1919, Sept. 9	122,489	John M. Lockwood, Jr., W. Hoboken, N.J.	Word "Chickin" for dolls
1919, Sept. 10	122,508	"Babs" Mfg. Corporation, Philadelphia, Pa.	See illus. 33—walking doll
1919, Sept. 16	122,755	Lester Clark Brintnall, Los Angeles, Calif.	Words "Sunny-twin" for dolls
1919, Oct. 21	124,054	Hazel D. Silberman, New York, N.Y.	Words "Phyllis May" for dolls & paper dolls
1919, Nov. 1	124,452	Trego Doll Mfg. Co. Inc., New York, N.Y.	See illus. 34—for dolls
1919, Nov. 18	125,063	Sig. I. Rothschild, New York, N.Y.	See illus. 35—for dolls & toys
1919, Dec. 2	125,515	Elsie Shaver, New York, N.Y.	See illus. 36—for dolls
1919, Dec. 2	125,516	Elsie Shaver, New York, N.Y.	Words "Olie-Ke-Wob" for dolls
1920, Jan. 22	127,483	Murdock-Mackay-Graham, Boston, Mass.	Words "Eski-Dollie" for dolls
1920, Feb. 14	128,597	Minnie M. Meldram, New York, N.Y.	See illus. 37—for dolls
1920, Feb. 20	128,704	Samstag & Hilder Bros., New York, N.Y.	Words "Colonial-Quality-Colonial Doll" for dolls
1920, Mar. 15	129,709	The Faultless Rubber Co., Ashland, O.	Words "Pat-Biddy" for dolls
1920, Mar. 15	129,754	The Toy Tinkers, Evanston, Ill.	Words "Flying Tinker" for dolls & toys
1920, Mar. 30	130,388	Notaseme Hosiery Co., Philadelphia, Pa.	Words "Little Kim" for dolls
1920, April 9	130,902	Kentucky Derby Co. Inc., New York, N.Y.	Words "Derby Kid" for dolls
1920, April 10	130,959	Federal Doll Mfg. Co., New York, N.Y.	Words "Roze Doll" for dolls
1920, July 30	151,045	Baron Henry Scotford, Atlantic City, N.J.	Word "Photodoll" for dolls
1920, Aug. 20	136,316	Baron Henry Scotford, Atlantic City, N.J.	Words "Peggy Newell's" at left of portrait, "Portrait Dolls" at right of portrait of woman
1920, Sept. 8	136,927	Charles Bloom Inc., New York, N.Y.	Word "Emmylou" for dolls, doll dresses & outfits
1920, Sept. 20	137,370	Marian Gardiner, Seattle, Wash.	Words "The Peggy Doll" for dolls, doll dresses & dress patterns
1920, Sept. 28	135,346	The Toy Tinkers, Evanston, Ill.	Representation of a manlike figure for dolls & other toys
1920, Nov. 9	139,398	E. I. Horseman & Aetna Doll Co., Inc., New York, N.Y.	Word "Pinafore" for dolls
1920, Nov. 12	139,570	Katherine Fisher, Chicago, Ill.	Words "Please and Thank You" for dolls
1920, Nov. 15	139,689	Wexler, Goldstein & Co., Philadelphia, Pa.	Words "Hug'm and Squeez'm" for dolls
1920, Nov. 26	140,192	McCrosky Bros., Oakland, Calif.	"Rock-A-Bye-Dolly" doll heads
1920, Nov. 26	140,193	May B. Moran, Kansas City, Mo.	"Wee-Wee" for dolls
1920, Nov. 29	140,379	Julia Greene, Philadelphia, Pa.	"Beddy-Bye" for rag dolls
1920, Dec. 27	141,532	Karl H. Rogers, Philadelphia, Pa.	"Bendo" for pliable, bendable dolls

sKooter Kid
9 (see 1915)

Maiden
America
10 (see 1915)

67

AMERICAN

Peakies
11 (see 1915)

JAM KIDDO
MADE IN U.S.A.
12 (see 1915)

Rastus
13 (see 1915)

1917, *Colonial Lady. One of 30 famous "Ef-fanbee" historical dolls made by Fleischaker & Baum. Collection Phyllis Hart Morse.*

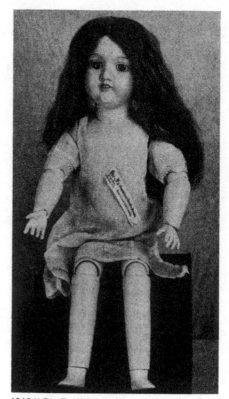

1919 *"Gie F A" Star of David Doll, a product of World War I. All wood body, feet and hands of aluminum. Collection Mrs. Chester Dimick, Gales Ferry, Conn.*

	Patent Date	Patent Serial No.	Patentee	Trademark
	1921, Jan. 6	141,894	Geo. Berkander, Providence, R.I.	"Shimmikins" for dolls
	1921, Jan. 6	141,896	George Borgfeldt & Co., New York, N.Y.	"Com-A-Long" for dolls
	1921, Jan. 12	142,140	J. G. Franklin & Sons Ltd. Dalston, London, England	"Rubbadubdub" toys made of India rubber, namely representations of animals, human beings, etc.
14 *(see 1915)*	1921, Jan. 31	142,956	Bob-Betty Belongings, Carlsbad, Calif.	"Bob Betty Belongings" for toys namely animals, birds & dolls made of rubber, cloth, hand decorated or colored & stuffed with cotton, Christmas tree decoration, namely stuffed rubber Santa Claus
	1921, Mar. 3	144,279	William Donahey, Chicago, Ill.	"Teenie Weenie" for cut-out dolls
	1921, Mar. 11	144,634	William H. Price, Jr., Akron, O.	*See illus. 38*—for dancing dolls
	1921, Mar. 28	145,355	Notaseme Hosiery Co., Philadelphia, Pa.	"Binkie" for dolls
	1921, April 15	146,226	Notaseme Hosiery Co., Philadelphia, Pa.	"Binkie Doll" with dolls shown draped over each letter, for dolls
	1921, April 21	146,488	Irokese Trading Corp., New York, N.Y.	"Dora" for dolls
	1921, July 21	150,763	The Miller Rubber Co., Akron, O.	"Pun-Gee" for dolls
	1921, July 22	148,761	John W. Glenn, Buffalo, N.Y.	"Glenn's" toys made of paraffin in the form of dolls, human figures, etc.
15 *(see 1915)*	1921, July 28	151,044	Norman Jacobsen, New York, N.Y.	"Bunintheface" for dolls
	1921, July 28	151,045	Norman Jacobsen, New York, N.Y.	"Minnehaha" for dolls
	1921, July 28	151,043	Norman Jacobsen, New York, N.Y.	"Brown Bear" for dolls
	1921, Aug. 18	151,928	Edith S. Smith, Waterloo, N.Y.	"Kuddly Kids" for cloth dolls
	1921, Aug. 29	152,301	Atlas Doll Co., Chicago, Ill.	"Toddles" for dolls
	1921, Sept. 1	152,461	George Borgfeldt & Co., New York, N.Y.	"Floradora" for dolls. Used since April 1, 1905. (These heads were made by A. M. Co. of Germany)
	1921, Sept. 7	152,669	Arthur Black, Toledo, O.	"Koaster Kid" for dolls
	1921, Sept. 19	153,064	George Borgfeldt & Co., New York, N.Y.	"My Girlie" for dolls
	1921, Sept. 19	153,063	George Borgfeldt & Co., New York, N.Y.	"Pansy Doll" in a pansy for dolls
	1921, Sept. 23	153,265	A. Strauss & Co., New York, N.Y.	"Our Pet" for dolls
	1921, Sept. 24	153,280	George Borgfeldt & Co., New York, N.Y.	"My Dearie" for dolls. Used since March 15, 1908
DEFENSE 16 *(see 1916)*	1921, Oct. 8	153,898	United Hosiery Mills Corp., Chattanooga, Tenn. . .	"Dixie Doll" over an oval in which are shown two dolls, for stocking dolls

Patent Date	Patent Serial No.	Patentee	Trademark	
				17 (see 1916)
1921, Oct. 18	154,265	Amy M. Eshleman, Lancaster, Pa.	"Aimee" for dolls	
1921, Oct. 31	154,802	Howard Larsen, Milwaukee, Wis.	"Jiggle-Wiggle" for dolls	
1921, Dec. 6	156,329	Clara V. Havens, New York, N.Y.	"Tubbins" for washable dolls, animals & doll clothes	
1922, Jan. 16	158,009	Percy Reeves, Chicago, Ill.	"Kiddie Kraft" for cut-out dolls	
1922, Jan. 31	158,667	Averill Mfg. Corp., New York, N.Y.	See illus. 39	
1922, Mar. 22	161,049	James A. Hayes, New York, N.Y.	"Flapper" for dolls	
1922, Mar. 29	161,442	Joseph Meer Inc., New York, N.Y.	"Mascotte Boudoir" for dolls	
1922, April 3	161,672	Cosgrove Bros. Inc., Milton & E. Milton, Mass. .	"Elizabeth" for dolls	
1922, April 10	162,066	Helene Sardeau, New York, N.Y.	"Ki-Ki" for dolls	
1922, April 17	162,421	Kammer & Reinhardt A. G., Waltershausen, Germany	"Naughty" for dolls & their parts	
1922, April 22	162,768	Rees Davis Toy Co., Chicago, Ill.	"Mitzi" for dolls	
1922, April 24	162,864	Wolf Doll Co., Inc. New York, N.Y.	See illus. 40	
1922, May 17	163,971	May Bliss Dickinson, Boston, Mass.............	"Mothercraft" for dolls, doll's clothing & doll bedding	18 (see 1916)
1922, May 20	164,144	Georgene Averill, New York, N.Y..............	"Mak-A-Dol" for dolls & doll outfits	
1922, May 31	164,722	Cora L. Scovil, New York, N.Y................	"Pin Personalities" for dolls	
1922, June 24	165,988	May Bliss Dickinson, Boston, Mass.............	"Children Well & Happy." Child holding a flag or banner, for dolls, doll's clothing & doll bedding	
1922, June 30	166,336	Lola Carrier Worrell, New York, N.Y.	Word "Flapper" in rectangle for dolls	
1922, July 1	166,383	Maurice M. Levy, Brooklyn, N.Y. (doing business as The Doll Craft Co.)	See illus. 41—for dolls	
1922, Aug. 14	168,212	The Flexie Toy Co., Broadalbin, N.Y.	"Baby Bunting" for dolls	
1922, Aug. 24	168,651	Kittie Sischo, Santa Monica, Calif.	"Tumblin' Tim" for dolls	
1922, Sept. 2	169,015	Jane Gray Co. Inc., New York, N.Y.	"Puss in Boots" for dolls	
1922, Sept. 12	169,351	Fleming Doll Co., Kansas City, Mo.	"Tum Tum" for dolls	
1922, Sept. 18	169,651	The Seamless Rubber Co. Inc., New Haven, Conn.	"Hula Maidens" for dolls	
1922, Oct. 9	170,502	Ontario Textile Co. Inc., Chicago, Ill.	"Kurnin-Kids" for dolls	
1922, Nov. 6	171,610	Mayotta Browne, San Francisco, Calif.	See illus. 42—for dolls	
1922, Nov. 27	172,598	Frank O. King, Chicago, Ill.	"Skeezix" for dolls	
1922, Dec. 4	172,921	The Wazu Novelty Co., New York, N.Y.	See illus. 43—for dolls & manikins used as dolls	
1922, Dec. 12	173,247	Samuel Robert, New York, N.Y. (doing business as Konroe Merchants)	See illus. 44—for dolls	19 (see 1916)
1922, Dec. 12	173,244	Samuel Robert, New York, N.Y. (doing business as Konroe Merchants)	"My Honey" for dolls	
1922, Dec. 14	173,319	Simonne Bouvet, New York, N.Y.	"Dad's Doll" for dolls	
1922, Dec. 27	173,896	Lansburgh & Bros. Inc., Washington, D.C.	"Lansburgh & Bros." for dolls & toys	
1923, Jan. 17	174,707	India King Stubbs, Monroe, La.	See illus. 45—for dolls	
1923, Jan. 31	175,338	George Borgfeldt & Co., New York, N.Y.	See illus. 46—for dolls	
1923, Jan. 31	175,339	George Borgfeldt & Co., New York, N.Y.	See illus. 47	
1923, Feb. 7	175,660	Lucille B. Kelley, Sidney, O. (doing business as Jimmy Boy Doll Co.)	"Jimmy Boy" for dolls	
1923, Mar. 10	177,228	Frank O. King, Chicago, Ill.	"Uncle Walt" for dolls	
1923, Mar. 10	177,544	Universal Feature & Specialty Co., Chicago, Ill. .	"DooDads" for dolls & puzzle games	
1923, Mar. 19	177,649	Lenore Boatright, San Francisco, Calif.	"Goo-Goo" for dolls	
1923, April 9	178,885	Tutt Mfg. Co., Los Angeles, Calif.	See illus. 48—for dolls	
1923, April 12	179,062	Seigenberg & Sher, Los Angeles, Calif.	See illus. 49—for dolls	
1923, April 14	179,130	American Character Doll Co. Inc., New York, N.Y.	"Petite" for dolls	
1923, April 24	179,614	Mah-Jongg Sales Co. of America, San Francisco, Calif.........................	"Mah-Jongg" for dolls	
1923, April 26	179,709	William Caldwell, New York, N.Y..............	"Skweez-Me" for dolls, rubber dolls, etc.	
1923, April 27	179,824	Schreyer & Co., Nuremberg, Germany	See illus. 50—for character babies, fabric, sheet metal, wood, cardboard doll head	20 (see 1917)
1923, May 1	180,003	Madame Georgene Inc., New York, N.Y.......	"Wonder" for dolls	
1923, May 29	178,652	Lola Carrier Worrell, New York, N.Y. (doing business as The Flapper Novelty Doll Co.)	"Floppy Flo" for dolls	
1923, May 8	180,331	Laura J. Eyles, Chicago, Ill.	See illus. 51—for dolls	
1923, May 12	180,536	Pearl P. Goerdeler, Brooklyn, N.Y.	"Bunny Hugtite" for dolls	
1923, June 12	181,883	Fleischaker & Baum, New York, N.Y.	See illus. 52	
1923, June 14	181,982	Davis & Voetsch, New York, N.Y.	"Dee Vee" for dolls & stuffed animals	
1923, June 23	199,008	Frank O. King, Chicago, Ill.	"Rachel" for dolls	
1923, July 18	183,382	Alma P. Hickman, Joplin, Mo.	"Billie Button Doll" for dolls	
1923, July 21	183,524	Ideal Novelty & Toy Co., Brooklyn, N.Y.	"Soozie Smiles" for dolls	
1923 July 31	181,134	George Lund, New York, N.Y. (doing business as George Lund Co.)	"Sandy" for dolls and animals cut-outs to be filled with sand	
1923, Aug. 1	183,936	The Nelke Corp., Philadelphia, Pa.	"Diggeldy Dan" for dolls	
1923, Aug. 7	184,187	Enrico Scavini, Turin, Italy	See illus. 53—for dolls, manikin dolls, human figures & grotesque character	
1923, Aug. 11	184,363	The Perfection Rubber Co., Cleveland, O.	"Daddy Boy" for rubber dolls	
1923, Oct. 6	186,675	Schoen & Yondorf Co. Inc., New York, N.Y. ...	See illus. 54—for dolls	21 (see 1917)

Left to right: 1925 Grace Storey Putnam Bye-Lo doll (courtesy George Borgfeldt Co., N.Y.); 1926 Bonnie Babe, 6" bisque with sleeping glass eyes, George Averill & George Borgfeldt & Co.; 1927 Patsy, a wardrobe doll manufactured by Fleischaker and Baum.

"Floradora" 1921.

	Patent Date	Patent Serial No.	Patentee	Trademark
"SAM-ME"	1923, Oct. 9	186,766	Ethel P. Westwood, New York, N.Y.	"Dolly Jingles" for dolls
	1923, Oct. 15	187,019	Helen Vincent Reader, Roosevelt, Wash.	"Gooky Girl" for dolls
22 *(see 1917)*	1923, Oct. 30	187,659	Aunt Jemima Mills Co., St. Joseph, Mo.	"Uncle Mose" for dolls. Renewed. Used since Dec. 1908
	1923, Oct. 30	187,658	Aunt Jemima Mills Co., St. Joseph, Mo.	"Diana Jemima" for dolls. Renewed. Used since July 1908
	1923, Oct. 30	178,955	Aunt Jemima Mills Co., St. Joseph, Mo.	"Wade Davis" for dolls. Used since July 1908
	1923, Nov. 5	187,985	George S. Carrington Co., Chicago, Ill.	"Bunny Boy" for dolls & toy animals
	1923, Nov. 5	187,986	George S. Carrington Co., Chicago, Ill.	"Doggy Dan" for dolls & toy animals
	1923, Nov. 5	187,988	George S. Carrington Co., Chicago, Ill.	"Ella Phant" for dolls & toy animals
	1923, Nov. 5	187,987	George S. Carrington Co., Chicago, Ill.	"Kitty Kute" for dolls & toy animals
	1923, Nov. 20	176,133	Ideal Novelty & Toy Co., Brooklyn, N.Y.	"Soozie Smiles." Renewed Nov. 20, 1943. For dolls
	1923, Dec. 22	190,040	Stella N. Webster, Los Angeles, Calif.	"Birthday" for dolls
	1924, Jan. 24	191,216	Berg Bros. Inc., New York, N.Y.	"Familee" for dolls
	1924, Mar. 3	193,176	Jeanette Doll Co. Inc., New York, N.Y.	"Little Red Riding Hood" for dolls
	1924, Mar. 8	193,453	Howard R. Garis, East Orange, N.J.	*See illus. 55*—for toy figures
	1924, Mar. 10	193,533	New York Merchandise Co., New York, N.Y. ..	"Pearlie" for dolls
	1924, Mar. 17	193,965	Shulman & Sons, New York, N.Y.	"Kiddy" toy dolls
	1924, Mar. 18	194,027	Mabel H. Slater, New York, N.Y.	"Pinky Winky Idol Eyes" with picture of an eye for dolls
Effanbee	1924, Mar. 20	194,132	Schoen & Yondorf Co. Inc., New York, N.Y. ...	"Sayco" for dolls
23 *(see 1917)*	1924, Mar. 20	194,131	Schoen & Yondorf Co. Inc., New York, N.Y.	"Mistah Sunshine" in circle for dolls
	1924, Mar. 21	194,234	Western Grocery Co., Marshalltown, Iowa	"Jack Sprat" for dolls
	1924, Mar. 22	194,243	Averill Manufacturing Corp., New York, N.Y. ..	"Mah-Jongg Kid" for dolls
	1924, Mar. 22	194,244	Averill Manufacturing Corp., New York, N.Y. ..	"Lyf-Lyk" for dolls
	1924, Mar. 22	194,245	Averill Manufacturing Corp., New York, N.Y. ..	*See illus. 56*
	1924, Mar. 28	194,584	Averill Manufacturing Corp., New York, N.Y. ..	"Sis" for dolls
	1924, Mar. 28	194,585	Averill Manufacturing Corp., New York, N.Y. ..	"Chocolate Drop" for dolls
	1924, April 8	182,320-182,321	Aunt Jemima Mills Co., St. Joseph, Mo.	"Aunt Jemima Dolls"
	1924, April 22	182,941	Estelle Allison, New York, N.Y.	"Baseball" and drawing. Renewed April 22, 1944 to Estelle Allison, Burlingame, Calif.
	1924, April 30	196,329	George Borgfeldt & Co., New York, N.Y.	"Bringing up Father" dolls of fabric, oil cloth, glass, etc., and mechanical toys
	1924, May 12	196,898	Frank Baum, Los Angeles, Calif.	*See illus. 57*
	1924, June 5	198,144	Elsie Dinsmore Landfear, Jersey City, N.J. (doing business as Kris Kringle Kid Co.)	"Kris Kringle Kid" for dolls
	1924, June 6	198,172	George Borgfeldt & Co., New York, N.Y.	"Felix" dolls of wood, rubber and textiles, etc.
Rosy-Posy	1924, June 9	198,326	Rice-Stix Dry Goods Co., St. Louis, Mo.	"Polly Prim" for dolls
	1924, June 23	199,007	Frank O. King, Chicago, Ill.	"Mrs. Blossom" for dolls
	1924, June 23	199,006	Frank O. King, Chicago, Ill.	"Puff" for dolls
24 *(see 1917)*	1924, June 25	199,135	Bernhard Ulmann Co. Inc., New York, N.Y.	"Stuftoys," stuffed dolls, stamped and tinted. Renewed 1944

Patent Date	Patent Serial No.	Patentee	Trademark
1924, June 28	199,288	Harold Munro, Providence, R.I.	"Katnips" rubber & celluloid dolls
1924, July 5	199,600	Helen Gordon Barker, San Francisco, Calif......	"Helen's Babies" celluloid dolls with crocheted costume
1924, Aug. 8	212,344	Kaufmann Department Stores Inc., Pittsburgh, Pa.	"Kaufmann's The Big Store" for dolls & toys
1924, Aug. 11	201,247	Hubert Leland, New York, N.Y...............	"Hell'n—Maria" for dolls
1924, Nov. 28	205,944	John Osborne, New York, N.Y.	"Totem Tom Tom" children's dolls
1924, Dec. 2	192,488	Bernhard Ulmann Co. Inc., New York, N.Y.....	Word "Stuftoys" for dolls, etc.
1924, Dec. 23	208,649	Ideal Novelty & Toy Co., Brooklyn, N.Y.	"Carrie Joy" for dolls
1924, Dec. 23	207,136	Ideal Novelty & Toy Co., Brooklyn, N.Y.	"Flossie Flirt" for dolls. Renewed April 1925
1925, Jan. 10	207,953	Inga Shilling Patterson, Washington, D.C.......	"Inga" for dolls
1925, Jan. 21	208,424	Adolphe Schloss Fils & Cie, Paris, France	"Berthoyette" for dolls
1925, Jan. 23	208,498	American Unbreakable Doll Corp., New York, N.Y.	See illus. 58
1925, Jan. 24	208,558	George Borgfeldt & Co., New York, N.Y.	"Bye-Lo" for dolls
1925, Mar. 17	211,147	Averill Mfg. Corp., New York, N.Y.	"Mi-Baby" for dolls
1925, Mar. 17	211,148	Averill Mfg. Corp., New York, N.Y.	"Lullabye" for dolls
1925, Mar. 31	211,896	Bing Werke vorm, Gebruder, Bing A. G., Nuremberg, Germany	See illus. 59—Dolls & mechanical toys
1925, April 3	212,141	Beatrice Jackson, Auburn, N.Y. (doing business as Novelty Doll Co.)	"Jack and Jill" for dolls with picture of boy and girl doll
1925, April 21	213,057	Arranbee Doll Co., New York, N.Y.	"My Dream Baby" for dolls
1925, April 28	197,822	Ideal Novelty & Toy Co., Brooklyn, N.Y.	"Flossie Flirt" dolls
1925, May 11	214,121	George Borgfeldt & Co., New York, N.Y.	"Ko-Ko" for dolls, toy figures & mechanical toys
1925, June 18	202,598	The Nelke Corp., Philadelphia, Pa.	See illus. 60—for dolls
1925, June 23	216,304	Unique Art Mfg. Co., Newark, N.J.	"Kid Samson" for mechanical figure toys
1925, Aug. 17	218,942	Elizabeth Adrian New York, N.Y.	"Jim-in-ee" for dolls
1925, Sept. 24	220,700	Albert Bruckner's Sons, Jersey City, N.J.......	"Dollypop" for dolls
1925, Sept. 30	221,014	E. I. Horseman & Co., Inc., New York, N.Y....	"Patty-Cake" for dolls. Used since Feb. 1918.
1925, Oct. 10	221,571	Walter B. Scott, Marblehead, Mass.	"Daddy Scott" for wooden toys namely human figures
1925, Nov. 13	223,211	George Borgfeldt & Co., New York, N.Y.	"Little Annie Rooney" for dolls
1925, Nov. 17	223,433	J. K. Farnell & Co., Ltd., Acton, London	"Alpha" dolls of textile materials
1925, Nov. 27	223,918	E. I. Horseman & Co., Inc., New York, N.Y....	"Hebee-SHEbees" for dolls
1925, Nov. 30	223,996	George Borgfeldt & Co., New York, N.Y.	"Jackie Coogan" for toy figures
1926, Jan. 9	225,698	Live Long Toys, Chicago, Ill..................	"Red Grange" dolls & footballs
1926, Jan. 9	225,699	Live Long Toys, Chicago, Ill..................	"77" for dolls & footballs
1926, Jan. 25	226,410	Harold S. Wittmaak, Erie, Pa.	"Rubber-oons" for rubber inflated dolls
1926, Jan. 27	226,523	H. C. White Co., North Bennington, Vt.	"Kiddie-Kar-Kid" for pull toy consisting of a doll upon a miniature child's vehicle
1926, Jan. 28	226,534	Albert Bruckner's Sons, Jersey City, N.J.......	"Tubby-Tots" for fabric dolls
1926, Jan. 28	226,535	Albert Bruckner's Sons, Jersey City, N.J.......	"Tubby" for fabric dolls
1926, Feb. 15	227,305	Hale Bros. Inc., San Francisco, Calif.	"Over the bridge to Fairyland" for dolls of wood, rubber, celluloid, bisque and metal
1926, Mar. 20	228,888	George Borgfeldt & Co., New York, N.Y.	"Bonnie Babe". The heads were made in Germany by Alt Bach & Gotchalk. Bodies made by Borgfeldt. Renewed March 1946
1926, Mar. 23	229,018	Annin & Co., New York, N.Y.	"Liberty-Belle" for dolls
1926, Mar. 26	229,224	M. J. Frank & Co. Inc., New York, N.Y.	"On-My-Lap" for dolls
1926, April 9	229,893	Mattie Thayer Basinger, Kansas City, Mo.	"Dolloyd" for paper dolls
1926, April 17	230,327	George Borgfeldt & Co., New York, N.Y.	"Buttercup" for stuffed & mechanical dolls
1926, April 29	230,864	American Character Doll Co. Inc., New York, N.Y.	"Bottletot, A. Petite Baby" for dolls
1926, May 3	231,041	Hills, McLean & Haskins, Inc., Binghamton, N.Y.	"Betty Bingham" for dolls
1926, May 17	231,747	The Moxie Company, Boston, Mass.	"Moxie" for dolls & toys
1926, May 21	231,969	Bayless Bros. & Co., Louisville, Ky.	"Honey Child" for dolls
1926, June 12	233,125	Heiss, Brush & Co. Inc., New York, N.Y.......	"Hankyland Dolls" for dolls
1926, July 1	234,015	Helen Haldane Wyse, Mineola, N.Y. (doing business as Bonser Doll Co.)	"I AM A Bonser Doll" for dolls
1926, Aug. 3	216,200	George Borgfeldt & Co., N.Y.C. .... Georgene Averill	"Bonnie Babe" (Georgene Averill transferred her trademark to Borgfeldt but both Averill's name & Borgfeldt also on Bonnie Babe dolls)
1926, Aug. 18	236,131	Jacobs & Kassler, New York, N.Y.	"Bisqueloid" for dolls
1926, Aug. 18	236,132	Jacobs & Kassler, New York, N.Y.	"Kiddiejoy" for dolls & toys
1926, Sept. 15	220,971	Yves De Villers & Co. Ltd., New York, N.Y....	See illus. 61—for dolls
1926, Sept. 30	237,980	Performo Toy Co. Inc., Middletown, Pa........	"Mickey" for toy figures for children
1926, Oct. 21	238,954	Ray W. Dumont, New York, N.Y.	"Widget" for dolls

NOSY ROSY

25 (see 1918)

26 (see 1918)

TOTS-TOIE

27 (see 1919)

GEORGIA PEACHES HomeGrown

28 (see 1919)

DALL WIG DOLL

29 (see 1919)

Gie-Fa

30 (see 1919)

31 *(see 1919)*

32 *(see 1919)*

33 *(see 1919)*

34 *(see 1919)*

35 *(see 1919)*

36 *(see 1919)*

Patent Date	Patent Serial No.	Patentee	Trademark
1926, Oct. 29	239,450	Louis Wolf & Co. Inc., New York, N.Y.	"Baby Tunes" for dolls
1926, Nov. 15	240,118	Harry J. Wolf, New York, N.Y. (doing business as Wolf Doll Co.)	*See illus. 62*
1926, Nov. 24	240,524	George Borgfeldt & Co., New York, N.Y.	"Featherweight" for dolls
1926, Nov. 24	240,523	George Borgfeldt & Co., New York, N.Y.	"Rolly-I-Tot" for dolls
1926, Dec. 3	240,913	Irwin & Company, Inc., New York, N.Y.	"Darling" for dolls, etc.
1926, Dec. 13	241,457	Zadek Feldstein Co. Inc., New York, N.Y.	"San-I-Toy" for dolls
1926, Dec. 17	241,611	Fleischaker & Baum, New York, N.Y.	"Bubbles" for non rubber composition dolls
1927, Jan. 27	243,423	The Curtiss Candy Company, Chicago, Ill.	"Baby Ruth" for wax, china, celluloid, fabric & stuffed
1927, Feb. 19	244,605	Dennison Manufacturing Co., Framingham, Mass.	"Nancy" for dolls
1927, Mar. 5	245,263	Arthur A. Gerling, New York, N.Y. (doing business as Gerling Toy Co.)	"Black Bottom" for dolls
1927, Mar. 18	245,987	Ideal Novelty & Toy Co., Brooklyn, N.Y.	"Twinkle-Toes" for dolls
1927, Mar. 22	247,056	Louis Amberg & Sons, New York, N.Y.	"Vanta" for dolls
1927, April 5	246,948	Averill Mfg. Corp., New York, N.Y.	"Bubbles" for dolls
1927, April 5	246,987	Strauss-Eckardt Co. Inc., New York, N.Y.	"Our Play Yard Pet" for dolls
1927, April 11	247,250	S. Blechman & Sons, Inc., New York, N.Y.	"Charm" for dolls, etc.
1927, April 15	247,460	Jeanne DeM. Brumback, White Plains, N.Y.	"The Cheerio Doll" for dolls
1927, June 22	250,945	Eleanor A. Spaulding, Swampscott, Mass.	"Mrs. Spaulding's Children" for dolls
1927, July 16	252,144	George Borgfeldt & Co., New York, N.Y.	"Rag and Tag" for dolls & toy figures
1927, Sept. 2	254,259	L. Bamberger & Co., Newark, N.J.	"IKWA" for dolls
1927, Oct. 14	256,079	Fleischaker & Baum, New York, N.Y.	"Mi-Mi" for dolls
1927, Oct. 14	256,080	Fleischaker & Baum, New York, N.Y.	"Patsy" for dolls
1927, Dec. 14	259,086	Twinzy Toy Co., Battle Creek, Mich.	"Twinzy" for toy dolls & figures
1927, Dec. 24	259,320	George Borgfeldt & Co., New York, N.Y.	"Jolly Jester" for dolls
1928, Jan. 3	259,631	Louise R. Kampes, Atlantic City, N.J.	"Kamkins-A Dolly to Love" for dolls
1928, Jan. 11	259,966	J. C. Penney Co., Wilmington, Del. & New York, N.Y.	"Mary Lu" for dolls & toys
1928, Jan. 23	248,002	Krestine Knudsen, Oakland, Calif.	"The Old Country Dolls" for dolls
1928, Jan. 23	260,486	George Borgfeldt & Co., New York, N.Y.	"Rosy-Posy" for dolls
1928, Jan. 28	260,795	George Borgfeldt & Co., New York, N.Y.	"BonTon" for dolls
1928, Feb. 15	261,693	George Borgfeldt & Co., New York, N.Y.	"Mimi" for dolls
1928, Feb. 17	261,835	Regal Doll Mfg. Co. Inc., New York, N.Y.	"Kiddie Pal Dolly" for dolls
1928, Feb. 20	261,995	Strauss-Eckardt Co. Inc., New York, N.Y.	"Our Dolly-Kar Pet" for dolls
1928, Feb. 20	261,941	The Children's Press, Chicago, Ill.	"Joey" for dolls
1928, Feb. 29	262,391	Lee M. Byrd, Oakland, Calif.	"Friendly Bugs" for dolls
1928, Mar. 22	263,582	George Borgfeldt & Co., New York, N.Y.	"Nifty" for dolls & toys
1928, April 19	265,088	George Borgfeldt & Co., New York, N.Y.	"Sugar Plum" for dolls
1928, July 12	269,444	George Borgfeldt & Co., New York, N.Y.	"Fly-Lo" for dolls
1928, July 13	265,248	Albert J. Clark, Los Angeles, Calif. (doing business as Clark's Dollar Stores)	"Dollar Store" for dolls, etc.
1928, July 18	269,787	Ideal Novelty & Toy Co., Brooklyn, N.Y.	"Peter Pan" for dolls
1928, Aug. 4	270,565	Louis Amberg & Son, New York, N.Y.	"SoBig" for dolls with pictures of doll stretching arms overhead
1928, Aug. 22	271,374	George Borgfeldt & Co., New York, N.Y.	"Mignonne" for dolls
1928, Aug. 30	271,755	Helen N. Gove, Williamsport, Pa. (doing business as Gove Mfg. Co.)	*See illus. 63*—for dolls & toy animal figures
1928, Sept. 4	271,897	Chihiro Katagiri, New York, N.Y.	"Branko" for mechanical acrobatic toys
1928, Nov. 2	274,713	Fleischaker & Baum, New York, N.Y.	"Lovums" for dolls
1928, Dec. 28	277,278	George Borgfeldt & Co., New York, N.Y.	"Gladdie" for dolls
1929, Jan. 24	270,247	Fanny Keeler, New York, N.Y.	"Keeler Dolls" for dolls
1929, Jan. 25	278,429	George Borgfeldt & Co., New York, N.Y.	"Just Me" for dolls
1929, Jan. 29	278,596	Ideal Novelty & Toy Co., Brooklyn, N.Y.	"Wendy" for dolls
1929, Feb. 8	279,039	H. Goodman & Sons Inc., New York, N.Y.	"Goody" for dolls & Paper dolls
1929, Feb. 14	279,330	Ideal Novelty & Toy Co., Brooklyn, N.Y.	"Tickletoes" for dolls
1929, Feb. 15	279,422	Frank W. Peterson, New York, N.Y. (doing business as F. W. Peterson Co.)	"Petson" for dolls & toy animals
1929, Feb. 26	279,961	S&H Novelty Co., Atlantic City, N.J.	"Peppy Pals" for dolls
1929, Mar. 28	281,486	The Curtiss Candy Co., Chicago, Ill.	"Chicos" for dolls made of China, wax, celluloid, fabric & stuffed
1929, May 13	283,940	Louis I. Bloom, Brooklyn, & New York, N.Y. (doing business as American Made Toy Co.)	*See illus. 64*—for stuffed dolls and other toys
1929, June 4	285,027	Ideal Novelty & Toy Co., Brooklyn, N.Y.	"Winsome Winnie" for dolls
1929, June 17	285,703	The Blue Bird Co., Baltimore, Md.	"The Blue Bird Co. Better Bilt Joycraft Toys" for toys namely human figures made of base metal
1929, June 27	286,253	Maxine Doll Co. Inc., New York, N.Y.	*See illus. 65*
1929, Oct. 30	279,785	Pat Page Inc., New York, N.Y.	"Komic Klown" pictured on figure of a clown doll
1929, Dec. 17	293,781	Lee Rubber & Tire Corp., Conshohocken, Pa.	"JolLeeJays" for sponge dolls & toy animals
1930, Jan. 29	295,323	Amos 'N Andy Doll Co., New York, N.Y.	"Amos 'N Andy" for dolls
1930, Feb. 10	295,828	Bert B. Barry & Associates, Chicago, Ill.	"Pinocchio" for dolls

Patent Date	Patent Serial No.	Patentee	Trademark
1930, Feb. 17	296,152	Violet D. Steinmann, Los Angeles, Calif.	"The Hart Doll" for dolls
1930, Feb. 25	296,467	Amos 'N Andy Doll Co., New York, N.Y.	"Amos 'N Andy Check 'N Double Check" in square
1930, Mar. 13	297,225	The Averill Co. Inc., New York, N.Y.	"Amos 'N Andy" for dolls
1930, Mar. 17	297,403	Arranbee Doll Co., New York, N.Y.	See illus. 66—for dolls
1930, Mar. 27	297,990	The S&H Novelty Co., Atlantic City, N.J.	"Amos 'N Andy" for dolls
1930, May 3	299,883	American Character Doll Co. Inc., New York, N.Y.	See illus. 67—for dolls
1930, May 17	300,724	I. B. Kleinert Rubber Co., New York, N.Y.	"Jiffy" for dolls & apparel
1930, May 27	301,342	Gre-Poir, Inc., New York, N.Y.	"Balsam Baby" for stuffed dolls & toys
1930, May 29	284,413	The Toy Pack Corp., New Haven, Conn.	"Toy Pack" for rubber dolls
1930, Aug. 4	304,181	Camile C. Blair, W. Los Angeles, Calif. (doing business as Ruffles Co.)	"Ruffles" for dolls
1930, Sept. 20	305,905	The Lamp Studio, Utica, N.Y.	"Lynda-Lou" for dolls
1930, Oct. 6	306,467	Sears Roebuck & Co., Chicago, Ill.	"Dainty Dorothy Doll" for dolls
1930, Nov. 15	307,914	Arranbee Doll Co., New York, N.Y.	See illus. 68
1930, Dec. 2	308,511	Joseph Kallus, New York, N.Y. (doing business as Cameo Doll Co.)	See illus. 69—for dolls
1931, Jan. 15	309,958	L. Bamberger & Co., Newark, N.J.	"Under the China-berry Tree" for rag dolls
1931, Jan. 24	309,970	Gaess & Hollander, Long Island City, N.Y.	"Phenox Products" for composition figures
1931, Jan. 28	310,478	Ideal Novelty & Toy Co., Brooklyn, N.Y.	"Honey Bunch" for dolls
1931, Feb. 3	310,673	George Borgfeldt & Co., New York, N.Y.	"Mary Ann" for dolls
1931, Feb. 3	310,674	George Borgfeldt & Co., New York, N.Y.	"Mary Jane" for dolls
1931, Feb. 12	311,012	Augusta Wasson Whitestone Long Island City, N.Y.	"Wassy" for dolls
1931, Mar. 19	312,288	George Borgfeldt & Co., New York, N.Y.	"Babykins" for dolls
1931, Mar. 25	312,518	Meyer Goldman, Philadelphia, Pa.	"Molly-'es" for doll apparel
1931, April 11	313,245	Victor Keney, Woodside, L.I., N.Y.	"Keeneye" for dolls
1931, April 21	313,591	Walt Disney Productions Ltd., Hollywood, Calif.	"Minnie Mouse" for dolls
1931, June 23	316,147	American Character Doll Co. Inc., New York, N.Y.	See illus. 70
1931, July 3	316,607	Morrison Manufacturing Co. Inc., Conway, N.H.	"Kink-A-Doos" for dolls made of parts to be fitted together
1931, Aug. 14	317,979	Ideal Novelty & Toy Co., New York, N.Y.	"Saucy Sue" for dolls
1931, Sept. 3	318,722	"Semperit" Oesterreichisch-Amerikanische Gummiwerke Aktiengesellschaft, Vienna, Austria	"Belinde" for dolls & toy human figures
1931, Sept. 5	318,792	Strauss Toy Shops, Inc., New York, N.Y.	"Miss New York" for dolls
1931, Sept. 14	319,032	S. S. Kresge Co., Detroit, Mich.	"Marjorie" for dolls
1931, Sept. 17	319,130	American Character Doll Co. Inc., New York, N.Y.	"Flex-O-Flesh" for dolls
1931, Nov. 6	320,850	American Character Doll Co. Inc., New York, N.Y.	See illus. 71—for dolls
1931, Nov. 7	320,884	Esther M. Ames, Yonkers, N.Y.	"Shavings Doll" for dolls
1931, Nov. 11	321,046	Vazah, Inc., New York, N.Y.	"Prosperity Pal" for dolls
1931, Dec. 10	322,004	Magyar Ruggyantaarugyar Reszveny Tarsasag, Budapest, Hungary	"Gumotex" for dolls
1932, Jan. 20	323,183	American Needlecrafts, Inc., New York, N.Y. ..	"Be Ba Bo" for stuffed cloth dolls
1932, Feb. 27	324,561	Ideal Novelty & Toy Co., Brooklyn, N.Y.	"Honeysuckle" for dolls

39 (see 1922)

40 (see 1922)

37 (see 1920)

38 (see 1921)

"House of Seco Dolls" 1937, papier-mâché heads, made in Germany, trademark by U.S. agent Strauss Echardt Co. Center top, Raggedy Ann 1918-1935, character created by author Johnny Gruelle in 1918, made by Georgene Novelty Co. Below, 1934 "Dydee", an Effanbee wetting doll made by Fleischaker & Baum Inc., Right 1934 Shirley Temple doll modeled by Herr Lipfert, made by Ideal Novelty & Toy Co.

	Patent Date	Patent Serial No.	Patentee	Trademark
	1932, Mar. 1	324,672	Portia Sperry, Nashville, Ind.	"Abigail The Log Cabin Doll"
	1932, Mar. 3	324,744	International Silver Co., Meriden, Conn.	"Toto" for toy figure representing a clown
41 (see 1922)	1932, Mar. 19	325,291	Ideal Novelty & Toy Co., Brooklyn, N.Y.	"Ideal" for dolls
	1932, Mar. 26	325,399	The Fair, Chicago, Ill.	"Baby Carol" for dolls
	1932, April 20	326,287	Ideal Novelty & Toy Co., Brooklyn, N.Y.	"Tru-Flesh" for dolls
	1932, May 4	326,750	S. H. Kress & Co., New York, N.Y.	"Janet" for dolls
	1932, May 4	326,748	Marion Greene, Montclair, N.J.	"Knit-Wit" for dolls
	1932, Aug. 9	329,426	Ottinger, Carew & McLaughlin, New York, N.Y.	"Boop-Boop-A-Doop" for dolls
	1932, Aug. 9	329,427	Ottinger, Carew & McLaughlin, New York, N.Y.	"Helen Kane" for dolls
	1932, Aug. 20	329,715	Ideal Novelty & Toy Co., Brooklyn, N.Y.	"Ducky" for dolls
	1932, Nov. 23	332,424	Stephen Slesinger, New York, N.Y.	"Toy of the Month" for dolls, etc.
	1933, Jan. 23	334,251	Leo Fisher, Highland Park, Ill.	"Maiden America" for dolls
	1933, Feb. 4	334,642	S. H. Kress & Co., New York, N.Y.	"Billy Boy" for dolls
	1933, Feb. 13	334,922	S. H. Kress & Co., New York, N.Y.	"Jo-An" for dolls
	1933, Feb. 13	334,923	S. H. Kress & Co., New York, N.Y.	"Suz-Ann" for dolls
	1933, Feb. 13	334,921	S. H. Kress & Co., New York, N.Y.	"Baby Rose" for dolls
	1933, Mar. 17	335,763	Bertha Behrman, New York, N.Y. (doing business as Alexander Doll Co.)	"Alice in Wonderland" for dolls
42 (see 1922)	1933, April 11	336,656	Pauline Margulies, Brooklyn, N.Y.	See illus. 72—for dolls
	1933, May 8	337,593	Best & Co. Inc., New York, N.Y.	"Best & Co." for dolls & toys
	1933, July 29	340,228	S. H. Kress & Co., New York, N.Y.	"Baby-Dot" for dolls
	1933, Sept. 13	341,554	Ideal Novelty & Toy Co., Brooklyn, N.Y.	"Snoozie" for dolls
	1933, Nov. 24	344,080	Bertha Behrman, New York, N.Y. (doing business as Alexander Doll Co.)	"Little Women" for dolls
	1933, Dec. 4	344,430	Anna Roosevelt Dall, New York, N.Y.	"Scamper" for dolls & toy figures
	1934, Jan. 5	345,680	Frank Passarelli, Mizpah, N.J.	"Pixy" for dolls
	1934, April 21	350,288	M. Pessner & Co., New York, N.Y...........	See illus. 73—for dolls & toys
	1934, May 22	351,676	Louis Marx & Co. Inc., New York, N.Y.	"Joe Penner" for metal dolls & toys
	1934, May 22	351,677	Louis Marx & Co. Inc., New York, N.Y.	"Suzabella" for metal dolls & toys
	1934, June 2	352,182	Ideal Novelty & Toy Co., Brooklyn, N.Y.	"Ginger" for dolls
	1934, June 22	353,030	Miller Rubber Co. Inc., Wilmington, Del. & Akron, Ohio	"Baby Glee" for dolls of rubber
	1934, June 22	353,029	Miller Rubber Co. Inc., Wilmington, Del. & Akron, Ohio	"Judy" for rubber dolls
	1934, June 22	353,031	Miller Rubber Co. Inc., Wilmington, Del. & Akron, Ohio	"Milly" for rubber dolls
Wazu	1934, Aug. 30	355,559	Arranbee Doll Co., New York, N.Y.	"Nannette" for dolls
43 (see 1922)	1934, Oct. 29	357,638	Evelyn Clayton Lewis, Dallas, Texas	"Teeny-Tiny" for dolls
	1934, Oct. 24	357,464	Ideal Novelty & Toy Co., Brooklyn, N.Y.	See illus. 74
	1934, Dec. 31	359,775	George Borgfeldt & Co., New York, N.Y.	"Kewpie" for toy figures & toy dishes
	1935, Jan. 30	324,401	Louis Wolf & Co. Inc., New York, N.Y.	"Perfection" for dolls & toys
	1935, Jan. 30	360,871	Louis Wolf & Co. Inc., New York, N.Y.	"Robin Hood" for dolls & toys
	1935, Mar. 1	362,054	The Shinn Sisters, White Sulphur Springs, W.Va. & Palm Beach, Fla.	"The Dollhouse—It's the smallest shop but it gives the greatest joy" for dolls & toy animals
	1935, Mar. 1	362,009	Bertha Behrman, New York, N.Y. (doing business as Alexander Doll Co.)	See illus. 75
	1935, Mar. 20	362,784	Jerome Hamburger, New York, N.Y.	"My Be Be Dolls" for dolls
	1935, Mar. 23	362,903	George Borgfeldt Corp., New York, N.Y.......	"Little Bright Eyes" for dolls
	1935, Mar. 26	363,008	Molly'es Doll Outfitters Inc., Philadelphia, Pa. ..	"Raggedy Ann" with picture of dress hanger for dolls, doll clothes, toys, etc.
	1935, Mar. 26	363,007	Molly'es Doll Outfitters Inc., Philadelphia, Pa. ..	"Self Help Educational Toy" for dolls, doll clothes & stuffed toy animals
44 (see 1922)	1935, April 1	363,290	Molly'es Doll Outfitters Inc., Philadelphia, Pa. ..	"Hollywood Cinema Fashions for Dolls" for dolls & doll clothes
	1935, April 17	363,890	Paragon Rubber Corp., New York, N.Y........	"Wee Wee" for dolls
	1935, April 24	364,133	Eugene Goldberger, Brooklyn, N.Y............	"Little Miss Movie Everybody Loves Me" around circle for dolls
	1935, May 9	364,722	Ideal Novelty & Toy Co., Long Island City, N.Y.	"Curly Top" for dolls
	1935, May 9	364,723	Ideal Novelty & Toy Co., Long Island City, N.Y.	"Our Little Girl" for dolls
	1935, May 28	365,537	Helen Seibold Walter, Staunton, Va.	"Just Folks" for dolls
	1935, June 12	366,082	George Borgfeldt Corp., New York, N.Y.......	"Henry" for mechanical dolls & toy figures
	1935, July 1	366,878	Santa Claus Inc., Chicago Ill. & Santa Claus, Ind.	"Santa Claus" for dolls & toys
	1935, Sept. 25	369,708	Militant Dolls Inc., Brooklyn, N.Y.	"Kaydet Doll" for dolls
	1935, Sept. 25	369,709	Militant Dolls Inc., Brooklyn, N.Y.	"Middy Doll" for dolls
	1935, Oct. 3	369,965	Ideal Novelty & Toy Co., Long Island City, N.Y.	"The Littlest Rebel" for dolls
	1935, Oct. 5	370,043	Joseph Coyle, Chicago, Ill.	"Ko Ko The Clown" for dolls
	1935, Oct. 9	370,188	Joseph Love Inc., New York, N.Y.	See illus. 76
	1935, Oct. 29	370,958	Mrs. Frankie L. McCulloch, Branson, Mo.	"Hill-Billy Doll" for dolls. In oval
	1936, Jan. 2	373,245	Blossom Products Corp., Allentown, Pa.	See illus. 77—for dolls
	1936, Jan. 2	373,261	Myers & Lindquist, St. Paul, Minn.	"Baby Pinn" for dolls
	1936, Jan. 16	373,717	Blossom Products Corp., Allentown, Pa.	"Quins" for dolls
45 (see 1923)	1936, Jan. 16	373,720	Blossom Products Corp., Allentown, Pa.	"Quintuplets" for dolls

Patent Date	Patent Serial No.	Patentee	Trademark
1936, Jan. 22	373,970	Paragon Rubber Corp., New York, N.Y.	"Sleepy Tot" for dolls
1936, Jan. 28	370,783	Torme Products Co.	Paper, cardboard, fabric cut-outs
1936, Jan. 30	374,272	Bertha Behrman, New York, N.Y., (doing business as Madame Alexander)	"Quints" for dolls
1936, Jan. 30	374,274	Bertha Behrman, New York, N.Y. (doing business as Madame Alexander)	"The Five Babies" for dolls
1936, Jan. 30	374,273	Bertha Behrman, New York, N.Y. (doing business as Madame Alexander)	"Quins" for dolls
1936, Jan. 30	374,269	Bertha Behrman, New York, N.Y. (doing business as Madame Alexander)	"Quinties" for dolls
1936, Jan. 30	374,271	Bertha Behrman, New York, N.Y. (doing business as Madame Alexander)	"Five Little Peppers" for dolls
1936, Jan. 30	374,268	Bertha Behrman, New York, N.Y. (doing business as Madame Alexander)	"Little Lord Fauntleroy" for dolls
1936, Jan. 30	374,270	Bertha Behrman, New York, N.Y. (doing business as Alexander Doll Co. & Madame Alexander)	"Quintuplets" for dolls
1936, May 4	568,558	Crescent Toy Co. Ltd., South Tottenham, England	Claim control for miniature representatives of human civilian persons, etc. wholly or partly of cast metal
1936, May 15	378,485	Eugene Goldberger, New York, N.Y.	See illus. 78—for dolls
1936, June 9	379,481	Joseph M. McConnell, Okmulgee, Okla.	"G-Men Dolls" for dolls
1936, June 10	379,506	Charles Colombo, New York, N.Y.	See illus. 79—for dolls
1936, June 10	379,507	Charles Colombo, New York, N.Y.	See illus. 80—for dolls
1936, Aug. 3	381,743	American Character Doll Co. Inc., New York, N.Y.	"Marvel Tot" for dolls
1936, Sept. 17	383,357	Ideal Novelty & Toy Co., Long Island City, N.Y.	"Sunbonnet Sue" for dolls
1936, Oct. 6	384,059	Ullstein Aktiengesellschaft, Berlin, Germany	Picture of man and little girl for dolls, games & toys
1936, Dec. 1	386,161	Ideal Novelty & Toy Co., Long Island City, N.Y.	"The Lifetime Doll" for dolls
1936, Dec. 23	387,057	Abraham & Strauss Inc., Brooklyn, N.Y.	"World's Fair" for dolls, paper cut-outs & toys
1936, Dec. 28	387,169	Bloomingdale Bros. Inc., New York, N.Y.	"Baby Sister" for dolls
1937, Feb. 8	388,641	E. J. Herte, Milwaukee, Wis.	See illus. 81—for dolls
1937, Feb. 19	389,129	Ideal Novelty & Toy Co., Long Island City, N.Y.	"Heidi" for dolls & accessories
1937, Mar. 17	390,177	Molly-'es Doll Outfitters Inc., Darby, Pa.	"Babyland Toys" for dolls
1937, Mar. 18	390,252	Strauss-Eckardt Co. Inc., New York, N.Y.	See illus. 82—for dolls & toys
1937, Mar. 23	390,536	Martha E. Battle, Chattanooga, Tenn.	See illus. 83—for dolls
1937, Mar. 24	390,573	Lottie Laurie McCall, Biloxi, Miss. (doing business as Mammy Lou Doll Co.)	"Mammy Lou" for stuffed black dolls
1937, April 23	391,734	Virginia Stowe Austin, Los Angeles, Calif.	See illus. 84—for doll or puppet, etc.
1937, April 28	391,942	Bertha Alexander, New York, N.Y. (also known as Madame Alexander, doing business as Alexander Doll Co.)	"Neva-Wet" for dolls
1937, April 29	392,003	Bertha Alexander, New York, N.Y. (also known as Madame Alexander, doing business as Alexander Doll Co.)	"Scarlet O'Hara" for dolls
1937, April 29	392,002	Bertha Alexander, New York, N.Y. (also known as Madame Alexander, doing business as Alexander Doll Co.)	"Teeny Twinkle" for dolls
1937, April 29	392,004	Bertha Alexander, New York, N.Y. (also known as Madame Alexander, doing business as Alexander Doll Co.)	"Princess Alexandria" for dolls
1937, May 1	392,153	Kimport Dolls, Independence, Mo.	See illus. 85—for dolls
1937, May 5	392,306	American Character Doll Co. Inc., New York, N.Y.	"Bottie Babe" for dolls
1937, May 6	392,371	Sam Kalner, New York, N.Y.	"Q-T" for dolls
1937, May 13	392,720	The Sun Rubber Co., Barberton, O.	"Wet-Ums" for wetting dolls
1937, May 28	393,387	Valerie McMahan, Washington, D.C.	"Gone with the Wind" by Valerie McMahan-Trademark for dolls
1937, June 2	393,519	Catherine A. Abt, Pittsburgh, Pa.	"Sister Catherine Doll" for dolls
1937, June 10	393,886	Bertha Alexander, New York, N.Y. (doing business as Alexander Doll Co.)	"McGuffey-Ana" for dolls
1937, Aug. 4	395,987	Georgene Novelties Inc., New York, N.Y.	"Little Cherub" for dolls
1937, Aug. 24	396,708	Charlie McCarthy, Inc., New York, N.Y.	"Charlie McCarthy Inc."
1937, Oct. 9	398,303	McLoughlin Bros. Inc., Springfield, Mass.	"Magic Doll" for dolls & costumes for dolls
1937, Oct. 11	398,355	Edith Holden, New York, N.Y.	"Bratchet" for dolls
1937, Oct. 28	374,505	Lenart Import Ltd., New York, N.Y.	"Lenart" for dolls
1937, Nov. 9	363,240	Bertha Alexander, New York, N.Y. (doing business as Alexander Doll Co.)	"Snow White" for dolls
1937, Dec. 6	400,539	Toy Creations Inc., Jersey City, N.J.	"Our Little Sister-Dillon Doll Creation" for dolls
1937, Dec. 21	401,099	Bertha Alexander, New York, N.Y. (doing business as Madame Alexander Doll Co.) . . .	"Annie Laurie" for dolls
1938, Jan. 20	402,132	Charlie McCarthy, Inc., New York, N.Y.	A silhouette picture of Charlie McCarthy
1938, Jan. 20	402,131	Charlie McCarthy, Inc., New York, N.Y.	"Charlie McCarthy" for dolls

46 (see 1923)

47 (see 1923)

TU-TANKH-AMEN DOLLS

48 (see 1923)

TUT MUMMIE

49 (see 1923)

Schuco

50 (see 1923)

AMERICAN

51 (see 1923)

52 (see 1923)

Lenci
53 (see 1923)

My Bunny Boy
54 (see 1923)

NURSE JANE FUZZY WUZZY
55 (see 1924)

Patent Date	Patent Serial No.	Patentee	Trademark
1938, Jan. 22	402,221	George Henry Hutaff, Jr., Wilmington, N.C.	"Bunny-Hop" for toy figures
1938, Feb. 19	403,235	Norcross, New York, N.Y.	"Susie-Q" for dolls
1938, Feb. 21	403,273	Famous Playthings Co., New York, N.Y.	"World of Tomorrow" with a picture of a spire and globe of world, for dolls
1938, Feb. 25	403,407	Ralph Freundlich Inc., Clinton, Mass.	"Dummy Dan" for novelty dolls or dummy representation of beings
1938, Feb. 26	403,460	Meyer Julius Hackman, Chicago, Ill. (doing business as Jock-O-Company)	"Jock-O The Life of the Party" with a monkey picture for novelty toy doll
1938, Mar. 7	403,769	Ideal Novelty & Toy Co., Long Island City, N.Y.	"Baby Snooks" for dolls
1938, Mar. 15	404,084	Ideal Novelty & Toy Co., Long Island City, N.Y.	"Princess Beatrix" for dolls
1938, April 9	405,072	Ideal Novelty & Toy Co., Long Island City, N.Y.	"Sonia" for dolls
1938, April 9	405,079	Norcross, New York, N.Y.	"Bobby-Q" for dolls
1938, May 7	406,086	Eve Bennet, New York, N.Y.	"Astro-Logical" for dolls & dummy representatives of beings
1938, May 27	406,810	Joy Doll Corporation, New York, N.Y.	"Maid of America" for dolls, cut-out figures, etc.
1938, June 17	407,589	L. Ray Fowler, New York, N.Y.	"General Goodwill" for dolls & stuffed toys & cut-out paper figures
1938, June 17	407,588	L. Ray Fowler, New York, N.Y.	"Dandy Goodwill" for dolls, stuffed toys & cut-out paper figures
1938, June 21	359,648	Hale B. Anthony, Rockport, Mass.	"Solomon Salt" for dolls
1938, July 19	408,654	Mildred Northern Miller, Lexington, Va. (doing business as Mildred Miller's Gift Shop)	"Brother Rat" for dolls
1938, July 26	408,921	Joy Doll Corporation, New York, N.Y.	"Girl of Tomorrow" for dolls, stuffed toys, cut-out paper figures
1938, July 26	408,922	Joy Doll Corporation, New York, N.Y.	"International Parade" for dolls, stuffed toys, cut-out paper figures
1938, July 26	408,923	Joy Doll Corporation, New York, N.Y.	"Miss 1939" for dolls, stuffed toys, cut-out paper figures
1938, Aug. 5	409,290	Yermie Stern Commercial Attractions, New York, N.Y.	Picture of figure in stocking cap for dolls
1938, Aug. 26	409,989	Edgar J. Bergen, Hollywood, Calif.	"Mortimer Snerd" across picture of Mortimer for dolls
1938, Oct. 24	411,983	Arranbee Doll Co., New York, N.Y.	"Debu 'Teen" for dolls
1938, Oct. 24	411,993	Josephine Aldrich Harris, Birmingham, Ala.	See illus. 86—for dolls
1938, Nov. 4	412,382	Louis Marx & Co., New York, N.Y.	See illus. 87
1938, Dec. 7	413,565	Sears Roebuck & Co., Chicago, Ill.	See illus. 88—for dolls
1939, Feb. 18	416,230	E. I. DuPont DeNemours & Co., Wilmington, Del.	"DuPont" for dolls, rattles and tops
1939, Feb. 20	416,245	Lawrence Gideon, Perry, N.Y.	"Design Styles" with picture of doll inside a triangle for doll kit including doll, patterns & materials to make clothing
1939, Feb. 24	376,558	George Borgfeldt & Corp., New York, N.Y.	"Baby Wiggles" for dolls
1939, Mar. 9	416,827	American Character Doll Co. Inc., New York, N.Y.	"Junior Deb" for dolls
1939, April 6	417,901	American Character Doll Co. Inc., New York, N.Y.	"Rock-A-Bye" for dolls
1939, May 31	419,993	American Character Doll Co. Inc., New York, N.Y.	"Hush-A-Bye" for dolls
1939, June 10	426,609	Walt Disney Productions, Hollywood, Calif.	"Jiminy Cricket" for figure dolls
1939, June 10	423,038	Walt Disney Productions, Los Angeles, Calif.	"Pinocchio" for dolls & toy figures
1939, June 27	421,001	Mary Hasell Lakopolanska, New York, N.Y. (doing business as The American Doll)	See illus. 89
1939, July 1	421,192	Metal Textile Corp., West Orange, N.J.	"Maggie" for paper dolls
1939, Aug. 29	423,108	The May Dept. Stores Co., New York, N.Y., Akron, Baltimore, Cleveland, Los Angeles, Denver (doing business as Famous Barr Co., St. Louis, Mo.)	"Baby Aristocrat" for dressed & undressed dolls
1939, Oct. 20	424,724	G. C. Hanford Mfg. Co., Syracuse, N.Y.	"Perky Prill" for paper dolls
1939, Dec. 12	426,500	Florence Sherman, New York, N.Y.	"The Clipper" for dolls
1939, Dec. 12	426,499	Florence Sherman, New York, N.Y.	"The Boy Friend" for dolls
1939, Dec. 15	426,617	Marjorie Gregg, Bridgeport, Conn.	"Real People" for dolls
1940, Jan. 8	427,243	Mollye Goldman, Darby, Pa. (doing business as Molly'es)	"Southern Belle" for dolls & doll clothes
1940, Jan. 8	427,245	Don Heyer, Inglewood, Calif.	"Billy Bug" for dolls, cut-out toys, enclosed in circle with figure
1940, Mar. 1	429,084	American Features Inc., Hollywood, Calif.	"Becky Bug" for dolls, cut-outs & games, enclosed in circle with figure
1940, Mar. 30	430,181	Julia Gray, Washington, D.C.	"Virginia Dare" for dolls
1940, April 15	430,761	Julia Cline, Shreveport, La.	"Julie Ann" for hand painted wooden dolls
1940, May 8	431,686	Ideal Novelty & Toy Co., Long Island City, N.Y.	"Poppa-Momma" for dolls
1940, May 14	431,898	Bertha Alexander, New York, N.Y. (doing business as Alexander Doll Co.)	"Butch" for dolls
1940, May 14	431,899	Bertha Alexander, New York, N.Y. (doing business as Alexander Doll Co.)	"Mother and Me" for dolls
1940, May 14	431,900	Bertha Alexander, New York, N.Y. (doing business as Alexander Doll Co.)	"Madelaine" for dolls

Patent Date	Patent Serial No.	Patentee	Trademark
1940, June 20	433,208	Arranbee Doll Co., New York, N.Y.	*See illus. 90*
1940, June 22	433,294	J. Swedlin Inc., New York, N.Y.	"Honey Lou" for dolls & stuffed toys
1940, June 24	433,312	Nantok Corp., New York, N.Y.	"Weepy Baby" for dolls
1940, July 2	433,632	Madeleine Schneidewind, Montclair, N.J.	"Susan Joy Adopt-Me-Doll" for dolls & dummy representations of beings
1940, Aug. 1	434,551	Milton Bradley Co., Springfield, Mass.	"Bradley" for dolls, doll clothes & toys
1940, Aug. 4	434,690	Toyad Corp., Latrobe, Pa.	"Foamflex" for rubber toys, namely dolls
1940, Aug. 7	434,751	Sam Kalner, New York, N.Y. (doing business as Well Made Doll Co.)	"My Bandbox Baby Doll" for dolls
1940, Aug. 16	435,069	Toyad Corp., Latrobe, Pa.	"Sleeping Pal" for rubber toys, namely dolls
1940, Sept. 7	435,762	Ideal Novelty & Toy Co., Long Island City, N.Y.	"Little Miss America" for dolls
1940, Oct. 9	436,776	Margit Nilsen Studios Inc., New York, N.Y.	"Deb-U-Doll" for dolls & mannequins
1940, Nov. 27	384,731	Richard G. Krueger, Inc., New York, N.Y.	"Krueger, N.Y." for dolls & toys
1941, Mar. 12	441,496	Toy Manufacturers of the U.S.A., Inc., New York, N.Y.	*See illus. 91*—claims use since Feb. 1, 1918
1941, Mar. 13	441,506	The Fair, Chicago, Ill.	"Blue Ribbon Baby with Peek-A-Boo Eyes" for dolls
1941, April 4	442,273	Nancy Ann Dressed Dolls Inc., San Francisco, Calif.	"Gerda and Kay" for dolls & doll clothes
1941, April 19	442,755	Harold Munro, Providence, R.I.	"Savme" for dolls, toy surgical instruments & toy badges
1941, May 19	443,699	George Pal, Hollywood, Calif.	"Puppetoon" for dolls & marionettes including figures & operating appliances therefore
1941, May 21	443,767	Ideal Novelty & Toy Co., Long Island City, N.Y.	"Gorgeous" for dolls
1941, June 23	444,775	The Sun Rubber Co., Barberton, O.	"Sunbabe" for rubber dolls
1941, June 23	444,776	The Sun Rubber Co., Barberton, O.	"Sunruco" for rubber dolls & rubber toys
1941, June 26	444,850	Bertha Alexander, New York, N.Y. (doing business as Alexander Doll Co.)	"Lov-Le-Tex" for dolls
1941, Aug. 9	446,111	Joseph Kallus, Brooklyn, N.Y.	"Cookie" for dolls
1941, Aug. 18	446,335	Girdner Provost, New York, N.Y. (doing business as Girdner Provost Co.)	"Piper Dolls" with three doll figures for dolls
1941, Sept. 17	392,882	J. Swedlin Inc., New York, N.Y.	"CUND" for stuffed dolls & figures
1941, Oct. 3	447,511	Lily Marianne Hubert, Bellport, N.Y.	"Lily Marianne Toys" for dolls
1941, Oct. 21	447,975	Dante Quinterno & Cia, Buenos Aires, Argentina (doing business as Sindicato Dante Quinterno) ...	"Tupa Isidoro Patoruzu" for dolls. Each name indicating a doll figure
1941, Oct. 27	448,162	Lolita Duncan Munford, Richmond, Va.	"Kuddle-Duddle" for dolls & stuffed dolls
1941, Nov. 12	448,595	Virginia Woodin, Arlington, Va.	"Dollydrop" in circle for dolls
1941, Dec. 12	449,436	Sayco Doll Corp., New York, N.Y.	"Baby Smoothie" for dolls
1941, Dec. 15	449,493	Nancy Ann Dressed Dolls Inc., San Francisco, Calif.	"Sunday's Child" for dolls
1941, Dec. 15	449,492	Nancy Ann Dressed Dolls Inc., San Francisco, Calif.	"Goldilocks" for dolls
1941, Dec. 15	449,495	Nancy Ann Dressed Dolls Inc., San Francisco, Calif.	"Polly Put Kettle On" for dolls & clothes
1941, Dec. 15	449,496	Nancy Ann Dressed Dolls Inc., San Francisco, Calif.	"Little Bo Peep" for dolls & clothes
1941, Dec. 15	449,497	Nancy Ann Dressed Dolls Inc., San Francisco, Calif.	"December Girl" for dolls & clothes
1942, Jan. 23	450,433	J. Swedlin Inc., New York, N.Y.	"Dreamie" for stuffed dolls & figures
1942, Jan. 26	450,487	Grace Neff, New York, N.Y. (doing business as Kate Greenaway Designs)	"Kate Greenaway Toys" for dolls
1942, Feb. 7	450,825	George Borgfeldt Corp., New York, N.Y.	"My Playmate" for dolls & toy animals
1942, Feb. 25	451,207	Ideal Novelty & Toy Co., Long Island City, N.Y.	"Plassie" for dolls
1942, Mar. 10	451,524	American Character Doll Corp., New York, N.Y.	"Little Love" for dolls
1942, Aug. 3	454,699	Sears Roebuck & Co., Chicago, Ill.	"Happi-Time" for dolls & toys
1942, Aug. 24	455,084	Angela Peterson, Parkersburg, W.Va...........	"Ima-Doll" for dolls & clothes
1942, Sept. 4	455,328	Dritz-Traum Co. Inc., New York, N.Y.........	"Peggy" for dolls
1942, Oct. 2	455,918	Domenick Ippolito, Glendale, Calif. (doing business as Hollywood Mfg. Co.)	"Mother Goose Story Dolls" for dolls
1942, Oct. 12	456,155	Nancy Ann Dressed Dolls Inc., San Francisco, Calif.	"Mother Goose" for dolls & doll clothes
1942, Nov. 21	456,955	Lord & Taylor, New York, N.Y.	"Gremlin" for dolls
1942, Dec. 24	457,585	Rosalie Campbell, New York, N.Y.	"Rosomax" for dolls & toys of leather, cotton, rayon & wool fabrics
1943, Jan. 29	458,229	Sears Roebuck & Co., Chicago, Ill.	"Dorable" for dolls
1943, Feb. 4	458,346	Roslyn Stock, New York, N.Y. (doing business as Tweets Novelty Co.)	"Tweets" for dolls

56 *(see 1924)*

57 *(see 1924)*

58 *(see 1925)*

59 *(see 1925)*

60 *(see 1925)*

	Patent Date	Patent Serial No.	Patentee	Trademark
61 (see 1926)	1943, Feb. 4	458,347	Henry Sussman, New York, N.Y.	"Admiration" for dolls & stuffed animal toys
	1943, Feb. 15	458,549	Lenore Porter, San Francisco, Calif.	"Swankee Dandee" for toy dolls
	1943, Mar. 27	459,423-459,428 incl.	Nancy Ann Dressed Dolls Inc., San Francisco, Calif. (assignor to Nancy Ann Dressed Dolls)	"Monday's Child" through "Saturday's Child" inclusive for dolls
	1943, Mar. 27	459,429-459,440 incl.	Nancy Ann Dressed Dolls Inc., San Francisco, Calif. (assignor to Nancy Ann Dressed Dolls)	"January Girl" through "December Girl" inclusive for dolls
62 (see 1926)	1943, Mar. 29	459,482-459,494 incl.	Nancy Ann Dressed Dolls Inc., San Francisco, Calif. (assignor to Nancy Ann Dressed Dolls)	"Little Miss," "Roses are Red," "Over the Hill," "School Days," "To Market," "He Loves Me," "Merrie Maid," "When She Was Good," "Sugar & Spice," "Ring Around a Rosy," "Princess Minon Ninette," "Prince Souci" for dolls
	1943, May 1	460,333-460,344 incl.	Nancy Ann Dressed Dolls Inc., San Francisco, Calif. (assignor to Nancy Ann Dressed Dolls)	"Boy Blue," "Mistress Mary," "Alice Sweet Alice," "Annie at the Garden Gate," "Elsie Marley," "Lucy Locket," "Curly Locks," "Queen of Hearts," "Pretty Maid," "Jennie," "Princess Rosanie," "Little Miss Donnet" for dolls
63 (see 1928)	1943, June 7	461,204	Nancy Ann Dressed Dolls Inc., San Francisco, Calif. (assignor to Nancy Ann Dressed Dolls)	"Lady in Waiting" for dolls
	1943, July 22	462,229	Richard Krueger Inc., New York, N.Y.	"Button Buddy" for stuffed dolls & toys
	1943, Sept. 24	463,625	Heirloom Needlework Guild, Inc., New York, N.Y.	"Sunny Jill" for stuffed doll and patterns for making stuffed dolls
	1943, Sept. 24	463,624	Heirloom Needlework Guild Inc., New York, N.Y.	"Sunny Jack" for stuffed doll and patterns for making stuffed dolls
	1944, Jan. 6	466,390	Indian Arts & Crafts Board, Washington, D.C. ..	"Navajo Arts & Crafts Guild" for dolls
	1944, Feb. 11	467,342	Ideal Novelty & Toy Co., Long Island City, N.Y.	"Lazy Bones" for stuffed dolls & animals
	1944, Feb. 28	467,812	Nancy Ann Dressed Dolls, San Francisco, Calif.	"Mary Had a Little Lamb" for dolls
	1944, Mar. 7	468,033	Ideal Novelty & Toy Co., Long Island City, N.Y.	"Pin-Up-Girl" for dolls
	1944, Mar. 27	468,716	Nancy Ann Dressed Dolls, San Francisco, Calif.	"Little Miss Muffet" for dolls
	1944, May 27	470,729	Nancy Ann Dressed Dolls, San Francisco, Calif.	"Alice Thru Looking Glass" for dolls
64 (see 1929)	1944, June 27	471,710	Nancy Ann Dressed Dolls, San Francisco, Calif.	"Little Miss Sweet Miss" for dolls
	1944, June 28	409,122	Jennie Graves, Medford, Mass. (doing business as The Vogue Doll Shoppe)	"Vogue Dolls Fashion Leaders in Doll Society" for dolls & clothes
	1944, July 18	472,351	J. Donald Biever, Philadelphia, Pa.	"Circus Parade" for toys simulating circus characters
	1944, Aug. 19	473,457	Parmor Products Co., Atlanta, Ga.	"Dixie Doodle" for dolls
	1944, Sept. 26	474,630	Helen Hartman, New York, N.Y.	"Hugables" for dolls
	1944, Oct. 7	463,982	Sire-Schindel Co., New York, N.Y.	"Huggy Wuggy" for stuffed chenille dolls & toys
	1944, Oct. 7	475,092	George Weber, Akron, O.	"Jerry" for dolls
65 (see 1929)	1944, Oct. 7	475,044	May Agnes Davis, Orange, N.J................	"Miss Victoria the doll that never changes her mind But never loses her head" for dolls
	1944, Nov. 3	476,060	Domenick Ippolito, Glendale, Calif., (doing business as Hollywood Doll Mfg. Co.)	"Garden Series" for dolls
	1944, Nov. 3	476,061	Domenick Ippolito, Glendale, Calif., (doing business as Hollywood Doll Mfg. Co.)	"Hollywood Lucky Star" for dolls
	1944, Nov. 9	476,292	Jolly Toys Inc., New York, N.Y.	"Jolly Toy" for stuffed dolls & toys
	1944, Nov. 14	411,792	Furty Novelty Co., New York, N.Y.	"Furtoy" for stuffed dolls & animals
	1944, Nov. 21	476,720	Cavendish Trading Corp., New York, N.Y.	"Cavencrest" for dolls & toys
	1944, Dec. 13	477,504	Gardel Industries, New York, N.Y.	"Mayfair" for dolls
	1945, Jan. 8	478,381	Joe Grand & Dick Huemer, Glendale, Calif.	"OOGLE" with picture of elephant for dolls
	1945, Jan. 24	478,959	Ideal Novelty & Toy Co., Long Island City, N.Y.	"IDEALTOY" for dolls & toys
	1945, Jan. 26	479,039	Ideal Novelty & Toy Co., Long Island City, N.Y.	"Bit of Heaven" for dolls
	1945, Feb. 8	479,568	Ideal Novelty & Toy Co., Long Island City, N.Y.	"Continental' for dolls
66 (see 1930)	1945, Feb. 9	479,616	Corinne Del Vecchio, St. Albans, N.Y.	"Lem and Effie" for dolls

Patent Date	Patent Serial No.	Patentee	Trademark
1945, Feb. 9	479,620	Gardel Industries, New York, N.Y.	"Birthstone Doll of the Month" dolls
1945, Feb. 9	479,619	Gardel Industries, New York, N.Y.	"Birthstone Doll" for dolls
1945, Mar. 8	480,660	Karavan Trading Co., New York, N.Y.	"Karavan" for dolls, etc.
1945, April 28	482,752	Margaret Ludeman, Centerport, N.Y.	"Lucky Horse-Shoe" for dolls
1945, May 22	481,685	Jane Alexander, Valley Stream, N.Y.	"Pluggin Jane" for dolls
1945, July 17	474,411	Lois Hendron, Marion, Ala.	"Cotton Tot Dolls" for dolls
1945, July 17	481,732	Bantam U. S. Toys Inc., New York, N.Y.	"Bantam U. S. Toys Inc." for stuffed dolls
1945, July 24	482,306	Api Ltd., New York, N.Y.	"Childhood Classics Beautiful Dolls" with picture of doll
1945, July 24	484,224	American Character Doll Co. Inc., New York, N.Y.	"Junior Miss" for dolls
1945, July 31	473,190	Hilda Moore, Asheville, N.C.	"Doing Toy" for puppet doll
1945, July 31	415,266	Boyce Wimberly, Yoakum, Texas	"Boyce" for dolls (inside a ball)
1945, Aug. 14	482,814	Selvy Creations Inc., New York, N.Y.	"Uffy-kins" for stuffed figures
1945, Sept. 4	480,676	Mills & Easley, New York, N.Y.	Doll holding a sign on which were words "Mary Frances"
1945, Sept. 4	485,400	Alice L. Clarke, Mill Valley, Calif.	"Nina" for dolls
1945, Sept. 25	482,570	L. A. Goodman Mfg. Co., Chicago, Ill.	"Bobbin" for plastic dolls
1945, Sept. 25	484,470	Grover Turner, Indianapolis, Ind.	"Carrol-Lina" for dolls
1945, Oct. 16	483,182	Lydia Jedwabnik, New York, N.Y.	"Lydart" for dolls
1945, Oct. 16	484,005	M. Ailetcher & Co., Lakewood, N.J.	"Susan Fran" for dolls
1945, Oct. 16	485,879	Mae Murphy, Chicago, Ill.	"Magic Doll" (in ball) for dolls
1945, Nov. 21	492,217	Anne Norton, Anderson, Ind.	"Dingle Doll Family" for dolls
1945, Dec. 4	481,227	Domenick Ippolito, Glendale, Calif., (doing business as Hollywood Doll Mfg. Co.)	"Nursery Rhymes" for dolls
1945, Dec. 4	481,229	Domenick Ippolito, Glendale, Calif. (doing business as Hollywood Doll Mfg. Co.)	"Toyland" for dolls
1945, Dec. 11	485,800	Umbriago Corp., New York, N.Y.	"Umbriago" for novelty doll heads
1945, Dec. 18	488,087	Julia Culbreath Gray, Washington, D.C.	"Gal of the Gay Ninties" for dolls
1946, Jan. 22	419,032	Paul Winchell, New York, N.Y.	"Jerry M. A. Honey" for dolls
1946, Jan. 22	419,030	L. Hitchcock, Los Angeles, Calif.	"A Lynne Creation" for dolls & toys
1946, Feb. 5	419,241	Gramercy Toy Co., New York, N.Y.	"Gramercy Toy Co." for toy dolls & animals
1946, Feb. 5	496,022	Zadek Feldstein Co., Inc., New York, N.Y.	"Snow Baby" for dolls, etc.
1946, Feb. 26	419,643	Umbriago Corp., New York, N.Y.	"Umbriago" for dolls and heads
1946, Mar. 8	497,871	Londonderry Products Inc., South Londonderry, Vermont	"The Brandon Life Toys of Destinctive Design" in circle with Christmas tree in center for wooden toys, pull toys and educational toys
1946 May 21	421,161	Irene Alma Edenburn, Chicago, Ill.	"Tiny Iney" for dolls
1946, May 21	495,638	Three in One Doll Corp., New York, N.Y.	"Trudy" for dolls
1946, May 21	496,792	Domenick Ippolito, Glendale Calif., (doing business as Hollywood Doll Mfg. Co.)	"Annabella" for dolls
1946, May 21	496,795-496,806 incl.	Domenick Ippolito, Glendale, Calif., (doing business as Hollywood Doll Mfg. Co.)	"Camellia," "Dottie Dimples," "Forget me Not," "Garden Lady" for dolls
1946, May 21	496,801-496,806 incl.	Domenick Ippolito, Glendale, Calif., (doing business as Hollywood Doll Mfg. Co.)	"Lady Elaine," "Lady Guinevere," "Lady Isolde," "Lady Lynette," "Lady of the Lake," "Lady Slipper" for dolls
1946, May 21	496,816-496,817	Domenick Ippolito, Glendale, Calif., (doing business as Hollywood Doll Mfg. Co.)	"Marie Helena," "Mary Mary Quite Contrary" for dolls
1946, May 21	496,819-496,820	Domenick Ippolito, Glendale, Calif., (doing business as Hollywood Doll Mfg. Co.)	"Masquerade," "Miss Gingerbread" for dolls
1946, May 21	496,822-496,823	Domenick Ippolito, Glendale, Calif., (doing business as Hollywood Doll Mfg. Co.)	"Miss Teeter Totter," "Muffie with her Spider" for dolls
1946, May 21	496,825	Domenick Ippolito, Glendale, Calif., (doing business as Hollywood Doll Mfg. Co.)	"Pat-A-Cake" for dolls
1946, May 21	496,830	Domenick Ippolito, Glendale, Calif., (doing business as Hollywood Doll Mfg. Co.)	"Queen Silver Bell" for dolls
1946, May 21	496,834-496,835	Domenick Ippolito, Glendale, Calif., (doing business as Hollywood Doll Mfg. Co.)	"Sleepyhead," "Star Dust" for dolls
1946, May 21	496,837-496,838	Domenick Ippolito, Glendale, Calif., (doing business as Hollywood Doll Mfg. Co.)	"Sweet Janice," "Sweet Spirit" for dolls
1946, June 18	483,572	Domenick Ippolito, Glendale, Calif., (doing business as Hollywood Doll Mfg. Co.)	"Grandma's Dolls"
1946, June 18	490,538	Audrey Kargere, New York, N.Y.	"Audrey Kargere" for dolls
1946, July 2	495,214	Elaine Cannon, Batavia, Ill.	"Little Hickory" for dolls
1946, July 2	496,084	Jos. L. Kallus, Port Allegeny, Pa., (doing business as Cameo Doll Products Co.)	"Baby Blossom" for dolls

67 *(see 1930)*

68 *(see 1930)*

69 *(see 1930)*

70 *(see 1931)*

71 *(see 1931)*

EMPRESS

72 *(see 1933)*

73 (see 1934)

74 (see 1934)

LITTLE COLONEL

75 (see 1935)

76 (see 1935)

77 (see 1936)

78 (see 1936)

Patent Date	Patent Serial No.	Patentee	Trademark
1946, July 9	483,078	Nancy Ann Dressed Doll, San Francisco, Calif., (assignor to Storybook Dolls Inc.)	"Birthday Dolls"
1946, Aug. 1	506,650	Albert M. Danzig, New York, N.Y.	Wreath inside of which are words "Me-Mi-Self-Doll" for dolls
1946, Aug. 13	422,824	The Three In One Doll Corp., New York, N.Y.	"Trudy" for dolls
1946, Aug. 13	482,252	Maxing Products Co., New York, N.Y.	"MAXING" for dolls
1946, Aug. 17	504,838	Revoc Inc., New York, N.Y.	"Punchinella" for dolls
1946, Aug. 20	423,088	The Three In One Doll Corp., New York, N.Y.	"Sleepy, Weepy, Smily" for dolls. Republished by registerer
1946, Aug. 27	481,226	Domenick Ippolito, Glendale, Calif., (doing business as Hollywood Doll Mfg. Co.)	"Hollywood Book Doll" for dolls
1946, Oct. 1	504,369	Ann Lorenzen, Atlantic City, N.J.	"Scar Belly" for dolls
1946, Dec. 3	501,832	Roger DeVries, Buenos Aires, Argentina	"Bahiana" for dolls
1946, Dec. 17	507,586	E. A. Jakku, Hood River, Oregon	"The Stampeder" for dolls
1946, Dec. 17	509,065	Anna J. Wiseman, Memphis, Tenn., (doing business as The Wiseman Co.)	"Memphis Mammy" for dolls
1947, Jan. 14	489,742	Roy Kropp, Cicero, Ill.	"Toggle Woggle" for animated toys in form of dolls, manikins & animals
1947, Jan. 21	488,504	Omer Boucquey, Saint Cloud, France	Picture of fat Kewpie type of baby above which is word "Choupinet" for dolls
1947, Jan. 21	492,807	Viking Toy Co., Larchmont, N.Y.	"Atomic Man" with picture of fanciful man with wings for dolls
1947, Jan. 21	516,081	Kohner Bros., New York, N.Y.	"Hit and Miss" in rectangle for animated toys
1947, Jan. 21	519,759	Kohner Bros., New York, N.Y.	"Bronco Bill" in rectangle for toys
1947, Jan. 29	516,535	Coronet Toy Mfg. Co., Seattle, Wash.	A crown plus words "Coronet Playtime Pals for the Nations Kiddies" for dolls, animals & characters
1947, Feb. 4	484,754	Nancy Ann Dressed Dolls, San Francisco, Calif., (assignor to Nancy Ann Story Book Dolls Inc.)	"Fairyland" for dolls
1947, Feb. 11	484,755	Nancy Ann Dressed Dolls, San Francisco, Calif., (assignor to Nancy Ann Story Book Dolls Inc.)	"Fairytale" for dressed dolls
1947, Feb. 25	494,189	Nancy Ann Dressed Dolls, San Francisco, Calif., (assignor to Nancy Ann Story Book Dolls Inc.)	"Goose Girl" for dressed dolls
1947, Feb. 25	518,078	Ideal Novelty & Toy Co., Hollis, N.Y.	"Honeyfoam" for dolls & toy rubber figures & animals
1947, Mar. 4	494,834	Gardel Industries, New York, N.Y.	"Melody Maids" for dolls
1947, Mar. 19	433,273	Dominick Ippolito, Glendale, Calif.	"Cowgirl" for dolls
1947, Mar. 19	519,304	Vogue Dolls Inc., Melford Mass.	"Vogue Velva Baby" for dolls
1947, Mar. 23	575,932	Sayco Doll Corp., New York, N.Y.	"Sayco" for dolls
1947, Mar. 25	428,592	Nancy Ann Dressed Dolls, San Francisco, Calif., (assignor to Nancy Ann Story Book Dolls Inc.)	"Marjorie Daw" for dressed dolls
1947, Mar. 25	492,763	Curran, Cushions & Textile Co., Downers Grove, Ill.	"Vegie Doll" for dolls
1947, Mar. 25	492,791	Republic Precision Mfg. Co., Chicago, Ill.	"Dollyo" for doll heads
1947, Mar. 25	494,835	Gardel Industries, New York, N.Y.	"Melo Dears" for dolls
1947, April 1	428,819	Nancy Ann Dressed Dolls, San Francisco, Calif., (assignor to Nancy Ann Story Book Dolls Inc.)	"Nellie Bird" for dressed dolls
1947, April 5	520,244	Vanity Doll Co. Inc., Brooklyn, N.Y.	"Wetsie Kins" for dolls
1947, April 8	488,424	Plymouth Wholesale Dry Goods Corp. of N.Y., New York, N.Y.	"Hearthstone" for dolls, toys, etc.
1947, April 8	494,688	Ned Lincoln, New York, N.Y.	"Haba-Hubba." "Haba-Hubba" in black head for dolls
1947, April 8	496,443	Julia Gray, Washington, D.C.	"Bible Story" for dolls
1947, April 22	501,338	Plastic Treasure Inc., New York, N.Y.	"Klippy" for infants toys in nature of plastic swinging doll
1947, April 29	494,717	Twinzy Toy Co., Battle Creek, Mich.	"The Man in the Moon" for dolls
1947, May 2	521,759	Show Doll Co., New York, N.Y.	"Lucky Oggie" for dolls
1947, May 6	496,793	Domenick Ippolito, Glendale, Calif. (doing business as Hollywood Doll Mfg. Co.)	"Beauty Rose" for dolls & clothes
1947, May 6	496,794	Domenick Ippolito, Glendale, Calif. (doing business as Hollywood Doll Mfg. Co.)	"Bonnie Blue Bell" for dolls
1947, May 6	496,810	Domenick Ippolito, Glendale, Calif. (doing business as Hollywood Doll Mfg. Co.)	"Little Nancy Etticoat" for dolls
1947, May 6	496,812	Domenick Ippolito, Glendale, Calif. (doing business as Hollywood Doll Mfg. Co.)	"Little Rose" for dolls
1947, May 6	496,814	Domenick Ippolito, Glendale, Calif. (doing business as Hollywood Doll Mfg. Co.)	"Lizbeth Long Frock" for dolls
1947, May 6	496,828- 496,829	Domenick Ippolito, Glendale, Calif. (doing business as Hollywood Doll Mfg. Co.)	"Pretty Kitty," "Princess Beauty" for dolls

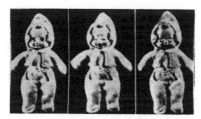

"Trudy", 1946 *creation of the Three-in-One Doll Corporation, displayed three different facial expressions as her head was turned.*

Left to right, 1937, Snow White doll; 1937 McGuffey Ana doll and 1937 Scarlet O'Hara doll.

Patent Date	Patent Serial No.	Patentee	Trademark
1947, May 6	496,833	Domenick Ippolito, Glendale, Calif. (doing business as Hollywood Doll Mfg. Co.)	"Sleeping Beauty" for dolls
1947, May 6	496,840	Domenick Ippolito, Glendale, Calif. (doing business as Hollywood Doll Mfg. Co.)	"Tiny Tina" for dolls
1947, May 6	518,390	R & E Doll & Novelty Co., New York, N.Y. . . .	"Wonder Skin" for rubber dolls
1947, May 13	496,808	Domenick Ippolito, Glendale, Calif. (doing business as Hollywood Doll Mfg. Co.)	"Little Girl Where Have You Been" for dolls & clothes
1947, May 27	523,095	Alice L. Clark, Mill Valley, Calif., (doing business as Nina Doll Co.)	"Sambo" for dolls
1947, May 27	523,094	Alice L. Clark, Mill Valley, Calif., (doing business as Nina Doll Co.)	"Black Sambo" for dolls
1947, May 27	429,933-429,934	Domenick Ippolito, Glendale, Calif. (doing business as Hollywood Doll Mfg. Co.)	"A Wee Bonnie Lassie," "American Beauty" for dolls & clothes
1947, May 27	429,935-429,941 incl.	Domenick Ippolito, Glendale, Calif. (doing business as Hollywood Doll Mfg. Co.)	"Little Blue Apron," "Little Miss Bunnie," "Little Red," "Little Shepherdess," "Miss Hollywood," "Nancy Lue," "The Bride" for dolls
1947, June 17	490,074	Nancy Ann Dressed Dolls, San Francisco, Calif.	"Little Betty Blue" for nursery rhyme doll
1947, June 24	430,849	Wiggle Me Toys Inc., Lynbrook, N.Y.	"Wiggle Me" for jointed toy figures of puppet type
1947, July 4	526,233	Imperial Crown Toy Co., Brooklyn, N.Y.	"Imperial Skin" for dolls
1947, July 29	508,911	Masco Corp., Chicago, Ill.	"Bull Fight" for magnetic toy figures. Picture of matador charging bull
1947, Sept. 8	497,045	Barbara Sager, West McHenry, Ill., (doing business as Sager Enterprises)	"Hug Toys" for stuffed dolls & toys
1947, Sept. 9	501,093	Sayco Doll Corp., New York, N.Y.	"Skintex" for dolls
1947, Sept. 16	519,025	A & L Novelty Co., New York, N.Y.	"AYANEL" for stuffed dolls
1947, Sept. 16	501,574	International Doll Co. Inc., Philadelphia, Pa.	"Precious" for dolls
1947, Sept. 23	519,396	Ideal Novelty & Toy Co., Hollis, N.Y.	"Softies" for hollow rubber figures
1947, Sept. 30	491,713	A. F. Greenwood Co., New York, N.Y.	"Lumy" for dolls
1947, Sept. 30	504,839	Domenick Ippolito, Glendale, Calif.	"Western Series" for dolls & clothes
1947, Sept. 30	509,829	Sarah S. Craig, Fayetteville, Ark., (doing business as Katie Kates Doll House)	Outline map of Texas inside of which are words "Texas Bluebonnet Doll" with two flowers
1947, Sept. 30	514,152	Tuffy Toys, Cleveland, Ohio, (assignor to Tuffy Toys, Inc.)	"Tuffy" for pull toys of metal, plastics & wood
1947, Oct. 7	433,368	Dominick Ippolito, Glendale, Calif.	"A Hollywood Doll" in five-point star, for dolls
1947, Oct. 7	501,231	At-A-Toy Co., Kansas City, Mo.	"At-A-Toy" for figures similar to human figures
1947, Oct. 7	500,309	Kib-itz Toy Mfg. Co., Pittsburgh, Pa.	"Kib-itz" for mechanical operated figures
1947, Oct. 28	433,835	Dominick Ippolito, Glendale, Calif.	"Cowboy" for dolls

79 (see 1936)   80 (see 1936)

81 (see 1937)   82 (see 1937)

83 (see 1937)   84 (see 1937)

Top, illustration #91, trademark of Toy Manufacturers of the U.S.A., Inc. Dolls from left to right, 1943 Nancy Ann dressed doll "Thursday's Child"; 1940 Magic Skin doll by Ideal Novelty & Toy Mfg Co.; and 1943 "Junior Miss" made to measurements of a four year old child.

Patent Date	Patent Serial No.	Patentee	Trademark
1947, Oct. 28	503,652	Haniford Doll Products, Bridgeport, Conn.	"Robin Maid Dolls" for dolls
1947, Oct. 28	504,835	Dominick Ippolito, Glendale, Calif.	"Little Friends" for dolls
1947, Oct. 28	526,234	Imperial Crown Toy Corp., Brooklyn, N.Y.	"Midge" for dolls
1947, Nov. 7	540,416	Imperial Crown Toy Co., Brooklyn, N.Y.	"Miracle Skin" for dolls
1947, Dec. 2	506,601	International Doll Co. Inc., Philadelphia, Pa.	"Little Designer" for dolls
1947, Dec. 2	507,606	Victory Mfg. Co., Philadelphia, Pa.	"Yarbo" for dolls, etc.
1948, Feb. 10	523,096	Alice Clark, Mill Valley, Calif., (doing business as Nina doll Co.)	"Little Black Sambo" for dolls
1948, Feb. 17 republished 1939, Aug. 22	393,430	McLoughlin Bros. Inc., Springfield, Mass.	"Miss America" cut-out books
1948, Mar. 30	521,458	Nasco Doll Co., Inc., Brooklyn, N.Y.	"Nasco" for dolls, etc.
1948, April 17	554,897	Ideal Novelty & Toy Co., Hollis, N.Y.	"Baby Coos" for dolls
1948, May 25	520,092	Herman Cohn, Baltimore, Md., (doing business as Herman Cohn Co. And the House of Puzzy)	Picture of girl (Sizzy) and boy (Puzzy) holding an arch with words "Sizzy & Puzzy" across the arch
1948, June 6	520,407	Majestic Doll & Toy Corp., New York, N.Y.	"dubl-Doody a Majestic Creation" for dolls & dresses
1948, June 22	511,997	Ideal Novelty & Toy Co., Hollis, N.Y.	"Bobby Sox" for dolls
1948, June 29	520,616	March W. Baker, Colorado Springs, Colo., (doing business as Colorado Springs Toy & Novelty Co.)	"Camptown Circus" for miniature toy circus
1948, June 29	523,596	Manufacture des Jouets de Luxe, Saint Etienne, France	Seal with words "Marqueet Modele Deposes, made in France"
1948, Aug. 17	515,372	Max Eckardt & Sons, New York, N.Y.	"Our Pet" for dolls
1948, Aug. 17	521,469	St. Nicks Workshop Inc., Chicago, Ill.	"Bend-O" for stuffed toys
1948, Oct. 5	499,582	Blanche Sturgeon, Santa Barbara, Calif.	"Fantasy Children by Sturgeon" for dolls
1948, Oct. 5	503,268	United Hosiery Mills Corp., Chattanooga, Tenn.	"Buster Brown" for dolls
1948, Nov. 2	370,333	McLoughlin Bros. Inc., Springfield, Mass.	"Jolly-Jump-Up" paper toy, republished
1948, Nov. 9	511,362	Walther Waks, Tassin, Switzerland	"Wakouwa" for toy figures and animals
1948, Nov. 9	521,436	Sam J. Ciffo, Brooklyn, N.Y., (doing business as Columbia Mfg. Co.)	"Baby Patty" for boxed drinking & wetting dolls
1948, Nov. 16	535,229	Dresco Products Inc., Chicago, Ill.	"T-Zee" for mechanical toys
1948, Nov. 23	521,051	Arranbee Doll Co., New York, N.Y.	"Angel Skin an R & B . . Quality Doll in fluted circle with flying stork
1948, Nov. 30	272,070	Bert B. Barry & Associates, Chicago, Ill.	Republished "Pinochio" for dolls

Patent Date	Patent Serial No.	Patentee	Trademark
1948, No. 30	528,824	Terri Lee Co., Lincoln, Nebraska	"Terry Lee" for dolls
1948, Dec. 21	524,702	Ruth Gibbs Inc., Flemington, N.J.	"Ruth Gibbs Godeys Lady Book Dolls" for dressed dolls. Used since May 1946
1949, Jan. 11	501,092	Sayco Doll Corp., New York, N.Y.	"Toughie" for dolls
1949, Jan. 11	529,394	Alma LeBlane, (doing business as Lenna Lee's Tiny Town Dolls)	"Tiny Town" for dolls, republished
1949, Jan. 11	377,915	Metal Textile Corp., West Orange, N.J.........	"Maggie" for paper dolls. Used since 1924
1949, Feb. 22	529,103	Winefred B. Sherman, Detroit, Mich.	"Little People" for dolls & doll clothes
1949, Feb. 23	574,371	Northwestern Mail Box Co., St. Louis, Mo......	"Little Deb" for mechanic animated figures
1949, Mar. 1	550,742	Sayco Doll Corp., New York, N.Y.	"Tubby" for dolls
1949, Mar. 1	551,895	Ideal Novelty & Toy Co., Brooklyn, N.Y.	"Linda Olive" for dolls
1949, Mar. 8	542,569	J. Halpern Co., Pittsburgh, Pa.................	"Halco" for dolls & toys
1949, Mar. 15	539,398	Crescent Toy Co. Ltd., South Tottenham, England	"Crescent" with crescent moon, for dolls
1949, Mar. 22	550,040	Robert Y. Grant Inc., Fitchburg, Mass.	"Swawky" for animated toy figure activated by blowing into figure
1949, Mar. 29	494,472	Unique Art Mfg. Co. Inc., Newark, N.J........	"Unique" for mechanical toys
1949, Mar. 29	514,091	V. G. Herber, Leavenworth, Kansas (doing business as Herber's Gift Shop)	"Leavenworth Kansas" for dolls. Picture of boy convict working on letter "W" of Leavenworth
1949, Mar. 29	523,261	Angus J. Grant, Findlay, Ohio	"Grant Toy Always Latest" for action toys
1949, April 1	576,472	Frank Satz, Beverly Hills, Calif.	"Sazbo" for dolls
1950, Jan. 10	545,632	Looby Loo Designers, Minneapolis, Minn.	"LOOBY LOO" for dolls, clothes & furniture
1950, Jan. 10	552,534	Beehler Arts, New York, N.Y.	See illus. 91a—for dolls
1950, Jan. 10	553,668	Beryl W. Boynton, Lafayette, Calif.	See illus. 92—for dolls
1950, Jan. 10	564,801	The Bar Rubber Products Co., Sandusky, Ohio ..	See illus. 93—for dolls & toys of plastic, rubber & latex
1950, Jan. 17	563,103	The Bar Rubber Products Co., Sandusky, Ohio ..	See illus. 93a—for toys, dolls, etc. of rubber, latex or plastic
1950, Jan. 24	564,622	Harlis Inc., Miami, Florida	See illus. 93b—for toys of miniature figures
1950, Jan. 24	570,497	Kestral Corp., Springfield, Mass..............	"Puncho" for inflatable figures
1950, Feb. 14	575,539	Grace Morse, Michigan City, Ind., (doing business as Grace Morse Doll Shop)......	See illus. 94
1950, Feb. 14	580,000	Robert E. Smith, New York, N.Y.	See illus. 94a—for dolls, puppets & toys
1950, Feb. 21	571,583	Ann Sperl, Kansas City, Mo.	See illus. 95
1950, Feb. 28	573,840	Domenick Ippolito, Glendale, Calif., (doing business as Hollywood Doll Mfg. Co.)	for dolls and doll clothes
1950, Feb. 28	575,751	Columbia Broadcasting System Inc.	See illus 96—for dolls
1950, Mar. 7	554,742	Unique Art Mfg. Co. Inc., Newark, N.J........	See illus. 96a—for toy cowboy figure in Jeep
1950, Mar. 7	570,163	B. Altman & Co., New York, N.Y.	Initials "B.A. & CO" for dolls, toys & games—See illus 96b
1950, Mar. 7	574,404	Bayshore Industries Inc., Elkton, Ind.	See illus. 96c—for toys, dolls, doll clothes, etc.
1950, Mar. 14	542,631	Nancy Ann Storybook Dolls Inc., San Francisco, Calif.........................	See illus. 96d—for dressed dolls
1950, Mar. 14	557,757	Richard G. Krueger, New York, N.Y.	See illus. 96e—for dolls, toys, etc.
1950, Mar. 21	555,167	Eugenia Doll Co., New York, N.Y.	"Burpee-Babee" for dolls
1950, Mar. 28	577,761	Raphael Weill & Co., "The White House," San Francisco, Calif......................	"Happy Holly" for doll
1950, April 4	57,913	Stombeck Becker Mfg. Co., Molene, Ill.	"Bill Ding" for wooden men & clowns
1950, April 11	543,542	Toy Manufacturers of U.S.A., New York, N.Y. ..	Picture of Uncle Sam's Hat full of toys on which is name Toy Mfrs. of U.S.A.
1950, April 11	555,166	Eugenia Doll Co., New York, N.Y.	"Bubbles/Babee" for dolls
1950, April 11	573,313	Alexander Doll Co. Inc., New York, N.Y.	"Divine-a-Lite" for dolls
1950, April 11	578,667	Tru-Life Toys Inc., New York, N.Y.	"Nappy" for dolls
1950, April 11	579,140	Edna Irene Sinker, Detroit, Mich., (doing business as Silent Pal Doll House)	"Silent Pal" for stuffed doll & playthings
1950, April 25	574,484	Beehler Arts, New York, N.Y.	See illus. 96f
1950, May 2	579,064	Wolf & Dressauer Co., Fort Wayne, Ind.	See illus. 96g—for dolls
1950, May 9	565,491	Imperial Crown Toy Corp., Brooklyn, N.Y.	"Betty Bubbles" for dolls
1950, May 23	577,713	Gail Novelty Co. Inc., Brooklyn, N.Y.	See illus. 96—for dolls & furniture
1950, May 30	525,833	Natural Doll Co. Inc., New York, N.Y.........	"It's A Natural" for dolls of human & animal form
1950, June 6	555,101	Ideal Novelty & Toy Co., Hollis, N.Y.	"Lovey-Coos" for dolls
1950, June 13	331,238	(Re-Issued from Registration Number—Dec. 31, 1935). Hazelle H. Rollins nee Hazelle Hedges, Kansas City, Mo...........................	"Hazelles" for marionettes & stages for same

85 (see 1937)

86 (see 1938)

87 (see 1938)

SUNSHINE

88 (see 1938)

89 (see 1939)

90 (see 1940)

Virga

91a *(see 1950)*

92 *(see 1950)*

93 *(see 1950)*

BARR   Conk & Carrie
93a *(see 1950)* 93b *(see 1950)*

Howdy Doody
94 *(see 1950)*

94a *(see 1950)*

95 *(see 1950)*

96 *(see 1950)*

Rodeo Joe

96a *(see 1950)*

96b *(see 1950)*

BAYSHORE
96c *(see 1950)*

STORY
96d *(see 1950)*

KRUEGER
96e *(see 1950)*

A Virga Doll
96f *(see 1950)*

Wee Willie Wand
96g *(see 1950)*

AMOSAMARA
97 *(see 1950)*

98 *(see 1950)*

99 *(see 1950)*

100 *(see 1950)*

101 *(see 1950)*

Patent Date	Patent Serial No.	Patentee	Trademark
1950, June 20	576,586	Arranbee Doll Co., New York, N.Y.	*See illus. 98*
1950, June 20	580,251	Peter E. Maurer, San Jose, Calif.	"Winkem-Blinkem" for dolls & stuffed animals
1950, June 27	583,289	Reliable Toy Co. Ltd., Toronto, Ontario, Canada	"Relco" for toy dolls & toys
1950, June 30	581,041	J. Swedlin Inc., New York, N.Y.	"Willie The Wolf" for stuffed doll & toys
1950, July 18	577,494	Dorothy T. Pletnik, Milwaukee, Wis. (doing business as Cheryl Lea Enterprises)	*See illus. 99*
1950, Aug. 15	567,183	Walter Burd & Esther Burd, Westfield, N.J.	"The Play Fair" for toys, games, dolls, etc.
1950, Aug. 15	579,655	Bergen Toy & Novelty Co. Inc., Hackettstown, N.J.	"Breton" for plastic figures
1950, Aug. 15	582,627	Domenick Ippolito, Glendale, Calif., (doing business as Hollywood Doll Mfg. Co.)	"Everyday Series" for dolls & doll clothes
1950, Aug. 15	529,275-579,288	Norma Mfg. Co., New York, N.Y. (Registered May 25)	"Norma Originals The Doll with an *Educational* Story" for dolls
1950, Aug. 22	583,123	Ed Schuster & Co. Inc., Milwaukee, Wis.	"Billie the Brownie" for dolls
1950, Sept. 5	581,103	The Toni Co., Chicago, Ill. & St. Paul, Minn., (assignor to Gillette Safety Razor Co., Boston, Mass., a corp. of Delaware)	"Toni" for dolls and doll hair wave set
1950, Sept. 12	560,692	Ruth Gibbs Inc., Flemington, N.J.	"Godey's March Family" for dressed dolls to typify dolls of Louisa Alcott is story about March family. These dolls wear styles of period 1830-98 featured in Godey's Lady's Book
1950, Sept. 26	587,031	Bertha Honeck, Milwaukee, Wis.	*See illus. 100*
1950, Oct. 3	585,168	Ideal Novelty & Toy Co., Hollis, N.Y.	"Talkytot" for dolls
1950, Oct. 10	587,811	Maison Blanche Co., Orleans Parish, New Orleans, La.	"Mr. Bingle" for dolls
1950, Oct. 10	574,440	The May Department Stores, (doing business under name "Kaufmann Dept. Stores")	"Kaufmann's" for toys, games & dolls
1950, Oct. 17	582,463	Ida Beebe, North Kingsville, Ohio	"The Pumpkin Man" for dolls
1950, Oct. 24	578,045	Miriam Rabb, Naples, Florida	*See illus. 101*—for dolls
1950, Oct. 31	589,139	Artisan Novelty Co., Los Angeles, Calif.	"Little Miss Gadabout" for walking dolls
1950, Oct. 31	532,959	Ideal Novelty & Toy Co., Hollis, N.Y.	"Baby Gurgles" for dolls
1950, Oct. 31	585,960	J. Swedlin Inc., New York, N.Y.	"Bebop" for dolls
1950, Nov. 7	586,001	Izetta Doll Mfg. Co. Inc., San Francisco, Calif.	"Izetta" for dolls
1950, Nov. 14	590,925 & 590,926	American Metal Specialties Corp., Hatboro, Pa.	"Amsco" & "Amsco" in oval for dolls & playthings
1950, Nov. 21	554,573	International Doll Co. Inc., Philadelphia, Pa.	"International Doll" for doll & clothes for same
1950, Dec. 5	587,728	Ideal Novelty & Toy Co., Hollis, N.Y.	"Tummy" for dolls, toys & stuffed animals
1950, Dec. 5	590,320	R. H. Macy & Co. Inc., New York, N.Y.	"Formula Baby" for dolls
1950, Dec. 19	593,154	American Character Doll Co., New York, N.Y.	"Tiny Tears" for dolls

English Dolls

Truly early English dolls are almost impossible to find outside of a museum. Like American doll manufacturers, English toymakers were rather slow in starting to compete with their French and German contemporaries. Toy distributors in England were content to buy German-made dolls and toys because they were so much cheaper than domestic products. Not until the outbreak of the First World War, in 1914, did English potters start to supply their own version of dolls, most of them fashioned after German models which were no longer available to toy distributors. In the 1914-1918 period, there was a Board of Trade Instruction to potters directing them to try their hands at dollmaking, and various potters acted on those instructions. The results were "very grotesque" in the words of one practical potter living and working at that time. But as time went on, English potters were able to supply dollmakers with heads and other doll parts needed to launch them into an ever-growing industry.

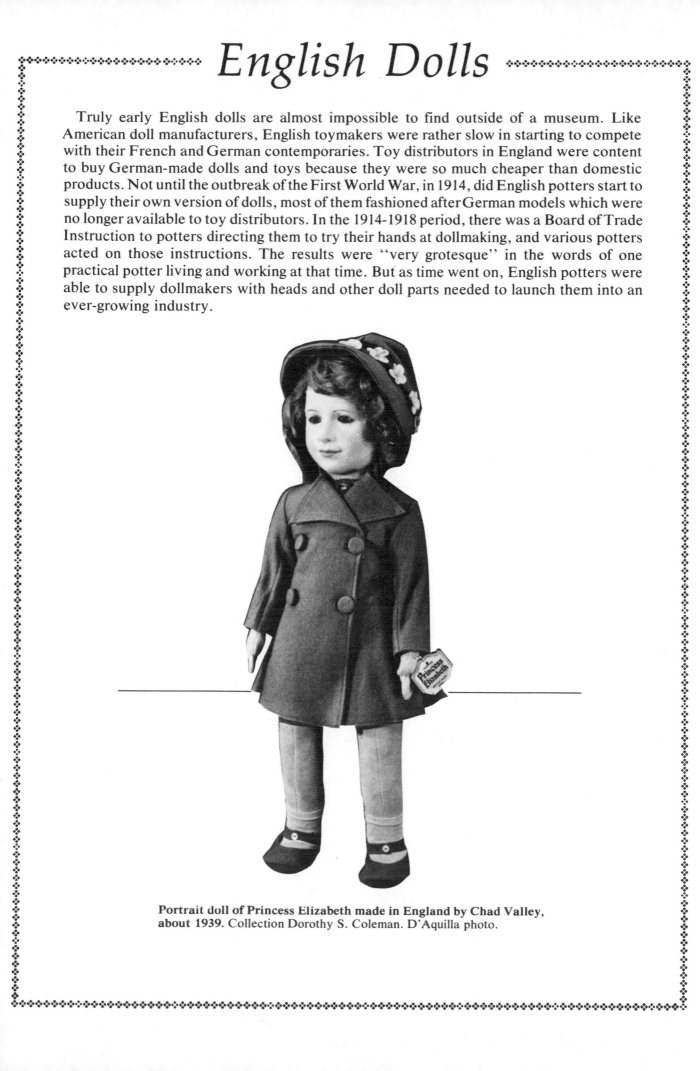

Portrait doll of Princess Elizabeth made in England by Chad Valley, about 1939. Collection Dorothy S. Coleman. D'Aquilla photo.

The English Wax Doll

by MARY HILLIER

Wax modeling was known to the ancient civilizations of Egypt and Greece and was probably introduced to Europe by way of the Roman invasion. Works in wax are on record in 16th century France, but it was with the works of art for the aristocracy in 16th century Italy and the impetus of the religious statuary in Southern Germany that fine modeling and portraiture established recognized schools of craftsmanship. Natural beeswax was then used, sometimes rendered more supple by the addition of a little animal fat or turpentine.

In England there were few native wax modelers; many of those who became famous in this craft were of foreign origin, such as the Huguenot Isaac Gosset (1713-99) who settled in London. The same was probably true among

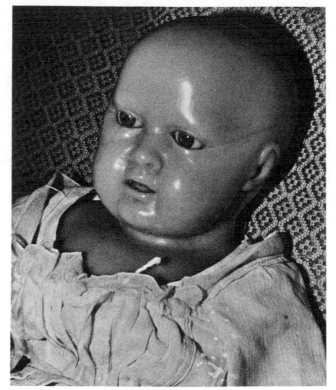

Fig. 1. Baby doll "Caroline Harris," ca. 1789, reputed to Mme. Tussaud. Private collection.

dollmakers; certainly several of the earliest and best known of London wax dollmakers had French or Italian forebears. But at least one old show-woman, Mrs. Salmon, was by all accounts "as English as roast beef and Yorkshire pudding."

The papers of the day described the racy exhibition she put on in an historic old house in Fleet Street in the late 17th century as "Mrs. Salmon's Moving Waxworks." Caractacus, Alexander the Great, and King Henry VIII were among the 140 life-size worthies depicted; the figure of "Old Mother Shipton," the witch, gave customers a kick as they passed by her.

Mrs. Salmon, besides being a modeler and toymaker, according to her advertisement also sold all sorts of molds and glass eyes and taught the full art of wax craft. Behind this robust personality was the shadowy figure of Thomas Bennier (or Besnier), a sculptor and modeler of French parentage who was "much imployed by Mrs. Salmon." He died in 1695, aged about 30. We presume he both helped and taught Mrs. Salmon, who herself lived to be 90, dying in 1740. Her exhibition changed hands, and was finally broken up after a burglary in 1827.

Another famous waxworks show in the late 17th century, rather in imitation of Mrs. Salmon's, was owned by Mrs. Mills. About the same period, Catharine Andras, one of four orphan sisters of French descent who ran a toy shop in Bristol, began to make wax dolls for sale. She became expert in modeling portrait waxes, and her likenesses of Lord Nelson in 1805 (now preserved in Westminster Abbey) and of Princess Charlotte at the age of five, made her famous.

It is still a mark of distinction to be invited to feature as a waxwork at Tussaud's Exhibition in London. Princess Anne and Capt. Mark Phillips, before their marriage, are two of the latest to join that famous throng.

Marie Tussaud brought her collection of waxworks and relics of the French Revolution to London in 1802. She had been taught the art in Paris by her uncle, John

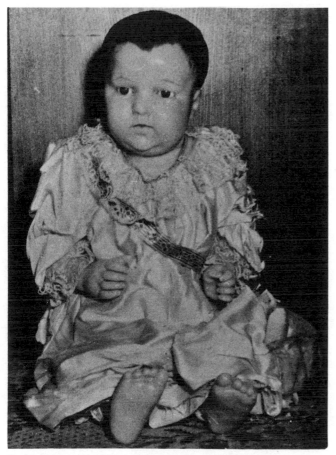

Fig. 3. Wax model "Dauphin," Nantucket (Mass.) Historical Museum.

Christopher Curtius, a brilliant man who had originally modeled wax figures to help him in his medical studies. He had established a profitable Exhibition of waxworks in Paris, and there Marie, as a child, had met such celebrities as Voltaire, Rousseau, Franklin, and Mirabeau. She had also learned the skills of both wax modeling and showmanship. When the sister of the ill-fated Louis XVI wished to learn the craft, young Marie was sent to teach her, and lived for a while with the royal family.

During the Terror, both Marie and her uncle were obliged to undertake wax models and death masks of some of the guillotine victims. This gruesome test of their skill later lent an especially morbid interest to the Tussaud Exhibition when it toured England and after it was settled in London.

Though it has never been proved that Mme. Tussaud made actual dolls, there are several references in early catalogs to "Infants" made by her; one was of her own little son modeled for the Duchess of York in 1802. Marie Tussaud had left her husband for good when she emigrated to England, but she took her two young sons with her. They grew up to carry on her waxworks.

However, wax dolls have been reputed to Mme. Tussaud. One *(Fig. 1)* is said to be the first wax doll she ever made. This doll measures 24 inches from top to toe. The head and bust, measuring 6¼ inches, is mounted by sew holes onto a stuffed body and legs of linen. The baby is quite bald, with fine quality blown glass blue eyes. No attempt was made to "prettify" the features which represent a chubby infant only a month or so old; parted lips reveal gums with the marked indent where the milk teeth should appear. She is dressed in her original baby clothes, including a linen "pocket" and handkerchief, identified as 18th century by experts at London Museum.

The doll is said to represent Caroline Harris, born November 22, 1798. Caroline lived to be 76, and her doll has ever since been passed down in direct descent on the female side of her family, with the tradition that it was made by Mme. Tussaud. The Harris family were Quakers and Caroline's father was a Corn Factor with dealings across the channel with France. Possibly there was some personal or charitable connection between the Harrises and Mme. Tussaud, for the Quakers of the period extended much help to French refugees.

The present owner recently made an intriguing discovery. Gently detaching the head from the body in order to repair the sew-strings, she found a little wire contraption within the hollow head which turned the pivot of the eyes and showed a wax eyelid delicately applied to the upper half of the glass eyes, causing the baby to "sleep." Originally this was no doubt worked from below by a stiff wire or cord which reached down through the body, an aspect forgotten when the mechanism was broken some 60 years before. *(Fig. 2).*

Another famous wax baby reputed to Mme. Tussaud is owned by the Nantucket (Mass.) Historical Association. This supposedly represents no less a person than Louis Charles, Dauphin of France, son of Marie Antoinette and Louis XVI, at the age of about one.

A letter at the museum dated 1852, states the wax figure was brought back from Paris as a present for Priscilla Coffin in 1796 by her sea captain father, Jonathan Coffin, who had purchased it from a nunnery in Paris as the work of Mme. Tussaud. Presumably it could have been made by her when she resided at the French court.

While there is no proof that either of these dolls was made by Mme. Tussaud, considering their date context, the quality of their workmanship and fineness of materials, they could have been. There seems no doubt

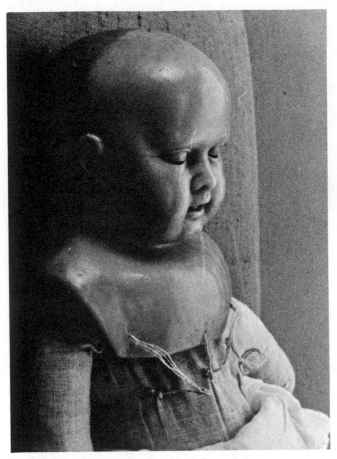

Fig. 2. Profile view of "Caroline Harris" wax baby.

that Mme. Tussaud, in her last years in Paris, was in hard financial straits, and she may have been glad to sell some of her early works or accept particular orders, as from the Harris family.

The wax doll as a popular plaything seems to have derived from such wax portrait models and waxworks made miniature.

Dr. Marsh at her Doll's Hospital as pictured in *Strand Magazine,* Dec. 1895.

During the 1780s, an Italian boy, Domenico Pierotti, was sent to England for medical treatment unobtainable in his own country. He lodged at Portsmouth with an aunt and uncle, called Castelli. They made a variety of things incorporating modeling and molding—wall and ceiling panelings coated with plaster; tailors' and milliners' figures of papier-mâché dipped in wax; and even wax-coated papier-mâché dolls. (See "The Pierotti Wax Doll, by Lesley Gordon, *SW* Feb '57.) Young Pierotti learned their skills and, years later, in London, passed them on to his son Enrico, known as Henry, who began to specialize in wax portrait models and dolls.

Henry claimed .o be the inventor of the Royal Model Doll-   Such beautiful dolls that will open their Eyes/ You may wash, comb, and dress them and not fear their cries."

He sold his dolls, along with imported French and German toys and novelty goods, at the Crystal Palace Bazaar in Oxford Street, an address which has sometimes led to the mistaken impression that his dolls originated at the 1851 Crystal Palace Exhibition. Early on, he advertised "Newly-invented Baby Dolls," and noted that "young ladies by sending their own hair" could have it implanted to form the wig . . . "likenesses modell'd and cast taken."

ENGLISH

Pierotti Italian Fortune Telling Doll, made for Bazaar. All Pierotti dolls shown here from the collection of Miss Irene Pierotti.

Typical Pierotti boy doll, 17".

Henry Pierotti died in 1872. The business was carried on by his son Charles William until 1892, when he died of lead poisoning. Essentially a home industry, the widow and sons of Charles William continued the business which lasted until 1935.

One of the last surviving members of the large Pierotti family, Miss Irene Pierotti, well remembers visiting the house at Hammersmith and seeing her uncles at work. (Her father was one of the non-dollmaking members of the family.) She recalls

Doll signed "Montanari Soho Bazaar," said to represent Princess Louise, 14½". Purchased at Dublin Exhibition 1853. Bethnal Green Museum, London.

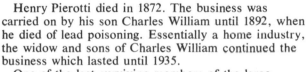

Wax doll signed "Santy Inventor 340 Long Room Soho Bazaar," ca. 1860, 31". Bethnal Green Museum, London.

Wax doll, unsigned, probably by Marsh, about 1870. Norwich Museum, England.

won a Prize Medal for her model wax dolls at the 1851 Exhibition. At the same time, Napoleon Montanari showed life-size figures modeled after Mexican Indians. Miss Maude Montanari, his granddaughter, believes he originally came from Mexico. (Though it has been generally accepted that Napoleon Montanari was Augusta's husband, Jo Elizabeth Gerken in her *Wonderful Dolls of Wax,* 1964, suggests from her research he may have been her brother or her brother-in-law.)

Some of Augusta Montanari's dolls represented the children of the Royal Family, and it was reported: "Undressed dolls sell from 10 shillings to 105 shillings. Dressed dolls are much more expensive." Perhaps expense was the reason Montanari dressed dolls are rare today. Mme. Montanari died of tuberculosis in 1864, at the age of 46.

Her son, Richard Napoleon, (born 1840) carried on the business, but his dolls tended to be of a cheaper variety. He perfected the London Rag doll which had a wax and muslin mask added to a stuffed head and body. Since he described himself as "Artist in Wax," it may be assumed he earned by other means than just dollmaking.

In 1875, he married a daughter of the artist James Pauley. Neither his son, also Richard Napoleon, nor

them as sweet, kindly old men who took great pride in their work and their artistry.

The dolls were made by the traditional method of pouring liquid wax into warm molds which had been made from original sculptures. Wax was warmed to blood heat in an iron cauldron over the fire in their kitchen range. Melted white lead and carmine for coloring was added until the desired tint was acquired. Then the wax was poured into molds set out along a 10-foot bench. After a thin layer of wax had set in the mold, the residue was poured away. Three separate pourings might be used to accomplish the required thickness of wax.

When finally the wax was cold and hard, the 3-part mold could be opened and the finishing touches given to the new heads, arms, and legs. Holes had to be cut for the eyes which were inserted from inside and sealed with wax. The addition of hair, eyelashes, and eyebrows called for great deftness. Women of the family cut out and stuffed the sewn cloth bodies and added head, arms, and legs by sew holes pierced in the wax.

The late J. C. Pierotti left a collection of family tools and some of the materials used in the business to the Toy Museum at Rottingdean. These, with some of the complete dolls and uncompleted parts, are a valuable asset in understanding the special art of wax dollmaking.

The Pierotti name was sometimes scratched on a doll as identification since the firm feared copyists. For the same reason, Mme. Augusta Montanari signed her dolls across the lower abdomen with an autograph in brown ink.

Mme. Montanari made a name for herself when she

Pierotti Christmas Tree Fairy, 18".

his daughter followed the family trade.

While it may appear that the "English" doll was anything but English in its origins, "English" was always the label used for the poured wax doll as against the continental type of wax over papier-mâché or composition. As the *London Graphic* reported in 1879, "England admittedly beats the whole world in dolls, wax dolls."

By that time there were many wax doll manufacturers in London, some of them in home industries similar to the Montanari and Pierotti family enterprises.

Herbert John Meech advertised as "Doll Maker to the Royal Family." Undoubtedly the publicity enjoyed by Queen Victoria's huge family of Royal children gave impetus to this most Victorian of toys.

Charles Marsh seems to have made dolls from about 1875. After his death his widow continued with a Doll's Hospital, a much needed service, considering how vulnerable wax dolls were to damage.

Charles Edwards is registered as a maker by 1853, and his son, John, was running a factory 20 years later which manufactured 20,000 wax dolls a week, some so superfine in quality they marketed at £ 50 each.

Last in the field came Mrs. Peck who, besides making dolls, specialized in fine models of the young Queen Victoria. An 1895 trade paper noted that she "had extended her premises." She continued until 1921, making and repairing dolls at The Doll's House, Regent St., London.

Wax dolls of the 1850 period have considerable personality. Later models introduced a tradition of prettiness, like the beautiful "a la Watteau" doll pictured. Unmarked, she resembles the Marsh dolls in coloring and type. Her original emerald green dress is in the fashion of a Wattcau shepherdess. The 12-year-oid girl who owned her died of typhoid in the 1870s.

By the end of the century, wax dolls were fast losing popularity, ousted by the great new variety of china and bisque-headed dolls.

Doll "a la Watteau," ca. 1871, in original clothes; unsigned, probably by Marsh. Privately owned.

Fig. 1

THE INCOMPARABLE MRS. BLOOMER

by MARY HILLIER

To me the name of bloomer had always conjured up the early days of bicycle riding and illustrations in old magazines of girls ludicrously garbed in plus-four-like suits perched stiffly up behind a high pair of handlebars.

It was left to a doll to educate me out of these misinformed ideas; a doll unique possibly in character and costume. She was bought at the 1851 Exhibition, that famous occasion when the Crystal Palace was erected in Hyde Park, London, in the hey-day of Victorian splendor.

No doubt the doll was an expensive and luxurious present since it was bought by the Duke of Northumberland for his children. When they had outgrown its charms, it was passed on to the gardener of the Estate for his young family. The family preserved it with pride and carefully kept it intact with all its possessions. The old lady who owned it, daughter of one of the gardener's children, assured me that she was never allowed to play with it and her mother kept the doll wrapped in a box lined with turpentine rags and sprinkled with pepper to keep moths at bay. (Hint for conservation!)

I doubt whether she was even allowed to lift the doll from its pretty wicker cradle with draped curtain head, for tucked away beneath the bottom mattress was a tiny card in faded handwriting which she told me she had never seen. It read: "This doll and accessories was purchased at the International Exhibition held in Hyde Park 1851. The Bloomer Costume worn by the same was introduced by Mrs. Bloomer of New York. Her name is Mary Caudle."

The doll herself is of a common type of the period. (Fig. 1.) She measures 24 inches from top to toe and, though time has added cracks to her wax face, she has a sweet expression with dark grey inset glass eyes, painted rosebud mouth, inset hair eyebrows and long ringlets of russet brown human hair.

"Mary Caudle's" Bloomer outfit consists of a shell pink skirt over long cream silk trousers, with matching jacket, waistcoat and wide brimmed hat. She has other clothes (Fig. 4) including an elegant low-cut dress, typical of the period, in narrow pink and white striped material with ribbon trimmings, dainty cambric drawers and underclothes, three pretty bonnets and two pairs of little kid shoes, one pair labelled "E. C. SPURIN, Juvenile Repository, 37 New Bond St." (a toyshop which stood nearly on the spot where Sotheby's now have their auction rooms). A wicker basket accompanying the doll in her wicker cradle, contains her Staffordshire china toilet set: jug and basin, sponge

Fig. 2

The above may be taken as a pictorial embodiment of the Bloomer doctrines.
"To such base uses may we come at last, Horatio"
Peregrine Perkes feels resistance to be in vain but comforts himself with the knowledge "that an absurdity however

Fig. 3

dish, soap dish, and foot bath, all ornamented with transfer-printed blue flower pattern and marked "DRESDEN FLOWERS Opaque China." (Fig. 5)

In 1851 Mrs. Dexter (Amelia) Bloomer of Seneca Falls, New York, was a sensation. At 21, she had married a Quaker in 1840–the same year as Queen Victoria married. She was an ardent advocate of the temperance movement and soon joined forces with Mrs. Elizabeth Cady Stanton, the American forerunner of Mrs. Pankhurst, preaching women's suffrage. The first Women's Rights Convention was held at Seneca Falls in July 1848, and a magazine called *The Lily* (founded 1849), and edited by Mrs. Bloomer, voiced both the evils of strong liquor and the rights of women to equality.

Early in 1851, Mrs. Stanton was visited by a young cousin, Mrs. Miller, who wore an outfit she had made for use in Switzerland on her honeymoon. The long full Turkish style trousers and a short skirt worn over the top reaching just below the knee appealed to Mrs. Stanton and Mrs. Bloomer both of whom imitated the fashion in their home town. The new-found style was described and recommended in the columns of *The Lily*. This was the beginning of a publicity and controversy which spread around the world.

Mrs. Bloomer herself was astounded and wrote: "At the outset I had no idea of fully adopting the style. No thought of setting a fashion; no thought that my action would create an excitement throughout the civilized world, and give to the style my name and the credit due to Mrs. Miller. This was all the work of the Press. I stood amazed at the furor I had unwittingly caused."

The Bloomer costume came in for both praise and ridicule. Doubtless it would have made less impact had it been just a fashion without its connection with this small band of fearless and emancipated American women. Their husbands apparently approved though Mr. Stanton wrote amusingly:

"The worst thing about it would be, I should think, *sitting down*. These ladies will expose their legs somewhat above the knee to the delight of those genelemen who are anxious to know whether their lady friends have round and plump legs or lean and scrawny ones." (A sentiment echoed some 100 years later when mini-skirts first appeared).

In England, *Punch* lampooned the costume in the cartoons of Leech (probably the source from which our doll was designed). Long skirts, tight-lacing, and numerous undergarments were then the fashion. Floor sweepers invented for keeping floors clean at the Crystal Palace exhibitions were never used since the floors were swept clean and polished by ladies trains.

A rare little book by Watts Phillips, *"My Wife Turned Bloomer"*, published in London (Fig. 2) by Ackerman, showed ten scenes of folding pages depicting the adventures of Mrs.

Fig. 4

Fig. 5

Peregrine Perks, converted to Bloomerism by her American friend, Mrs. Colonel Nathan Sparkes.

This satire foresaw that if women wore trousers, other masculine habits would follow, such as drinking, smoking, carriage-driving and even, perish the thought, intellectual hobbies. In one scene the cook and maid have forsaken their household chores for the delights of literature and philosophy. Finally the ultimate absurdity (to the 1851 masculine mind), men were shown taking over the women's place, doing the cooking and laundry and minding the babies whilst their womenfolk are tub-thumping. (Fig. 3)

Peregrine Perks feels resistance to the movement is in vain and comforts himself with the thought that "an absurdity however Potent wears itself out in the end and leaves what is good and true to vindicate itself."

Plays on the stage, articles in the papers, musical scores, and Staffordshire china figurines, and Currier & Ives prints, spread the cult, and ladies wearing Bloomer costume even appeared in London's West End. Mrs. Bloomer herself never visited England or it might have been seen how misrepresented this serious lady was. After three years or so the American group gave up wearing the Bloomer costume as Mrs. Bloomer felt that the dress "was drawing attention from what we thought to be of far greater importance: the question of women's right to better education." She died in 1894, a pioneer in Women's Enfranchisement. By that time other dress reformers had revived the idea of Rational dress for women, and the use of the divided skirt or the old bloomer costume with modifications had become the vogue for the new cycling craze.

The name and style became imbedded in our consciousness. Only this week, in a London Bond Street window, I saw two all black Bloomer costumes. Amelia Bloomer herself would have been prouder for the recognition of her enfranchisement ideas.

With acknowledgement and thanks to Charles Neilson Gattey, author of *The Bloomer Girls* (Coward McCann, Inc., publishers), who allowed me to use facts from his book.

20th Century DOLLS MADE IN England

by MARY HILLIER

THROUGHOUT THE 19th century, the German pottery industry, especially that centered in Thuringia, turned out doll heads in such numbers and so cheaply that there was little point in English makers competing. Not until the outbreak of the 1914 War, when gradually the Continental stock in English shops was exhausted, did English potters seek to supply their own version of doll— usually a rather poor copy of German types. Staffordshire potters found it difficult to emulate the beautiful and skillful German modeling.

In my researches on English dolls, Arnold Mountford, Curator of Hanley Museum, and Mr. George Sherratt, descendent from the famous line of potters whose name he bears, have been extremely helpful.

Mr. Mountford told me that there were no locally-made dolls in the Museum, but that recently a head was presented marked "GOSS 9." I have since seen a doll made up with such a head. In his history of the Goss firm, M. J. W. Willis-Fear wrote: "Another idea tried at this time [World War I] in an attempt to help recoup the firm's fortunes was the manufacture of china dolls' legs, arms, and faces, as the chief supply for high class quality china dolls had ceased when war was declared on Germany in 1914. Apparently these Goss china dolls were just beginning to successfully capture the English toy market *despite their relatively high prices* [author's italics] when the war ended in November 1918 and the German toy industry promptly revived its former specialty, forcing the Goss factory to cease this line as the German dolls were considerably cheaper."

Mr. Mountford also passed on information on a more recent venture. The Diamond Tile Company, Ltd., of Brook St., Hanley, founded in 1933,

Top: Melba doll dressed. Bottom: Melba doll undressed to show construction of the body.

manufactured earthenware dolls and doll heads from June 1 to September 15, 1942, copying from German baby dolls, as part of the current war effort, but in 1943, this firm was fined £ 300 "for manufacturing earthenware dolls and dolls' heads otherwise than under the authority of a license issued by the Board of Trade, contrary to article I of the Domestic Pottery Order 1942."

A contemporary press reported: "Originally the company was engaged in the manufacture of tiles and tile surround. After the outbreak of war [1939] that trade became slack, and dolls and doll heads were produced as a sideline by the defendants, Germany having previously controlled the trade." Obviously the dolls they made must be uncommonly rare.

From various correspondents came reports that dollmaking had been carried on at the Howard Pottery, Norfolk St., Shelton, from 1925; at the Blue John Factory, Union St., Hanley, from 1939; and at the Doric China Company, China St., Fenton, before 1934 when a fire destroyed their factory. J. W. Ridgway at the Cauldon Works, Shelton, made dolls during the World War II period and perhaps it was some of these that were marked "N.T.I." and marketed in Canada and the United States by the Nottingham Toy Industry, Ltd. (*See* Dorothy Coleman's *Collector's Encyclopedia of Dolls,* 1969.)

Melba Dolls

Mr. George Sherratt, a practical potter himself, now retired, told me that there was an actual Board of Trade Instruction to Potters in the 1914-18 period to try their hands at dollmaking, and that various firms acted on that instruction. The first trial dolls were "very grotesque." He was able to give a firsthand account of actual dollmaking since Mayer & Sherratt, Clifton Works, Longton,

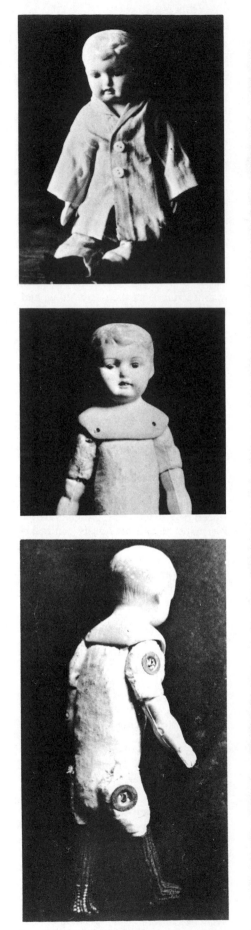

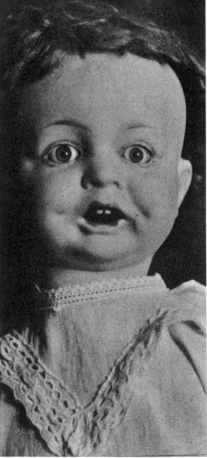

Top: DPC boy doll dressed in contemporary striped pajamas. Middle and bottom: DPC boy doll undressed to show construction. Note metal discs that fasten the joints to the body.

Top: Nonsuch doll in a seated position. Bottom: Close-up of the Nonsuch doll's curious features.

made the doll heads marked "England," and/or "Melba."

Thinking the market for such dolls may not have been widespread, I advertised in Staffordshire papers for anyone possessing a doll head marked "England," "Melba," or both. This produced no dolls, but an informative letter came from a Mrs. Bryan, who said she was engaged in the factory at that time (1916) and that "there were different kinds of heads: baby dolls and heads that had to be cut out at the crown to have hair put on. Also dolls that had eyes that opened and shut; these also had to have crowns cut out and slits made for the eyes."

Mr. Mayer, now nearly 90 years old, recollected there were two sizes of "Melba" — an ordinary standard size and one smaller. As the mixture was a pink felspar, the finished product was called earthenware rather than bisque, which is made from china clay.

As soon as my book was published, the Melbas began to appear. Two dolls marked MELBA and CLASSIC were owned by Mrs. Tustin, of Spratton, England. The Melbas measured 16 inches, had china legs and arms on a stuffed body, rather plump dumpy faces, blue glass eyes, and fair hair. The Classic was rather sweet and pretty with blue glass eyes and black hair; she measured only 12 inches. Dr. Julia Boyd of Godalming, only ten miles from my home, produced an 18-inch Melba with blue eyes and "two left legs." (Actually all the legs seem to have been made in the same rather shapeless mold.) Her body was made of rather cheap "war-time" standard cotton. The impressed mark on her neck was

$$\frac{\text{IN MELBA}}{4 \ \text{ENGLAND.}}$$

DPC Dolls

Several collectors found small rather insignificant little dolls made up with poor style heads marked "DPC ENGLAND." Mr. Mountford thought this probably stood for Dresden Porcelain Co., Longton. One given to me was an engaging little boy in contemporary striped pajamas. The curious feature of this little chap—he measures only 8 inches — is the oddly jointed amateurish body, stuffed with coarse straw and made up rather like a Teddy Bear. The limbs are fastened on with old-fashioned "bachelors' buttons," as these metal discs were called. His blue eyes and two little white teeth are painted on; pottery is poor and matt surfaced.

Nonsuch

From Mrs. Aitken, Kingston, England, came an especially interesting

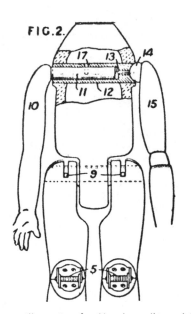

FIG.2.

Patent illustration for Nunn's walking doll.

discovery. Her grandfather, John Sneed, had been British representative for a firm of German Christmas card, makers until the 1914 war broke out. He then teamed up with G. L. Nunn, who had been a representative in England for a German dollmaking firm and was also out of a job. Together they decided to produce dolls in Liverpool. Neither of them was a potter, but they realized dolls would be in short supply, and that they could find local talent for the technical side. They produced the NONSUCH.

Mrs. Aitken says the doll was modelled after a German doll with, real hair which had been used as a hairdresser's model and then given to her mother to play with. The features and expression of the NONSUCH which Mrs. Aitken owns are curious, a little like a cariacature; obviously the head must have been made from one of the realistic type of dolls, perhaps KR or some lesser known maker, such as Wislizenus. The overlarge arms and legs are clumsy papiermache.

Nunn's Walking Dolls

Mr. Sneed sold out his share of the business, but it seems Mr. Nunn was the inventive half of the partnership, for we find him in 1922 taking out a patent (#186,232, Nov. 15 '22) for a walking doll. This was made with spring hinges at the knee joint on legs pivoted to the body so that they could move freely. (See patent diagram pictured here.) The late Queen Mary is said to have admired Nunn's Patent Walking doll when it was shown at the Wembley Exhibition in London, in 1924.

True Portrait Doll

By Marie Matheson

THE early decades of the 19th century marked a period of portraits. Everyone of importance had his picture done—by Sir Thomas Lawrence or some other leading painter by preference, or by lesser artists when "the best" were not available. A Mr. Lodge, for instance, is credited with eight volumes of pictures. Portrait galleries flourished, supported and encouraged by the king. When every room allotted to such exhibits at Somerset House was crowded, a second British Institution was formed. Here, in the special room where ladies' portraits were placed after their initial showing, *LaBelle Assemblee*, the *haut monde* reporter of the day, records in 1828 an exhibit of wax figures as "the interest of the exhibition to juvenile visitors".

That wax was becoming a popular medium for portraiture is shown, too, by the success Madame Tussaud, refugee from the French Revolution, was meeting in the establishment of her famous wax works in London.

Among fine artists who worked in wax was Richard Cockle Lucas (1800-1893). A member of the Royal Academy, he worked also in ivory and marble, specializing in his wax work in figures of living people. His genius in this medium is indicated by the attribution to him, in 1911, of a wax bust long considered the work of de Vinci.

The identification and naming of portrait dolls has long been a subject of debate among collectors. Such dolls should by rights bear a resemblance to the personage whose name they carry. Many of them do. Others have been assigned names of well known persons to whom they bear no likeness at all, solely for the purpose of identification among collectors. It is this arbitrary naming that has caused many a casual doll to become accepted as the true portrait of a named person. Only intensive research can determine whether the doll is actually a true portrait or a "so-called" portrait.

But of Lucas's work, there can be no question. His "dolls" were actually portraits. The doll pictured, when it came from England to Mrs. A. Sanborn in California, carried identification papers which attest it a representation of the Marchioness of Blandford, made by Lucas, in 1832. In checking further the identity of the

15" wax figure portrait of the Marchioness of Blandford, by Lucas, 1832, with head, arms, and feet of poured wax in the rather dark color of natural beeswax, though traces of coloring remain, inserted glass eyes, and hair inserted individually into the wax as in later Montanari type, linen body.

Enlargements of profile and back of head.

subject, the new owner consulted the ladies magazines of the day for social notes on this illustrious family, as well as Burke's Peerage.

In June 1816, *La Belle Assemblee* reported on a Drawing Room held by Her Majesty to receive congratulations on the marriage of her Royal Granddaughter Princess Charlotte. "Among the Nobility and Gentry present", it reads, "was the Marchioness of Blandford: white satin petticoat with magnificent gold lama draperies, elegantly ornamented with gold cord and tassels; train of purple satin, trimmed with a full lama border; headdress of feathers and jewels."

In March 1817, the same publication carried: "Died at his seat at Blenheim, Oxfordshire, George Spencer, 4th Duke of Marlborough, Marquis of Blandford, etc. His Grace was born the 26th of January 1738. He was found dead in his bed at seven o'clock in the morning."

His eldest son George (1766-1840) who succeeded him as the 5th Duke of Marlborough, and who is known for the enormous sums he spent on his gardens and his library of early printing, took the additional name of Churchill by Royal License in 1817.

In January 1819 comes the marriage announcement in *Lady's Magazine*: "George, Marquis of Blandford, to Lady Jane Stewart, oldest daughter of the Earl of Galloway. The bride was given away by her father; and her two sisters, Lady Caroline and Lady Louisa Stewart, together with Lady Caroline Spencer Churchill, assisted as bridesmaids."

In Burke's Peerage of that same year, is listed Lady Jane, the cousin and wife of George, Marquis of Blandford, who became the 6th Duke of Marlborough.

The dates of the above entries—and the 1832 date of the doll—would indicate that the figure might well represent Lady Jane, the granddaughter-in-law of the Marquis who died in his bed, and the daughter-in-law (or possibly granddaughter-in-law) of the Marchioness who was so elegantly gowned for the Queen's Drawing Room. Lady Jane was destined in course of time to become the great-grandmother of today's Sir Winston Churchill.

All this — the popularity of wax figures in the 1830s, the master hand of Lucas at work during that period, and the presence of Lady Jane, Marchioness of Blandford, of suitable age to be represented by the figure—bear out the doll's identification.

For doll collectors, the importance of the 1832 date lies in the fact that the hair of the doll was individually inserted in the wax head in the so-called Montanari method — some twenty years before the Montanaris appeared on the doll scene.

Post-Coronation Dolls

By Marjory Ames

LONG in advance of the Coronation of Queen Elizabeth II, preparations were begun by English dollmakers for the making of commemorative dolls in Her Majesty's likeness. Permits from the Privy Purse, from the Lord Chamberlain's office, acceptance by the Coronation Souvenir Committee, were only the beginnings of governmental red tape to put these Coronation dolls into production. Hours of research and conference with authorities went into the exact reproduction of robes, regalia, postiches and coloring for the dolls. But the design of the dress itself had to be left to the maker's discretion, for no advance information was given out on the gown the Women of the Royal School of Needlework were then embroidering for Her Majesty to wear. Two companies only produced Coronation dolls in the collector class—the Chelsea Art Doll Makers, who developed an 18″ portrait doll, and I. & R. Ottenburg, whose lovely 12″ Queen Elizabeths were also made in limited quantity.

After the Coronation, the Chelsea Art Doll Makers, 21 Carlyle Square, Chelsea S.W.3, London, brought out a post-Coronation doll in which details were changed to conform with the actual gown and bearing of the new Queen at the ceremony. The position of the arms, hands and fingers in which the Queen held the sceptre and orb in the Coronation Procession leaving the Abbey, was now copied exactly. The gown, too, of this "after" doll, followed in detail the famous "White and Gold Lily" gown worn by the Queen at the Coronation. The rich embroideries were hand done by the renowned needlewomen of the Baleares from photographs or drawings of the actual gown. (The Baleares include those islands of Majorca, Minorca and Iviza, long famous for export of Majolica ware and silver filigree.) Over five thousand pearls, and the same number of gold beads were, with exquisite craftsmanship, incorporated into each gown. The regalias for this model are of silver, fashioned by an artist-jeweler exactly to design, with semi-precious stones and enamel. So exact are these exquisite miniatures that the words "Honi soit qui mal y pense" can be read with a magnifying glass on each link of the chain of the Garter.

Each post-Coronation doll is made to order, individually molded by Mary Nicoll, and numbered. Still available, though in limited number, they sell in this country for $300, taxes and duty included.

The man responsible for the manufacture of these dolls is Captain Xavier Puslowski, director of the Chelsea Art Doll Makers. Captain Puslowski's interest in dolls was fired some fifteen years ago, when, on behalf of the Polish President, he was called on to present two Polish folk dolls, made by a Polish artist, to the little Princesses, Elizabeth and Margaret. So delighted were the Royal children, and so intrigued was the Captain himself with the dolls, that he decided then and there to learn to make similar dolls himself. He studied the art in all its phases, and with Russian-born society dressmaker, Mrs. Lydia Sherwood, has turned out some of England's finest, most gorgeously gowned portrait dolls.

The Coronation dolls are no doubt his finest endeavor. Meticulous care was taken in their production, and the best of English, Polish and Italian artists contributed to their perfection of detail. Halima Nalecz was responsible for the design and robes; Felix Stawinski, the regalia; Peter Isaia, the postiches; Mary Nicoll, the coloring and figure; and Mario Ricciardi, the sculpture. Ricciardi's model of the Queen's head was chosen from the submitted work of six important artists for its close resemblance to the Queen, as well as its charm and beauty.

Any Coronation doll—and perhaps the post-Coronation doll especially, with its complete exactitude — has everything to recommend it as an "antique of the future"—beauty, elegance and artistry. It is a tribute to tradition and an appeal to the heart. For the investing collector, it is all this, plus an insured increase in historical value.

Left, frontispiece to Queen of the Pirate Isle, 1886; Center, frontispiece to Little Wide-A-Wake, 1885, both showing typical Greenaway figures. Right, authentic doll, copy of one of the five sisters from Kate Greenaway's book, Under The Window.

A Kate Greenaway Doll

By ETHEL A. McPHAIL

Doll with cloth body of material printed with Kate Greenaway figures. On the forearm can be seen the identical figures as shown on front of Birthday Book and Hand-in-Hand button.

KATE GREENAWAY, famous English artist and illustrator of children's books, was born in Hoxton, England, March 17, 1846. Her father excelled as a wood engraver and from him she no doubt inherited her talents. Her first public exhibit consisted of six tiny woodcuts at the Dudley Gallery, London in 1868. The public who passed them by with a careless glance, or perhaps a nod of admiration, never once dreamed she would rise to be world famous, beloved by children as well as adults in the century to come. She died after a lingering illness at Hampstead, a suburb of London, November 6, 1901.

Collectors of dolls have been at a difference of opinion as to whether there was ever a Kate Greenaway doll, meaning a doll designed by her and sold commercially as such. The writer has no evidence that there was ever such a doll but we are showing here a picture of one that certainly can be called a "Kate Greenaway" doll. The cloth body is made from material with Kate Greenaway illustrations as taken from the "Kate Greenaway Birthday Book for Children." The head is china with legs and arms of bisque. The shoes are of a brown color, painted on. It apparently dates from the period of the A.B.C. dolls, namely the late 1880s. The small illustrations on each forearm are taken from the cover of the first edition of the Birthday Book, 1880. This particular illustration we have found nowhere else, excepting on an old brass

button (see illus.). This button has been called "Hand in Hand" and was made in Germany. The doll's head is marked Germany. Where, we wonder, was the material made?

As the daughter of a poor family, Kate Greenaway's dolls were very inexpensive, costing for the most part only a half-penny. She had a giant 'Guaraca' said to have been given her for learning a piece of piano-forte music, so entitled, and then in vogue. Her dolls covered a wide size range from the Guaraca right on down to the Dutch manikins which were the very smallest. On them she performed those tentative experiments of making their clothes which was to color her work twenty years later when she made all the costumes for her living models before she drew and painted them for her book illustrations.

Her first loves were the Royal Family, Queen Victoria, Prince Albert and the Royal Princes and Princesses. She was profoundly interested in the doings at Buckingham Palace and it remained for her to execute Queen Victoria's Jubilee Garland in 1887—a very rare and choice item for the Greenaway collector to acquire today.

The dresses she made for her Royal Family and other dolls were made from gauze bonnet linings, just then going out of style. She supplemented this with scraps of net and lace, salvaged from her mother's store. Her dolls of wood and china were kept in a cupboard in her room when she was not playing with them on the mantel-

Hand-in-Hand, German button depicting same figures as shown on Birthday Book and cloth-bodied doll's forearm.

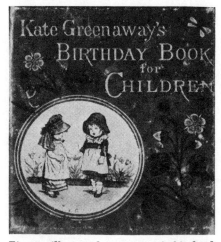

Figures illustrated on cover of this book correspond to figures on material in cloth-bodied doll.

The First Patented British Paper Dolls

By Luella Hart

piece. The china dolls' clothes were all removable and if they had been preserved for us, no doubt we would see the muffs with blue ribbons on either side, the frills, sashes, long black mitts, the pinafores and the mob cap, the capes and the high-waisted dresses for the little girl dolls; and for the boy dolls, the three-quarter length pants buttoned onto the blouse, or the smocked Russian blouse and the pork-pie hats.

This is Greenawayland, with its lovely old fashioned houses with red tiled roofs and peacock green gates leading into beautiful gardens. Her dolls were all very short-lived and passed away with the exception of "Doll Lizzie" made of brown oak, legless and armless; and "One-Eye" equally devoid of paint and retaining one rag arm. These two seemed immortal. These fascinating facts about her dolls were in her autobiography which her biographer, Marion H. Spielman had when he did her biography in 1905.

A great many ceramic and plastic dolls have been made to represent Greenaway illustrations. The cloth doll (see illus.) with authentic costume even to the color of the plumes on the hat and the ribbons on either side of the muff, is a copy representing one of the five sisters in "Under the Window." The Kate Greenaway expression in this face is well portrayed.

Further proof of Kate Greenaway's love for dolls even after she reached adulthood is displayed in the many times she used them throughout her books. Listed below is a partial check list of her books in which dolls can be found: Almanack for 1884, 1888, 1892, A Apple Pie, The Alphabet, Birthday Book (see illus.), Book of Games, Little Ann, Marigold Garden, Queen of the Pirate Isle (see illus.), Spelling Book, Spielmann Layard "Kate Greenaway," Topo, Trot's Journey, Under the Window, Harper's Bazaar November 18, 1893, Ladies Home Journal November 1900, Little Folks Magazine and Little Wide-a-Wake for 1885 (see illus.)

Fig. 1.

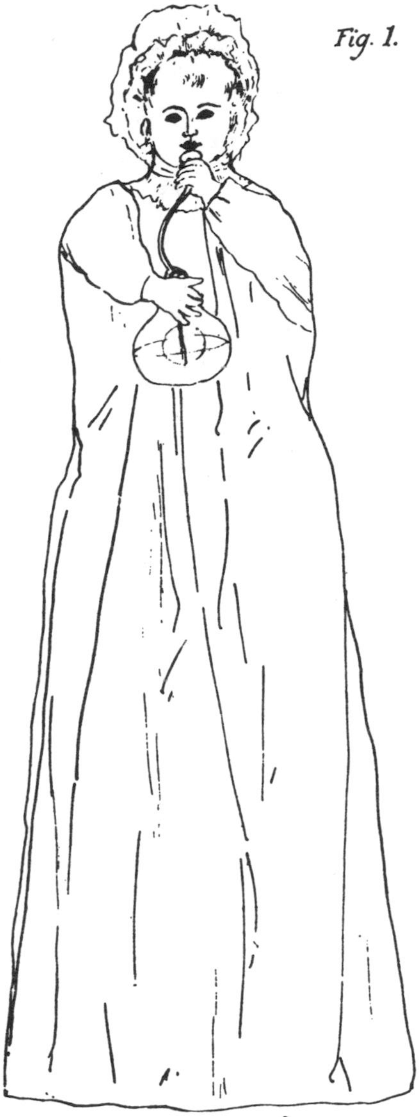

TO England goes honors for inventing the one-sided figure to be cut out of paper for which many different garments were provided so costume could be changed. These 8" paper figures, with several sets of clothing, were first put on the market by English firms in 1790. Their cost was said to have been three shillings and they were known as English mannequins.

Germany and France imitated the invention. France found them far less expensive for advertising their luxurious fashions than dressing and circulating the fashion lady doll.

Raphael Tuck and Sons Company, publishers to her Majesty (Queen Victoria) first applied for the right

Figures 1 & 2 reproduced from original patent papers of nursing doll; below, head and shoulders of actual doll. On back of head are the words "Raphael Tuck & Sons, Publishers to her Majesty, R.T.S. Trademark, Patent Applied For".

Fig 2.

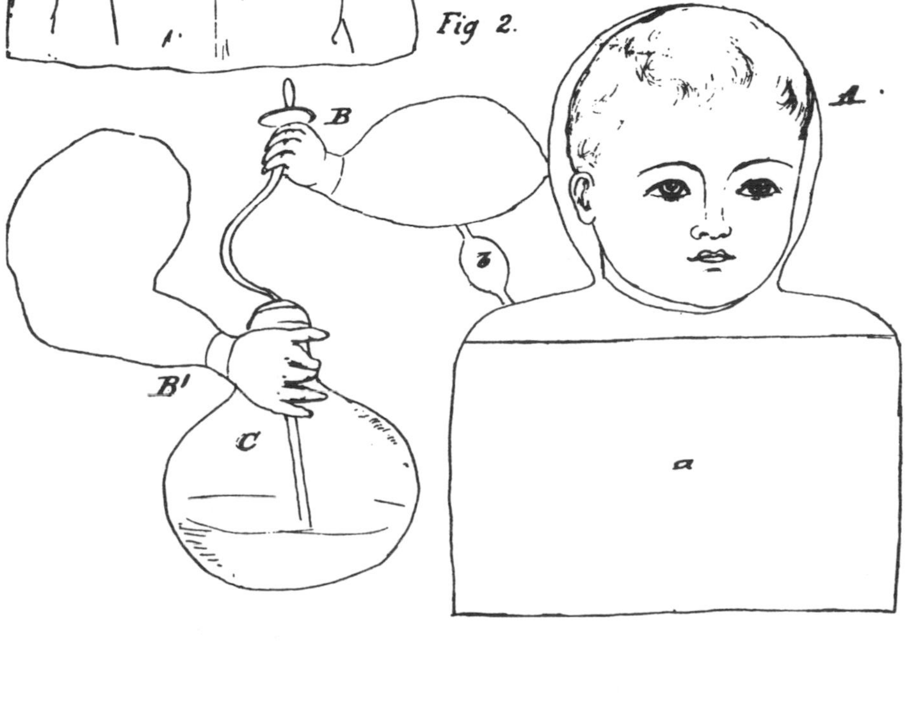

Early English paper doll, or mannequin, circa 1790, from an artist's sketch.

to patent a paper doll. On June 9, 1893, A. Tuck and F. P. Scott, submitted drawings and specifications for patent No. 11,367. It called for a colored toy to be cut from a sheet of cardboard, of which one portion represents a baby's face, arms and nursing bottle. Another portion is a pattern for a long robe and bonnet to be cut from tissue paper to fit the baby.

Mrs. Lloyd Brown of Oakland, California, known for her famous collection of dolls representing every country belonging to the United Nations, is also a collector of fascinating paper dolls, and the first copyright paper doll of Great Britain, pictured here, is from her collection.

Five months after taking out the baby doll patent, on November 30, 1893, A. Tuck again received a patent (No. 23003) for cardboard dolls printed in colors, provided with a number of changeable dresses and hats. These two patented paper dolls by the Tuck company are among the most sought for paper dolls not only because they are the first of their kind but also because Raphael Tuck has become a leader in the field.

The second patented English paper doll, by Tuck, direct from the patent papers.

French Dolls

In the late 19th and early 20th centuries, Limoges was the center of porcelain manufacturing in France. And since dolls were made of porcelain, one would naturally assume that there were many doll manufacturers located in this area. But this was not true. According to André Girard, successor to M. Moynot of *Bébés et Jouets,* there were never more than two or three companies at Limoges making doll heads. Most of the doll heads made in Limoges were sideline products of porcelain manufactories, with but one exception, the firm of *Bébés et Jouets.* This firm was founded in 1899 when the *Bébé Jumeau, Eden Bébés* and *Bébés Bru* all joined forces and formed the *Société Française de Fabrication Bébés & Jouets,* better known to collectors as *S.F.B.J. Bébés et Jouets* supplied the ceramic parts from which the S.F.B.J. dolls were made. Several firms in Paris purchased doll heads and parts from Limoges factories and assembled them with bodies and costumes in their own shops. If the dolls bear a maker's mark at all, it might be that of the pottery where the ceramic parts were made or the name of the shop where it was assembled; on some occasions it will bear both marks. The trademarks listed at the end of this chapter will be of great value to collectors in identifying their French dolls.

Bisque head doll made by Lanternier in Limoges, France, about 1916.
Collection Dorothy S. Coleman. D'Aquilla photo.

Lettre d'un Bebe Jumeau a sa Petite Mere

Recently found in an old Jumeau doll box was a little 16-page booklet, about 4 by 6½ inches, extolling the advantages of Jumeau babies. Its six color plates are reproduced here in black and white; and a complete translation is given. The booklet is undated, but it can be assumed, from information on the back cover, that it appeared between 1880 and 1884. This reads: BABY UNBREAKABLE/ E. JUMEAU/ Gold Medals at Paris, Philadelphia, Sydney, Melbourne, etc./ All Jumeau babies carry the name of the maker, in full, on the back. The gold medal was won in Melbourne in 1880; the "etc." would hardly have covered the important gold award won in New Orleans in 1884. Thanks go to Genevieve Angione, who shared with us this rare booklet, and to S.M.P. and C.F.A., who translated it.

Letter of a Jumeau Baby to her Little Mother

Mademoiselle,

You are, I know, a charming little girl. You have the quality of making everyone who draws near you love you, and you are cherished by your good parents to whom you are a pride and joy. I know, too, that you love to work and study, and it is to reward you for your progress that Madame, your mother, has just purchased for you my humble and blonde person.

It is with joy, my kind little lady, that I become your baby, for I am sure I will have in you the best and most attentive of little mothers. I am convinced that you will never let me want for anything, and that I will soon have, thanks to your fairy fingers, an ample provision of elegant dresses, of chic hats, of tiny shoes, and of linen whiter than snow—all this to do you honor when you take me into society or on a walk.

Yes, I promise myself to spend some happy days in your company. I will be so docile, so complaisant, and above all so little demanding that you will not be long in cherishing me for I want to be not only your dear unbreakable baby, but also a friend who will know how to console you when your heart is heavy with troubles.

Just as I am docile, I have many other qualities which make me a baby preferable to all others. First, I am discretion itself. Deaf and dumb at birth, you can be certain that I will never repeat any of your words, nor the least of your actions. My big blue eyes, which are so beautiful, will not let you guess my emotions and will not betray my sentiments. Then, too, I am unbreakable, a priceless quality, which I inherit from my father, M. Jumeau, the best of fathers and the most famous of manufacturers.

This excellent man, full of solicitude for his countless family of babies, demands of all those who leave his shop, a strength which will resist all tests. It is necessary for us to pass in review, my companions and me, before we leave his factory. With a severe face, he examines us with the most scrupulous attention. He makes us exercise our limbs in order to insure their vigor; and turn our little heads of bisque to try their firmness.

Woe to the unhappy one which does not answer to his expectations; it is pitilessly sent back to the factory with these terrible words: "Destroy immediately this camelote!" [Trash.] Camelote! What an insult for a well-born baby's self-respect! It is good only for those frightful German babies, that word. They are ugly and ridiculous enough, these German babies, with their stupid faces of waxed cardboard, their goggle eyes, and their frail bodies stuffed with hemp threads! I would rather be mute, just as I am, than to have come from my breast, like them, the cry of an animal.

I am not a fighter but I assure you, Mademoiselle, that if I find myself one day face to face with one of them, I will break it like glass, this card-

Baby Jumeau chosen by her little mother.

Little mother makes baby Jumeau kneel.

Little mother washes baby Jumeau's face.

The unbreakable Jumeau baby shatters her fragile rivals. This picture also appears on the cover of the booklet.

Little mother and baby Jumeau in the Tuileries.

Examination of Jumeau babies before shipping.

board baby which smells of tallow and wax. Ah! I am a true French baby!

I beg your pardon, dear little mother, for allowing myself to be carried away by a just anger. I will try not to do that again. I will return to my numerous qualities.

Besides my sturdiness, I am so quiet that I never have to be fed, and I fear neither water nor falls. You will be able to comb my hair and wash my face as often as it pleases you, I will never complain. I am not like certain little children who scream like a peacock every time that their toilet is made. It is very naughty to cry for that. It is so pleasant and so healthful to be clean.

My limbs are so supple and so well articulated that you will be able, according to your fancy, to have me take any number of different posi-

tions. I stand perfectly erect; I can sit down, and kneel. My legs separate or draw close together at will. My arms are as supple as my legs, and my head—my pretty blonde head—turns in every direction.

You will say, perhaps, that I am scarcely modest, that I boast too much. That is true, but we Jumeau babies are proud of the perfections our papa has given us. Besides, I also know how to recognize our faults. First of all, we lack speech, and we have heads so hard we can learn nothing. I confess it to you in advance; do not waste your time and wear out your patience teaching us to read, it would be useless trouble. Understand me well, I will never learn anything. I am beautiful, magnificent, admirable, but intelligence is lacking in me.

Frankly, isn't this preferable to

you, my little mother? In this way you will make your baby what you wish without its answering you with the slightest impertinence while if I were intelligent, lady! I . . . But I do not wish to concern myself with this grave question, I prefer to end this letter, this already long letter by telling you again that I am the happiest of babies to have as my little mother a girl so nice as you.

And also, it is with joy that I call myself for life,

Your beautiful Jumeau baby,
Zizi

P.S. If after some too violent shock, my head should happen to break, do not weep. Go find my father, M. Jumeau. Clever doll surgeon that he is, he will put another one on me and I will not be any the worse for it afterward.

Bebe Jumeau Dolls

A verbatim translation from *"Notice Sur la Fabrication Des Bebes Jumeau Dans L' Usine de Montreuil-Sous-Bois,"* or Making of Bebe Jumeau Dolls in the Factory of Montreuil-Bois. Translated by Pierre A. Durandet of Paris.

THE MAKING OF BEBE JUMEAU

About the Making Itself

Moulding of the Heads: The heads of the Bebe Jumeau doll are made of bisque, which is a kind of paste made of Kaolin. The Kaolin is put into water to "macerate" for a long time. The more decomposed it is, finer and nicer will be the bisque. The water is drained from the paste which is then put between cylinders, to get a sheet the thickness of which is the same as the heads will be when completed. These are cut into square pieces to fit the head moulds. This is a very delicate stage of the making. When the moulds have been used 50 times they are thrown away.

After a certain time the heads are taken off the moulds. The holes for the eyes are made. When the heads are of large size the ears are placed securely.

Cooking: The heads are put on special trays, 3 dozen in each, piled up in a big oven and allowed to "cook" 27 hours. Then they are taken away to cool gently. They are now white bisque. Every head is polished with sand paper by women and then they are ready to be sent to the decorating department.

Painting: Mineral pigments only are used in the composition of the paint. Two coats of pink paint are spread over the head. When it is dry, the cheeks are colored with red, lips with a deeper red. Eye lash and eye brow are drawn. When this is done they are returned to the oven to bake 7 hours more at a lower temperature. That is why they are called bisque. In French the word "Biscuit" means cooked twice. After this the heads are ready for eyes.

Eyes: They are made with the help of a torch, working by gas, with different kind of glass. A stick of black glass is used to make the prunelle, then a blue or brown glass is used to produce the iris, a very thin stick of spun glass will make the tiny rays which radiate from the prunelle on the iris. When that is finished a piece of white enamel blown into shape is made in a mould, in which the iris is set. When it is done, melted crystal

A Jumeau head made on an old mold and given to Mrs. Hart when she was researching the subject in Paris.

is spread all over the eyes to give a bright appearance, and to make them look like human eyes. When they have cooled they are cooked in an oven to make them unbreakable.

Finishing the Heads: Eyes according to size are placed in special eye boxes. These are set with wax into the eye orbits. Plaster is then spread inside the head so the eyes cannot move. Breakage is very important. Every head is thoroughly checked.

The Body: The body is made of several layers of papier-mache held together with glue. Framework of metal is covered with this material. The body is composed of two parts, front and back and the two parts are joined together. The same is done for the limbs. Face side and back side are made separately. After having been moulded they are assembled and then left to dry. It takes a couple of days according to the weather.

Caps are fixed up on the body where the limbs will be attached as well as on every articulation. Then they are sent to the painting department. A white coat is first spread on the different parts of the body. When dry it is polished. Five coats of paint were used, plus one of varnish.

Assembly Department: A hook inside the body held in place by a framework. Elastic tape is passed through the thighs and through the arms at the shoulders. This elastic also passes through the neck into the head where it is screwed in such a way that the head can turn around.

A "calotte" of cork is stuck into the top of the bisque head onto which a wig is affixed. Now the Bebe Jumeau is finished, but before leaving the factory it has to be baptised. That means the name "Jumeau" has to be put on the back.

Other Dolls Made in the Factory: Dolls made with kid, stuffed with wood powder. Talking Bebes who say "Daddy" and "Mummy."

Dressing Department: Mrs. Emile Jumeau is in charge of this part of the fabrication of the Bebe Jumeau.

The workshop is not situated in Montreuil but in Paris, Rue Pastourelle, with huge show windows. Costumes of all kinds are shown; satins, velvet, silk, old lace, are used and Mrs. Jumeau belongs really to the world of the haute couturiere (high class dress maker).

History of Jumeau Company

Mr. Emile Jumeau, the actual manager of the firm was an architect, and was not supposed to take the firm over. His father established the firm in 1843 and was making Parisian dolls. It was the type known as kid dolls. He had two sons, Georges and Emile. As Georges died around 30 years of age, Emile took over the business and really succeeded. In 1875 the annual gross was 150,000 francs ($75,000). In 1885 the annual gross was 1,000,000 francs or $500,000 in actual gold money.

List of the Different Prizes Won by Bebe Jumeau

1844	PARIS	Honorable Mention
1851	LONDON	First recompense
1855	PARIS	Silver medal
1867	PARIS	Silver medal
1873	VIENNA	First recompense
1876	PHILADELPHIA	First recompense
1878	PARIS	Gold medal
1879	SYDNEY	First recompense
1880	MELBOURNE	Item
1884	NEW ORLEANS	Item
1885	ANTWERP	Diploma of honour
1885	PARIS	Gold medal

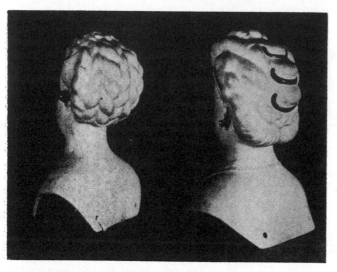

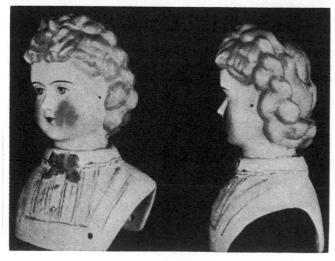

Dating Parian Dolls

by MARIE MATHESON

BECAUSE of an almost total lack of markings on early china and Parian doll heads, those who seek their age and era look to their hair-dos for an indication of date. Fashion books of various periods reveal how closely molded doll heads adhered to the current hair styles, and attest to the practicality of such dating.

The late 1860s and early 1870s marked a period of great interest in fashion. France was centering her advertising—and building her reputation as the fashion center of the world—on constantly changing "latest" styles in dress. Hair styles kept pace in elegance and rapid change, and magazines rushed them into print.

This was a time, too, of great competition among dollmakers. France was manufacturing lovely bisques of the lady style, known as fashion dolls. Germany, turning out porcelain parts for dolls to be assembled elsewhere—many in France—met competition by concentrating on the latest in coiffures.

A close connection between hair styles used on doll heads and those pictured in fashion plates is evident. Comparison under a magnifying glass will frequently show an identical likeness, even to the number of waves and curls. Often features of the doll and the pictured model are markedly similar.

One doll, an "autoperipatikos" or walking doll, patented in 1862, has a Parian head with brown molded hair in the same style as pictured in Peterson's Magazine for September, 1862. While the patent may have been used for several years, such novelties were short-lived, being frequently changed and improved. It is safe to assume the span of production of this particular model dated only a few years beyond its beginning.

The repeated argument that molds were often used for years may be true of the later and cheaper so-called "Godey-type" heads, which were made by the thousands, but it is questionable if it applies to the fancier type produced in this earlier period of stiff competition. With the swing from the fantastic hair styles of the 1830s to the severe lines of the 1840s, to the lovely hair-dos of the 1860s and 1870s, no competitive dollmaker would purposefully produce dollheads several years out of date.

Harper's Bazar, November 2, 1867, announced to the American public they had perfected arrangements with leading European fashion journals—*"especially with the Bazar of Berlin which supplies the fashions to the newspapers of Paris"*—whereby fashions would be published here simultaneously with their appearance in Paris and Berlin. The italicized words supply the link to the doll head-fashion plate simularity. Though the fashions may have been Parisian, the steel engravings were made in Germany. So German dollmakers were assured of being the first to review the latest styles in print. Quite possibly they had access to material before publication. Incidentally, in spite of promises, a comparison of Harper's Bazar here and Der Bazar from Germany shows a lapse of several months in the printing of identical engravings.

ILLUSTRATIONS

Above, left: The braided chignon, as shown in Harper's Bazar, July 8, 1871, was the most popular hair style of the period. It was often caricatured, ridiculing the increasing use of false braids. Exact duplicate in Parian below. *Right:* elaborate roped chignon is similar to that of Parian "Isobel" below. *Below:* Another coiffure from Harper's Bazar, 1871, is composed of "braids in the back, brought across the front crepes to form a coronet." Bow of blue grosgrain ribbon on top of plaits in back is duplicated in Parian doll head below. Note simularity of features in model and doll.

The Limoges Mark on Dolls

by LUELLA HART

LIMOGES, France, located about two hundred and thirty miles southwest of Paris is regarded as the chief porcelain center of Europe. The making of earthenware, introduced to the town in 1736, was supplanted by the manufacture of porcelain when kaolin (porcelain clay) was found in the neighborhood in 1768.

In 1840, there were thirty porcelain factories in Limoges and its region; in 1882, there were forty-two. United States imports of Limoges porcelain were only slightly superior to those of English earthenware in 1842, when the United States imported 753 cases of French porcelain and 621 of English earthenware. But ten years later, the United States imported 8,594 cases of French porcelain and only 353 cases of English earthenware.

This development was due largely to the initiative of David Haviland, an American, who settled in Limoges in 1842 and set up a workshop for decorating porcelain.

"Limoges," an identifying mark placed on any quality porcelain article manufactured there for the past one hundred years—be it table service, vases, figurines, or dolls — indicates the district, and does not refer to one specific company.

With so many manufactories turning out porcelain, it is to be expected that doll heads would be among items produced, and the occasional doll head found, bearing the word "Limoges," bears out this supposition.

However, according to M. Andre Girard, successor to M. Moynot of *Bebes et Jouets,* there were never, at any one time, more than two or three companies at Limoges making doll heads.

The present President of the Limoges Chamber of Commerce, in cooperation with M. Longequequeue, mayor of Limoges, informs us: "Several firms made dolls of porcelain here. Among them, in the early 1900s. was the House of Lanternier. [Their heads are marked A. L. & Cie for Alfred Lanternier & Company.] The firm is still in operation at 14 Rue Cruveilher, Haute Vienne, Limoges, but they no longer make dolls. Today, J. Chateau of 86 Rue du Pont Saint Martial, whose trademark is a small castle, with the word 'Limoges,' is the only firm here making porcelain figures—but they are figurines, *not* dolls."

Bebes et Jouets

Most of the doll heads made in Limoges were sideline products of porcelain manufactories, but one of the exceptions—a factory that made only doll heads — was the firm of *Bebes et Jouets.* This was formed in 1899 when the *Bebe Jumeau, Eden Bebe,* headed by Fleischman and Bloedel, and *Bebe Bru,* owned by Paul Girard, combined into a sort of union called *Societe Francaise de Fabrication Bebes & Jouets,* or "S.F.B.J." Later, other companies strengthened their positions by joining this "union."

After M. Girard, of *Bebes et Jouets,* had examined the photograph and a rubbing of the marking from Miss Rowena Godding's doll Celestine (see illustration), he stated that without doubt the head was made in their porcelain factory at Limoges, which operated there until the war of 1914. These heads were sent to the Paris branch of the factory to be placed on bodies. He added that if the body of the doll, so marked, had been of kid or leather, it would have been made during the regime of his grandfather in the Bru factory in the 1800s. Since the body of Miss Godding's doll was of papier-mache, it was undoubtedly assembled between 1900 and 1905 by Jumeau.

The story of the development of the bodies of Jumeau dolls is an entire research project in itself. Briefly, the early kid bodies built over wire frames, in 1843, were stuffed with sawdust. When the doll was forced into a sitting position, the gussets leaked sawdust badly, and the construction was soon changed. A wood base, over which kid was fitted like a glove, was another step. The papier-mache body came later in 1885.

After 1914, the *Bebes et Jouets*

Limoges Doll at the Brooklyn Children's Museum

THE WORLD'S oldest museum for children — in Brooklyn, New York—celebrated its 65th anniversary in December with the opening of a year-long exhibition of rare dolls and toys, many of them brought out from storage for the first time. This is the first phase of a rehabilitation program which will bring some dynamic new exhibits and redesigned facilities to the museum.

The head of the walking doll pictured is marked Limoges/FRANCE. Arms and legs are composition. Dressed in her original finery, she responds to the turn of a key by pulling a wooden dogcart. (SW, April '63, pictured and described a similar winding device, patented by Roullet & E. Decamps, June 28, 1892, and a German adaptation of it. Both were used on walking dolls—no cart—with Simon & Halbig heads.)

"Celestine", a 28" tall Limoges marked doll, made by *Bebes et Jouets* (Jumeau) in their Limoges factory. "Limoges, France" appears under hairline at back of bisque head; intense blue stationary eyes are shadowed by long spidery black lashes; open mouth, teeth show. Body of papier-mache, hands dainty, with two middle fingers molded together. Original red suede shoes and light brown stockings. *Collection of Rowena Godding.*

porcelain factory was established in Paris where it produced dolls until 1955. At that time, the factory was sold to a firm specializing in porcelain, because, says Mr. Girard, sadly, "There is no longer a demand for dolls with porcelain heads. Now it is plastics, plastics, plastics!"

In tracing the mark on Miss Nina Webb's doll (see illustration) which bears in addition to the word "Limoges," the hand signed name "E. Tusson," a rather baffling problem presented itself. Mrs. Gordon Bennett of Oakland, California, reported a Limoges doll in her collection marked "D. E. Masson, Alece, Limoges, S. C. Lorraine," and Mrs. Earle Andrews, another well known collector, a Limoges doll with the mark "Depose/ Fabrication / Franciase / Favorite / No. 12/Ed Tasson/R/Alec/Limoges." While markings are often barely legible, the possibility was present that three Limoges marked dolls could bear such similar names as "E. Tusson," "D. E. Masson," and "Ed Tasson."

French sources solved the mystery; there was no error in reading the makers; the three names do appear. It seems in 1917, M. Masson, a sculp-

tor, made the original model for this doll. M. Gillet reduced it in size for the House of Lanternier. The variations from "D. E. Masson" evidently occurred in the Lanternier factory for M. Masson, in one instance at least, brought legal action against the firm for changing the letter "M" to "T," thus giving "Tasson" instead of "Masson." There are also examples signed "Nialonos Gilletti." Mr. Gillet is now employed by the Haviland Manufactory at Limoges, but he is no longer making dolls.

Within twenty years, we are told, doll collectors may expect to find on the market some 15,000 to 20,000 porcelain doll heads, creations of times past. But the collector then must be prepared to pay high prices for these treasures now in storage, being "kept

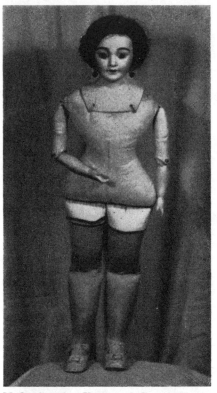

Made by the House of Lanternier in Limoges, circa 1917, this doll head is signed "E. Tasson". Eyes are deep brown, earrings are red hearts. Body of doll, much older than the head, was originally kid, but was recovered with cloth some 40 years ago. A wigmaker in Toronto, through association with a doll hospital for whom he occasionally made doll wigs, often obtained dolls, heads, or bodies for his granddaughter, who was the original owner of this body. *From the collection of Nina Webb, Paris, Ontario.*

on ice" for tomorrow's pleasure. These may, or may not, be Limoges marked, but they will be of the porcelain or bisque currently in disfavor in Europe.

Some years ago I was told, on what seemed to be top authority, that when the Societe Francaise de Fabrication de Bebes et Jouets stopped making Jumeau porcelain doll heads, shortly after World War II, some 20,000 were stored away in their factory near Paris, and that "by 1980, collectors would be queueing for them."

Recent news of a "seeming flood" on the American market of doll heads, presumably Jumeaus, from the "J" on the head, made me wonder, supposing the storing-away had been done, if the stores considered the time for profit-making already come, and set me quizzing in Paris.

However, the mystery only deepened when two former executives of the Societe Francaise de Fabrication de Bebes et Jouets, failed to accept the "storing-away" story. This is what they told me.

M. Jean Maynot: "The 20,000 is incredible. I suggest that when the S.F.F.B.J. ceased to make porcelain heads, say in 1946, there couldn't have been more than a thousand around; very probably fewer. If there is anything like a 'flood' of porcelain 'J' heads in the United States, I could credit your suggestion of counterfeiting. It would, however, be very difficult to imitate an old Jumeau, *especially the eyes;* but skilled, artistic craftsmen could make a good job of it. It would be costly, but these dolls have been fetching high prices, so the counterfeiters could stand that. Risks of legal proceedings would be reduced as the 'J' was not a registered trademark. I thought once of making imitations myself of old Jumeau porcelain heads and, of course, marketing them as such, but for various reasons, I renounced the idea."

M. Andre Girard: "I can't believe 20,000 Jumeau porcelain heads were stored away. I know buyers of old Jumeau dolls in France, and such dolls, they say, are very scarce at the moment. The last porcelain heads made when I was with the firm had the number 301. [M. Moynot had corroborated that.] When the S. F. F. B. J. finished making porcelain doll heads, there may have been a few hundred '301's' around. I don't know what happened to them."

Both M. Girard and M. Moynot wonder how many doll collectors in the United States could, independently of its mark, identify a Jumeau.

F. G. Mark on French Dolls

by LUELLA HART

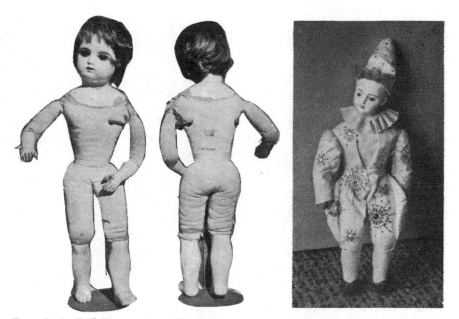

STAMPED on the bodies of several dolls owned by Mr. and Mrs. Gordon Grimes of Corona, California, are the markings "F.G." or "F. Gesland", followed by "Brevete S.G.D.G." The Grimeses enlisted the writer's help in identification, and in the ensuing research not only was the Gesland story uncovered, but also the meaning of the S.G.D.G. mark which has long puzzled doll collectors.

According to the French Patent office, these initials stand for "without guarantee of the Government". They explained: "We make no examinations or research as to whether the idea of a patent is actually original. It is the responsibility of the applicant for a patent to do the research himself or to employ an agent. If he prefers not to take time for a patent search, he must mark his product "S.G.D.G." to protect the government and indicate that he himself is responsible for possible infringements."

As for information on the Gesland firm, the Grimeses were fortunate to find, inside the bisque head of one of their dolls, an advertising circular of the Gesland firm. Written in French, and printed on both sides, it described the company and its products.

Briefly translated, Gesland was the sole distributor of his dolls; they were sold in Paris only from his salesrooms which had been located since 1874 at 5 and 5 *bis* Rue Beranger. (The firm had been established in 1860). Salesrooms were open every day from 8 a.m. till 8 p.m. and on the day before Christmas and on New Year's from 8 a.m. to 11 p.m. The workshop was at 62 Rue d'Avron.

Gesland dolls, read the circular, were the strongest ever made. They had metal joints instead of the usual rubber, and were the only type made with feet, arms, and bust of hardened wood. They could sit, and kneel, and had long flowing hair. Prices were listed for bisque head dolls, undressed, in sizes from 12 to 31 inches; with removable satin dresses, in the same size range; and for dressed dolls, with necklaces, earrings, and ribbons, in sizes from 10 to 31 inches.

Sold separately were bisque heads, unbreakable heads, real hair wigs, Tibetan wool wigs, dolls' petticoats, shoes, dresses, coats, drawers, hats, pelisses, baptismal dresses, bonnets, pinafores, corsets, baby clothes. In addition, the firm offered talking dolls,

Two Gesland dolls, marked "F.G." both with swivel heads, bisque shoulders, stockinette bodies, composition legs and arms to knees and elbows, ball joints. Pierrot, also marked "Bebee Gesland", from Grimes collection; doll shown back and front, courtesy Mrs. Vincent Mosley, Tarentum, Pa.

sleeping dolls, negro dolls, and walking dolls; they produced, in all, over 200 models, ranging from 6 to 39 inches tall. They also conducted a repair service.

To substantiate the information in the circular, Mr. Alex Potter, a researcher in Paris, was called upon. He found that 5 Rue Beranger—an historic building dating from 1752—now houses an elementary school. However, in consulting the janitress, Madame Chapuis, he was in luck. Her husband, Roger Chapuis, born in

Label on body of "Mr. Bum" (Grimes collection): F Que De Bebes Gesland/ B to S.G.D.G./ Reparations en Tous Genres/ 5 & 5 bis Rue Beranger/ A L'Entresol/ Paris. Head model is 210; applied pierced ears, nose painted red, twisted mouth has hole for cigarette.

1912, had worked for the Geslands for years, and was able to supply additional facts about dolls and company.

For the doll wigs, he said, real hair was gathered from hairdressers all over France; in a period when French women wore their hair long, children's hair was utilized. The doll heads were imported from Germany and were of deluxe bisque. Hands and feet were of *paraquetine* (hardened wood), covered with a kind of cellulose paint, steeped and drained. The outstanding feature of the dolls was the body. The framework of both body and limbs was of steel covered with tin, with rivets at the joints to facilitate movement. This framework was covered with kapok, then with stockinette or fine lambskin. The dolls could be made to assume lifelike positions.

At one time, M. Chapuis, recalled, there were 50 workers on the premises and 200 outside workers who made clothing, shoes, hats, and doll accessories in their home. For holiday trade, he said he and his entire family worked long hours to fill orders for export; their dolls went to all parts of the world.

Mr. Gesland died during the First World War; Madame Gesland continued the business until her death in 1924. Though production of dolls stopped then, a Madame Proffet, who had long worked for the Geslands, continued to repair the dolls in her home at 11 Rue Beranger. She died in 1949.

NOTE: There has been much confusion over the S.F.B.J. mark and the S.G.D.G. mark. The former refers to the Societe Fabrication Bebes et Jouets, the name taken by the combine of the Jumeau, Bru, and Eden Bebe manufacturers. The S.G.D.G. mark indicates *Sans Garant du Gouvernement*. Many firms used these letters; only one was entitled to the trademark S.F.B.J.

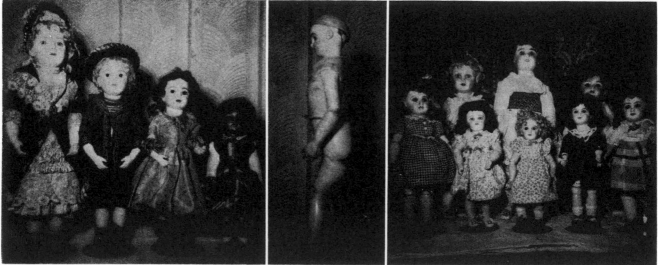

Left, four Bru dolls; Center, marked Steiner, brass lever back of left ear opens and closes eyes; Right, front row 2nd from left is a Steiner doll with all wood body; others are all Jumeaus; Back row: left to right, papier-mache with colorless blue eyes, word "Junis" in a diamond; "R.D." mark, probably Roullet and Decamps; marked "Limoges, France."

French Doll Trademarks 1885-1928

By LUELLA S. HART

IN seeking to identify 19th and 20th century French dolls in time and by maker, the markings on the doll itself provide the most accurate source of information. Marks or labels may appear on the neck of the doll, under the wig, on shoulders, bust, leg, or on either back or front of the body. In mechanical dolls, markings may be found on the mechanism, or on the key used to wind the mechanism. Sometimes tags fastened to an arm or a costume, or affixed to the box in which the doll was packed were the only labels used.

When a maker stamped his name or that of his firm on a doll, indentification is, of course, apparent. Few enough were so obliging! More manufacturers preferred to use a trademark or trade-name — a practice which leaves the seeker for information with the important clue, but not always the solution, to positive identification. When dolls bear no marks at all, identification is dependent on speculative comparisons or on exhaustive, though not necessarily conclusive, patent search.

The doll researcher may turn to patent papers to learn the material used and the method of construction of a particular doll, the date of its invention and the inventor's name. The Design Patent will reconstruct the appearance of the doll. But it is the Trademark Registry papers which accurately translate the mark

Left, Pink lustre china, painted molded eye, marked Brevet DSCDC/Maison Huret/Boulevard Montmarte 22/Paris/Exposition 1855/Nap. III Emperor; Center, French Fashion Doll, small "D" incised near cork at back of head; Right, another marked S5B at base of shoulders, head swivels but is flush to shoulders.

"Louise" Jumeau, an Emile Jumeau doll, trademark 24407, 1886.

or label on the doll to the maker's name and place of business.

Besides picturing the device chosen as the trademark and furnishing a full description of it, trademark papers often supply the informative date as to when the trademark was first used, as well as the date of registry. For example, Emile Jumeau, of Paris, registering his first doll trademark in the U. S. Patent office, "Bebe Jumeau," in November 1888, claimed its use since 1840.

A doll *patent* was issued in France as early as 1824, but French doll trademarks were not registered until 1885. It is interesting to note that seven years earlier, a Frenchman, Charles Bertan, had taken out trademark #15,333 in London, England, on a swimming doll trade-named "Ondine." One of these "Ondine" dolls is in the collection of Mrs. Berdie Ortner of Chicago, Illinois.

To search out and assemble the complete list of French trademarks issued for dolls from 1885 to 1900 is a task of no mean proportions. Only a researcher as mindful of the importance of the material and as devoted to the subject as Mrs. Hart would have undertaken the months of detail involved. The result of her research represents a real and lasting service to the collector and student of French dolls. Not only is the listing in itself an invaluable reference, but the amount of new and hitherto unrecorded material contained in the accompanying notes will set the seal of positive identification on many a doll whose origin has up to now been in doubt.

The size, color, and location of the stamp or label, the type of doll on which it was used, as well as the name of the manufacturer claiming the trademark and the date of registration are to be found in the accompanying descriptions, translated from the orginial trademark papers on file in the Patent Office in Paris.—THE EDITORS.

The French Doll Before 1900

(1) The first patent for a doll taken out in France seems to be that issued to M. Maelzel on January 21, 1824 for a mechanism for a talking doll. This provided for a bellows to work as the doll's arms were lifted, producing the "spoken" words "Mama" and "Papa". . . . A *patent* for a gutta percha doll body was taken out on December 16, 1950 by Miss Calixto Huret of Paris. Here the joints were furnished with a spherical part to insure smooth movement; bodies were used with porcelain heads, probably imported from Germany. . . . Among United States *patents* issued to French doll makers, #507,174 was granted on October 24, 1893, for a walking doll,

to Claude Joseph Simonet of Paris, France, assigned to Fleischmann and Bloedel of Furth, Germany and Paris, France. (This same patent had been granted the year before in Paris to Claude Simonet, with the same assignees). Another United States patent, dated June 26, 1900, was issued to Etienne Rodolphe Verdier and Sylvain Gutmacher of Paris, to protect a process for manufacturing unbreakable dolls and doll heads as a substitute for porcelain heads.

(2) The Jumeau doll dominates the toy field before 1900. The first Jumeau factory, in 1835, was in the Plaza de Bosges. Doll bodies were made here, and assembled with bisque heads imported from the Thuringen province of Germany. In 1843, the Jumeau doll body built over a metal framework was of such excellence as to win top award at the Universal Exposition in Paris the following year. (Messrs. Belton, and M. Brouillet, as well as Emile Jumeau exhibited dolls at the French Industry Fair of 1844 which survive in celebrated collections today.)

In 1850, bisque heads were made for the first time in France at a Jumeau factory in Montreuil, which employed workmen brought from the porcelain center of Limoges. However, the Jumeau doll head with the mark "Limoges" was created in a branch factory of the same firm actually in the district of Limoges.

Jumeau's sleeping eye, fully jointed doll was developed in 1851 and won an award that same year. The Queen Victoria doll, also of 1851, created a sensation, both in France and in England. About that time the son of Emile Jumeau entered the business, and the dolls of Napoleon III and Eugenie were made. The War of 1871 temporarily interrupted doll manufacture, but as soon as possible, the Jumeaus, father and son, repaired the war damage to their factory, and continued in business.

Up to 1870, Jumeau had led the field, although Steiner at 60 Rue Davron had created a beautiful doll. After 1870, Paul Girard with "Bebe Bru," and Fleischmann and Bloedel with "Eden Bebe" were active competitors. In 1899, Jumeau, Bru (with Mr. Girard), and Eden Bebe combined to form the Societe Bebe et Jouets, or "S.F.B.J." (Fleischmann headed the Jumeau factory before the 1914 war as director.)

Today there is still one Jumeau factory, located at Montreuil-sous-Bois, employing some three hundred persons, but they are no longer making bisque dolls. The bisque and porcelain sections of the business have been sold to another firm whose output is confined to vases and similar items. No one in France today is making bisque dolls, Mr. Girard states, all have turned to plastics.

The "F.G." found with the Jumeau mark has long confused collectors.

A Fleischmann and Bloedel "Eden Bebe", a bisque that arrived from Paris just in time to be photographed for this story.

A key to wind the mechanism of this doll bears initials R.D. Head marked "S. H." Now properly identified as a Roullet and Decamps doll on which a German head from Simon Halbig was

Now according to the conclusions of M. Girard and M. Moynot (of the Jumeau firm), these initials stand for Fernand Gautier. Before 1900, Fernand Gautier and his brother had a factory at Vincennes, a Paris suburb not far from Montrieul. This company made dolls for Jumeau and stamped the identifying "F.G." along with the Jumeau mark. This practice was continued until the business was ceded to Jumeau. (Hitherto, collectors have felt the "F.G." stood for F. Greffier, who was making dolls in the early days of the Jumeau company. However, he was not working with Jumeau, nor did he make dolls or parts for the Jumeau firm.)

(3) Jean Roullet and Ernest Decamps, in addition to their own line of dolls, made mechanical and non-mechanical bodies for Jumeau, and also for Simon Halbig Company of Germany. *Any doll bearing the Jumeau mark and "R.D.", indicates that the head was made by Jumeau and the body by Roullet and Decamps. Any Simon Halbig doll marked "S.H." and "R.D." indicates a similar combination of makers.* This information, which sets aright the popular misconception that "R.D." is purely a manufacturing mark to indicate the model, has been furnished by M. Gaston Decamps, the son of Ernest, who is still living. He has been for a long time distressed that the Roullet and Decamps dolls should have been misattributed to other makers. The Roullet and Decamps trademark "R.D." used on dolls is without government warranty. Their trademark, for their "L'intrepide Bebe," issued in 1893, is shown among those in the following list.

#22465. Mark to be affixed to dolls and their cardboard containers, registered Sept. 3, 1885 at 1:25 p.m., at the commercial court of the county of Seine, by Monsieur Falck (Adolphe), trader in Paris and doing business there in the name of Falck-Roussel. This mark is in different sizes. It is applied in any color.

#22466. Mark to be affixed to cardboard containers of jointed baby-dolls, registered Sept. 3, 1885 at 1:25 p.m. at the office of the commercial court of the county of Seine, by Monsieur Falck (Adolphe), trader in Paris, and doing business there in the name of Falck-Roussel. This mark is in different sizes. It is printed in any color.

#23102. Mark to be affixed to dolls, registered January 14, 1886, at 10:20 a.m., at the office of the commercial court of the county of Seine, by Monsieur Sommer (Jacques - Adolphe) manufacturer in Paris. The imprint constituted by this mark is 16 millimeters in diameter. It is applied in color.

BÉBÉ JUMEAU

#24407. Mark to designate baby-dolls, registered August 31, 1886 at 1:05 p.m. at the office of the commercial court of the county of Seine, by Monsieur Jumeau (Emile), maker in Paris. This mark is printed in gold on the manufactured articles, and in any color on the wrappings. (See Note 2).

#24866. Mark to be affixed to embroideries and dolls, registered November 22, 1886 at 10 a.m. at the office of the commercial court of the county of Seine, by Madame Deropkine (Alexandrine), trader in Paris. This mark is in different sizes. It is printed in any color.

#26856. Mark to be affixed to doll's heads, registered October 14, 1887, at 3:30 p.m., at the office of the commercial court of the county of Seine, by Monsieur Delcroix (Henri), manufacturer at Montreuil. This mark is in different sizes. It is stamped into the material.

.PARIS

PAN

#26857. Mark to be affixed to doll's heads, registered October 14, 1887 at 3:30 p.m., at the office of the commercial court of the county of Seine, by Monsieur Delcroix (Henri), manufacturer at Montreuil. This mark in different sizes. It is stamped into the material.

PARIS

G D

sizes. It is stamped into the material.

#26858. Mark to be affixed to doll's heads, registered October 14, 1887 at 3:30 p.m., at the office of the commercial court of the county of Seine, by Monsieur Delcroix (Henri), manufacturer at Montreuil. This mark is in different sizes.

#26859. Mark to be affixed to doll's heads, registered October 14, 1887 at 3:30 p.m., at the office of the commercial court of the county of Seine, by Monsieur Delcroix (Henri), manufacturer at Montreuil. This mark is in different sizes. It is stamped into the material.

H D

PARIS

BÉBÉ MOUJIK

MARQUE DEPOSEE
J B

#27993. Mark to be affixed to boxes containing baby - dolls, registered April 25, 1888 at 2:10 p.m., at the office of the commercial court of the county of Seine, by Monsieur Berner (Jacques), trader in Paris. This mark is in different sizes and colors.

#28498. Mark to be affixed on dolls made with hide, and on baby-dolls, July 18, 1888 at 10 a.m. at the office of the commercial court of the county of Seine, by Monsieur Schneider junior (Benoist), maker in Paris. This mark is in different sizes and colors.

"LE PETIT FRANÇAIS"

BÉBÉ INCASSABLE ARTICULE

Fabrication absolument Française

(Modèle et Marque Déposée)

Douz N°

#28689. Mark to be affixed to boxes containing jointed dolls, registered August 21, 1888 at 3:30 p.m., at the office of the commercial court of the county of Seine, by Monsieur Marseille (Francois-Emile), maker at Maisons-Alfort. This mark is in different sizes and colors.

#29177. Mark to be affixed to boxes containing baby-dolls, registered November 9, 1888 at 1:10 p.m., at the office of the commercial court of the county of Seine, by Monsieur Remignard (Frederic), trader in Paris. This mark is in different sizes and color.

PARIS-BÉBÉ
Breveté

#31524. Mark to be affixed to baby-dolls. Registered October 21, 1889 at 11:05 a.m., at the office of the commercial court of the county of Seine, by the Societe Danel et Compagnie, makers at Montreuil-sous-Bois. This mark is in different sizes and colors. It is applied by means of a damp stamp or by any other suitable method.

PARIS-BÉBÉ
CREATION 1889

Seul Bébé de la Fabrication Française offrant des garanties de solidité et de fonctionnement supérieures à ce qui a été fait jusqu'à ce jour

Suppression de l'inconvénient de la monture en caoutchouc

Application du Ressort-Métal breveté donnant une durée certaine et une garantie véritable de solidité

#31525. Mark to be affixed on wrappings containing baby-dolls, registered October 21, 1889 at 11:05 a.m., at the office of the commercial court of the county of Seine, by the Societe Danel et Compagnie, makers at Montreuil-sous-Bois. This mark is in different sizes and colors.

#31596. Mark to be affixed to baby-dolls and their wrappings, registered October 29, 1889 at 3:20 p.m., at the office of the commercial court of the county of Seine, by Monsieur Steiner (Jules-Nicolas) maker in Paris. This mark is in different sizes and colors.

French Doll Trademarks
[Continued from preceding page]

#3291. Mark to be affixed to boxes containing baby-dolls, registered August 6, 1892 at 9 a.m., at the office of the commercial court of Marseilles, by Monsieur E. Pelletier at Marseilles. This mark measures 34 millimeters each way. It is printed black on a white background.

IDÉAL BÉBÉ

#4453. Mark to designate baby-dolls, registered October 23, 1895 at 3 p.m., at the office of the commercial court of Marseilles, by Messieurs Bertoli Brothers, traders at Marseilles.

EDEN-BEBE

#33072. Mark to designate toy babies, registered March 31, 1890 at 2:40 p.m., at the office of the commercial court of the county of Seine, by the Fleischmann and Bloedel Company, toy makers, Paris. (See Note 2).

BÉBÉ MASCOTTE

#33645. Mark to designate jointed toy babies registered June 3, 1890 at 3:30 p.m. at the office of the commercial court of the county of Seine, by the May Brothers Company, industrialists, Paris.

#36686. Mark to designate toy babies registered July 4, 1891 at 10 a.m., at the office of the commercial court of the county of Seine, by Monsieur Girard (Paul), industrialist, Paris. This mark consists of the name, independent of any distinctive form. (See Note 2).

#36987. Mark to be affixed to the shoes of dolls, registered August 28, 1891 at 1 p.m., at the office of the commercial court of the county of Seine, by Monsieur Jumeau (Emile) maker of dolls and toy babies, Paris. This mark is in different sizes. It is applied by means of a stamp.

BÉBÉ-SOLEIL

#37041. Mark to be affixed to toy babies and to their wrappings, registered September 7, 1891 at 2 p.m., at the office of the commercial court of the county of Seine, by Monsieur Guepratte (Jean-Marie), maker of Paris. This mark is in different sizes and colors.

BÉBÉ FRANÇAIS

#37075. Mark to designate toy babies, registered September 11, 1891, at 10:30 a.m., at the office of the commercial court of the county of Seine, by Danel and Company, manufacturers, Montreuil-sous-Bois.

Bébé Favori

#38191. Mark to designate baby-dolls and other toys, registered February 8, 1892 at 3 p.m., at the office of the commercial court of the county of Seine, by Messieurs Cosman Brothers, makers, Paris.

Bébé le Favori

#38192. Mark to designate baby dolls and other toys, registered February 8, 1892 at 3 p.m., at the office of the commercial court of the county of Seine, by Messieurs Cosman Brothers, makers, Paris.

LE PARISIEN

#39514. Mark to designate dolls and baby dolls, registered August 12, 1892 at 1:30 p.m., at the office of the commercial court of the county of Seine, by Monsieur Lafosse (Amedee-Onesime).

"L'INTRÉPIDE BÉBÉ,,

#40643. Mark to designate dolls and toy babies registered February 4, 1893 at the office of the commercial court of the county of Seine, by the Roullet and E. Decamps Company, makers, Paris. (See Note 3).

#41360. Mark to be affixed to toy babies and to their boxes and wrappings, registered May 1, 1893, at the office of the commercial court of the county of Seine, by Monsieur P. H. Schmitz, Paris. This mark is in different sizes and colors.

Splendide Bébé

#41436. Mark to designate jointed and other baby dolls, ordinary dolls, clowns, games, toys, etc., registered May 10, 1893 at 10 a.m., at the office of the commercial court of the county of Seine, by Messieurs Cosman Brothers, makers, Paris.

BÉBÉ FAVORI

#41518. Mark to designate dolls nude and dressed baby dolls and various toys, registered May 24. 1893 at 3 p.m., at the office of the commercial court of the county of Seine, by Monsieur Gatusse (Clement) maker, Paris.

#47043. Mark to designate dolls, registered May 3, 1895, at 11 a.m., at the office of the commercial court of the county of Seine, by Mme. Lafosse (Marie) maker, Paris. This mark consists of the above name, independent of any distinctive form.

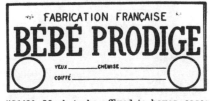

#51420. Mark to be affixed to boxes, cases and other packings for dolls or baby dolls registered October 17, 1896 at 1:10 p.m., at the office of the commercial court of the county of Seine, by E. Jumeau and Company, Paris. This mark is 0.053 millimeters high and 117 millimeters wide. It is printed black on a white background.

#51421. Mark to be affixed to boxes, cases, and other packings for dolls or baby dolls, registered October 17, 1896 at 1:10 p.m., at the office of the commercial court of the county of Seine, by E. Jumeau and Company, Paris. This mark is 70 millimeters high and 122 millimeters wide. The background is golden, the frame white, bordered in black, the same as the strip carrying the words "Chemise . . Yeux . . . Coiffe", and the scroll covering part of this golden strip; the words "Jouet National Bebe Jumeau", are in white letters framed in black; the other words are printed in black.

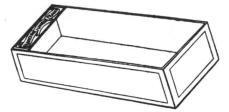

#51422. Mark to be affixed to boxes, cases and other packings for dolls or baby dolls, registered October 17, 1896, at 1:10 p.m., at the office of the commercial court of the county of Seine, by E. Jumeau and Company, Paris. This mark is 54 millimeters high and 117 millimeters wide. It is printed in two colors (gold and black) on a reddish background.

#51423. Mark to be affixed to boxes, cases, and other packings for dolls or baby dolls, registered October 17, 1896 at 1:10 p.m., at the office of the commercial court of the county of Seine, by E. Jumeau and Company, Paris. This mark is 11 millimeters high and 88 millimeters wide. The background is gold, the streamer blue, white and red, the inscription is in gold and black letters.

#51424. Mark to designate dolls and baby-dolls, registered Oct. 17, 1896 at 1:10 p.m., at the office of the commercial court of the county of Seine, by E. Jumeau and Company, Paris. This mark is characterized by a small strip fixed inside the box containing the product and on which the label may be stuck.

BÉBÉ OLGA

#51557. Mark to designate dolls, registered October 31, 1896, at midday at the office of the commercial court of the county of Seine, by Monsieur Ballu (Ernst), trading agent, Paris.

AMOUR-BÉBÉ

#52026. Mark to designate dolls, registered December 10, 1896 at 3 p.m., at the office of the commercial court of the county of Seine, by Monsieur Guillet (Louis), Paris.

"BÉBÉ TRIOMPHE"

#56876. Mark to designate baby-dolls, ordinary dolls, etc., registered February 11, 1898 at 11 a.m., at the office of the commercial court of the county of Seine, by the Fleischmann and Bloedel Company, manufacturers, Paris.

BÉBÉ LE SELECT. V.G.
BÉBÉ MÉTROPOLE. V.G.
BÉBÉ MONOPOLE. V.G.
BÉBÉ EXCELSIOR V.G.

#62919 to 62922. Marks to designate baby-dolls, registered June 27, 1899 at 3:10 p.m., at the office of the commercial court of the county of Seine, by Messieurs Verdier and Company, makers, Paris.

BABY PHÉNIX-BABY BÉBÉ-LIÈGE

#63872 to 63874. Marks to designate dolls and baby-dolls, registered October 21, 1899 at 2:10 p.m., at the office of the commercial court of the county of Seine, by Monsieur Mettais (Jules), maker, Paris.

POUPÉE MERVEILLEUSE

#64701. Mark to designate dolls and baby-dolls, registered January 12, 1900 at 2:15 p.m., at the office of the commercial court of the county of Seine, by Monsieur Mettais (Jules), maker, Paris.

#453. Mark to designate baby-dolls, registered April 18, 1900 at 2 p.m., at the office of the commercial court of Versailles, by Mme. Ricaillon (Caroline), living at Argenteuil. This mark is in different colors and forms. It is applied to the products and also to their boxes, wrappings, etc.

#67807. Mark to designate baby-dolls, ordinary dolls and toys, registered November 14, 1900 at 10 a.m., at the office of the commercial court of the county of Seine, by Messieurs Sylvain Thalheimer and Company, Paris. This mark is in different colors.

#131042-45, renewal. By S.F.B.J., 1911. Provinces of France represented by costumes.

"BÉBÉ MODÈLE"

#70426. Mark to designate dolls and baby-dolls, registered June 10, 1901, by M. Mettais (Jules), maker, Paris.

"BÉBÉ PARISIANA"

#75122. Mark to designate baby-dolls, dolls and all accessories, registered June 13, 1902, by the Societe Francaise de fabrication de bebes-jouets, Paris.

BÉBÉ MODERNE LE SÉDUISANT

#79963; 79964. Mark to designate baby-dolls and dolls, registered June 5, 1903, by the Societe Francaise de fabrication de bebes-jouets, Paris.

#86685. By M. Bonnal, 1904, "Le Petit Francais". Dark bisque, large eyes with no pupils, swivel head, jointed body of composition and wood.

ETOILE BÉBÉ

#85556. Mark to designate baby-dolls, dolls, games and toys, registered June 22, 1904, by MM. Bernheim and Kahn, Paris.

BÉBÉ L'UNIQUE
BÉBÉ LE RADIEUX
BÉBÉ LE SPÉCIAL
BÉBÉ LE PETIT FRANÇAIS
BÉBÉ LE GLORIEUX

#86682-86686. Marks to designate toys, registered September 28, 1904, by M. Bonnal (Claude-Valery), Vincennes.

EDEN-BÉBÉ

#88618. Mark to designate baby-dolls and dolls, registered February 16, 1905, by the Societe Francaise de fabrication de bebes-jouets, Paris. Renewal of registration.

Poupon Parisiana
Bébé Parisiana
Poupée Parisiana

#89828-89830. Marks to designate toy-dolls, registered April 20, 1905, by the Societe anonyme de Comptoir General de la Bimbeloterie, Paris.

#91052. Mark to designate articles such as baby-dolls, dolls, toys, etc., registered July 17, 1905, by the Societe Francaise de fabrication de bebes-jouets, Paris.

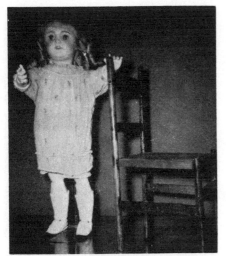

#91052. By S.F.B.J., 1905. "Celeste", bought in Paris in 1919, and dressed to order by Roberts, 72 Avenue Victor Hugo. (Roberts now concentrates on baby clothes.) Pale green georgette dress, embroidered orange flowers, matching flower earrings in orange, sash under dress in front shows through material, bow in back. Cording finish on bottom, neck, sleeves.

CENTIL BÉBÉ

#90861. Mark to designate dolls and toy-dolls, registered June 30, 1905, by M. Naneau (Hippolyte), Paris.

L'HEUREUX

#92337. Mark to designate dolls, toys, household articles and all bazaar articles, registered October 25, 1905, by M. L'heureux (Louis), Paris.

L'Idéal

#94891. Mark to designate toy-dolls, registered March 16, 1906, by Mlle. Fouillot (Blanche), Paris.

#14004. Mark to designate many products, among which are dolls, registered May 3, 1906, by the Societe Gebr. Stollwerch. A.G., Cologne-on-Rhine, Germany. This mark is affixed to samples, labels, packing materials, etc.

Bébé Mondain

#95901. Mark to designate toy-dolls, registered May 30, 1906, by the Societe Bernheim et Kahn, makers, Paris.

#97596. Mark to designate dolls, shoes and soles for dolls, registered August 24, 1906, by the Societe Francaise de fabrication de bebes et jouets, Paris.

'Bébé l'Avenir'

#15284. Mark to designate dolls and baby-dolls, registered October 17, 1907, by the Societe Gutmann & Schiffnie, Nuremburg, Bavaria.

#15419. Mark to designate toy dolls or animals in felt, plush, linen, velvet or similar materials, registered November 22, 1907, by the Firme Margarete Steiff of Giengen - on - Brenz, Wurtumberg. This mark is in the form of a button fixed in an ear of the doll or the animal.

Bouton dans l'oreille.

#12. Mark to designate dolls, registered Dec. 10, 1908, at the office of the commercial court at Bauge, by Mme. Demarest (nee Marie-Felicienne Gosse) of Clefs. This mark is affixed by an appropriate means, and in any color, to boxes or other containers of the products, and to the packages and packing material. [Clefs is a village in the county of Maine-et-Loire.]

BÉBÉ PROPHÈTE
BÉBÉ ORACLE
LA FÉE AU GUI
LA FÉE BONHEUR
LA FÉE AU TRÈFLE
LA FÉE AUX TRÈFLES

#116268-116273. Marks to designate baby dolls and dolls of all kinds, registered Sept. 28, 1909, by Mme. E. Cayatte (nee Marie Mommessin), 219 Rue Lafayette, Paris.

#116274; 116275. Marks to designate baby-dolls of all kinds, registered Sept. 28, 1909, by Mme. E. Cayatte (nee Marie Mommessin), 219 Rue Lafayette, Paris. These marks in various colors.

JOLI BÉBÉ

#119973. Mark to designate jointed dolls, registered March 25, 1910, by MM. Damerval (Jules), 212 Faubourg Saint-Martin, and Damerval (Charles), 81 Rue du Theatre, Paris.

LA PARISIENNE

#120914. Mark to designate dolls, registered May 10, 1910, by M. Kratz-Boussac (Henri-Othon), 14 Rue Martel, Paris.

#122068. Mark to designate dolls, registered July 19, 1910, by Societe Au Bebe Rose, 44 Rue Fontaine, Paris. The registered trademark is printed in violet.

#122611. Mark to designate dolls, registered August 16, 1910, by the Societe Gebaulet freres, 37 Rue de Turenne, Paris, This mark is in various colors.

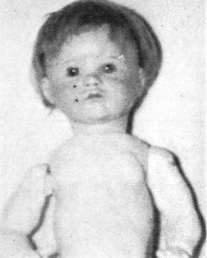

#91052. By S.F.B.J. 1905. "Pouty", bisque head.

"BÉBÉ-COIFFURE"

#18964. Mark to designate baby-dolls or dolls, registered March 10, 1911, by the Societe Gutmann and Schiffnie, Nuremburg, Germany.

BÉBÉ-OLGA

#127385. Mark to designate dolls, registered March 22, 1911, by M. Ballu (Ernest), 76 Rue Saint-Denis, Paris.

PARIS-BÉBÉ

#128025. Mark to designate dolls and baby-dolls, registered Abril 13, 1911, by the Societe Francaise de fabrication de bebes-jouets, 8 Rue Pastourelle, Paris.

#129427. Mark to designate all sports articles and all toys, notably those in plush, velvets or fur, registered June 13, 1911, by M. Dieckmann (Max), 24 Rue de Paradis, Paris.

S. T. F.

BÉBÉ EUREKA
BÉBÉ LE RÊVE
PARADIS BÉBÉ

#130965-130967. Marks to designate baby-dolls, registered September 6, 1911, by the Societe La Parisienne, 39 Rue de la Roquette, Paris.

BÉBÉ PRODIGE
BÉBÉ JUMEAU
BÉBÉ FRANÇAIS

#131041-131045. Marks to designate baby-dolls and dolls, registered September 12, 1911, by the Societe Francaise de fabrication de bebes-jouets, 8 Rue Pastourelle, Paris. Marks in various colors. [Marks of #131044-5, "Fabrication, Jumeau, France", pictured Aug. '57 Spinning Wheel, were renewals.]

„Steiff"

#19647. Mark to designate toys in felt or similar materials, registered September 13, 1911, by the Societe Margarete Steiff Gesellschaft G.m.b.H., of Geigen-in-Wurtemberg, Germany.

#131186. Mark to designate baby-dolls and toys registered September 22, 1911, by the Societe Francaise defabrication de bebes et jouets, 8 Rue Pastourelle, Paris. This mark is in various colors.

MAGIC BÉBÉ
BÉBÉ STELLA
BÉBÉ LUX

#131251-131253. Marks to designate baby-dolls, registered September 27, 1911, by the Societe "La Parisienne", manufacture de bebes et jouets, 39 Rue de la Roquette, Paris.

NINI KASPA

#138200. Mark to designate an artistic, jointed, unbreakable baby-doll, registered July 3, 1912, by M. Bernhold (Julius), 9 Rue des Petites-Ecuries, Paris.

BÉBÉ TRIOMPHE

#143317. Mark to designate baby-dolls, registered February 12, 1913, by the Societe Francaise de fabrication de bebes et jouets, 8 Rue Pastourelle, Paris. Renewal of registration.

LE TROTTIN

#145043. Mark to designate dolls and baby-dolls and especially a walking doll, registered April 16, 1913, by Mme. Le Montreer (nee Henriette-Joseph), 9 Rue Charlot, Paris. ["Trottin" means dressmaker's errand-girl.]

"MONA LISA"

#22882. Mark to designate dolls and toys in general, registered January 8, 1914, by the Firme Gutmann and Schiffnie, Nuremberg, Germany.

#147757. Mark to designate baby-doll's shoes, registered July 22, 1913, by M. Alart (Eugene), 134 Rue du Temple, Paris. This mark in various colors.

Below, #22488. By Geo. Borgfeldt & Co., 1913, Kewpie, Rose O'Neil. *Right,* #19647. By Margareta Steiff, 1911.

UN POULBOT
UNE POULBOTTE

#148034; 148035. Marks to designate all toys and notably dolls of all kinds, registered August 2, 1913, by M. Poulbot (Francisque), 11 Rue de l'Orient, Paris.

#148666. Mark to designate dolls made of fabrics, registered August 29, 1913, by M. Pintel, Junior (M.), 74 Rue de la Folie-Regnault, Paris. This mark is blue, white and red, and is the design of a ribbon with which armlets, necklets, etc. are made.

MAL'OTO de ma Poupée
MAL'AUTO de ma Poupée

#148805; 148806. Marks to designate dolls' dress-boxes, registered September 9, 1913, by M. Rouard (Charles), 137 Rue du Faubourg-Saint-Denis, Paris.

KEWPIE

#22488. Mark to designate dolls of all kinds registered September 30, 1913, by Geo. Borgfeldt & Co., 7 Kostlergasse, Vienna, Austria.

Marque de Fabrique

#23337. Mark to designate dolls, combs and other articles in celluloid, registered April 22, 1914, by the Compagne Rheinische Gummi und Celluloid Fabrik, Mannheim-Neckarau, Germany.

#148034, 148035. By M. Poulbot (Francisque), 1913. Poulbot, a humorous artist (1879-1946) known throughout France for his drawings of Paris urchins.

#23368. Mark to designate dolls in general, registered April 29, 1914, by MM. Rehbock and Loewenthal. Fuerth, Bavaria.

MON TRÉSOR

#156762. Mark to designate dolls, baby-dolls, trousseaux and dolls, dress-boxes, and all toys in general, registered June 3, 1914, by M. Rostal (Henry), 5 Rue du Tresor, Paris.

„LE BÉBÉ "

#156971. Mark to designate all ready-made articles, dresses, trousseaux, babies' garments in general and all clothes and accessories of baby-dolls and dolls, registered June 13, 1914, by M. Rocher (Marius), 19 Fontaine-au-Roi, Paris.

LE VICTORIEUX

#159214. Mark to designate baby-dolls and dolls, registered December 15, 1914, by M. Le Montreer (D.), 9 Rue Charlot, Paris.

LA POUPÉE FRANÇAISE

#9835. Mark to designate all kinds of dolls, registered December 31, 1914, at the office of the commercial court of the city of Lyons, by M. Cornet (Marius), 8 Rue Constantine, Lyons.

TRÉSOR

#158101: 158102. Marks to designate dolls, baby-dolls, trousseaux, dolls' dress-boxes, and all toys in general, registered July 27, 1914, by M. Rostal (Henry), 5 Rue du Tresor, Paris.

DURAN MARX

#160374-160376. Marks to designate dolls, toys and games, registered March 1, 1915, by Mme. Duran (Max), 25 Rue Fourcroy, Paris.

GALLIA

#162214. Mark to designate dolls or objects related to their clothing, registered July 28, 1915, by Mlle. Desaubliaux, 8 Rue de la Tourelle, Boulogne-sur-Seine.

PANDORE

#162227. Mark to designate toys, dolls, fashion objects, clothing, writing-paper, perfumes and in general all products and objects in the classes 12, 15, 38, 44, 52 and 54, registered July 29, 1915, by Mlle. Thomson (Valentine), 134 Rue de Grenelle, Paris.

#162676. Mark to designate dolls of any kind, registered September 17, 1915, by Mlle. Verita (Gabrielle), 40 Avenue de la Bourdonnais, Paris.

#163430. Mark to designate dolls and various toys, registered November 24, 1915, by Mlle. Guerin (Marthe), 301 Rue de Vaugirard, Paris.

LUTECIA BABY

Made in Paris

BÉBÉ GLORIA

Made in Paris

#163706; 163707. Marks to designate dolls registered December 15, 1915, by M. Koch (J.-Cesar), 52 Rue des Petites-Ecuries, Paris.

#163694. Mark to designate dolls, and particularly heads, arms, and legs, registered December 14, 1915, by M. Lejeune (Louis-Aime), 66 Avenue de Bois-Guimier, Saint-Maur-des-Fosses.

La Poupée de France

#164234. Mark to mark toys, registered Feb. 7, 1916, by M. Gautier (Louis), 68 Rue de Rivoli, Paris.

La Poupée des Alliés

#164735. Mark to designate dolls, registered March 24, 1916, by Mme. Perrin, 19 Rue Theophile-Gautier, Paris.

#164790. Mark to designate dolls, registered March 30, 1916, by Mme. Perrin, 19 Rue Theophile-Gautier, Paris.

FAVORI = BÉBÉ

#164929. Mark to mark dolls and baby-dolls, nude or dressed, and various toys, registered April 14, 1916, by M. Sadin (Arthur), 220 bis, Rue Marcadet, Paris.

MANOS.

MARQUE DEPOSÉE

#165126. Mark to designate dolls, registered April 29, 1916, by Mlle. Fauche (M.), 57 Avenue de Suffren, Paris.

#165882. Mark to designate dolls, registered July 1, 1916, by Mlle. de Wouilt (Renee), 9 Rue du Printemps, Paris.

POUPÉES GAULOISES

#26453. Mark to designate dolls or other toys, registered July 11, 1916, at the office of the commercial court at Bordeaux, by Mme. Louit (nee Jeanne de Montaigut) 136 Rue Terre-Negre, Bordeaux.

#166905. Mark to designate toys, registered September 22, 1916, by M. des Loges (Hubert), 9 Rue Gustave-Courbet, Paris.

EXCELSIOR BÉBÉ

#167155. Mark to designate baby-dolls and dolls, nude or dressed, and various toys, registered October 14, 1916, by M. Ortiz (Joseph), 5 bis, Rue Beranger, Paris.

#158102. By M. Rostral (Harry), 1914, "Mon Tresor". 30", kid body fashion lady, even has separate kid toes.

La Vraie Parisienne

#167192. Mark to designate dolls, registered October 18, 1916, by M. Perier (Henry), 1 Rue Lincoln, Paris.

#167193. Mark to designate dolls and other toys registered October 18, 1916, by M. Perier (Henry), 1 Rue Lincoln, Paris.

J'HABILLE MES SOLDATS
J'HABILLE MES POUPÉES

#167387; 167388. Marks to designate toys in papier-mache, registered November 3, 1916, by the Societe Ch. Ramel et Cie., 16 Rue de la Tour-d'Avergne, Paris. [Ch. may possibly indicate Charles.]

PATRIA

#167432. Mark to designate clothed dolls, registered November 7, 1916, by Mme. Lebel (nee Rachel Stapfer), 81 Avenue de Villiers, Paris.

PLASTOLITE

#168227. Mark to designate a plastic paste, and articles molded with this paste, such as the head and body of dolls and other objects, registered January 19, 1917, by M. Gault (J. Roger), 27 Rue Taitbout, Paris. This mark can be flat, indented, or in relief.

"VITA"

#169491. Mark to designate a mechanism to give movement to the eyes in artificial heads; also artificial eyes and heads of dolls, animals and mannequins, registered April 23, 1917, by M. Laffitte (Andre), 17 Boulevard Haussman, Paris.

17101. By M. Hieulle (Edmond). 1917. "Montreuil Sur Bois, France, D.L." mark. Men dolls depict periods of Louis XV, Napoleon, 1831, 1840, and 1871. Moustaches molded in the bisque.

#168866; 168867. Marks to designate dolls and all kinds of toys, registered March 10, 1917, by the Societe Sussfeld & Co., 21 Rue de l'Echiquier, Paris.

PARFAIT-BÉBÉ
PARIS

#170856. Mark to designate dolls and toys, registered August 6, 1917, by M. Hieulle (Edmond), 1 Rue Marbeuf, Paris.

#191. Mark to designate dolls, registered August 20, 1917, at the office of the commercial court at Le Puy, by M. Cortot (J.), 51 Boulevard Gambetta, Le Puy.

MONTREUIL-BÉBÉ

#171010. Mark to designate dolls and toys, registered August 22, 1917, by M. Hieulle (Edmond), 1 Rue Marbeuf, Paris.

PARFAIT - BÉBÉ
PARIS
MANUFACTURE FRANÇAISE
DE POUPÉES ET JOUETS

#171083. Mark to designate dolls and toys, registered August 25, 1917, by Mme. Crosier (Aline), 23 Avenue de Breteuil, Paris.

#171190. Mark to designate dolls and toys, registered September 7, 1917, by M. Hieulle (Edmond), 1 Rue Marbeuf, Paris.

TANAGRA

#171393. Mark to designate dolls and all kinds of toys, registered October 4, 1917, by M. Levy (Albert), 14 Rue Rougemont, Paris.

MA JOLIE

#172080. Mark to designate dolls and dolls' heads. Unbreakable, washable, non-inflammable, and light in weight, registered November 20, 1917, by M. de la Ramee (Max-Henri-Marie), 44 Rue Carnot, Suresnes.

KEWPIE

#174998; 174999. Marks to designate dolls and all kinds of toys, registered June 25, 1918, by Geo. Borgfeldt & Co., 43 Rue de Paradis, Paris. [#174998 is a renewal of registration.]

YERRI et SUZEL

#176150. Mark to designate all toys, and all propaganda or souvenir articles, notably trinkets, charms and mascots, and particularly trinkets, charms and mascots in the form of figurines or dolls dressed in the costumes of Alsace or Lorraine, and detached pieces of such articles; the products and materials used in their manufacture or aiding such use; or photographs, post cards or brochures. Trademark registered July 20, 1918, by the Societe Rene Schiller & Co., 24 Rue Saint-Marc, Paris.

LIBERTY

#175199. Mark to designate a doll, registered July 26, 1918, by M. de Roussy de Sales (Georges), 22 Rue de Levis, Paris.

MIGNON

#175288. Mark to designate dolls, heads of dolls, articles connected with dolls, registered August 10, 1918, by M. Arena (Felix), 6 Rue de la Smala, Paris.

#175508. Mark to designate dolls and various rag-made animals, registered September 6, 1918, by the Societe Binder & Co., 11 Rue Villedo, Paris.

#1754. Mark to designate toys, dolls, decorative objects, and any other objects for use by children, registered May 6, 1918, by Mlle. Brunot (Marguerite), 38 Boulevard Bon Accueil, Algiers, North Africa.

ENTRÉE DES ALLIÉS
à STRASBOURG

#180167. Mark to designate a toy, registered May 7, 1919, by M. Dubois (Paul), 36 Rue de Montmorency, Paris. (Translation of Mark: "Entry of the Allies to Strasbourg," shows influence of 1914-18 war.)

#179699; #179700. Marks [used separately] to designate baby dolls, dolls, and other toys in plastic, registered April 25, 1919, by the limited company "Les Bebes de France", 14 Rue Drouot, Paris.

LES POUPÉES DE FRANCE

#180202. Mark to designate dolls and toys and any articles in plastic, registered May 7, 1919, by M. Levi (Edmond), 19 Rue Saint-Paul, Neuilly-sur-Seine, near Paris.

PYGMÉE

#1781139. Mark to designate toys, registered March 10, 1919, by M. Savary (Andre), 11 Rue Campagne-Premiere, Paris.

Le Petit LARDON
SAC de TERRE
PILEFER
COCO
COCO
L'Infernal brise-tout
SANSONNET
NINI
NINI
La Princesse
MOUTCHOU
MOUTCHOU
La Mouche
LILI
RINTINTIN
NÉNETTE
BABA
FANFOIS
ZIZINE
MOMO

#174950-174966. Marks to designate all toys, and particularly dolls and charms, and mascots of all kinds, and all kinds of reproductions of such articles in whatever form, registered June 18, 1918, by Mme. Poulbot, 54 Rue Lepic, Paris. [Is this the wife of the M. Poulbot (#148034-5) who died in 1946?]

#893. Mark to designate all miniature articles of furniture for dolls, and children's toys, registered October 12, 1918, at the office of the commercial court at Beauvais, by M. Merz (Emile), 45 Rue Sadi-Carnot, Beauvais.

LA PARISETTE

#176286. Mark to designate dolls, registered November 15, 1918, by Mme. Coquillet (widow), 14 Rue Mandar, Paris.

EXPRESSION

#176324. Mark to designate a doll's head, registered November 18, 1918, by M. de Roussy de Sales (Georges), 22 Rue de Levis, Paris.

#178377. Mark to designate toys and fancy goods, registered March 18, 1919, by Messrs. Hirschler (Fernand-Calmon) and Hirschler (Paul-Moise), 44 Rue de Londres, Paris.

#275. Mark to designate toys, registered March 11, 1919, by M. Jean (Elie), 76 Rue Saint-Jean, Caen.

BOUQUET DE LA VICTOIRE

#18752. Mark to designate a toy and a decorative object, registered February 6, 1919, by M. Michel (Severin), Saint-Mitre, near Saint-Just, Marseilles.

#178811 [Modestes]; #178812 [Espiegles]. Marks to designate movable eyes for dolls, registered January 3, 1919, by M. de Roussy de Sales (Georges), 22 Rue de Levis, Paris.

LA MADELON

#1523; #1524. Marks to designate toys, registered January 4, 1919, by M. Martin (Alfred-Francois-Xavier), 47 Boulevard de la Reine, Versailles.

#180005; 180006; 180007. Marks to designate games and toys of all kinds, registered May 5, 1919, by M. Gratieux (Fernand), 82 to 96 Avenue des Moulineaux, Billancourt, near Paris.

#178375. Mark to designate dolls, registered March 18, 1919, by Mme. Consuelo Fould, 15 Rue Treilhard, Paris.

LA MIGNONNE

#179481. Mark to designate dolls and other articles, registered April 18, 1919, by the limited company "Les Arts du Papier", 168 Rue Vercingetorix, Paris.

#1559. Mark to designate toys in general, registered April 22, 1919, by M. Foucher (Rene), 5-7 Rue de Paris, Sannois.

#179482. Mark to designate dolls' heads and other articles, registered April 18, 1919, by the limited company "Les Arts du Papier", 168 Rue Vercingetorix, Paris.

#179043. Mark to designate toys in wood and other materials, registered April 29, 1919, by M. Sedard (Eugene), 7 bis, Rue Quesnay, Sceaux, near Paris.

L'HIRONDELLE

#179668. Mark to designate all toys and particularly roller-skates and scooters, registered April 24, 1919, by M. Brunet (Valentin-Victor), 49 Rue de Villiers, Montreuil-sous-Bois, near Paris. [Hirondelle means "swallow"].

"POUPARD" ART

#182144. Mark to designate toys of all kinds and in all materials, chiefly papier-mache, registered June 25, 1919, by M. Bellet (Henry), 50 Rue Planchat, Paris.

SPLASHME
MISS YANKEE

#182241 [Splashme]; **#182239** [Miss Yankee]; **#182240.** Marks to designate dolls, toys and other articles, registered June 30, 1919, by Messrs. Geo. Borgfeldt & Co., 43 Rue de Paradis, Paris.

MANOTA

#182392. Mark to designate toys, registered July 5, 1919, by the Mauger and Montera Company, 19 Rue Daguerre, Paris.

KLIPTIKO

#27158. Mark to designate toys, and particularly parts for building objects, registered July 17, 1919, by the William Bailey Company, 38 and 39 Weaman Street, Birmingham, England.

#113. Mark to designate toys, registered July 18, 1919, by M. Charrie (Jean), Rue Lespinasse, Marmande, County of Lot-et-Garonne.

#182852. Mark to designate games and toys, registered July 18, 1919, by Pierre Levy and Company, 67 Rue de Turenne, Paris.

#11495. Mark to designate toys, registered November 14, 1919, by the Lyons French Toy Company (formerly the Joffre School), 263 Rue Garibaldi, Lyons. ["Joffre School", is mysterious, possibly the premises were at one time used by a school.]

#187791. Mark to designate doll, registered January 9, 1920, by M. Vormus (Roger), 38 Rue de Chateaudun, Paris.

KISSMY

ARTISTE

#184672 to #184674. Marks to designate dolls, toys and other articles, registered October 3, 1919, by MM. Geo. Borgfeldt & Co., 43 Rue de Paradis, Paris.

JOLI GUY
ROSETTE
MUGUETTE

#184905 to #184907. Marks to designate dolls, registered October 15, 1919, by Messrs. Laquionie & Co., Societe des Grands Magasins du Printemps, 64 Boulevard Haussmann, Paris.

Le Joujou Français

#184951; #184952. Marks to designate toys of all kinds and in all materials, registered October 15, 1919, by M. Lepinay (V), 22 Passage des Petites-Ecuries, Paris.

HOLLIKID   TUMBLE-BO
LOTTA-SUN   WINKIE

#18872 to #188281. Marks to designate dolls and other articles, registered January 21, 1920, by Messrs. Geo. Borgfeldt & Co., 43 Rue de Paradis, Paris.

MYSTÈRE

#194582. Mark to designate dolls, dolls' heads, dolls with movable eyes, dolls' heads with movable eyes, and mechanism for dolls' movable eyes, registered July 13, 1920, by Belleville & Co., 4 Rue Capron, Paris.

BÉBÉ PARISIANA
BÉBÉ MODERNE
LE SÉDUISANT
BÉBÉ PARFAIT

#180036 to #180039. Marks to designate baby dolls and dolls, registered January 14, 1920, by the Societe Francaise de Fabrication de Bebes-jouets, 8 Rue de Pastourelle, Paris.

#11632; #11633. Mark to designate a toy, registered February 12, 1920, by Messrs. Badin (Antonin) and Guibert (Antoine), 233 Grande-Rue, Oullins, Rhone.

FUMS UP
THUMBS UP

#28325; #28326. Marks to designate dolls, toys and other articles, registered March 12, 1920, by M. Hamley (John Green), 86 and 87 High Holborn, London.

#189672. Mark to designate dolls, registered February 24, 1920, by M. Marcoux (Charles), 23 Rue Buffon, Montreuil-sous-Bois, Seine.

#318. Mark to designate dolls and various toys, registered March 23, 1920, by M. Olivier (Fernand Paulin), 26 Rue d'Arches, Mezieres. ["A La Clinique des Poupees, translates to 'Dolls' Hospital.'"]

#190883. Mark to designate dolls and various toys and other articles, registered April 1, 1920, by Messrs. Borgfeldt & Co., 43 Rue de Paradis, Paris.

1

3

Dolls pictured here are all French, but not all of the period under discussion. Mrs. Verne Hollander is the owner of the marked S.F.B.J. doll, *Figure 1*. The Jumeaus, *Figure 2*, are some of the last made; picture was furnished by former president of the firm, M. Moynot. *Figure 3* is an "R.D." marked swimming doll, owned by Mrs. Cecil Perry. Roullet Decamps took out several patents; used the R.D. mark on his dolls. *Figure 4*, courtesy of the Lila Benton Doll Hospital, Inc., is marked with "J" on head and shoulders, a Jumeau renewal.

4

JEANNE D'ARC

#679. Mark to designate dolls, baby dolls, and any toys, registered August 20, 1920, by Mademoiselle de Raphelis-Soissan (Marguerite), 8 Rue Pierre-Blanchet, Poitiers.

" TANAGRETTE "

#11945. Mark to designate dolls and all articles in this class, registered February 12, 1921, by M. Durand (Octave), 72 Rue des Gros-Grès, Colombes, near Paris.

#6947. Mark to designate toys, and notably baby dolls in papier mache, registered February 21, 1921, by M. Lefebvre, senior (Alexandre), 23 Rue Jacques-le-Paire, Lagny, Seine-et-Marne.

#6832. Mark to designate dolls and toys, registered February 25, 1921, by Messrs. Geo. Borgfeldt & Co., 43 Rue de Paradis, Paris. [Standing Kewpie doll, right arm raised]

#7721. Mark to designate toys and games and notably a special type of doll, registered March 10, 1921, by M. Dreifuss (Isidore), 63 Rue des Vosges, Strasbourg, Bas-Rhin.

MIGNON

#194057. Marks to designate dolls, doll's heads, and such articles, registered June 29, 1920, by Messrs. Arena (Felix) and Lafond (Michel), 16 Rue Jean-Nicot, Paris.

POUPÉES DE PARIS
Les Poupées Parisiennes
LES POUPETTES

#194486 to #194488. Marks to designate dolls and other articles, registered July 10, 1920, by Messrs. Manuel (Gaston) and de Stoecklin (E), 137 Rue de Vaugirard, Paris.

#8988. Mark to designate dolls and toys, registered April 6, 1921, by Messrs. Geo. Borgfeldt & Co., 43 Rue de Paradis, Paris. [Seated Kewpie doll, elbows on knees, hands under chin.]

LE PAPILLON

#8624. Mark to designate dolls, registered April 2, 1921, by the Societe Francaise de Fabrication de Bebes et Jouets, 8 Rue Pastourelle, Paris.

#10220. Mark to designate dolls and toys, registered April 27, 1921, by Mademoiselle Lambert (Cecile), known as Edmee Rozier, 21 Rue du Chateau, La Garenne-Colombes, Seine.

BABET

#17140. Mark to designate dolls, and doll accessories, such as wigs, shoes, clothing, under-garments, registered September 22, 1921, by the Societe Francaise de Fabrication de Bebes et Jouets, 8 Rue Pastourelle, Paris.

Bébé l'Avenir

#17845. Mark to designate baby dolls and dolls, registered in Paris, October 5, 1921, by the Societe Gutmann et Schiffnie, Nuremberg, Bavaria, Germany.

#22373. Mark to designate dolls and other toys, registered January 7, 1922, by Mme. de Kasparck (Jeanne), 11 Rue Villedo, Paris.

BÉBÉ JEANNETTE

#35649. Mark to designate dolls and toys, registered September 26, 1922, by Mademoiselle Cortot (Jeanne), 3 Rue de la Loi, Liege, Belgium. Renewal.

#40540. Mark to designate dolls, toys and other articles, registered January 15, 1923, by Messrs. Geo. Borgfeldt & Co., 43 Rue de Paradis, Paris. [Standing rabbit, in waistcoat, right arm raised]

DANCING KEWPIE SAILOR

#25323. Mark to designate dolls and toys, registered March 4, 1922, by Messrs. Geo. Borgfeldt & Co., 43 Rue Paradis, Paris.

#25324. Mark to designate dolls, toys, and other articles, registered March 4, 1922, by Messrs. Geo. Borgfeldt & Co., 43 Rue Paradis, Paris.

THUMBS UP! HAUT LES MAINS!

TOUCHE DU BOIS! TOUCH WOOD!

#19652; #19653. Marks to designate mascots made of any material, registered November 10, 1921, by M. Nalty (Herbert), doing business as Gourdel Vales et Co., 57, Great Marlborough Street, London.

FUMSUP

Lisette

MARQUE DEPOSEE
P.V

#29503. Mark to designate dolls in all kinds of fabric, registered May 15, 1922, by Mademoiselle Lelievre (Yvonne), 23 Rue de Constantinople, Paris.

MISS DANCING

#39253. Mark to designate doll, registered September 21, 1922, by M. Lilienthal (Michel), 9 Rue d'Isly, Paris.

Peter Rabbit Acrobat

#40541. Mark to designate dolls and toys, registered January 15, 1923, by Messrs. Geo. Borgfeldt & Co., Rue de Paradis, Paris.

GABY

#42422. Mark to designate doll and other articles, registered February 20, 1923, by M. Bertrand (Rene), 3 bis Rue des Beau-Arts, Paris.

BEDTIME

#42813. Mark to designate dolls and toys, registered February 27, 1923, by Messrs. Geo. Borgfeldt & Co., 43 Rue de Paradis, Paris.

MARQUISETTE BSGDG DEPOSE

#44619. Mark to designate dolls, registered March 14, 1923, by M. Noel (Charles-Marie-Paul), 19 Rue du Rempart, Saint-Etienne.

NINON
SELECT
GABY

#47099 to #47102. Marks to designate dolls, dolls' heads, and similar articles, registered May 17, 1923, by the Societe Bonin et Lefort, 46 Rue Fontaine-au-Roi, Paris.

HAPPY HOOLIGAN

#47366. Mark to designate dolls and toys, registered May 23, 1923, by the Societe Geo. Borgfeldt & Co., 43 Rue de Paradis, Paris.

#47367. Mark to designate dolls, toys and other articles, registered May 23, 1923, by the Societe Geo. Borgfeldt and Co., 43 Rue de Paradis, Paris.

LA POUPÉE LINA

#48890. Mark to designate dolls and other toys, registered June 21, 1923, by M. Mariage (Maurice), 12 Rue Saint-Merri, Paris.

LA VÉNUS

#53413. Mark to designate dolls made of fabric, registered September 20, 1923, by M. Carvaillo (Adrien), 29 Rue du Sentier, Paris.

#68434. Mark to designate wigs for dolls and all articles associated with dolls, registered August 7, 1924, by M. Bossuat (Etienne), 28 Rue Notre-Dame-de-Nazareth, Paris.

SERAPHIN

#56752. Mark to designate a lucky doll, registered December 6, 1923, by M. Thieck (Francis), 95 Boulevard Exelmans, Paris, Jean Born & Co., 3 Cite d'Hauteville, Paris.

NIFTY

#57716. Mark to designate dolls, toys and other articles, registered December 26, 1923, by Messrs. Borgfeldt & Co., 43 Rue de Paradis, Paris.

Zina

#62513. Mark to designate all doll articles and accessories, registered March 24, 1924, by M. Lambert (Andre), 24 Rue Philippe-de-Girard, Paris.

OLYMPIA   MARQUE DEPOSEE

#62530. Mark to designate toys, especially dolls, registered March 25, 1924, by M. Muller (Pierre), 1 Rue du Marche, Levallois, Seine.

KiPMi #63250. Mark to designate dolls of all kinds, registered April 10, 1924, by Mademoiselles Couin (Raymonde), 37 Rue Amiral-Mouchez, Paris, and Camgrand (Therese) 22 bis Rue Laugier, Paris.

SCARAMOUCHE
IDÉE NOM et USAGE
DEPOSÉS
en toutes matières

#65122. Mark to designate mascot-dolls, registered May 20, 1924, by M. Le Prince, (Ange), 32 Rue Saint-Sulpice, Paris.

JEANNINE

#67125. Mark to designate dolls and toys, registered July 5, 1924, by Madame Violon (Jeanne), La-Varenne-Saint-Hilaire, Seine.

LUTETIA

#65983. Mark to designate dolls, registered June 7, 1924, by Mademoiselle de Brzeska (Aline), 115 Avenue Marigny, Fontenay-sous-Bois, Seine.

La Poupée "NICETTE"

#66725. Mark to designate a doll in fabric, registered June 19, 1924, by M. Perrimond (Gaston), 14 bis Avenue Borriglione, Nice.

LA NÉGRESSE BLONDE

#68779. Mark to designate dolls, statuettes, registered August 13, 1924, by the "Au Perroquet" Company, 3 bis Rue des Beaux-Arts, Paris.

TI-KOUN

#73529. Mark to designate all toys, and particularly dolls of all kinds, registered December 9, 1924, by Madame Schlisler (Jeanne), nee Dumay, 96 Rue Chardon-Lagache, Paris.

#72573. Mark to designate dolls and toys of all kinds, registered November 20, 1924, by the "Chantilly" Company, 16 Rue Michel - le - Comte, Paris.

BYE-LO-BABY
FELIX THE CAT

#75644; #75645. Mark to designate dolls and toys, registered January 27, 1925, by Messrs. Geo. Borgfeldt & Co., 43 Rue de Paradis, Paris.

#75643. Mark to designate dolls, toys and other articles, registered January 27, 1925, by Messrs. Borgfeldt & Co., 43 Rue de Paradis, Paris.

JANUS

#82999. Mark to designate dolls' heads, games, and toys, registered June 16, 1925, by Mademoiselle Mabit (Louise-Adrienne), 60 Rue Beaunier, Paris.

LE JOUJOU PNEU

#83970. Mark to designate baby dolls, animals, and fish in supple rubber, registered July 6, 1925, by M. Zierl (Paul, Lucien), 19 Avenue Claire, Coeuilly-Champigny-sur-Marne, Seine.

#84036. Mark to designate dolls, registered July 9, 1925, by Mademoiselle Loudouze (Genevieve), 29 Rue de Trevise, Paris.

LES DEUX GOSSES

#84047. Mark to designate dolls, games, and various toys, registered July 10, 1925, by Mademoiselle Mabit (Louise-Adrienne), 60 Rue Beaunier, Paris.

BÉBÉ OLGA

#93156. Mark to designate dolls, registered February 2, 1926, by the Etablissements Gerbault, Brothers, 85 Rue de Turenne, Paris.

MOGLETTE

#93162. Mark to designate dolls and other articles, registered February 2, 1926, by M. Kahn (Lucien), 6 Rue Carnot, Montreuil-sous-Bois, Seine.

BICOT

#93555. Mark to designate dolls, registered February 12, 1926, by Madame Lubecka (Julienne), 12 Square Delambre, Paris.

#93418. Mark to designate dolls, registered February 4, 1926, by M. Giotti, 7 Rue de la Prefecture, Nice.

PARIS-BEBE

#93492. Mark to designate baby dolls and dolls, registered February 9, 1926, by the Société Francaise de Fabrication de Bebes et Jouets, 152 Rue de Paris, Montreuil, Seine. Renewal of registration.

#95351. Mark to designate artistic dolls, mascots, toys, signets, and their accessories and parts (bodies, heads), registered March 10, 1926, by M. Guillon (Silas), 53 Rue de Ponthieu, Paris.

BÉBÉ PRODIGE
BÉBÉ FRANCAIS
BÉBÉ JUMEAU

#102338 to #102340. Marks to designate baby dolls and dolls, registered August 24, 1926, by the Societe Francaise de Fabrication de Bebes et Jouets, 152 Rue de Paris, Montreuil, Seine, [Renewal of registration.]

#103906. Mark to designate a doll, registered October 8, 1926, by M. Carles (Jean), 1 Rue Alberti, Nice.

MON BABY
JOLI BÉBÉ

#109126; #109127. Marks to designate dolls, dolls' heads, and toys, registered January 22, 1927, by the Bonin and Lefort Company, 46 Rue Fontaine-au-Roi, Paris.

LES ORIGINAUX
DE VOVONNE

#110522. Mark to designate peasant dolls, registered March 17, 1927, by Madame Spaggiari (Yvonne), 103 Rue Caulaincourt, Paris.

LES POUPÉES DE MITOU

#104359. Mark to designate mascot dolls, fan-dolls, luxury dolls, registered October 29, 1926, by Madame Bruent (Anne, Marguerite), 22 bis Rue Laugier, Paris.

BATHILDE   MOUSMÉ   TRUDY

YVETTE   SUZEL   CLAIRE

JOSEPH   ARLETTE   MARIE-JEANNE

#108046 to #108056. Marks to designate costumed dolls holding bread trays, liqueur trays, trays for visiting cards, menus and so on, registered November 16, 1926, by Madame Rassant, nee Blum (Elisa), Rue de la Bouverie, Brou (Eure-et-Loir).

#117455. Mark to designate mascot dolls, registered August 18, 1927, by M. Dedieu (Louis), 51-53 Rue du Faubourg-Saint Denis, Paris.

DE LIAUTY

KEWPIE

#124101. Mark to designate dolls and toys, registered January 10, 1928, by Messrs. Geo. Borgfeldt & Co., 43 Rue de Paradis, Paris. [Renewal of registration.]

#108532. Mark to designate dolls, registered January 28, 1927, by M. Sanders, (William, Webb), Chateau de Nermont, Chateaudun, Eure-et-Loir.

#130549. Mark to designate mascot dolls and dolls registered May 3, 1928, by Madame Douch... (Germaine), 3 bis Rue des Beaux-Arts, Paris.

#133310. Mark to designate dolls made of material, (turtle leather), registered June 22, 1928, by M. Darcy (Robert), 28 Rue Feydau, Paris.

L'IDÉALE

#130896. Mark to designate dolls made of fabrics, registered May 7, 1928, by Mademoiselle Rigot (Marie, Georgette), 84 Rue de l'Hotel-de-Ville, Paris.

#138588. Mark to designate dolls and animals, toys made of fabric, registered October 12, 1928, by M. Brogi (Amilcare), Avenue de la Gauloise, Coeuilly-Champigny, Seine.

Puppel's Mary
NOVELTY

#131730. Mark to designate dolls and mascot dolls, registered May 21, 1928, by Madame Douche (Germaine), 3 bis Rue des Beaux-Arts, Paris.

German Dolls

For years the German toy industry dominated the world market supplying dolls to almost every country in Europe, and sending even more to the United States. The Germans had a marvelous faculty for creating dolls that looked like real babies and children. Best known to doll collectors are the names of *Simon & Halbig, Armand Marseilles, The Brothers Heubach,* and *Kammer & Reinhardt.* There were many others, as the list of marks found at the end of this chapter will testify. Not only were German dolls preferred over all others because of their life-like appearance, they were also far cheaper than American, English or French dolls. The doll manufacturers discussed in this portion of our book were the most prolific producers. Consequently, there is hardly a collection of any size that doesn't include at least one example of their artistry. While collectors lean more toward dolls made by *Armand Marseilles,* it would not be correct to say that *A.M.* dolls were superior or more popular than *Heubachs, Simon & Halbig,* or *Kammer & Reinhardt.* The name of *George Borgfeldt & Co.* of New York City on German-made dolls is difficult to comprehend until one realizes that this firm represented many German doll manufacturers in the United States.

Bisque head character boy doll with jointed composition body purchased in Munich, Germany, in 1958. Collection Dorothy S. Coleman. D'Aquilla photo.

Superb example of a wax-covered German doll; high-quality artificial eyes, blonde mohair braids and coiffure; 25 inches tall. Collection Shelburne Museum, Inc., Shelburne, Vermont.

German Wax-Covered Dolls

by LILIAN BAKER CARLISLE

STARTING WITH a kettle full of boiling dirty grey pulp and ending with a be-ringletted and be-flounced, rosy-cheeked blooming doll seems almost like magic to us today. But in the latter part of the 19th century it was an everyday occurrence in the quaint, quiet little toy-making villages of Germany. Wax-covered dolls were the pride and profit of Sonneberg and neighboring towns near the northern border of Bavaria. In the final quarter of the 19th century, an incredible two million dozens of dolls were annually exported all over the world from Thuringia.

In addition to the waxen babies, countless numbers of other kinds of dolls were produced in Germany—not to mention the bisque beauties from France and the penny woodens and solid wax dolls for which England was famous. Since World War II, the Thuringen section of Germany has been under Soviet administration, and one wonders what the families who made dolls and other toys for countless generations are doing today.

Fortunately for us, *The Wonderland of Work,* by C. L. Mateaux published about 1877, captured in words and pictures the technique of producing the wax-covered dolls and illustrated the procedures with a page of wood engravings.

Would it surprise you to learn that in the German toy-maker system of division of labor, 30 pairs of hands were employed in producing an ordinary doll head? Only the head, mind you—all the rest of the doll was made by other workers.

The first pair of hands in our progression belonged to the designer —an important and artistic member of the team. His job was to model a pattern for the new doll. In large, well-lighted workrooms, seated at tall workbenches called bankers, young men spent hours at this task. Their bankers could be screwed up or down, or revolved to allow the artist to work on any part of his model. In front of him were two lumps of clay. One he used as a tool cushion, plunging his bone modeling sticks into the clay as

he finished with them. The other lump of clay, under his skilled hands, metamorphosed into a doll head. He patted and dabbed away at the soft wet clay until the shapeless grey mass assumed the form of a pretty, though expressionless face which appealed to the modeler. He marked on it a few careful lines with a piece of red chalk and turned it over to Worker Number Two, who was responsible for making an exact mold or copy of it.

After the original clay model dried and hardened, the molder would lay it, face upwards, in a dish of wet clay, carefully pressing the clay into every corner of the back of the head up to the red lines the modeler had drawn as a boundary. He then built a clay wall all around the mass, somewhat higher than the uncovered face of the model. Another worker assisted him by holding the clay walls together while he fetched a vessel full of melted sulphur or plaster-of-paris from the stove, the contents of which he poured all over the face. As soon as the sulphur or plaster was cold, the dish was turned over and the clay removed, leaving the doll's face buried in the sulphur. This procedure was repeated, building up the clay wall again, pouring sulphur or plaster-of-paris and making the mold for the back of the doll's head.

In another room, an uninviting papier-mache broth, consisting of torn scraps of paper which were once old cotton rags mixed with water, boiled away in a great cauldron, gradually cooking until it became soft and clear. A worker then squeezed and strained the dirty water out of the pulp and mixed powdered clay and a little glue in it until the whole looked like a great lump of baker's dough. The dough was rolled, banged, and beaten into long, cake-like shaped loaves. Another worker picked up the loaves, laid them on a board, and flattened them with a big rolling pin, just as a cook does with pie crust. The paste was then cut into square pieces and piled on top of one another with a little powdered clay sprinkled like flour between each square to keep them from sticking together.

The next workman removed the little pile of soft squares and pressed them into one of the hollow half-head molds. The mold was passed to another man who, with a soft wet sponge and a little bone tool, fitted the soft paste neatly into every crevice of the mold so that it would turn out an exact counterpart of its shape. He pared off the rough edges of dough with a knife, gently slipped the half-head out of the mold and laid it aside. When the face and back-of-the-head pieces were thoroughly dry, the two halves were neatly glued together.

The next workman was a rough and heartless surgeon, for his job was to set the eyes. He ran a sharp knife around each cranium and kicked the piece out with a sharp rap of a hammer. If the eyes were to be fixed or stationary, the worker with a quick twirl of his knife cut out a couple of almond-shaped holes and popped in the eyes which were slightly warmed so they would stay in place until a little melted wax could be poured into the hollow skull to seal them fast in place. If the doll's eyes opened and shut, a much longer operation was involved.

The matched pair of blown glass eyes was first firmly fastened to the ends of a long piece of curved wire, something like a fork, with a heavy ball of lead fastened in the middle of it; it was the shifting weight of the lead which drew down the sleeping part of the eyeball when the doll was laid down. The eyes, half of the eyeball covered with wax for the eyelids, were carefully placed, then the wire

fastened in place by means of plaster-of-paris and sealing wax dropped in liberally. A slice of cork or piece of sponge was glued in and so located as to prevent the hard lead support from hitting the inside of the dimpled chin every time it slipped up or down. Last of all, some chips of wood were dropped in to keep the whole set-up firm; then the sliced-off top of the head was replaced and glued on again.

Originally nearly all glass doll eyes were made in England, principally at Birmingham, but by the final quarter of the 19th century the bulk of them were being manufactured in Germany. The exact method of blowing the eyes was a closely guarded German trade secret, but it was known that each eye was blown separately, and that ordinary ones costing a few pennies the

dozen were made of white enamel—that is, of glass with an opaque white substance mixed with it. A spot of black, or more often of blue which was by far the favorite color, placed in the centre of the enamel orb represented the pupil. Hundreds of large cases filled with dolls' eyes, packed according to size, were shipped out of Germany to doll makers every year. England, however, continued its manufacture of the costly blown glass eyes used in expensive dolls. They were fashioned exactly as though they were artificial eyes for grown persons, and cost as much as a guinea a pair (equal to $5 at the time).

After the eye-setting, the doll heads passed into the hands of several young women who carefully filed away rough spots and ugly mold seams and

The Manufacture of German Wax Dolls: 1. Making the model. 2. Joining the head. 3. Setting the eyes. 4. Waxing the head. 5. Painting the face. 6. Hair-dressing. 7. Sewing on the head. 8. Dressing. (From "The Wonderland of Work," by C. L. Mateux. Published by Cassell, Petter, Galpin & Company, London, Paris and New York; ca. 1877.)

then splashed them all over with a fiery sort of paint, almost the color of a scraped carrot. Next they were handed over to a man standing before a huge vessel full of steaming, boiling wax, clear and white. He took each head and gave it one or more wax dips; the more dunks the better the wax doll was likely to be. The flaming red paint now shown slightly through the clear white wax and gave to the face a soft, lovely, delicate pink complexion. The expressionless heads were then dusted with sweet-scented violet powder to make their waxen skins easier to beautify further.

The dolls then journeyed to the painting room where their cheeks grew rosy and their lips reddened. Many busy people waiting to receive their batch of new heads sat along the sides of a long table running along the center of the cool, comfortable work room. One, with a stroke and a flourish, gave the doll two little bowed cherry-colored lips; his neighbor delineated the eyebrows; the head passed from hand to hand, each worker doing his or her own special task. Finally, the head with blushing cheeks and pink-lined nostrils was sent to the frau hair-dressers, whose nimble fingers effected the final transformation of the staring bold-faced doll, for it was the graceful coiffure which gave the doll its gentle, soft, pleasant look.

The doll's hair was the costliest part of her construction, although tresses varied in texture and value. Black hair, never very popular with young customers, was really human hair. However most children wanted a doll with shining, glossy blonde curls made of a soft, silky kind of mohair. These tresses were a specialty of a house in London that did little else than manufacture this hair which was purchased by dollmakers in Germany and France, as well as England. Ready-made wigs of mohair, or of natural hair glued to a net foundation, or of raw wool braided and boiled to wave it were available for cheaper types of dolls, but for the wax-covered queens only individually rooted hair was acceptable.

When the mohair arrived from London it was tied in soft silken bundles, cut to different lengths, and ready for use. Rows of bald heads, perched on miniature hair-dressers' blocks, were lined up before the girls who were trained for this particular work. Each girl held a small bundle of hairs in her left hand, all of the same length and carefully combed out like a fringe. In her right hand, pressed to the doll's head, she held a blunted blade with which she deftly tucked in the even roots of the hair, pushing the blade a little way down into the wax, then as dexterously switching away the bundle. This operation was continued until the tresses began to be quite thick, when she took up a little iron roller, pressed it to the doll's scalp, and rotated it gently and firmly over the surface closing up the gashes she had made with the blade. The procedure was patiently repeated until the pinky foundation was hidden and covered by soft hair. Eyelashes in the more expensive dolls were rooted in the same manner; cheaper dolls had to make do with a painted fringe of lashes.

The head was now finally finished. There still remained the hands, feet, and body. If wax hands and feet were used, they were fashioned in the same manner as the head—that is, modeled, then cast into molds. The bodies, frequently of common white calico stuffed with sawdust, were neatly made by women and children. Some of the daintier bodies were formed of pinky soft kid or snowy thin sheepskin, carefully stitched, sewn, and jointed. The home craft of doll-body making gave a livelihood to many poor people in the humble, pine-scented villages in Germany, but that is another story.

ARMAND MARSEILLE DOLLS

by GENEVIEVE ANGIONE

Everyone doing doll research is hampered by great lapses in documented evidence concerning many firms whose work we know mostly from examining their dolls. That is why we are forever poking about in old letters, magazines, books, directories, and catalogues. Hearsay is never the best source of information, but all of it is welcome, simply because it gives us something from which to work and against which to check.

In 1945, Robert Raffety of Chicago, who now runs the M & R Doll Hospital there, had the good fortune to encounter a man who had worked in the mold room of the Armand Marseille factory during the last years of its operation. At that time Mr. Raffety was not particularly interested in dolls or antiques, but his mother was a doll collector. He became friendly with this fellow worker, brought him home, and made notes of what the man told them about his work in the A. M. factory at Koppelsdorf. These notes and the picture of the town were made available by Mr. Raffety for this article.

The Koppelsdorfer said that the elder Marseille was born in the 1840s in Riga, before it became part of Latvia. He had been a successful butcher before he entered the porcelain field about 1890. His given name, and that of his son and his grandson who followed him into the doll business, was *Herman.* The name "Arm-

and" was used only as a business identification. Whether the "Marseille" was also assumed is not known, but it is surprisingly French, in a business where French was important, for a Latvian German!

Researchers have long known there were family ties between many of the doll making firms, and this seems to have been the case here. The worker said the Heubach whose porcelain factory was also in Koppelsdorf was a brother-in-law to Armand Marseille. In fact, there was a great rivalry between the two, not on a business basis, but in the matter of horses. Heubach apparently was never as personally wealthy as Marseille for in the early 1900s when Heubach is said to have had four horses, Marseille had a stable of thirty.

Although Mr. Raffety's informant had not been with the firm from the begining, he was convinced the porcelain works had been originally started to manufacture tableware. These first efforts must not have been quality products for little was ever said about the days before A. M. entered the doll field. But from then on, all awards and prizes for dolls were displayed with great pride in the factory offices, and the company gloried in the quality, variety, and volume of their doll production.

It is little wonder we find so many A. M. dolls today, for even after the elder Marseille died in the early 1920s, and on into 1926, the firm still

turned out 1,000 heads a week. From 1926 through 1928 the volume dropped steadily to nothing.

The man recalled several details about the firm which ordinarily would not appear in any material available to us now. For instance, he said the firm imported English coal because German coal did not fire evenly to the temperature they desired. (This single expense must have been terrific!) It took 60 hours of continuous firing to bring their porcelain kilns up to 2600°, and they could be fired up to 5000°.

Tiny heads were made four to a mold; medium sizes were three to a mold; the large ones were molded individually. The coloring of the highlights, lips, cheeks, etc., was done by whole families, including small children, yet these home workers barely made a living. (It is surprising that the old German "home industry" system was still in operation at such a late date; the independent French worker had opposed it successfully generations before.)

Although they did not make kid bodies or bisque forearms, the man said, A. M. did make completely jointed papier-mache bodies, including bodies with jointed ankles. The latter were not too popular, however, for a factory-strung body will stand alone, and jointed ankles made the dolls fall over too easily.

The word "highlights" in the statement about coloring may very likely refer to the jointed bodies. Collectors have long noticed the variation in coloring on the knuckles of the hands, often very different on the same doll, and amateurish outlining of toenails and fingernails of the doll bodies. These could have been the tasks of children who were not trusted with the valuable heads.

Other interesting items: At least during his employment there, the man said, the German Steiner heads were produced by A. M. He also explained that the Gibson Girl and the Barbary Coast Gent were not made in quantity because the long necks of the girls broke in the greenware state coming out of the molds, and the moustaches of the gents stuck to the mold so that hundreds of them had no upper lip.

Although late-comers to the porcelain field, A.M. dolls are found in great profusion, a surprising number of faces, and an unbelievable variety of novelty and "character" types. Armand Marseille was evi-

View of the Village of Koppelsdorf as it appeared on a picture postcard, ca. 1900. Arrow points to the A. M. factory. Home of Heubach of Koppelsdorf, brother-in-law of Armand Marseille, is in lower right hand corner.

dently a man with great competitive spirit, wise to fundamental merchandising tricks, well supplied with money and dedicated to making more of it.

Dollers continually comment on the fine quality of A.M. bisque. At the same time they complain bitterly about the cheapness of many of the bodies and the vapid, dollish features of the large jointed dolls. A.M. was selling dolls in a highly competitive market as toys for children, and he must have been a very practical man. Little girls wanted pretty dolls from Santa Claus and their purchase was a big item in Christmas shopping budgets, so he made the dolls the children wanted.

If the 1890 starting date is correct, it would account for the detailed identification and country of origin marks generally found on A.M.'s. Many are also incised D.R.G.M. (Deutches Reiche Gesetz Musterschutz) indicating that he had applied for German patents. These were evidently originals because the warning initials appear horizontally on the back of the shoulder plates and are squeezed in vertically on some swivel necks with the same faces.

It is difficult now to establish any progressive framework of Armand Marseille production. We find a great variety of sizes, with closed mouths, open-closed mouths, open mouths with teeth, with both swivel and shoulder heads, and many of them in combination with intaglio eyes, set or sleep eyes, without eyelashes or with them. [Open-closed mouths are those with parted lips, with or without teeth and/or tongue, but always with no opening into the head. Intaglio eyes are incised by the mold so they are deeply pitted in the pupil.]

The production pattern formation is further hampered by the fact that some of the open-closed mouth faces also appear with open mouths on quite similar original bodies with only a slight change or no change at all in the model number. Added to all that, some shoulder head faces turn up on swivel necks; some shoulder heads are found on cloth bodies with composition arms and legs, while others are on original kid, kidette, or kidaline bodies from a period when both shoulder heads and kid bodies had supposedly outlived all popularity.

Besides all the features which seem to be indicative of production economies to undercut the market price-wise, A.M. was also quick to ride the prevailing bandwagon. His head 370 appeared with and without fur eyebrows on bodies marked "Floradora," and with D R G M or DEP added to the multitude of information incised on the plates. Their quality was poor but they sold well because we are still finding them.

The deliberate assembly of A.M. dolls over a period of years makes one wish there was some personal description of the man available. He lived from the 1840s to the 1920s, so he was not young when these doll heads were pouring out of his Koppelsdorf kilns.

No. 1—Beatrice

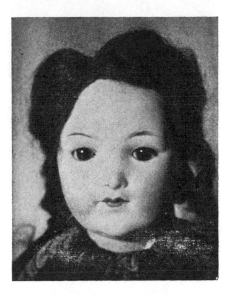

No. 1, *Beatrice,* 24½" tall, has some unusual features. Up under the wig she is lightly incised: Armand Marseille, Germany. Below the holes used to tie the weights for the sleep eyes, the number 700 appears, with the French 7 which has the crossbar like our F. Below that: A 9 M. She could have been made for the French trade, or on specification by a French body-maker. She is very un-German looking.

The closed mouth is red with orange overtones; her brown sleep eyes are heavily lashed under the waxed lids, and she has eyelashes painted around the eye socket. The eyebrows are done in the light German mode rather than the heavy French fashion. She does not have pierced ears, however, which helps to place her in the 1890s.

Except for the ears, the head appears to be early, but the body belies this. If it is original—and the head is perfectly seated in the neck socket— the closed mouth could simply be an indication that A. M. had not yet assembled porcelain workers experienced in open mouth work.

This body was originally spring strung, and the arms still work perfectly. The spring attached to the head and one leg snapped. In restringing, it was discovered that the other leg was strung with the customary large hook to an inside wooden chest bar. Other dolls found with springs have all been open-mouthed.

The body quality is satisfactory but not good when compared to other old German bodies. The thigh and upper arm balls are built onto the parts, but they are a thin wash of plaster over cardboard which did not hold up like the wooden balls. The enamel is a sturdy golden tan rather than the dainty German pink.

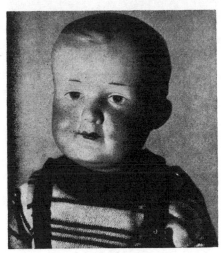

No. 2, Infant Barry

No. 2—Barry

No. 2 Barry, an infant, is a good example of this. The incised mark on his swivel neck is in three lines: 500/Germany/ A 2 M, which fairly well fills up his little neck. Vertically, on the right side, clearly incised, are the patent warnings: D R G M.

On a typical pink bent-leg baby body, he sits 8⅜". The blue intaglio eyes have no highlight dots; the eyelids are well defined; and the one-stroke eyebrows match his reddish blonde painted hair. The all-over complexion is baby pink without much cheek contrast.

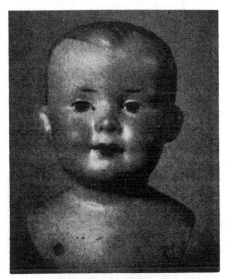

No. 2-A, Child Barry

No. 2A—Barry

No. 2-A Barry, a child shoulder head, has shoulder incised in four lines: 600/ A 3/O M / Germany / D R G M. The head is 3½" high and 2½" across the shoulders under the plate.

Although he has four sew holes, the liberal application of glue still on the underside suggests that he, too, was late, and was originally glued to a cloth body with composition arms. He could be much like Bernadette, No. 3.

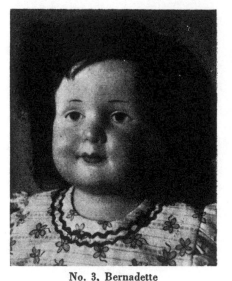

No. 3, Bernadette

No. 3—Bernadette

No. 3 Bernadette, 13". Boldly incised across the entire shoulder plate in four lines: 640/ A 3 M / Germany / D R G M. Her blue intaglio eyes are very deep but have no white highlight; the lids are well defined; the one-stroke very short eyebrows are light brown. Her mouth is a soft light rose color; the overall complexion is soft pink; and there is little cheek contrast. The old mohair wig may or may not be original.

Her body is similar to another all-original doll in the group. The torso is a rather flat cardboard roll which extends almost to her seat and is stuffed with some sort of linters. A small rear end of linters was added and the entire assembly covered with sized pink muslin. The stuffed cloth upper legs are sewn to the front edge of the seat and some wire arrangement can be felt through the body which helps her to sit down. The above-elbow arms and to-knee legs are a plaster and papier-mache mixture with a smooth matte finish more like a dye than paint.

No. 4, Polly

No. 4—Polly

No. 4 Polly, 11½", could have been dressed as a boy or a girl, as is often the case. Incised up under the wig is: Made in Germany. In two lines below and in plain sight is simply: 390/A 7/O M. The threaded blue eyes are set; the eyelashes are painted; and the eyebrows are both molded and painted. It is interesting to note that the German mark does not show under the wig, and the eyebrows are painted like many of the smaller French dolls, almost meeting in the center. The open mouth is a soft orange pink and the four tiny teeth appear to be molded to the upper lip. The white blonde mohair wig is original and does not appear to have been barbered by a child.

The torso is the cardboard box again, but could have been an earlier model than Bernadette because the wood and composition arms are

strung through wooden joints attached to the body under the composition shoulder plate. This is not the full wooden cylinder found in many kid-bodied shoulder heads with jointed composition arms.

The one-piece composition legs with wooden knee balls are strung with rubber through the wooden caps that finish off the stuffed thighs, which make re-stringing quite a problem. The elbow balls in the wristless lower arms and the entire upper arms are wood. Either she is an early open mouth or the limbs were left over from early production before the cheap composition bodies took over. The old blue and yellow beads on her talkbox strings point to the early date. The shoes of soft tan leather could be original.

No. 5, Bernice

No. 5—Bernice

No. 5, Bernice, 13½". Under the wig she has no marks. Across the center back "Made in Germany" is incised, and below that only A 3 M. Her blue intaglio eyes resemble those of old Gebruder Heubach's with a tiny drop of white bisque on the upper lid as a highlight. The eyelids are well molded; the brows are one-stroke in light brown. The entire face is pink without much contrast in the cheeks, and the lips are a pretty orange-pink without the darker center line often found in closed mouths. The dark human hair wig is not original.

The body fits well and is in such fine proportion it could be original. If it is, the quality would incline one to believe that the head was bought from A.M. by somebody still manufacturing good bodies. The built-in thigh and upper arm balls are wood and, like many old pale pink German jointed bodies, the fingernails and toenails are not outlined in red.

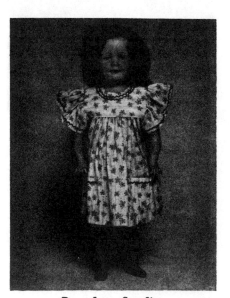

Bernadette, Standing

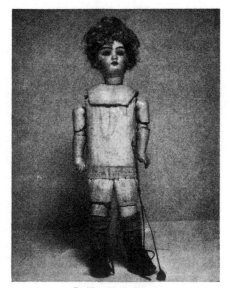

Polly, Full View

No. 6—PATRICE, 19" tall

No. 6—PATRICE, 19" tall

Patrice's head is incised in four lines: 590 / A 5 M/ Germany/ D R G M. Her dark gray threaded sleep eyes have no hair lashes, but eyelashes are painted around the socket. The pale brown brows are multi-stroked but without the depth of color found in similar French eyebrows. The open-closed mouth has a molded ridge under the upper lip which could have been used for upper teeth like one very popular S.F.B.J. child.

However, every A.M. specimen thus far has had the entire mouth painted a soft orange pink. The complexion is pale but warm, and the cheeks are in good contrast. The very pale blonde mohair wig could be original, and a larger duplicate in the group has a similar attractive wig also in excellent condition. The duplicate has the same eyes but they were factory set.

Patrice is on a replacement body, but the companion doll is evidently all original and the body quality is very good for A.M., with wooden shoulder and hip balls. Here again it is possible that the companion may have been a head which was bodied, wigged, and dressed by some factory which had to buy heads. The original chemise, shoes and socks are superior to the general German quality.

Patrice is carrying a very late, tiny A.M. Known among collectors as a "teenage" body, it is rubber-strung at hips and shoulders with little hooks protruding from the limbs. This 4¾" blue sleep-eyed specimen has a closed mouth. With bent arms, straight legs which always have white painted socks and brown, heeled, one-strap shoes, these dolls were made by many firms in the second decade of our century. The wig is a replacement.

Armand Marsielle Dolls

No. 7—Patrick and Pierre

No. 7—PATRICK and PIERRE

Patrick and Pierre are also 590 A.M.'s. Patrick, on the left, is like Patrice but one inch shorter. Pierre is the open-mouth version and is marked exactly like the other two. He is 16 inches tall. Patrick's eyes are blue-gray, but the later Pierre's are blue. There is no proof that either body is original, but Pierre has his original wig, of soft brown mohair with a "gravy bowl" cut, straight around the head.

No. 8—Albert, 14" tall

Albert's swivel neck is incised in four lines: 1894 (a date which appears on many A.M. heads); then A M 1½ DEP, and on two lines, "Made in Germany." The set brown eyes have painted lashes; the medium brown brows are very glossy multi-stroke; and the open mouth has four teeth added. The white blonde mohair wig was made to appear like a boy's by putting the sewed part far to the left. The head is "greasy" bisque which is commoner in S&H than in A.M. heads. The color is pale without much cheek contrast.

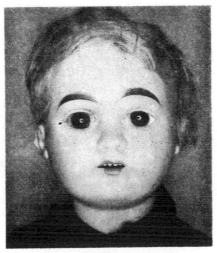

No. 8—ALBERT, 14" tall

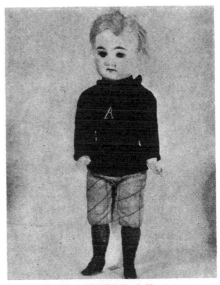

No. 8—ALBERT, full view

All original, he is peg-jointed at hips and shoulders with rubber, and his straight legs have high molded black boots, with heels and yellow laces, and painted brown stockings. The padded tan pants and knitted blue jersey suggest a cricket suit, but if he had any equipment, it is long since lost. The clothes are tacked and sewed to a body of fair quality. The one-piece arms are not especially well molded, but the very attractive legs and feet are superior.

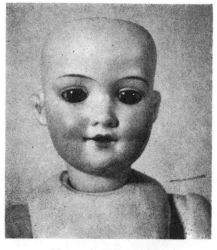

No. 9—BABY BETTY

No. 9—Baby Betty

Baby Betty's head is marked "from stem to stern." Penciling the deep incising was not difficult. Not shown in either picture are the holes above each ear for the tied-on domes with the large center hold for a mohair yardage wig rather than a wig on a gauze form. This economy was practiced in the trade from the time of the bug-eyed papier-maches. Perhaps it was used to market "seconds," because both old shoulder heads and good bisque heads are found with excellent wigs; the cut holes were covered by wigs.

The quality of bisque is excellent, the brown sleep eyes have painted lashes only, the brows are one-stroke in medium brown and the teeth were added back of the open mouth. The upper lip is so deep and "fleshy" the mouth appears closed in pictures. The ears are especially well shaped and molded. The body is obviously not original.

The name of this doll is misleading because it is by no means an infant as the word "baby" implies in English. The fact that a patent was applied for suggests that it was the incised oval bearing a special name which was the point of the patent. Whether A.M. made it this way for their own line and with other names incised for body manufacturers makes a most interesting speculation. Proof would be even more intriguing.

No. 10—Hindu Boy

No. 10, Hindu Boy, 17½". This name is said to have been on this lad's original box. Incised in four lines: 1894 A M/ DEP/ Made in Germany/ 2½. The dull bisque is tobacco brown; the brown sleep eyes have brown waxed lids, painted eyelashes and multi-stroke black brows. The open mouth has teeth added after baking and the lips are bright scarlet. The close-curled wig is made of black knitting yarn which was glued right to the head and dome without a gauze cap. Again, the ears are well molded and prominent.

The reddish brown body is fully jointed, the stick leg type, with wooden kneeballs embedded in papier-mache-and-plaster lower legs. The shoulder balls are wood and are part of the wooden upper arms. Finger- and toenails are not outlined.

His original clothing is detailed and

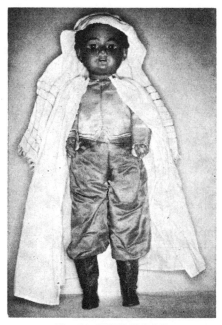

No. 10, HINDU BOY

interesting. The white head scarf is of fine white cloth, chainstitched in silk at the ends in yellow, red, and blue stripes to form a "Roman" border; edges are fringed. It is held on by a wire halo, covered with gold braid.

The flowing cape is the same white material with a narrow gold braid loop at the neck. The clothes, which fasten with hooks and eyes, are cotton-backed satin, and the jacket is lined with lightweight buckram. The jacket is deep aqua bordered with chainstitched double rows of yellow silk. The wide, pleated, body-fitting belt is cerise; the "bloomer" pants, a vivid Prussian blue. He wears long black stockings and high, dark tan kidette boots with yellow paper soles. He just invites display with a nice, hide-covered old fashioned toy horse!

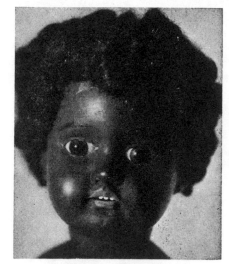

No. 11, CLEONIE

No. 11—Cleonie

No. 11, Cleonie, 13". In two lines, the first up under the tightly glued hair, she is incised: 1894 A M / 2/O DEP. There is no "Made in Germany," but she may have had a tag or label for entry into the U.S.A. Her brown eyes are set and the one-line black eyebrows shine on her dull black face. The open mouth is bright red and the teeth were added, not molded, to the lip. The original tightly curled black hair is a very good mohair wig.

The torso is a heavy molded shell which seems to be the mixture of plaster and papier-mache; the wristless lower arms and lower legs are of the same material. The wooden shoulder balls are added to the wooden upper arms, but the hip balls appear to have been turned on the ends of the wooden thighs.

CLEONIE, Standing

No. 12, AMERICAN INDIAN

No. 12—American Indian

No. 12, American Indian, 11". This "Red Indian" is a completely German product. Incised in three lines: A.M./xGermany/ 4/0. The dark brown eyes are set, with painted eyelashes and one-stroke brows which are pitch black. There is a frown molded above the straight, sharp nose. The open mouth is a deep henna color and the teeth are added. The complexion is dull reddish tan without cheek color. The black mohair is loosely glued to the dome and hangs loose over the bisque.

There are large holes above the ears. Instead of the tie-on dome, this size was frequently used for a cheap stringing arrangement. Hard wires were hooked to short leg rubber and anchored in these head holes, with the wig covering the wire grip outside the head. In this doll the holes were ignored and a short hard wire

was hooked over the back of the head. It extends through the head where it is hooked to the pegged rubber extending between the arms. It gives every evidence of being pre-World War I.

The composition body is painted the same reddish tan as the face and is peg-jointed at the hips as well as shoulders. Yellow painted slippers with heels are slightly inaccurate moccasins. The original suit is made of thin tan felt trimmed with multicolored fringe. The stapled black belt is oilcloth; the headband, pink and yellow cotton edging attached to a bronze-gilded paper crown. The clothing is tacked to the body, but it apparently was not childproof because most of these dolls turn up nude.

AMERICAN INDIAN, Full View

137

No. 13—Wee One

No. 13, Wee One, sits 3⅝" and is 5" overall. Because it is so small, the marking is difficult to read but it appears to be, incised in three lines: A M / Germany/ 351-/10/0. The tiny, irisless eyes are set; there are black eyelashes and brows and the little open mouth has two bottom teeth. The cap of hair is painted black. The complexion color is a deep chocolate brown with a matte finish, and does not seem to have been fired the second time as true bisque should be.

The typical bent-leg infant body is rubber, strung with wire hooks protruding from the arms and legs, and the finish is glossy.

GERMAN

Armand Marseille's

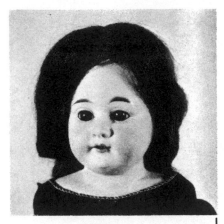

PRIZES and SURPRISES

by GENEVIEVE ANGIONE

Anyone who handles dolls in quantity, with sharp observation, eventually gets to have a "feeling" about many varieties, and A.M. is high on that list. Although A.M. dolls don't have a family resemblance, as Jumeaux do, or the childish features which set apart Gebruder Heubachs, or the "character" faces we associate with K*R, or typical lips, like Kestners, there is something "A.M.-ish" about them. They generally look like nothing but a German doll, yet the *feeling* is there.

The faces vary; the coloring covers a wide range from pale to high; they show up with every type of eyebrow—but they say, "Another A.M.," even before the mark is checked. Almost without exception, there is something about the bisque which responds to examining fingers; there is rarely the feeling that the head is thin and may break; the nose is frequently retrousse; there is often a dimple dot in the chin, and the mouth seems to be deliberately full-lipped and pleasant.

If there is a doubt in anyone's mind that German doll manufacturers were in business for any other purpose than to make money, the seemingly inexhaustible quantities of marked A.M.'s still in circulation should dispel the thought.

The same face and/or number appears on swivel necks from life-size to minute, then turns up in all sizes of shoulder heads. The 1894 marking is

a good example of this. The numbers 370 and 390 show up in everything, from pale to very high coloring (indicating that it was used over a long period), and in both swivel and shoulder heads. DEP. is often combined with 3200 in shoulder heads, and D.R.G.M., a size number, and even a patent number mark up the backs of the heads in a jumble of incisings which mean little to any of us.

One logical explanation is that A.M. fired in such quantities that heads were marked to be suitable for filling a wide variety of orders. If we remember that there was a continental price war for quantity orders, many things make more sense.

BENE

Bene: Marked across the back plate in one line: A.M. 95-6 DEP., with four unused sew holes. Many things about this slightly turned shoulder head indicate that it was for export, and that it was early.

The A.M. is in old fashioned curling script instead of the bold block letters. The coloring is peachy instead of the German pink. The excellent brown eyes are factory set and they are not the blown German type but have a paperweight look. The upper and lower painted eyelashes are full; the eyebrows are multi-stroke, glossy, and resemble the French. This may be an early attempt to produce an open mouth because it is not as well done as thousands of later A.M.'s.

The pitch black body is made of felt and copied after the wafer-jointed kid bodies, with a waistline in back and a 4-piece shaped buttocks. The knee wafers permit the lower legs to drop quite well, but the seat wafers are sawdust clogged and not flexible enough to allow her to sit—also a fault of the kid bodies. The neck and arm edges are machine overcast in white. The below-elbow bisque arms are very well molded and in far better proportion than the average German doll has, with rather chunky hands like the French ones.

BRENDA

Brenda: Marked in three lines: made in Germany/ A.4 M./ and a large Z down at the neckline with a slight indenture across the diagonal like a European 7. Like Bernice, No. 5 in April *Spinning Wheel*, the bisque is very fine, but the coloring in this instance is quite pale. The eyes are intaglio without the white dot of bisque, rimmed with blue; both the upper and lower eyelids are well molded, but have no painted lashes. The eyebrows again are single strokes in light brown. The open-closed mouth has four beautifully molded teeth. She could be a cheerful little sister to the pensive Bernice. The "made in Germany" indicates she was made after 1891, and that is enough to know about such a pleasant little face.

On first glance she resembles anything but an A.M., and she may have been a special order for a body manufacturer because in six or seven years not a single body or shoulder plate has been found in the proper proportions with a small enough neck hole to seat the head properly.

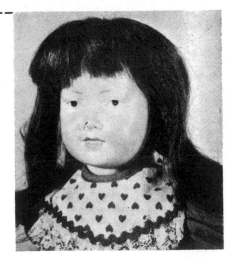

FUR-EYEBROWED

This fur-eyebrowed 5-inch head, with 11¼-inch circumference, is a good example of many A.M. characteristics. The luminous quality of the bisque is well illustrated; the retroussé nose and pleasant mouth show to advantage; and the incising is a classic example. In six lines: D.R.G.M. 377439/ Made in Germany/ D.R.G.M. 374 830/374/ a ¾" uncut oval with incised O/ A.7 M./ 390. Under the oval there are also the punched holes through which the sleep eyes could be tied for safe shipping. The blue sleep eyes have dark blonde lashes so soft they may be made of raw silk.

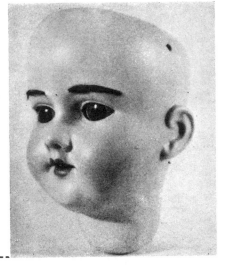

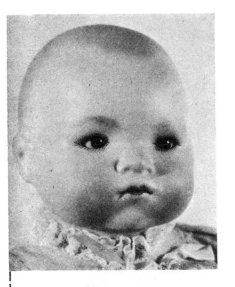

DREAM BABY

Dream Baby: Marked in three lines: A M/ Germany/ 341/4 down into the rim of the flange neck. It dates about 1924 or 1925; nevertheless, the bisque is beautiful and the coloring is much more subdued than the 351 swivel neck infant doll described, but not illustrated, under "Barney," at right.

Dream Baby's hair is such a light wash it appears to be water-colored, and the eyebrows barely show.

The pretty sleep eyes are blue and the upper and lower lashes are painted.

Dream Babies came on cloth bodies, but not the fairly good quality muslin used on many Byelos; nor did they have the overlapping legs. The shapeless stuffed body has straight, center-seamed, sewed-on legs which end in soft, fat feet. The sausage-like arms have composition baby hands. The unbleached cloth is of thin, poor quality, although fairly sturdy. It would probably classify as low-count muslin.

BARNEY

Barney. Swivel neck infant, marked in four lines: Germany/ G 326 B/ A.O.M./ D.R.G.M. 250. On page 4, *Dolls, Makers and Marks,* Elizabeth Coleman suggests that the G.B. indicates Gabriel Benda.

Except for the quality of the bisque, there is nothing about this infant head to indicate A.M. but the pin dot dimple in the chin. The slightly molded hair and the blonde brush stroke treatment of the head and the multi-stroke eyebrows strongly suggest Kestner. The coloring is medium and attractive; the sleep eyes are very dark brown, and the two bottom teeth are doubtless molded in. The bent limb baby body probably is original, of good quality, but unmarked.

It is interesting to note that A.M. also issued a swivel neck infant with two lower teeth in an open mouth, incised in three lines: A.M./ Germany/ 351/3K. The top lock is more definitely molded in a curl and the hair is sprayed almost orange. It has one-stroke eyebrows, blue sleep eyes, upper and lower painted lashes.

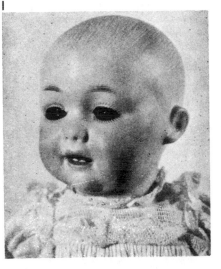

QUEEN LOUISE

Queen Louise: This is a suggested project for all dollers interested in German jointeds. She is marked in two lines with the distinctive: Germany/ Queen Louise. This is a 1910 U.S. registered trademark of Louis Wolf & Co., doll assembler and wholesaler in Sonneberg, Germany. Assemblers sometimes also made bodies, but all of them bought heads in the open market from any or all porcelain factories.

This particular doll has an A.M. *feeling* about her and only one small clue. Up at the top of the head there is *always* an odd incised figure. It is 305, the 5 raised slightly above the 30. So many A.M. heads have a 300 number (just as Kestners, for instance, have 100 numbers), this crooked mark could be A.M.'s identification to Wolf.

The bisque is extremely fine; the coloring is pale and pretty. The sleep brown eyes have both painted and mohair lashes; the eyebrows are multi-stroke and glossy. The nose and mouth are typical of A.M. and there is a suggestion of the chin dimple. The wig is made on a gauze form from beautiful mohair which may not have been dyed because it has bleached naturally where exposed to bright light. Out of every ten dolls marked "Queen Louise," only one or two have this head which is so superior to all the others that identification would be valuable. Do you have one?

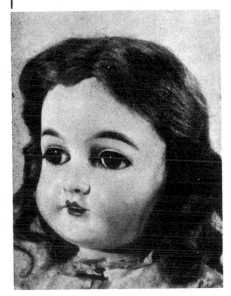

GOO-GOOS AND PIXIES

by GENEVIEVE ANGIONE

Modern psychiatry seems to hold with Armand Marseille, the ex-Latvian retired butcher who moved like the wind into the highly competitive field of doll making. Motivation research indicates that when adults choose dolls as gifts, they pick the ones which appeal to them and try to influence the child's choice if she is present. Adults could buy these cheap little goo-goos and pixies the year 'round without competing with the Santa Claus Christmas doll ideal. The adult appeal is still there; collectors now hunt them relentlessly.

It is difficult to establish a specific starting date for these charmers. Some women remember them from about 1910 but cannot say definitely that they were *new* then. Butler Bros. Nov. 1916 Catalogue #1443 carries a wholesale listing for dealers: "*The Happy Family:* in six styles, 9 inches, asstd boys and girls, bisque heads, asstd expressions, striped and solid color dresses and rompers, painted shoes and stockings." The accompanying small line drawings resemble some of the marked R.A.'s and Heubachs. They have painted eyes and hair, incredibly flimsy bare cardboard bodies and the original clothing is often made of felt. They look like hastily made competition for a fad which may have already waned.

Because the bodies are in two styles, they will be described here once, and identified with the specific dolls pictured.

Most of the fat little torsos are nothing but stem-molded cardboard, with the two halves joined by wire staples at intervals down the juncture. A pasted paper strip straight down the front, under the crotch, and up the back hides the staples from busy fingers. A light wash of calcimine or a thin coat of paint completes the job. The neck holes are completely open, often with ragged edges; the arm and leg holes are roughly molded in, which accounts for the need of the center body seam.

The bent arms and fat legs are molded from an unknown mixture of papier-mache, glue, plaster, and perhaps fine sawdust. They are very pulpy and break easily; water is disastrous to them. The stringing holes in the limbs are probably bored and the whole doll is held together with two short pieces of rubber glued and pegged into these holes. Sometimes short hooks hold the head to the arm rubber; in others, a long hook attaches the head to the hip rubber. In most of the all-bisque heads these wires have a spiral top forced up into the neck, although some have a hole molded in the back of the neck through which the wire could be bent. The wigged dolls often have two molded holes above the ears; apparently these were never used since the wires extend up over the head in back, under the wig.

The molded composition bodies are more attractive and durable but are not common in the smaller sizes. Some of these, too, have a wash of calcimine, while others have a light coat of oil paint or a good coat of paint resembling enamel. All of which indicates a wide variety in price. The arms and legs are painted unless specifically mentioned otherwise.

Since collectors are so conscious of markings, it is interesting to note that in several instances the same face was used with a different hairdo. The bisque, incidentally, is always good and sometimes the superlative A.M. quality. The decorating is consistently good and subdued, with none of the "high" coloring associated with late German products. The painted hair on the bisque heads varies from blonde to darker honey blonde, but the wigs are another story. Some are mohair on gauze foundations but many are just mohair glued to the cardboard dome and the head. The mohair is fair to good quality, straight, waved, or pencilpoint curls in brown, brassy gold, taffy blonde, and light blonde.

ILLUSTRATIONS

No. 1—10 inches; sleep brown eyes; 8½" circ.; enameled composition body with bare feet. Marked in five lines: 253, S.B., Germany, A. O M., D.R.M.R. [German patent applied for]. The head is held with a plug; clothing appears to be original. Wig replaced.

No. 2—9½ inches; paint blue intaglio eyes; 7½" circ.; washed composition body, painted limbs, blue shoes. Marked in four lines: 253, A 5/0 M, Germany, D.R.G.M. [German patent granted] 24811 (the last two figures are not quite clear). This is the same face as No. 1 but with uncut eyes; both have "watermelon" lips.

No. 3—sits 6½ inches; paint blue intaglio eyes; 7" circ.; bent arm and leg infant body is original, painted composition with bare feet. Marked in four lines: S B 252, Germany, A 6/0 M, D.R.G.M. Watermelon mouth.

No. 4—7 inches; paint blue intaglio eyes; 5½" circ.; washed composition body, painted limbs, blue shoes with heels. Unused stringing hole above mark in three lines: 210 A 11/0 M, Germany. Small mouth.

No. 5—7 inches; paint blue intaglio eyes; 5½" circ.; painted composition body, bare feet. Hole above mark used for stringing. Marked in three lines: 320, A 11/0 M, Germany. The "Mohawk" hair-do is well molded; watermelon lip.

No. 6—6½ inches; paint blue intaglio eyes; 5½" circ.; washed cardboard body, painted limbs, tan shoes. Spiral wire into head. Marked in three lines: 320, A 11/0 M, Germany. Watermelon lip but, without the Mohawk molded hair, it is a different doll.

No. 7—6½ inches; paint blue intaglio eyes; 5½" circ.; washed cardboard body, painted limbs, brown shoes. Spiral wire into head. Marked in three lines: 255 D R G M 2, A 11/0 M, Germany. Molded "boy" hair; watermelon lip.

No. 8 — 6½ inches; paint blue intaglio eyes; 5¾" circ.; washed cardboard body, painted limbs, brown shoes. (Also in washed composition body with bare feet.) Spiral wire into head. Marked in three lines: 322, A 11/0 M, Germany.

No. 9—10 inches; sleep blue eyes; 8" circ.; enameled composition body with slender limbs, paint black shoes. Head strung with plug; taffy mohair wig on gauze. Marked in four lines: Armand Marseille, Germany, 323, A. 4/0 M. Full goo-goo lips.

No. 10—7½ inches; sleep blue eyes; 6½" circ.; washed cardboard body, painted limbs, blue shoes. Wire over head; blonde mohair wig on gauze. Marked in four lines: Armand Marseille, Germany, 323, A 8/0 M.

No. 11—6½ inches; sleep blue eyes; 5¼" circ.; washed cardboard body, painted limbs, black shoes. Wire over top of head; mohair curls glued to dome and bisque. Marked in five lines: A 253 M, Nobbi Kid, U. S. Pat., Germany, 11/0.

No. 12—7½ inches; sleep blue eyes; 5" circ.; enameled body with slender limbs, bare feet. Wire over top of head; mohair "bob" on gauze. Original clothing is organdy. Marked in four lines: Just Me, Registered, Germany, A 310 11/0 M. Has "rosebud" mouth.

Records through the years indicate that the 253 face appeared in many types and sizes, and the 323 face, with both blue and brown sleep eyes, was the goo-goo standby in a great variety of sizes.

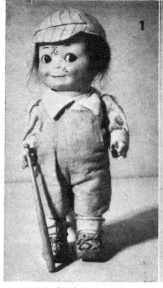

253/SB/AM—10"

253/AM—9½"

252/SB/AM—Sits 6½"

210/AM—7"

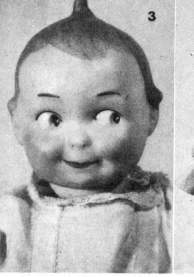

Mohawk/320 AM—7"

320/AM—6½"

255 DRGM/AM—6½ "

322/AM—6½"

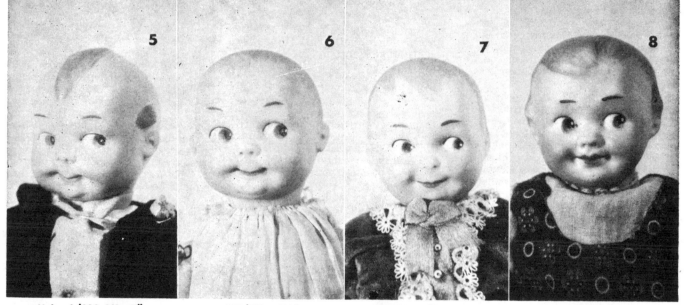

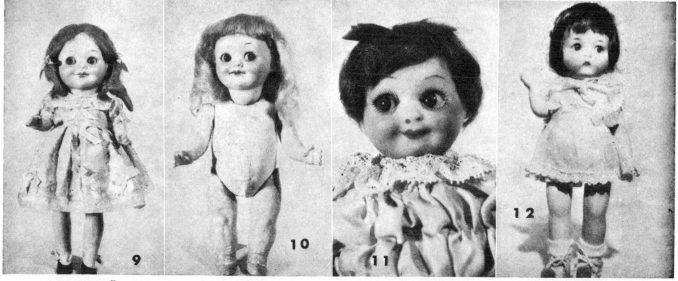

323 AM—10"

323 AM—7½"

A253/Nobbi Kid—6½"

A310M/Just Me—7½"

COMPETITION for GOO-GOOS?

by
GENEVIEVE ANGIONE

It is a dangerous game to do too much guessing in doll investigating because some serious researcher may prove you wrong before your print is dry. There are times, however, when assumptions must be made simply to have some platform from which to operate.

With this thought in mind, this month's little dolls are presented for what they seem to be — competition for the tremendously popular and still numerous Armand Marseille dolls known to modern collectors as "goo-goos." The squat bodies with the fat legs and the impish faces almost invariably remind outsiders, especially comic strip buffs, of the Katzenjammer Kids.

Just as our toy counters today reflect the grinding competition for the dollars spent on children, the American dollar was vied for with great gusto by the German dollmakers. There is more than a little evidence, too, that they helped each other with heads and/or bodies to make complete dolls.

Many of the bodies on these competitive items are exactly like the bodies on the A.M. models, but so far not one has been found with a manufacturer's mark on the body. The same standards used for the A.M.'s apply to these dolls and descriptions

will follow the same pattern with notes on the manufacturers of the heads.

No. 1—7 inches; sleep brown eyes; 6" circ.; washed cardboard body, painted limbs, tan shoes. Head strung with wire over the rim; blonde mohair glued to cardboard dome; redressed. Marked in four lines: 133/ S superimposed over H/ Germany/ 2.

The face of this doll looks exactly like A.M.'s model #323. It also has the same good bisque, the good, well-set eyes and the slightly high pink complexion. In *Dolls, Makers and Marks,* the Colemans identify this S over H as the mark of Hermann Steiner, also shown as Herm Steiner, 1924, Sonneberg. Koppelsdorf and Sonneberg were not very far apart, in that section of Thuringia which dipped down into Bavaria.

Numbers 2 through 5 are Heubachs, and this is the old Gebruder (brothers) Heubach firm which, besides a great variety of dolls, also produced untold thousands of the popular bisque "piano babies" and other appealing children figurines so much loved by our mothers and grandmothers around the turn of the century. On these dolls the Heubach mark is the domino-shaped oblong with HEU in the top and BACH in the bottom half. The Colemans give the business address as Sonneberg

although the factory was in Lichte near Wallendorf, quite a distance away.

No. 2—6½ inches; convex molded eyes with large half-pupils and rims of gray blue; 5½" circ.; sturdy composition torso is washed, painted limbs, black shoes. Head wire strung, probably with a coil; painted blonde hair with a tiny molded curl in front. Original dress is thin felt with white cotton collar and black sateen belt; usual tacked-on gauze pants are missing. Marked in three lines: 30 6/0 11 (poorly incised)/ 95 HEU BACH 94/ Germany.

No. 3—7 inches; sleep brown eyes; 5¾" circ.; washed cardboard body with center staples, usual painted limbs, bright tan shoes. Head, strung with wire over the rim, also has two small holes above each ear and is the old type with a sloping cut and high domed forehead. Human hair wig may be replacement, but little printed dress could be original; no pants but tack holes are visible. Marked in four lines: 9573/5 over a line over 0/HEU BACH/ Germany. This is one type of watermelon lip.

No. 4—7 inches; sleep gray eyes; 5¾" circ.; washed cardboard body with center staples, usual painted limbs, tan shoes. Head strung with wire over the rim; straight mohair

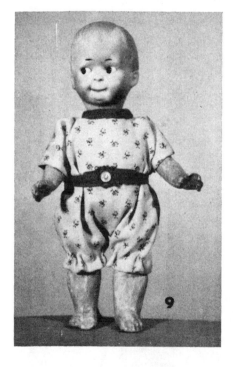

No. 6 — 7½ inches; intaglio blue eyes; 6″ circ.; composition torso and limbs painted; blue shoes with gilded buckles. Head wire strung. Molded "bob" is light blonde with blue band across top of head. Redressed. Marked in two lines: R 46 A/ 12/0.

No. 7 — 6½ inches; blue intaglio eyes; 5⅜″ circ.; unpainted stapled cardboard body; poor quality arms and legs are painted; black socks, tan shoes. Head wire strung; molded hair is light blonde; dress probably original. Marked in two lines: R 45 A/ 13/0.

This firm has not been satisfactorily identified although quite a few dolls, some of them infants with most attractive molded-on bonnets, bear this mark.

No. 8—6½ inches; blue sleep eyes; 5¼″ circ.; washed composition torso, painted limbs with tan shoes. Has been restrung with neck plug; human hair wig is replacement; redressed. Marked in three lines: S superimposed over W/ in lower section of S, Germany/ 208-12.

This is the mark of Strobel & Wilken, a Cincinnati, Ohio, firm with offices in New York City (Dolls, Makers and Marks, pg. 71). Kammer and Reinhard and Heinrich Handwerck made dolls for them but they carried the S.W. mark.

No. 9—7½ inches; molded eyes with half-pupils only; 5¾″ circ.; washed composition body, painted limbs and bare feet. Head wire strung; boy-cut molded hair is tinted blonde. True watermelon lip. Marked in three lines: Germany/ E H 27x 15/0/D.R.G.M.

This mark is unfamiliar and leads to speculation because the E. I. Horse-

man Company of New York was very active at this time. Their 1924 infant actively competed with the Bye-Lo and it could be that the middle initial of this firm was necessarily deleted in this small head.

No. 10—6 inches; painted blue eyes; 5¼″ circ.; washed composition body, poor quality painted limbs with blue shoes. Head wire strung; molded "bob" tinted reddish blonde. Dress with Dutch border print is probably original; undies missing. Marked in one line: 33 12/0.

With the exception of this last doll, which is quite ordinary, all these heads are very good German bisque and the molding and decorating is well done. In Nos. 1, 8, and 10 the color is slightly heightened, but all the others are pale and most attractive.

wig glued on dome. All original. Gauze, lace-trimmed pants still tacked on; 2-piece dress and tie-on hat are white-trimmed teal blue thin felt; flowers are red and white. Marked in four lines, the name in fancy printing: Elizabeth/ 6 over a line over 0/ HEU BACH/ Germany. "Rosebud" mouth.

No. 5—7½ inches; blue sleep eyes; 5¾″ circ.; entire body is enameled and composition torso is excellent; pale orange socks, bright tan shoes with heels. Head strung with wire over the rim; two holes above ears. Human hair wig is replacement; original gauze chemise. Marked in four lines: 10542/ 4 over a line over 0/ HEU BACH/ Germany.

Brown eyed bald baby, 2 lower teeth, head marked "J.D.K. Made in Germany" 12" and 32" doll with inset eyebrows, all original even to box she came in, head marked "16½ Made in Germany, D.D.K. 215", body marked "Excelsior No. 7".

Flirting Eyes, Bye-Lo Babies, and Kewpies were only the glamorous special attractions of a firm which produced year in, year out, thousands of popular kid-body, bisque head . . . .

Kestner Dolls

From the 1890s to the 1920s

by HELEN BULLARD and CATHERINE CALLICOTT

The exact time the Kestner family began making dolls is not known. About 1860 Henry Kestner, son of the Kestner then making the doll of that name in Germany, came to the United States, and settled in Nashville, Tennessee. His granddaughter, who now lives there, is certain that the J. D. Kestner firm was well established in doll manufacturing when her grandfather left Germany, but nothing is definitely known of the first Kestner, nor his son, who took over the business. It was *his* son, Adolf, a gandson of the original Kestner, who inherited the business about 1890 and operated it until the family's interest was sold during the 1920s.

The company was located in the German state of Thuringia, at Waltershausen, during the period when Thuringia was a busy center of doll manufacturing—at one time 25,000 workers were employed in local doll factories.

From the 1890s, Kestner dolls were imported into the United States and Canada by Geo. Borgfeldt & Company of New York City exclusively. Mr. Fred Kolb, now chairman of the board of today's Geo. Borgfeldt Corp., after more than fifty years with the company, is the primary source of information on Kestner dolls in this country.

According to Mr. Kolb, who first visited the factory in the early 1890s, the first Kestner doll imported by the Borgfeldt Company was all bisque. These 1890 dolls are presumed to have been the little girl type with jointed bodies, curly wigs, and fixed, painted eyes. Unlike most of their contemporaries in Germany, the Kestner factory manufactured their own doll heads. Kestner also made kid body dolls, dolls with muslin bodies, and character baby dolls. Kestner manufactured the first Rose O'Neill Kewpie dolls in 1912, in bisque. Kewpies were phenomenally successful and were produced in many sizes.

15" bald head baby, painted hair, 2 upper teeth, marked "Hilda 15 J. D. K.Jr. 1914, ges gesch n. 1020 Made in Germany 11" and *right*, 21" baby, head marked "Made in Germany J.D.K. 211".

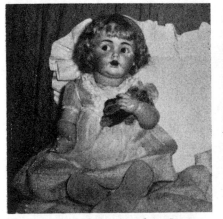

Flirting Eye doll purchased in Germany 40 years ago as gift to grand-daughter of president of Soo Chow University in China. Bisque arms and head, composition body, original blonde wig, brown eyes, 26" tall, marked "257 J. D. K. 64 Made In Germany Flirting Eye".

Head marked "J.D.K. 214", large crown sticker on chest. Two dolls in *center*, of type advertised in *Ladies Home Journal* Dec. 1910, featuring inset fur eyebrows: left, 21" jointed kid body, large trademark sticker on chest, head marked "Deo S 195"; right, 24" tall, fur eyebrows, original wig, head marked "K. Made in Germany 14 J.D.K. 215". *Right*, bisque head and forearms, unjointed kid body, cloth feet, probably oldest of dolls shown, 26" tall, marked "K" on head.   Photos by McNeill and Mabel Stokes

Another great Kestner success was the Bye-Lo Baby, introduced in 1924. Its popularity won for it the nickname "Million Dollar Baby." The first Bye-Lo Babies, with composition body and turning bisque head, proved expensive to produce and only a few were made. Then Mrs. Grace Story Putnam designed the Bye-Lo Baby which is more familiar today, with flange neck, soft cloth body, and outspread fingers. Mr. Kolb writes, "Regarding Bye-Lo, Borgfeldt controlled this item, and other factories besides Kestner made them." Though the Bye-Lo was imitated, Mrs. Putnam's dolls were all clearly marked.

The Gibson Girl, offered in 1900, was one of Kestner's outstanding dolls and is now considered the most valuable of all.

Kestner made at least one celluloid doll. According to Mr. Kolb, "Mr. Kestner had some models and dies made for a celluloid head which was produced for his exclusive use by the Rheinsche Gummi and Celloloid Fabrich." This doll was made up with celluloid head, hands, and feet, on a kid body, with the J.D.K. mark on the shoulder head, followed by numbers. This was one of the last types of doll manufactured by Kestner.

Two fine descriptions of Kestner dolls appeared as advertisements in mail-order catalogs. The one in Sears, Roebuck & Company's catalog for 1910 read:

"Our 'Dainty Dorothy' Brand
Made by the Celebrated
Kestner of Germany, the Peer of
All Doll Makers.

"Kestner, the manufacturer of this doll, is known for the excellence of manufacture, the fine quality features and the general superiority of

his dolls. His goods are the standard by which all others are judged. The heads are of absolutely the finest quality bisque with open mouth showing teeth, and moving eyes with natural eyelashes. Fitted with long curly wig, parted on the side and tied with a bow of good quality ribbon. Has papier-maché legs tinted in natural color fitted with good quality removable colored lace stockings and ribbon tied sandals to match. Best quality bisque forearm, riveted elbow, shoulder, hip and knee joints, allowing free movement of arms and legs. We buy these dolls direct from Germany and save at least one-third for you. This doll we guarantee to please for many years. Come in 5 sizes, each carefully packed for shipping.

18½"—$1.75
28" — 4.98"

The second advertisement is from Montgomery Ward's 1911 catalog:

"Koestner* Kid Body Doll

"This doll must be seen to be appreciated. The illustration does not begin to do it justice. It is the handsomest doll we could buy and sells at a much higher price retail. You will not be disappointed in this doll, it is well worth the price and with care will last indefinitely.

"Koestner's Patent Joint Kid body dolls cannot be shipped by mail. These dolls are made with extra fine quality kid, full formed, stout bodies, half cork stuffed, riveted hip and knee joints, composition arms with ball-jointed shoulder, elbow and wrist, large fine quality bisque head with teeth, moving eyes, eye-lashes and fine sewed wigs, fitted with shoes and stockings.

Length 23"—$4.25
28"— 6.60"

Koestner, Kostner variously appear, but Kestner is the correct spelling.

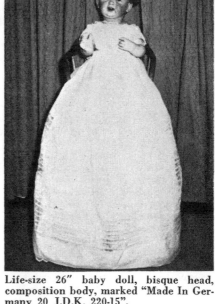

Life-size 26" baby doll, bisque head, composition body, marked "Made In Germany 20 J.D.K. 220-15".

Kestner dolls before 1891 are extremely difficult to identify and date, but fortunately some have a "K" marked on the head. The marking "Germany" or "Made in Germany," which appeared when 1891 import laws required, seemed to stimulate further identification. The Kestner crown trademark is one Mr. Kolb suggested that the manufacturer have registered in this country, and it was adopted on December 24, 1895. A paragraph in the application to the Trademark office reads: "The class of merchandise to which this trade-mark is appropriated is dolls, and the particular description of goods comprised in such class on which it is used is kid-body, bisque-head dolls." Various head markings are found in the accompanying picture captions.

Simon & Halbig — *Master Craftsmen*

by GENEVIEVE ANGIONE
Photographs by the Author.

SIMON & Halbig, in fifty or more years of operation in Thuringia, Germany, up through the 1920s, made millions of dolls, in wide variety, with many markings. They supplied all markets, from exclusive toyshops to peddler's pushcarts. It is not surprising that S&H dolls are found so frequently today, but the finer heads are few and far between.

At this late date one can only speculate about the vast difference in heads from the same factory. Some creative genius in the early days of the firm may have been responsible for a line of quality heads, or the designs and specifications may have come from customers. Many doll assemblers laid siege to the vast middle market between ordinary German dolls for the little girl gift trade and the much more expensive French dolls. Some modern collectors feel that the bisque clay was also supplied in some instances since many of the old heads are of a superlative quality when compared to German heads in general.

The good dolls are found in fractional proportion to the common type, but specimens available clearly indicate that extremely fine dolls were made by the firm from the very beginning. It is this *beginning* which cannot be pinpointed for S&H. All but one of the dolls discussed in this series on quality S&H dolls have swivel-necks, an invention credited to Emile Jumeau in the 1860s. Apparently this was not protected by patents, for both French and German firms followed his lead. Because the picture is so clouded, qualifying words such as "early" and "late" must always be interpreted with reference to the specific dolls under consideration.

Here, "early" and "old" bisque will refer to the type used in the 1860s and 1870s. (While this is old for swivel-necks, it is not old for original bisque shoulder heads, etc.) "Old" kid, on the other hand, is the thick, long-wearing type used in many kinds of bodies before and after 1860. The common, paper-thin kid, often used in combination with cheap cloth by the Germans in the 1890s and early 1900s is "late." (The Germans are accused of buying glove scraps and skins not of glove quality. The exquisite French kid cannot truly be dated at all.)

MELISSA is a 13″ German Fashion doll. The bisque is beautiful in both the swivel-necked head and the shoulder piece; the set eyes are threaded blue; the eyebrows are fine and shiny; the closed lips, painted to

---

Identifying S&H Dolls

In order to simplify this study, this skeleton outline is provided covering the dolls illustrated.

Shoulder heads, ears pierced thru head
Melany — S & H
Heidi — S 5 H

Swivel necks, bisque shoulder plates
Melissa — closed mouth, set eyes — S H 3 908
Melody — open mouth, sleep eyes — S 9 H 908

Swivel necks, composition bodies, closed mouths
Fran — paint eyes — 151 S&H 1
Olivia — set eyes — 719 S&H DEP
Olivia II — sleep eyes — 719 S&H DEP
Margie — set eyes — S 7 H 769 DEP
Laurel — set eyes — S 12 H 939
Laurie — set eyes — S 10 H 949
Sydney — sleep eyes — 1488 SIMON & HALBIG

Swivel necks, composition bodies, open mouths
Midge — set eyes — S&H 119 DEP
Mathilda — sleep eyes — S 15 H 939
Marlene — flirt eye walker — S.H. 1039 **Germany** DEP 7 ½
Carol — sleep eyes — 1079 1 ½ DEP S&H **Germany**
Celine — sleep eyes — 1079 S & H DEP 8
Celina — sleep eyes — 1079 S & H **Germany** DEP 8
Rhea — sleep eyes — S.H. 1079 14 ½ DEP
Lillian — sleep eye — 1159 S & H DEP 6
Ruby — sleep eyes — SIMON & HALBIG 1249 DEP **Germany** 7
Willie Lee — sleep eye — **Germany** SIMON & HALBIG S&H 6

---

look slightly parted, are a lovely rose color, complementing the rosy cheeks. The ears are pierced through the head, and the base of the neck is lined with kid, French style.

The bisque head is uncut, so Melissa has only a lightly incised line which would have been a cutting guide. The incised mark is close to this line and reads: S H 3, and under it, 908. This same mark is incised at the front base of her shoulder plate.

The shapely arms are bisque above the elbow, topped with scalloped kid and fastened to the drill upperarms. The fingers are slightly spread and each nail is indicated in rose color. The hips are machine sewn with red thread and the lower legs are attached by hand, with a covering braid band added, edged with rows of red stitching. The legs are back-seamed and the foot is made like the kid-body feet — a triangle of cloth forms the upper part and there is a separately sewn sole. No toes are indicated, however. The body is sawdust stuffed.

The original blonde mohair wig is thinning but is quite adequate. The tiny braids have been curled into buns

above her ears and are held in place with stitches through the gauze cap. She has been redressed.

MELODY, also a German Fashion, is a 25″ issue of the same doll. Offhand it would seem she is a later issue because her mouth is open, but the body, which appears to be original, is an old type. The bisque is of the type commonly called "greasy" because it shines even when dirty. The sleep eyes are threaded blue-gray with a dark outer rim and large pupils; the eyebrows are fine and very shiny; the open mouth has coral colored lips and two small, very square teeth, quite unlike the usual rounded German type. The nose is small and rounded and shows up well in this size. The ears are pierced through the lobes and appear to be applied although they do not have the telltale surrounding wafer of bisque found in French dolls.

Like Melissa, Melody is incised: S 9 H, and under it, 908. Her shoulder plate may also be marked but the kid has not been stripped off to verify that marking.

The top cut is completely out of the back half of the head so the forehead extends up to the top of the head. The original flat-bottomed head cork remains, with a glued-on cork plug at the base on the underside to keep it from slipping off. This may have been an early attempt at cutting the tops of the heads to lighten the shipping and import weight since no inside rim is provided on which to glue a cork or plaster or cardboard dome. Consequently the wig foundation had to be firm and deep and it was glued onto the bisque.

The heavy kid body is odd. The shoulder plate is glued to an underbody of cloth which extends to the waist. A kid "jacket" fits over the cloth body, with wide strips glued across the shoulder on each side to hold the head securely. At the waist, the cloth body is joined to the kid hip and abdominal section; the pinked upper jacket hangs free.

As in Melissa's small drill body, the lower legs are hand-sewn at the knee, but without any covering braid. The feet are made the same, but the toes are indicated in the kid with hand stitches. The arms are entirely of kid, hand-sewn across the elbow joint. The hands are hand-sewn from the outside, with each finger separate. The thumb is an added hand-sewn unit.

OLIVIA, an 18" jointed, also has an uncut head with the incised line to guide the cutter. Below the cutting line the mark is incised: S & H 719 DEP. (For the photograph, the line and the mark have been penciled to show clearly.)

The bisque is good but of a dull variety; the brown eyes are set; the closed mouth is a deeper tone of the cheek color; the chin has a dimple. As

MELISSA

in the first two dolls, the nose is rounded and childish. The ears are thick, appear to be applied, and are pierced through the lobes.

Above the cutting line the head has been left white, but it has a depressed area about the size of a quarter instead of the rounded top like Melissa. A hole at the back of the depression, about the size of a pencil, may have fit over a peg which held it upright

in the kiln. It seems to be too small for the hank mohair type of wig used on cheaper dolls with cardboard domes. Her present real hair wig is a replacement.

Because this head was broken, the holes above the ears have been used to string the doll. The elastic cord is attached to a loop in the wire at the base of the neck. The wire extends up through the head, out the side holes,

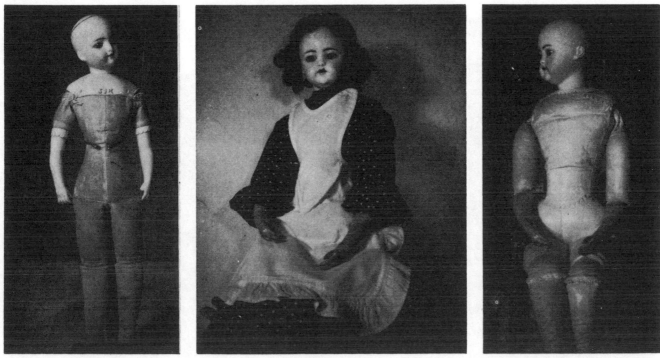

MELISSA   MELODY   MELODY

and is then twisted together on top and flattened. This technique makes a sturdy doll with no strain on the neck hole.

LAURIE, 18″, another doll with a beautiful "greasy" bisque head, has set brown eyes like Olivia's, closed mouth and cheeks of a lovely color, ears pierced through the lobes, and the cute little rounded nose.

The mark is just below the head cut: S 10 H, and below it, 949.

Like Melody, her forehead extends to the top of her head, but she is a later doll because she has the familiar inside rim around the top of her head to which a dome could be glued. In this case, however, the opening has a cork which is cut like the French doll corks, and it fits down into the head to prevent slipping.

The wig may not be original although it fits so perfectly to the cork and to the head it could have been a "special order." The foundation is toupé cloth and the naturally curly light brown hair still retains its ability to curl tighter in damp weather. The fine jointed body was cut in half for the insertion of a "talker" box; the pull strings come through the metal-bound holes in the left abdomen.

MIDGE, 20″, is included because she may be another variation of Olivia. The mark below the head cut is S&H 119, with DEP below it, indicating that she, too, was made for export. Midge has an open mouth, which accounts for the puffier cheeks, but she has the slight double chin, the dimple, the same kind of thick ears, pierced through the lobes, and the same small, rounded nose. The bisque in this head, however, is different and, we think, later. It is not soft and smooth like a hard type of paste, but hard with a crispness.

MIDGE

In her picture, the mouth appears to be closed, but it is an early open mouth, before perfection of the technique which narrowed the face and spread the lips so the teeth could be seen. Other early open mouths, made by other manufacturers, had this same fault. Apparently it was a problem common to all dollmakers.

The fact that the number on Midge is 119 and on Olivia it is 719 is worth mention. Molds were very expensive and were used as long as possible. We have come to identify *dolls* by these numbers, but it is entirely possible that S&H identified *customers* by incised numbers. In all these dolls the marks are in a form of script and done very lightly. In later dolls the marks are deep and clear-cut in print form.

OLIVIA, left and below.

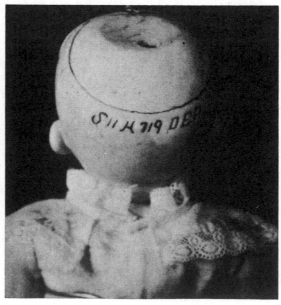

LAURIE

| CELINE | CELINA | RHEA |

CELINE, 20 inches, is a fine example of a lovely old doll. She has enormous threaded blue sleep eyes; eyebrows diagonally ridged in the bisque and beautifully painted; pierced ears; full cheeks; full upper lip; deep chin dimple; and a soft, childish double chin.

She is marked up at the head cut rim: 1079. Below that, S&H (in script), then DEP and below it, the size figure, 8.

Although she resembles some of the old, closed-mouth S&H dolls, there are two "new" features besides the open mouth. The old dolls did not have the molded-in eyebrow ridges. Also she has the two holes on either side of the figure 8 in the back of her neck through which strings to tie the eyes protruded. This simple safeguard on sleep-eye dolls reduced breakage in shipping, especially on the rough ocean passage to America.

CELINA, 20 inches, has the same markings in the same places, but with the addition of *Germany* in italics just above the tie holes. This definitely dates her after 1895.* This mold, then, had been used before, but if Celina had been purchased by markings alone by a collector who had admired Celine, she would have proved disappointing. Why aren't the two dolls twins? Why is the old one so unusual, the later one so ordinary? We can only study, compare, and guess a little.

Celine is made of very fine bisque. The old clay may have shrunk less in the kiln and, quite likely, more time was allowed for the initial drying in the greenware state before it encountered the heat. Surely the entire production was better—her coloring is delicate and appealing; the eyebrow painting is beautifully done on the French order; the eyes are much larger and of better quality; and her original red-brown mohair wig, which matches the eyebrow color, is still in adequate condition. It is entirely possible that this doll was made in Germany for some French firm or for sale

in France by some German wholesale firm which competed on their own ground with the more expensive French dolls. There is no doubt of her origin, but we cannot now determine her original destination.

Celina, on the other hand, is of poorer quality bisque. Either the clay shrunk of its own accord, or production speed-ups in the early 1900s sent the head to the kiln too damp. The coloring is the late type generally referred to as "high" because the whole face has a deeper flush than the old dolls, and the cheeks are consequently more dollish than human. The eyebrows are plain, the eyes are smaller and a very common threaded blue. The upper lip is not full enough. This defect pulls the mouth too far open, exposes too much of the four teeth, and leaves toothless gaps at each side. Her wig, a replacement, offers no basis for comparison.

With all this in mind, let's consider the next doll, Rhea. Fortunately this was a one-owner plaything and was purchased direct from the woman who had cherished her many years. Rhea was brought from Paris in 1901 by fond grandparents for the only little girl in the family. They were very anti-German, even then, and Rhea was always referred to as "the big French doll." But is she?

RHEA, 31 inches, is marked high up under her wig: S.H./1079/ 14½, and then, down in the middle of her neck, DEP. The wig covers the factory mark and only DEP shows.

There is no doubt that this doll fulfilled her destiny as an export product. Comparison with other 1079 S.H. dolls shows many points of superior production. Special attention was given her pretty open mouth, and the lips appear to be painted by hand instead of through a masking stencil. The large brown sleep-eyes are of good quality and the eyebrows are ridged in the bisque as are Celine's. The ears are pierced. The wig is worthy of special mention. It is extra-

ordinarily thick, and the ash blond mohair curls have not gone limp. (The child was not permitted to comb it, though the doll was a constant companion for years.)

The body is perfect and is of excellent quality, with large extra shoulder balls between the arm socket and the upper arm, which add an attractive width to the shoulders. The bisque helps the doll detective. It is not quite as fine as that used in Celine's head, but it is superior to that used for Celina's. Like Celine though, Rhea has no *Germany* incised in her mark.

These comparisons uphold the widely-held theory that many French firms had doll heads made in Germany from French clay, and that bodies were also made there to French specifications. These S&H dolls are definitely, completely German. There are many instances, however, of so-called "French" dolls purchased by visitors to Paris which are half-and-half.

One local doll whose history is thoroughly authenticated has a marked Jumeau body and a German head. The wig is still so firmly glued to the bisque that the marking cannot be checked, but the same doll has passed through our hands several times on German bodies and with different marks. Besides having the same face, these dolls had two other things in common: lovely thick ash blond wigs like Rhea's, and plaster domes instead of the common cardboard type. Our records show that two were marked: N / 17 / Made in Germany; and K / 1/2 / Made in Germany, plus size numbers. All of them were of high quality bisque with Celine's pretty coloring, and the wigs were glued onto the bisque rather than on the plaster domes so that the country of origin was not obvious. We have never had one on a Jumeau body, but all the bodies have been the best German quality, and all have been finished in the light yellow color found on many of the old unmarked

French bodies.

CAROL, 10 inches, has Celina's head in a small size, without tie holes and with all of her poor production qualities as compared to Celine and Rhea. The wig is the one exception. Because it is so small, it may have been made from the leavings of the better wigs. The mohair is superior to Celine's, but not as pale blond as Rhea's. Even in this small size, however, the ears are pierced—not a popular fashion in dolls in the 1900s.

If the body is original, which it appears to be, she could be one of the early dolls which complied with the "country of origin" law on American imports. The body is wristless; the elbow and knee balls are incorporated in the lower limbs; the neck socket, upper arms and thighs are of wood, and the color is the high quality pale yellow with tinted knees.

WILLIE LEE, 18 inches, is not common. The baked-on color is pitch black; the sleep-eyes are rather flat and dark brown; the eye wax is also colored very close to black. This is not a "white" doll painted, as many of the brown ones are. The features are African, with a wide nose, short upper lip, and a very wide, full mouth. The six teeth are small, like those used by the French, and may be the one real clue she carries with her.

The mark is: Germany / SIMON & HALBIG / S&H / 6, and is mostly covered by the wig cap.

This particular doll is not an early issue. The firm name is written out above the initials used on the old dolls; the word *Germany* appears; and she has the two holes, on either side of the number, through which the eyes were tied. The body is late.

It is quite possible, however, that the old mold, with just S&H / 6 was made for some French firm which exported to the French African colonies. The additional information could have been added to comply with our laws when it was re-issued. The great popularity of the Aunt Jemima, Cream of Wheat's Rastus, and other Negro rag dolls may have prompted this bit of competition in bisque. At this late date it is difficult to come to precise conclusions.

The soft black mohair wig is original and tends to fall into little locks with no kink in the hair at all. The body is enameled pitch black and is an ordinary German jointed without the wooden parts found in the fine old bodies.

Germany had a firm hold on the doll industry for many years, and it was mainly German dolls that filled the holds of ships in such ports as New York and Philadelphia. This top place in world trade was originally built on a price advantage through the "cottage industry" system, which flourished in Thuringia. Most of the work was farmed out on a family piecework basis. No family, and in

CAROL

many instances, no village, made complete dolls — precluding bootlegging of parts which could be combined and sold in competition with the master firm. Materials were parceled out with meticulous care and any spoilage deducted from the payment.

The always independent French, on the other hand, would have nothing to do with this system, even though it meant thousands of imports from Germany to cut into French employment. From the earliest days of cooperative industrial work, the French employer had to provide a shop or factory, and the workers went home at night without a care. This difference of opinion about employment added mightily to the antagonism between the two countries.

One of the results of the relentless international competition was the combining of French companies. In France in 1899, they eventually tried to save the doll and toy industry on a national basis by forming the S.F.B.J. firm in which the companies pooled their assets. In Germany, however,

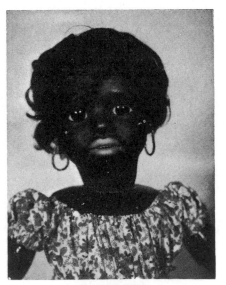

WILLIE LEE

the effort was strictly competitive and individual. Small firms died out and the giants grew bigger— notably S&H.

* With these dolls, we encounter the "country of origin" law, passed by the United States in 1891. There was, as always, an interim for compliance, here creating a twilight zone for some of the bisque head dolls. It is generally believed that the first dolls to comply with this law were stamped. The odd placement of the word *Germany* in some heads is good evidence that their makers immediately added the words to heads already in production. Speedy handling through U. S. Customs could mean an important sales advantage. However, no one knows how many thousands of completed dolls, warehoused abroad, or in transit, or piled in our retail store stockrooms, escaped stamping. (Some firms used stickers, which soon washed off.)

There is much evidence, too, supporting the theory that many firms, proud of fine workmanship, particularly in the bisque shoulder heads, marked them "Germany" before the law required it. Thus is confusion compounded. The word *Germany* incised in the bisque of a swivel head dates it after 1891, but the lack of it does not necessarily place it prior to that date. If *Germany* is hidden under the glued-down kid shoulder pieces on a shoulder head, the date is variable; but if it is clearly in sight above the kid edge, then 1891 is the earliest possible date to allow it—most likely it is later.

As with many other German doll firms, mystery surrounds the early days of S&H. Records that might pinpoint the beginnings of this busy factory have succumbed to wars, and to time itself. Collectors, to determine the firm's production, must turn to the study and comparison of available dolls. Too often they think only in terms of its later Simon & Halbig days. The older S&H dolls with the delicately incised script initials are unimpeachable witnesses, with or without time specifications. Some, like Melany, show close relationship to dolls of later date or different size.

Melany is 13 inches tall, with a 3½ inch shoulder head, lightly incised S&H, in the usual position on the lower front edge of the plate. The ears are exposed and pierced through the head. The painted blue eyes are convex; the eyebrows a single stroke of medium brown. The old red eyeline is very fine; in place of lashes, the top lids are outlined in jet black. The yellow hair, drawn back from the brow without a part, falls into nicely molded locks at the shoulders in back. A black "Alice" band crosses the center skull to the ear tops. There are four sew holes.

The bisque is pale, peachy pink, dry and dull in texture, not at all like the pale smooth bisque of the later Melissa. Their bodies, however, prove Melany and Melissa are sisters beyond doubt.

These two dolls are the same size; both have cloth bodies and above-

MELANY; the two Melanys together; MINIATURE MELANY, pictured just ½" less than actual size.

elbow bisque arms which are rouged at knuckles and elbows. The arms are attached from the inside to the cloth arm tops, and the hands are cupped. (Melissa's fingernails are outlined, Melany's are not.)

This early sawdust-stuffed body, made of sized cotton instead of the later tough drill, is also center-seamed back and front to provide a smooth, shaped waist at the sides. The legs are seamed in back, attached by hand at the base of the body and sewn by hand at the knees. Besides the type of material used in their manufacture, the bodies show another unusual feature — the use of kid scraps. Melissa's arms are kid capped; Melany has kid feet. Seamed only in the back, the kid is machine-sewn to the leg ends; the soles are overcast to the feet without any toes indicated.

Recently a miniature shoulder head in the author's collection was discovered to be a Melany infinitely reduced. The head is only ⅞ inch; the entire factory-made doll, 3½ inches tall. The "Alice" band, the hair-do, and coloring are alike; only the sew holes and pierced ears are missing in the tiny one.

For those who only vaguely understand bisque casting, a word of explanation. The model for a new doll head is generally made in a large size; not only is it easier to work in these proportions, but molds can decrease the head to any desired size, but cannot be used to increase the size. Every mold produces a smaller head than the head from which it was made. Surprisingly few successive molds are required to bring a head of human proportions down to doll size; from doll size to miniature is an even shorter process. Shrinkage of all

materials in each state of the work makes the difference.

This process accounts for several things collectors notice in dolls; it is also responsible for noticeable differences in beautifully made reproductions when they are compared with the originals. An old miniature may bear a haunting resemblance to a large doll, but features such as comb marks, manufacturers' incised marks, and convex eyes disappear in the smaller editions. This cannot be helped. Every cook knows that a greased and floured pan will deliver a perfect cake. It takes a smooth mold to deliver a good head. Plaster of Paris forms a silken smooth surface next to the object being molded. To re-etch comb marks or to touch up trademarks would break the required smooth surface and the heads would not release freely from such molds. Inasmuch as the bisque slip is only "set," not hardened, when it leaves the mold, additional handling outside the mold is not practical.

Who made the tiny Melany? Nobody knows, but the economy and fantastic drive against waste in German factories points directly at S&H. The cloth in her body is excellent and far superior to the crude, sized, pink cotton used in so many later small dolls. Undoubtedly this is scrap material which was either purchased for a song or, more likely, left over from some other S&H doll operation.

Another slightly larger china head miniature in the author's collection, of a known pre-1850 date, has a body of similar material.

The doll industry of the 1880s left almost no records to indicate the obstacles it met and the means it took to sur-

mount them. Rather our heritage has been a profusion of puzzles, mysteries, and problems.

S&H seems to have spanned almost the whole period of German bisque doll head manufacture, from shoulder heads through the multi-marked swivel-necked heads of the late 1920s. There are samples of every kind and quality of bisque in the heads still available; there is every style and type of feature painting, every head cut, dome, wig, eyes, teeth; bodies are myriad.

We know many dolls with S&H marks embodied features that were covered by both French and German patents. Common sense indicates, even at this distance in time, that no firm could have transgressed industrial and national lines in such a public business as doll manufacturing without authority from patent holders. The doll Marlene, shown here, is a case in point; she appears to combine patent features from both countries.

MARLENE is a 17-inch, swivel neck, flirty-eye, bisque-headed walker, incised SH (in script) — 1039 — Germany — DEP — ½.

The face has the "high" coloring generally associated with the later dolls, but the ears are pierced. The snappy brown eyes have lashes of thread, or something other than hair. The thick, light blond mohair wig is original and of the old construction. The open mouth shows four small French-type upper teeth.

The body is beyond question original and not the usual German construction. The arms are bent and in one piece, with swivel-top, French-style hands. The head is attached only by means of a hook to the arm rubber, a necessity which undoubtedly accounts for the unjointed elbows. The unbroken span of rubber holds the head well.

The trunk is cut off at the lower third; the legs are straight with open tops, and the area between the body and the legs is covered with kidskin panties glued to the base of the torso and to each leg top. The body color is very much like the Jumeau undercoat but without the cinnamon-speckled Jumeau varnish finish. This varnish is colorless.

The walker mechanism is a key-wind clockworks type with the winder shaft protruding from the left side of the body and through an opening in the kid. The mechanism seems to be a copy of or an adaptation from the Roullet & E. Decamps Patent #222661, of June 28, 1892, described by Luella Hart in her studies on French patents.

The chief point of the patent is that the weight of the head and body, when the doll is standing on her feet, releases the brake on the spinner so that the spring can go into operation. The main portion of the mechanism is attached to the inside back wall of the torso; rods on each side of it extend down into and are fastened to the inside of the legs.

Side-by-side comparison of this S&H with her much larger R.D. companion indicates that the German doll is possibly a simplified or refined version of the French patent. The chief visible points of difference are that the R.D. winds from the right side of the doll and the leg attachment is more complicated. The original patent calls for attachment of the rods to half a ball joint at the top of each leg. In the patent sketches, the inner half of the ball top is shown cut away, but in the doll itself, it is the outer half that has been removed and the attachment made to the inner side of the crotch half of the ball. In the German doll, the entire ball joint has been removed and the rods enter the hollow tops of the legs.

The changes in mechanism in the S&H are typical of German engineering ingenuity and would materially reduce costs. On the R.D. doll, the company initials are incorporated in the key design, whereas the German key has an open top. No date can be found on the R.D. example used in comparison; the head may be a replacement, so it is of no help. But the R.D. could have been made in the late 1880s while the patent was pending. The registration of the patent in 1892 ties in with the S&H; her ears are pierced, while the head is marked "Germany" and also DEP to cover export to France.

The flirty-eye mechanism, apparently of German patent, deserves special mention. The eyes are suspended on a hard wire which hangs from the top of the forehead. The wire is held in place by a string tied through a small

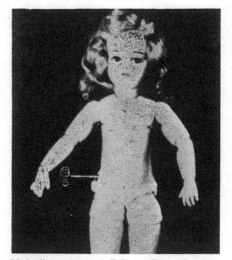

Midriff section of R.D. walker showing key on right side, R.D. initials on key design.

hole in the bisque which is covered by the front of the wig. There is a cork imbedded in plaster on each wall of the head to absorb the shock of the freely shifting eye bar. From her files, Dorothy S. Coleman, of Washington, D. C., kindly supplied the information that in German patent records under the year 1890, she has found an S&H patent registered for "right and left moving eyes."

That is a good description of Marlene's eyes but, once again, they are a forward step from the original patent. The pinhole in the bisque caused breakage in the assembly line and lead to various other patents covering self-contained flirty-eye mechanisms which could be used in any head.

With all this information, the questions still pile up. Did S&H make the walker for the patent owner, or for a lessee, or for their own distribution? Was she made in other versions than this pseudo-French style? Was she made after or simultaneously with the original? Did all of them have S&H flirty eyes?

One thing is certain—in this model her German origin was disguised enough to mislead the casual doll buyer, and her wig covered her German mark so completely it could not be easily found.

A larger doll like Marlene is illustrated and described in *Dolls of Three Centuries,* by Eleanor St. George. Apparently her wig had not been removed because she is not identified as S&H or by the number 1039.

The second doll illustrated here is another puzzle. The body is not original because the head is not properly seated in the neck hole as it would be in a factory assembled doll. The head, however, is all that concerns us.

MATHILDA: This head has a 13½ inch circumference; the face is quite long, measuring 5¾ inches from top of head to chin. It is incised close to the head cut: S 15 H-939. The dark brown sleep eyes have long thick, hair

lashes and the eyebrows are painted in a Jumeau manner. There are six small, French-style upper teeth in the open, rather bee-stung mouth the French admire. The ears are pierced.

The face tinting is very even and pleasing, more flesh colored than the customary pink-and-rose G e r m a n combination. The bisque is also very unusual for a so-called German doll. It is thick and coarse, closely resembling the coloring, textures, and density of bisque used in an old, all original and unmistakably French doll, Mary-Jo, in the author's collection, which predates marking of any kind. There is, in fact, such similarity that Mary-Jo's head now appears to be one of the old French doll heads long suspected of German manufacture.

Mathilda's wig is original and in excellent condition. It is the old bronze-brown m o h a i r, still well curled. The lining is very deep, extending below the ears, and the inside is still heavily coated with dark glue of the type used in furniture making.

These two dolls, Marlene and Mathilda, have similar dimpled double chins, the same rounded noses, and a definite resemblance. Could it be that the numbers 939 and 1039 are not a coincidence? If 39 was the identification S&H used for the French firm for whom they were made, the 939 of Mathilda would date her in the 1880s, where she seems to belong, and the 1039 would place Marlene in the early 1890s, borne out by the added "Germany" on her head along with the pierced ears which were soon after to be out of style. Mrs. Coleman's date of 1890 for the flirty eye patent adds further date proof.

Carefully compiled records of doll markings and other characteristics reveal many things when they are cross referenced. A doll marked 839 or 1139 would surely help to stabilize the tentative background of these two types. Since company records are not available, we have little alternative but to reconstruct them for our own information, and then share them with all "dollers."

Lillian: 18 inches, with brown sleep eyes which have heavily waxed lids and thick blonde thread eyelashes, she has an open mouth with four tiny teeth, pierced ears with original blue earrings, and she has her original cheap cotton factory made shift. Incised in four lines down the back of her head: 1159 S & H (in script) DEP 6, with the two eye-tie holes on either side of the size number. The bisque is the later dull type.

Her upswept blonde human hair wig is a German replacement; her clothes are new.

Her body, however, is not padded at all. She has the high molded bust, the narrow waist and molded hips commonly associated with the Gibson Girl figure. But the body is a puzzler. It is in pristine condition; almost the color of a Jumeau body but without

LILLIAN

LILLIAN'S HAIR

OLIVIA II

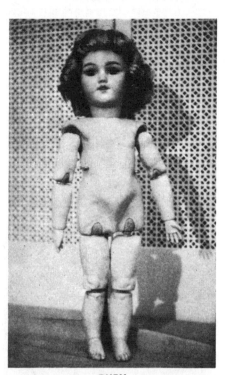

RUBY

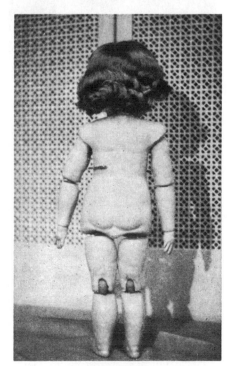

BACK DETAIL

the cinnamon flecks in the paint. The hands are very German, both in shape and in the decorative nail and knuckle painting. Compared side by side with a marked Jumeau body with the same bust, waist, and hips, this body has the long-limbed appearance of a young woman, whereas the Jumeau appears to be a developed teenager.

This is the body sometimes referred to as the "pregnant" doll, a misnomer if ever there was one. It has all the appeal of the "swan body," so admired in the Gibson era.

The tiny teeth, the French button-on-a-wire earrings, the incised DEP, and the body color all point to at least a partial French market for this attractive young lady.

Olivia II: 20″ tall, she is incised around the head cut: S & H (in script) 719 DEP. She has a closed mouth, heavy French eyebrows, large threaded blue sleep eyes with heavily waxed lids and pierced ears. Because her original dome and wig were re-

moved, it is impossible to tell whether or not she had the plaster dome so often used when the heads were first cut to reduce the import duty which was figured by weight. She has a German jointed body of good quality, but whether it is original is not known.

The first Olivia was pictured and described in the December '62 issue.

Although she is considerably larger than Olivia with the uncut head, the faces are exactly alike and the bisque is of the same superior type. Through an accident of workmanship her eye holes were cut rather wide and it gives her a sweet, childish look. The original Oliva's eye holes are small in proportion and that, plus dark brown eyes, gives her the quizzical look collectors admire without knowing exactly why.

Ruby: 16-inches, incised in five lines down the back of her head, SIMON & HALBIG 1249 DEP Germany 7, with the eye-tie holes on each side of the size figure. Of the eight dolls in this series, Ruby alone has "Germany" in her mark.

The face is much the same as Celina's 1079 (S.W. Jan.-Feb. '63) except that it has the molded eyebrows. The molded eyebrows *did* appear on the earlier Celine, however, which was also marked 1079. Both Ruby and Celina are of the later, harder type bisque.

It is the body which is especially interesting. Every dollmaker dreamed of the truly indestructible doll; many have advertised such a doll, yet none of them really wanted such a thing because it would automatically reduce their sales of replacements. This might be one of those dreams.

To tool up for this radical departure from ordinary doll body construction must have cost a small fortune. The patent information is not available in the author's files, but either someone high up in the doll business invented this body or was completely sold on it because it eliminated piecework stringing. It would be interesting to find some of

the original advertising for this one!

The most appealing feature of this body is the shoulder formation, surely a boon to the doll dressmaker. In this body the shoulder measures 1¾ inches from the neck to the outer edge, and the overhang is so pronounced that sleeves would not readily get caught in the joint. Because the rubber ball joints have hardened through the years, it is impossible now to determine just how much lifelike action the body had.

The exaggerated abdominal molding, as well as the odd shape of the thigh might have been necessary in order to hold the inserted balls in place. Movable hard stems with a shaped top protrude from the leg, thigh, forearm, and upper arm sections. These tops were fitted into the hollow rubber ball joints and the rubber appears to have been anchored in place.

La belle France slips into the picture when the legs are examined. The lower legs closely resemble the shape of many French doll legs, and the feet are certainly not German at all. They are narrow, dainty and straight edged under the arch. German doll shoes fit poorly but French shoes fit admirably.

It is interesting to note that another one of these dolls is on display at Maretta Wilcox's Doll and Toy Museum in Bergen, New York. It has the same SIMON & HALBIG 1249 head and is also a size 7. It is quite possible, in order to test the sales appeal of this body, it was only made in this one size. Reports of larger or smaller duplicates would be most helpful.

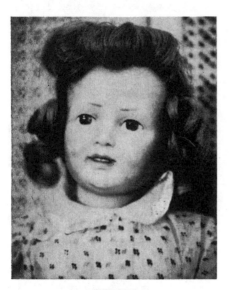

FRAN

FRAN: This 18-inch girl is a most unusual type for Simon and Halbig. The 3-line incised mark on the middle of her head is simply: 151 S & H 1. She has brown painted eyes of a generous size with unexpected one-stroke blonde eyebrows. The pretty open-closed mouth has four small teeth painted in, her cheeks have deep dimples, and a little round chin bone is indicated. The bisque is the finest "greasy" type and the coloring is delightful. Like Sydney, she has a high, flat head cut which requires a very small dome.

The blonde human hair wig and the German jointed body are replacements but in good proportion and the neck hole is exactly right for the swivel neck.

Since nothing seems to be known about this head, only one note in

passing—many infant collectors will recognize "151" as an identification often used for baby dolls credited to Kestner. But these infants have both open and closed mouths, all bisque heads or cut heads with mohair wigs, and all of them seem to have glass eyes, either set or sleeping, with the usual shaped and feathered eyebrow painting.

Like Sydney also, Fran is one of the few S&H dolls without the number "9" in her mark.

LAUREL

LAUREL: 19-inch, closed mouth, set threaded vivid blue eyes, heavy French-type eyebrows and pierced ears. Incised in two lines on the center back of the head, S 12 H 939. This is the glowing, greasy bisque with excellent tinting in soft colors.

The wristless jointed body is the pale yellow color and construction often found on German dolls for the French trade. Many doll collectors are convinced these bodies were made in France because the hands are especially un-German. Large, chubby, childish hands are a French doll characteristic, whereas most German dolls have "doll" hands which are quite out of proportion even in the 36- and 48-inch sizes. Laurel has closed fingers which are so much more practical than the open-fingered German doll hand.

Head Especially Interesting

The head is especially interesting because it is almost an exact duplicate of Olivia's but with a different number. It is uncut; like Olivia's, the cutting line is incised, the complexion paint stops at the cutting line, and there is the same depressed area at the top with the same pencil-sized hole.

Laurel came with her original stringing roughly intact and she has been restrung following the old pat-

tern. Stout cord comes out the holes above each ear, crosses the bulge of the head and goes down into the larger hole in the crown. The cords extend down into the body after being knotted firmly. A single piece of leg rubber crosses this tied loop and the leg wires are closed over the raw rubber ends.

This brings up an interesting speculation. Rubber was doubtless expensive since it had to be imported. Twine was a common, cheap commodity. This method of stringing eliminated costly wires as well as much elastic yardage because the rubber was cut after the leg wires were closed on each doll and this prevented any waste whatever. Is this a fine example of French "economy"?

Belton-type fanciers will also notice that this head is similiar in many ways to those mysterious creations.

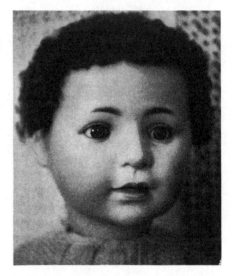

SYDNEY

SYDNEY: 23 inches, blue sleep eyes, closed mouth, incised: 1488 and the familiar SIMON & HALBIG in large letters level with the ear lobes. Directly below the lettering, in the center of the neck, there is an oval hole in the head instead of the commoner tie holes for the eyes. The head is almost full bisque of excellent texture, with only a comparatively small top piece removed. Like so many S&H dolls, there are ⅛-inch holes in the bisque up close to the cut line. They must have been provided for stringing wires or cords which eliminated the usual neck plug; they are too small to hold the stabilizing bar for a walking mechanism.

The wig is short reddish curls of fur on animal hide. Although it fits well it undoubtedly is not original because the glue does not match particles attached to the bisque. From the hatch lines on this head glue, the original wig must have been the typical German mohair on a gauze backing usual to this type.

The hole in the back of the head may indicate that this was made by S&H for someone else. The oval hole measures ¾-inch in length and ⅝-inch in width, which is quite large enough to carry an incised mark belonging to some other firm. This method has been observed before. A bisque "cookie" of the proper size and shape was incised with the required mark and kiln fired with a thin bisque rim all around so that it could be glued firmly in place.

Was It a Stock Head?

The speculation naturally arises: was this a stock head belonging to S&H, or was it made from molds owned by one or more smaller firms, each of which wanted its own mark fastened in that oval hole? S&H could have reserved the right to market a given number themselves or any which were not paid for in a stated period.

If Sydney's body is original, and that is a big IF, even though it is almost mint, it just contributes to the mystery. This particular toddler jointed body with the very short thigh pieces has been found many times on dolls with Heubach-Koppelsdorf heads. However, it is not likely that such an old porcelain manufacturer would have had to turn to S&H for production.

HEIDI

HEIDI: 15 inches tall, is another high quality shoulder head lightly marked on the edge of the front plate (in script), S 5 H. She has a closed mouth, blue sleep eyes with heavily waxed lids and ears pierced through the head.

The sawdust stuffed cloth body is stiff legged with the knees indicated only by large stitches; the above-elbow bisque arms have rather large, almost open hands. The head is high cut, and the old blonde mohair wig is done in two braids in back.

This doll appears to be in almost original condition. The huge black silk taffeta bow is attached to a tiny round black velvet cap. There is a white blouse with lace trimmed cuffs under the tight-fitting, laced black velvet bodice which is trimmed at the top with sequins and metalic thread embroidery. The large over-collar buttons in front and is trimmed with the same lace as the cuffs. It also has a twill tape harness which fits under the arms and ties in back to hold it firmly in place over the bosom. The plain red wool shirt is just gathered at the waist and braid trimmed at the hem.

She wears long pants, a petticoat, stockings of lacy weave, and black slippers without ties, all of which appear to be factory made.

MARGIE

MARGIE: 16-inch, this little girl is incised in one line along the head rim: S 7 H (in script) 769 DEP. She has a closed mouth, set brown eyes, pierced ears with the familiar holes above each just below the rim. The bisque and the decorating are both fine. Her forehead extends up to the top of her head and the cut is rather steep on the diagonal. The light brown old mohair wig is over a cardboard dome.

The German jointed body has more torso and abdominal shaping than the later German bodies but the wristed hands are German. Like Laurel, she has the heavy eyebrows so much admired by the French, and a tightly glued wig would have hidden her Teutonic origin from French shoppers.

If her clothes are original they were a special dressing job because her brown velvet coat is lined and her little brown velvet hat is trimmed with the same brown and gray checked taffeta from which her dress is made.

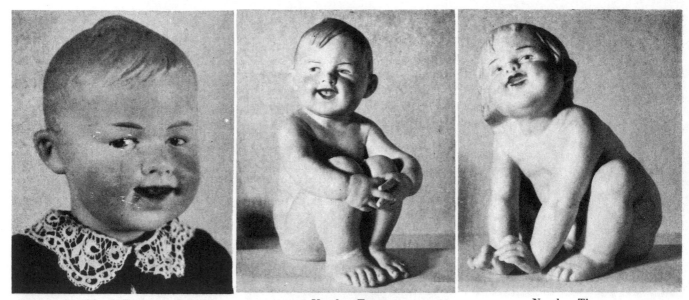

No. 1, Lenny   Number Two   Number Three

THE BROTHERS HEUBACH

by GENEVIEVE ANGIONE

What can be said in the United States about a firm established in a German hamlet in 1820? Records are understandably very sketchy and not too many people really care about it.

In *Dolls, Makers and Marks,* Elizabeth Coleman says Jean Paul and his brother, Ernest Christian Conrad Heubach, may have been "later owners" but they were young boys in 1820. The trade address was Sonneberg, but the actual factory was in Lichte, near Wallendorf, north and west of Sonneberg. Like its neighbor, Koppelsdorf, Sonneberg was close to the old Bavarian border and, presumably, to necessary transportation.

Doll collectors can thank German pride in workmanship, industrial competition, and the law for the markings which help to identify the much wanted dolls and piano babies at this

late date. Apparently very little left the Gebruder Heubach factory without being marked in one or several distinctive ways, both incised and stamped.

Heubach Marks

Fig. 1 seems to be the traditional marking and the combined G H initials in the lower half of the disc is quite definite. At times this trademark is found in combination with *Fig. 2,* the Heubach square, to form an oblong which is often minute in size but unmistakable.

The peculiar lettering of "Germany" in *Fig. 3* is also unquestionably a Heubach mark. Just as clowns never copy the make-up designs which identify their fellow showmen, even though these designs are not formally copyrighted, the German dollmakers honored the markings of their com-

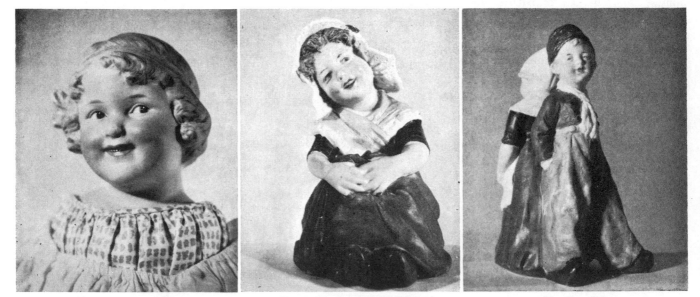

No. 4, Smiling Girl   No. 5, Smiling Dutch Girl   Number Six

Fig. One   **Fig. Two**

Germany

Fig. Three

petitors. Heubach incised deeply, and although some doll heads have only a size mark and this odd "Germany", countless comparisons of faces, hair molding, intaglio eyes, etc. leave no doubt about their origin.

A fourth mark, stamped on some heads and some figurines, is a small circle with MADE IN GERMANY in modern print between the two rings which form the circle. In most instances this circle is printed in the same shade of vivid green used by the workmen to mark some of the heads for piecework payments (like the red Jumeau workmen markings). There are instances, however, where the circle, printed in red, is combined with the *Fig. 1* mark. So, either green or red is authentic, combined with any of the three incised marks or with just the size figure.

To the best of available knowledge, the Gebruder Heubach firm had nothing whatsoever to do with the Heubach-Koppelsdorf porcelain w o r k s . Hearsay has it that the Heubach of Koppelsdorf was the brother-in-law of Armand Marseille. Fact or fancy, actual comparison of the workmanship of these two companies settles the argument. "A Heubach" is a Gebruder Heubach, and "a Heubach-Koppelsdorf" is just that.

Gebruder Heubach dolls are cherished by many collectors (the late Martha Thompson, for instance) because they frequently appear to be miniature portraits of real children rather than commercial dolls. Collectors have long suspected, too, that the Brothers Heubach, perhaps with a fine sense of economy peculiar to Germans, used some heads not only for figurines and piano babies but for dolls as well. Through the years rather conclusive proof of this has been accumulated.

Lenny

No. 1, Lenny — 4 inch swivel head with an 8¾ circ., incised in three lines: 5/79 Heubach square 11/ Germany. Fine grade, heavy bisque; intaglio eyes with molded highlight dot, blue iris; open mouth; one-stroke eyebrows in light brown; nicely molded hair tinted lighter brown.

No. 2 and *No. 3*—Lenny's face on an appealing piano baby boy and the same face with hair remolded for a little girl. These came in several sizes, commonly ranging from 4 to 5 inches up to 12 inches in ordinary sizes, judging from the specimens found. All had the incised disc, *Fig. 1*, sometimes augmented by a printed red or green circle to conform to the country-of-origin law.

Smiling Girl

No. 4, Smiling Girl — 5½ inch shoulder head with a 10 inch circumference above the bow, incised in two lines: the Heubach disc, Germany/ 1850. Stamped in green to the left of the incised Germany is the figure 58. Two smaller heads, 3½ inches high with 6 inch circumference, have incised figures 75 or 78 in place of the stamped green 58. Same general description as Lenny; these hair bands and bows can be either blue or pink.

The Smiling Girl is most commonly found as a shoulder head, ranging up to 6 inches or better. However, the head was also issued in a swivel neck up to tennis ball size.

Smiling Dutch Girl

No. 5, Smiling Dutch Girl—One of a pair of seated 6½ inch figurines, this face is strikingly similar to the doll above, with the head more tilted and the hair remolded at the front of the bonnet. Both the girl and her seated boy companion are incised with the disc but have no "Germany" mark, so presumably the figurines came first. They were also issued as a standing, back-to-back unit, *No. 6*.

Reference should be made to the difference in the quality of dolls and figurines or piano babies. Old timers talk about "the cry of the bisque." This is a hollow, slightly screeching sound which is produced when a finger is rubbed lightly and quickly over the bisque article. The original slip may have been the same but the figurines are a thinner shell than the doll heads. Besides being thicker, the dolls have an all-over complexion coat padded onto the smoothed outer surface, but the inside has the same texture to the touch as the figurines, a little unpleasant like very fine sandpaper.

It will be noticed that no mention has been made here about the bodies of the dolls pictured. The reason is simple: they show every indication of being replacements.

Nothing would interest the Heubach collector and student more than some definite information about the source of Heubach doll bodies. Some of the dolls under discussion here are on their original bodies and they are mostly a sorry lot.

It would be incorrect to call some of them "composition" bodies; they are more like compressed punk or pulp with plaster added to bind it. Hip and shoulder jointed in many instances, they are difficult to restring without a high speed drill because

they break under handboring pressure and melt if water is used to soften the plugs which hold the rubber. The body paint is poor quality, generally without a glaze; they attract dirt like magnets and wash down to the peculiar composition even when care is exercised.

The cloth bodies are not models of workmanship either. Made of sized bright pink or white muslin, they are outside-stitched with white or red machine overcasting. The hands are some form of composition; the feet are either the same material or crudely formed of cloth.

Nothing discourages a true collector, but it is amazing that while excellent workmanship and bisque characterize the Heubach heads right up to the last, few of the bodies are comparable to those of vastly inferior competitive dolls.

Another surprise is the difficulty encountered trying to find a substitute body for a Heubach swivel head. The original bodies must have been especially made because the necks of Heubach heads are longer and smaller at the base than other German heads of the same period. Seating them in the neck hole of a body from another doll is often impossible, and dozens of bodies can be tried before a satisfactory one is found — not right, just satisfactory.

It has been generally assumed that intaglio or painted eyes, closed or open-closed mouths indicated earlier dolls simply because it was thought all manufacturers followed the leaders into open-mouth, sleep-eyed production as quickly as possible. Continuous records, detailed descriptions, and relentless comparisons seem to undermine this theory. At some time in their productive life, Heubachs colored the slip pink. This simple economy eliminated the first step in the decorating procedure because no complexion coat was needed. These dolls are most accurately pinpointed by a glance inside the head or under the shoulder-plate.

This one small clue is valuable because the pink bisque was used in painted eye and sleep-eye dolls and also in closed and open mouthed heads. The most logical conclusion is that some firms continued to make the "older" type heads to beat the competition in the important item of cost. They simply had to be cheaper because they eliminated so many extra assembly steps, plus the outside cost of eyes and blinker bars. They are also lighter in weight, easier to pack and ship with less breakage.

Heubach's cunning seems to have been the appeal of the faces which resembled children rather than dolls. Eye appeal sells dolls today, whether for a collection or for a child, so when these dolls were assembled and dressed, few people examined the bodies. Once Heubach established this psychological fact, what inducement did they have to improve the bodies? None whatsoever.

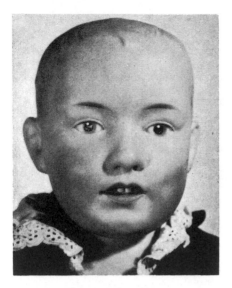

NO. 7—HERBIE

No. 7—*Herbie.* 6-inch shoulderhead of pink bisque. Deeply incised in the center back with the typical Heubach "Germany". Intaglio eyes with molded highlight dots and blue iris; open-closed mouth with two molded upper teeth; subdued, attractive coloring; single stroke brown eyebrows and lighter brown wash on the molded hair. Note the very childish, dollish nose. Substitute body.

NO. 8—WIND-UP WALKER

No. 8 — Wind-up Walker. 3½-inch swivel head with 8-inch circumference; incised in three lines: 3/Germany/76 Heubach disc 04. Open mouth with two molded lower teeth; intaglio eyes with molded highlight dot and blue iris; one-stroke brown eyebrows; lighter brown wash on well molded hair.

A wooden plug into the head holds it on a wood shoulder piece 1¼-inch wide and ½-inch thick, inserted and nailed in a 2-layer rolled brown cardboard chest. Gray cardboard skirt is glued at waistline with gauze, and the base is covered with 3-inch sized muslin with narrow lace, glued around

the lower edge. Two large pressed tin wheels protrude from 2½-inch slots in circular wooden base. Two ⅝-inch metal "balance" wheels are attached back and front with wire brads. Metal key in left side of skirt cannot be removed. Composition arms, mounted on extension wires in the wooden shoulder, are prebored for use on rubber and peg strung infant bodies.

This head (referred to as "Willoughby" sometimes) also came on crude-bodied walkers which, when wound up, waddled from side to side and managed to move forward.

- - - - - - - - - - - - - - - - - -

NO. 9—WHISTLER

No. 9—Whistler, all original. 2¾-inch flange-neck head with 6⅛-inch circumference. Incised in three lines: 23 8/0 / Heubach square / Germany. Pursed open mouth; intaglio eyes with molded highlight dot and blue iris; one-stroke eyebrows and blonde wash on molded hair. The composition above-elbow arms with cloth tops are attached to the stuffed pink cloth body which has boxed squeaker in front portion. Crudely pin-jointed straight cloth legs are attached on lower outer edges of body. Original blue "romper" suit is of the early 1900 period.

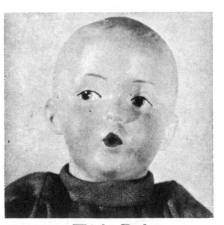

Whistler Head

Because the settlement of old estates keeps a slow but fairly constant supply of figurines coming into the open market, and because there are so many all bisque and bisque headed dolls available for study and sale, collectors are inclined to think of Heubach only as producers of bisque. This is part of our terminology problem because they were founded in the early 1880s as a Porcelain Works, which naturally implies that they also made glazed or so-called "china" objects as well. It is only by a happenstance or *era* that the market for their superb bisque objects reached a peak during the years of Heubach's greatest production.

For years the author has turned over countless large and small glazed objects looking for any of the Heubach marks; a piece finally came to light at a small antiques show on a dreary spring day in an up-state New York village. It has *Figure One* on the under side and, because the outer rim of the mark is definitely raised, it apparently was impressed on the piece rather than being incorporated in the mold.

No. 10. This small pin dish, 3¼ inches long and 2¾ inches wide, is pleasantly shaped, with an oval base. Originally there was a wide gold wash on the molded rim decoration, but most of that has worn off. The center picture of a little girl is still in perfect condition and under high magnification the small portrait looks like a handpainted fill-in on a black decal outline—just like an item in a coloring book. The painted area must have been well fired because it is not at all worn, even though the dish has been well used.

The top of the bonnet and the coat shoulder are tomato red. The round ribbon rosette and the smaller ruffle on the bonnet are yellow, the large ruffle is white, and the tied chin bow is magenta. She has brown hair, blue eyes with high pupils, and an excellent complexion. The front of her coat was painted to represent dark fur trim. The combination sounds a little outrageous but it is attractive, and typical of the period.

This marked and glazed piece proves there had to be others; Heubach was a mass production firm and this is not a worker's whimsy. The double problem is: Where are the glazed pieces and how have we, as collectors, missed them? Information about other marked and glazed Heubach items would be gratefully received.

Among the Heubach items nothing was more popular than their great variety of Piano Babies. To people who like them, these charming bisque children are irresistible; but even in

No. 10. Marked pin dish.

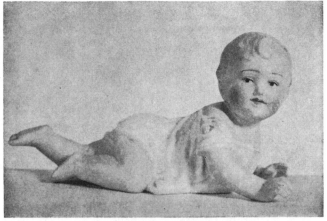

No. 12. Marked crawling child.

No. 13. Marked puppy.

their own day they were known as "dust collectors" to those who did not. Without exception, in all the years of the author's experience, the bisque in anything of this type from Heubach was the finest, whether the object was marked or unmarked. Always pure white, it is extremely fine grained and "sharp" to the touch. That is, it has a slightly metallic "cry" when rubbed with a fingertip.

No. 11. This unmarked child sits up 10½ inches high, measures 8¼ inches from the back to the toes, has a head circumference of 11 inches and is 13 inches around the body. The dress is white with a pink trim around the neck and both the neck and sleeve edges are trimmed in relief with standing dots of white, a substance which could be applied in droplets and yet in the firing hardened like the bisque.

The deep intaglio eyes have blue rims, pupils, highlight dots, and black lid linings. The open-closed mouth has a white center; the molded brows match the blonde hair in color; and the complexion is a beautiful tone, padded to an even perfection.

The arms and legs are applied to the molded head and torso—a greenware operation—and there is only a small round hole in the lower front of the dress for escaping gas to leave the hollow body during the firing.

This same child appears in several different positions—flat on its back playing with raised feet, etc., and we have no choice but to credit them to Heubach when they are carefully compared to marked pieces. No other firm used such deep intaglio eyes, or the beautifully shaped heads, hands and feet, or matched the quality and workmanship in this field.

No. 12. This crawling child has what amounts to a fifth Heubach mark. It is incised on the under side in three lines: DEP., the super-

imposed G over H in a raised circle, and 7285. The familiar initials in this instance fill the entire circle and the top half-daisy is missing entirely.

It is 4¾ inches long, with a 4-inch head circumference. The intaglio eyes have painted pupils and lid linings but no colored irises; and in this case the decorator did not follow the molded brow lines, but used a single blonde stroke higher on the forehead. The molded right shoulder bow is pink, and white dots in relief line the neck of the dress. The molded blonde hair and the complexion are very good.

Both arms and at least the bent leg are applied since the faint joining lines are visible on the under side; in this one the small gas hole in the base is below the number.

No. 13. The most unusual of all the Heubach pieces the author has ever found is this sad puppy. Incised on the under side with figure "1" and also stamped with the circular mark in red, he is presumably later than the other illustrated pieces. From the back to the right front paw he is 7¼ inches long, 6 inches high at the head. It is 5¼ inches across the head to the tips of his ears.

The bisque is very white and sharp;

No. 11. Unmarked Piano Baby.

the black trim shades to gray on the head, and there is some brown shading below and above the eyes. The intaglio pupils are very deep, with large white relief highlights. The eyes are brown and have both upper and lower lid linings. There is a small, round gas hole in the base under the stamped mark.

These gas holes are important, especially for novices. They are not "pour holes" from which the unset slip was poured in the original molding. Because these creations have applied parts, they have adequate pour holes from an arm or a leg opening, hence these small holes for gas to escape during firing, can be almost as small as the sew holes on some shoulder head dolls.

The quality of the bisque and the workmanship are the most important factors, but if there is a hole which accepts anything larger than the sharpened end of a pencil, be sure the piece is marked or get outside advice before making a purchase. Many types and sizes of modern pieces (this includes the past 10 or even 20 years) on the market resemble the old ones. Some of them do have small gas holes as well as painted black and red numbers which look like old German figures, or oval holes which will permit the entry of an entire cupped hand. Still others are open shells entirely without the closed bases which characterized the best of the old type. Some of these recent products enter this country with labels which are soaked off, or stamped marks which can be buffed off, so it has truly become a "buyer beware" situation.

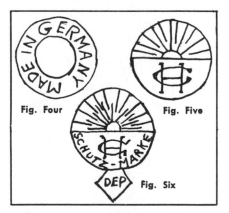

Fig. 4 is the previously described double circle which may be stamped in red or green, either alone or with some other portion of the marks. *Fig. 5* may frequently have been *impressed* rather than incised because the surrounding circle is often depressed. *Fig. 6* is stamped on some glazed pieces, impressed on others, and may have been the original pattern from which *Fig. 1* was later designed because the broken straight lines would not have molded well. As the century progressed, incised numbers were more common.

Perhaps the most interesting feature about *Fig. 6* is that it contains the

words "Schutz Marke" which is German for "trademark." It has been suggested that the superimposed "G" and "H" might be the mark of another firm than Gebruder Heubach. This clear, old mark seems to end that controversy.

A duplicate of the author's pin dish was reported by Roslyn South. Still in mint condition, hers has the gold border intact and the same little girl with very different coloring. Constant comparison has led to the belief that the decorators were allowed great latitude in coloring to provide as wide a variety as possible in the same basic design.

A round dish, 2¾ inches in diameter, colored like the author's oval dish, was reported by Mrs. W. E. Foster.

The most beautiful piece to join the author's collection is by all odds the lovely seated lady from Mrs. Ruth L. Givens. The oval base holding the chair is 6 x 7 inches and is stamped in the center on the under, unglazed surface with *Fig. 2* in dark green. The number 53 is incised above the trademark and 7527 is incised along the front of the oval underneath. She is 8 inches to the top of her hat bow; her skirt extends 1 inch beyond the base.

The coloring is soft and subtle. The hat brim, the folded scarf in her hand, the dress (especially in the deep folds), her slippers and foot pillow are tinted with a warm beige color. The sleeveless jacket and long gloves are pale blue with a hint of gray; the pillow under her elbow is sand with a deep green printed design; the chair frame is ivory; and the balance of the figure is white, including the seat of the chair.

Most importantly, she is signed. With a stylus, between the back legs

of the chair, she was marked while still in the soft, greenware stage: K. Ameallor.

Front and back views of Cinderella and Doves.

From Germany came word of another delightful piece but it has not been established that it is signed. This one has a name and says on the front in German: Cinderella and the Doves.

An American wife in Germany with an officer husband, Mrs. Mabel B. Burelbach, supplied some small pictures which show a beautiful young girl, in a little printed cap, off-the-shoulder blouse and very full skirt, kneeling to feed two birds. She is flanked on the right by a large water jug and apparently is dawdling on her way to the well. She is barefooted and there is a heavy braid of blonde hair down her back. The base is like that of the very formal lady. A quote from the letter which came with the pictures:

"Heubach was a name we'd never

Seated Lady (front view).

Seated Lady (back view).

heard until we picked up our little figurine in a shop, oh, probably almost a year ago (early 1968). We have some of the Danish figurines and on first sight we thought this might be one. The colors and quality of workmanship are quite similar. Before we had time to examine it, the dealer said, 'That's Heubach.' So, it wasn't Royal Copenhagen or Bing & Grondahl, but we liked it and brought it home.

"Meanwhile, having become Heubach conscious, we found a dog, a very typical Boxer. He is dated 1911 and has the artist's name, Fischer, impressed beside the date on the base. He sits on his haunches and leans forward, looking as belligerent as boxers do in life. He has black markings on a white background. Glazing is the same high quality as the little girl." (Author's note: Memory seems to say that white Boxers are outlawed by modern standards but 1911 is a long time ago.)

Glazed Pointer.

Miss Hupp, a well-known doll collector, also sent a picture and information about another, larger Heubach dog "which has been in our family as long as I can remember—at least over 60 years. Strange to say, I had never bothered to look for marks on either of them. It is also glazed china, white with the same soft gray underglaze markings and has an open mouth with a soft salmon-pink tongue." She sketched a complete *Fig. 1* as his marking.

"He looks like a Short-haired Pointer with a cropped tail," she continued, "and is beautifully molded with muscles and ribs showing. He crouches low in the front and has his hindquarters arched up as if barking at something. He is about 8¾ inches long and 4½ inches high. On the bottom of one foot there are four numbers, possibly 3220. People often ask if he isn't Royal Copenhagen."

As both Mrs. Burelbach and Miss Hupp suggested, most people also presume that the seated lady is Royal Danish or Royal Copenhagen.

Word came from several parts of the country concerning vases decorated with three white daisies and all marked Heubach in the *Fig. 2* design. One was added to the author's growing collection of this fine porcelain through Mrs. Louise C. Wilson.

A soft blue-gray in color, the vase is 8½ inches high, 2⅝ inches in diameter both across the base and across the top opening, it is 14 inches in circumference at the widest part. The decorating appears to be free-hand because the closest inspection does not reveal any underlying pattern marks. The white daisy petals are shaded with the same blue-gray at the juncture with the yellow centers; the stems and bud are the soft green used in both the mark and the pillow of the seated lady illustrated in the previous article. It is a charming piece but filled with live daisies it is a lovely decoration in any room.

Another "Copenhagen" type was reported by Mrs. L. W. Charkey. It is a 6¼ inch oval in "off white and blue," which has a raised bird in flight molded on the left side. The head extends over the bowl of the dish and the spread wings encompass a small portion of the bottom rim and almost the entire top rim. It is marked with *Fig. 2* plus the incised number 1928 and a single 2. In this instance, 1928 should not be mistaken for the year; Heubach had incised numbers into the thousands for identification purposes.

Sharp-eyed Mrs. Dorothy S. Coleman, primarily interested in dolls but aware of the search for glazed Heubach pieces, found the beautifully decorated and perfectly marked inkwell and sent it as a gift. She apologized for the large chunk out of the rim directly above the cluster of flowers on the front. As the picture shows, this has been mended by a porcelain repair artist; now the search is on for the metal top which it should have.

Made of shell-like white porcelain, highly glazed, 2½ inches square measured across the feet, this piece is exquisitely hand-decorated. The front bouquet of flowers includes a gay array of colors and the curving stem at the top left of the cluster is repeated on the three other sides, pointing both left and right. The gold trim is duplicated on all sides and, as can be seen in the "Made in Germany" circle in the picture of the base, workman #11 wanted credit for the job. The brush slipped and left an added dab of gold behind it. The presumption is that the flower painters were a breed apart and did not have to mark their pieces in order to be paid.

The picture also shows that the bottom was glazed and only the four feet were roughened by the floor of the kiln. The roughening in this instance is an advantage because it keeps the little working piece from slipping on a desktop.

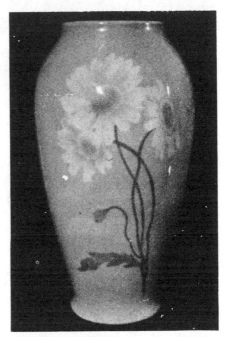

Daisy Vase.

Inkwell (front view).

Inkwell (underside).

Top tier: Snow Baby orchestra (saxaphone, drum, tuba, concertina, flute, and director). **Lower tier, left to right:** small, on side; double, boy and girl on one sled; baby on beige sled; medium "double" baby, have arms around each other in back; boy skater; girl on tummy on sled; tiny boy on wooden skis; small, standing with straw for balance.

Snow Babies

by HARRY WILSON SHUART
Illustrations from the collection of Mrs. Richard H. Mosher, Worthington, Ohio

LITTLE CHINA Snow Babies, one of today's popular collectibles, evolved from the German candy toys of the early 19th century, known as *tannenbaumkonfekt,* which were used to adorn the Christmas tree. These confections were made of gum tragacanth, flour, and sugar, molded into figures, and painted with vegetable coloring. The most appealing of these sugar characters became known as the *zucker puppe* or sugar doll, which along with polar bears and igloos, was used to decorate snow scenes beneath the holiday tree.

Eventually these Christmas tree figures came to be made of marzipan, a sweetmeat compounded principally of almond paste. Marzipan figures were especially popular with confectioners in Lubeck. In time, the old confectionary firm of Johann Moll of that city, seeking further novelty, commissioned the porcelain factory of Hertwig and Co. to recreate these popular marzipan babies in sugar bisque.

The Hertwig company was founded at Katzhutte, Thuringian, in 1864, as a porcelain and fine stone china manufacturer. They were best known for china doll heads bearing such names as "Agnes," "Bertha," "Edith," "Helen," "Pauline," etc. The London Directory for 1884 listed them as "makers of china dolls." Hertwig and Co. produced dolls and figurines of porcelain up until 1939.

According to Herr Keil, Director of the Deutches Spielzeugmuseum of Sonneberg, Germany, although snow babies were originated and produced by Hertwig and Company, the major portion of the manufacturing was carried on in the Thurxingen village

Left right: Lovely girl skier, wooden skis and ski pole; smaller boy skier, wooden skis and ski pole; two small babies on one sled; tall jointed snowbaby "doll"; medium-size baby, pushing smaller baby on beige sled; medium-size baby on side; large baby, sitting, waving.

of Ohrdruf, near Gotha, by the firms of Christian Frederick Klurg, Klen & Hahn, and Bahr & Proschild. Snow babies were very popular knick-knacks, and reached their peak of export between 1906 and 1910. These items are extremely rare, even in Germany. Their manufacture was an example of an old art which called for the porcelain ingredients to be beaten by hand instead of by machine.

Bisque *tannenbaumkonfekt* failed to impress the children who naturally enough preferred the candy version, but they were well received by hausfraus who used them to adorn their cottages during the Christmas season —and could save them safely for another year.

Hertwig produced the small figurines spattered with glittersand to simulate snow—they also resembled the familiar sugered marzipan. Most of the figures were 1 to 2 inches tall, though larger figures, up to 6 inches, were made for display in shop windows.

Other German china factories began producing similar "sugar babies," some equal to those Hertwig made, others quite inferior, especially those of a yellow gesso which were made by Moller and Duppe. Later Japanese versions were the cheapest of all in appearance.

For many years these little china German figures were exclusively exported by the Nurnberg firm of Craemer and Company. In the United States they were sold by such well established firms as Schall and Co. and Westphalia Imports, both of New York, and by confectionary and baking suppliers in the German communities of New York, Philadelphia, and Milwaukee. Their popularity dwindled during the late 1930s, and the second World War ended their importation.

Following the cessation of hostilities and the death of the last owner of the Hertwig firm, the government of the German Democratic Republic took over full operation of that business. All former merchandise was deemed "old fashioned," and new lines of items have been produced in their stead.

Thus, the Snow Baby, or the Sugar Baby, freely available a quarter of a century ago, is becoming a decidedly scarce item. In Europe, these miniatures are even rarer since, for over a period of forty years, the greatest number of those manufactured was exported to this country.

Top tier, left to right: Boy on toboggan; boy skater; baby on polar bear; snowman; baby standing on red sled; santa on sled; **Lower tier:** 2 Japanese (?) examples, one on back, one on tummy; small, standing; fat baby, sitting; girl with large snowball; baby pulling sled with 3 penguins on it; baby on side; baby, standing; baby, standing.

Top tier, left to right: Snowman with black hat; snowman with black hat; snowman with black hat, asleep; medium pair on sleds; baby, standing; pair on one base, dancing; baby, standing. **Lower tier:** Baby sitting on brown sled; small elf with pointed cap and beard; snowman with black hat, red scarf; baby on tummy; snowball or igloo, penguin on top, tiny girl climbing side, tiny face peeking out window; baby sitting on red sled; baby on red and white sled; small pair, boy and girl, on separate sleds.

More about Snow Babies

by JEAN H. CROWLEY

Except as noted, all illustrations from the author's collection. Photographs by John Kircher, Omaha, Nebraska.

Fig. 1: Snow Children group, 5" in length, produced by Galluba & Hoffman, Thuringia, Germany, Ca. 1888. Fig. 2: Mark on base of Snow Children group shown above.

THOUGH SNOW FIGURES were being produced as early as the 1880s, their peak of popularity was not reached until the first decade of the 1900s, continuing into the 1920s. The pride the Germans took in their workmanship is most apparent in these early figures. There was lifelike detail in the faces, excellent coloring, and proper firing even though these figures were simple novelties, intended at first for use in Christmas scenes and later as party favors and cake decorations.

The first Snow Babies were dressed in the familiar allover white bisque grout snowsuit and hood, bore no country of origin mark, and had no mitten or shoe distinction. In fact, these appendages were simple stubs, covered with snow. Facial features were excellent. The porcelain factory of Hertwig & Co., Thuringia, Germany, is credited with the manufacture of the original Snow Baby.

The first Snow Children, predominently blue-grey snow clad figures of the pre-1900s, were comparatively short lived. Intended as mantel ornaments, they are exquisite pieces of craftsmanship. In contrast to the all white helmeted Babies, the Children often wore snow hats, with their finely modelled hair partially exposed Definitely of German origin, they, too, rarely bear any mark other than

4-figure impressed numbers on the larger pieces. However, a rare factory marked piece with its mark is pictured here *(Figs. 1 and 2)*, a product of the firm of Galluba & Hofmann, of Thuringia, ca. 1888. Other known examples similarly marked include figures of two children building a snowman, a boy and girl pushing a snowball, and various single children molded to tan bisque sleds.

As Hertwig & Co. increased Snow Baby production, the figures began to appear in more varied positions—skiing, sledding, tumbling, etc. Hands and feet became defined. Shoes were brown. Figures were produced in at least two grades. In time, Hertwig commissioned smaller factories to produce Snow Babies for them to help them meet the demand.

With the increased production, pastel colors and brown shoes were often applied to exposed smooth bisque surfaces. Babies continued to predominate, although Children were manufactured, too. Some figures were clad in allover white snow, others in white snow jackets and caps with smooth bisque pastel pants or skirts. Occasionally a Snow Baby from this period will be found with a "Germany" mark; most bear no country of origin. Some are pre-1891 examples which did not require a mark, while the rest were no doubt packed in boxes sufficiently

Fig. 5: Snow Babies post card designed by Ellen H. Clapsaddle and printed in Germany, ca. 1910, for the International Art Publishing Co., New York-Berlin. Collection Mrs. R. H. Mosher, Worthington, Ohio.

marked to satisfy Customs. Too, the allover bisque grout would have been impossible to stamp upon, and only when a figure appears on a base, or sled, is there the chance of a mark being found.

Also included in this early group are the rare Snow Baby Angels *(Fig. 7)*—and fortunate the collector who finds one! Dressed in allover white bisque grout snowsuits, they have pale pink smooth bisque wings. Of all the snow pieces, Angel Babies are the most sought.

Another of the earlier babies is the Snow Baby Doll. These hip and shoulder jointed dolls were made in several sizes, ranging from 2½ to 6 inches. (A larger, cloth-bodied Snow Baby shoulder-head doll has been attributed to the 1880s.) These dolls are scarce, perhaps little girls rejected them as play dolls—who wanted a doll already dressed, and in a snowsuit at that?—and they were not profitable for the manufacturer. Most of those which survive were probably saved as Christmas decorations to be brought out each year.

Early Snow Babies and Children were featured in several issues of the *Ladies' Home Journal.* In the December 1911 page shown *(Fig. 6)*, Snow Babies were used as a cake decoration. In the december 1912 and the December 1920 issues, Snow Children and Snow Babies were shown as individual party favors, glued or nestled atop bonbon boxes. They were cake decorations again in the December 1922 issue, where they appeared sitting and skiing around an igloo-shaped cake.

The all white Snow Babies pictured in *Fig. 3* are excellent examples from the same early period. The tumblers, approximately 3 inches long, have identical flesh-tinted faces and are obviously from the same manufacturer. The 5-inch skier, a rare "pouty," with wooden pole and skis, and the 4½-inch boy with original metal sled are possibly products of a different factory. While these, too, are exquisitely detailed, their faces are more highly colored and they have intaglio-type eyes and red eyelines. The boy with sled is the only marked piece of the group; "Germany" is impressed on the underside of his grey bisque base. The Snow Baby Dolls, one a 4¼-inch elastic strung, the other a 3½-inch wire strung, have faces similar to those of the tumblers but their shoes are white.

In 1910 the International Art Publishing Co., of New York and Berlin, produced the artist-signed Ellen H. Clapsaddle Christmas postcards, Series No. 1118, depicting snowsuited babies engaged in winter activities. Whether actually intended as Snow Babies or designed out of sheer coincidence,

they are now emerging as the Snow Baby postcard. *(Fig. 5)*

—LATER BABIES—

The early Depression years brought a new and final group of snow pieces. Germany was ready with these inexpensive fun-type little figures and America happily responded. Used again in Christmas scenes, as well as package tie-ons, table favors, and decorations, they offered manufacturers a wide scope for their imagination. Colors, when used, were varied and bright. There were Eskimo babies playing musical instruments, skiing, sledding, riding airplanes, dancing, skating, caroling, sliding down ledges, riding polar bears, sitting in igloos, playing with penguins and seals, astride reindeer, sailing boats, as well as Babies in simpler poses—standing, sitting, tumbling.

This last group of simple-posed Babies, approximately 1½-inches long, represents the "copies" from an earlier day. Although no less lovable, they lack the more permanent features of their predecessors, and they have hand and shoe distinctions which the earliest Babies did not. Their shoes are black or brown.

Snow polar bears in all shapes and sizes abounded, as well as quaint snowmen, usually wearing black top hats. Santa also appeared in various shapes, not always a "snow" Santa, but at least mounted on a snow base.

The Japanese also produced snow figures; some were flagrant copies of

Fig. 3: Snow Babies. Back row, left to right: two jointed Snow Baby dolls; Snow Baby with sled; Snow Baby on wooden skis. Foreground: Tumbling Snow Babies.

Fig. 4. Left: Snow Children sliding down a snow bank. Right: Snow Mother pushes her Babies in a bright red carriage.

Fig. 6: Snow Babies decorated a Mistletoe cake in this illustration from the "Ladies' Home Journal," December 1911 issue. Reprinted by Special Permission of the "Ladies' Home Journal," Downe Publishing, Inc.

the German ones, others original.

All the German snows of this period bore a stamped "Germany" mark in black, red, purple, or blue. The under-side of even the tiniest baby was smooth and the stamp was easily applied. Possibly import laws were firmer. Japanese pieces were also marked, usually in black or red, and sometimes impressed. However, the stamps were not fired, and time and an occasional washing could remove them. To the beginning collector or dealer, the "Germany" is a guarantee that the snow piece is not a product of the ever-clever imitator. Japanese pieces, however, were much in the minority, Germany having been by far the leading producer. (Incidentally, the snow pieces encased in the spherical snow weights were Japanese, even though many of the weights themselves were made here in America.)

Common sense and a careful study under a magnifying glass produce good results in recognizing the differences in origin. The German modellers and painters of these late pieces did their work well. The faces of their snow

pieces and the variety of activities their snow people engaged in are extremely appealing. But in the rapidity of production, the firing was hasty—often just enough to keep the colors from rubbing off—and the pieces chipped and broke easily. Still, thanks to their owners' care, many excellent pieces survive. In defense of the manufacturers, it must be remembered that these were not meant to be lasting collectibles, and that their retail prices ranged from 15 to 35 cents. Truly ap-

Fig. 7: Unmarked Snow Baby Angel; ht. 1 5/8". Collection Mrs. William Johnson, Omaha, Nebraska.

pealing, these snow figures of the late 1920s and 1930s are just as desirable to collectors as their predecessors—sometimes more so.

Pictured in *Fig. 4* are two snow pieces from this later period. The children on a yellow ledge (2½ inches long) wear black pants and blue skirt, brown shoes; the "Germany" stamp in black. The Snow Mother pushing two babies in a bright red carriage measures 2½ inches tall; her "Germany" stamp

is purple. Her snow covered shoes are unusual for this period, only proving there are exceptions to most everything. Her original price was 50 cents—higher than most.

During this period, "no snows" appeared—colorful bisque pieces, often exact duplicates of the snow pieces, except the snow was omitted—manufactured by the same factories. B. Shackman & Co., N.Y., imported Snow Babies and No Snows, and illustrated them in their catalogs over a number of years.

For Those of us old enough to remember the hostility felt toward Germany after the outbreak of World War II, it is easy to understand why shopkeepers and importers quietly packed away any marked German items. No one wanted them. (A few less patriotic dealers may have removed the "Germany" altogether, which could account for some of the unmarked, smooth underside pieces found today which should rightfully bear a stamp.)

The last snow pieces produced—the tiny 1 to 1½ inch assorted Eskimo Babies and Bears, stamped in blue—were wholesaled to storekeepers in dozen or gross lots. How many of these little figures were packed away for years in warehouses is anybody's guess.

Just before going to press we received a letter from Mrs. Crowley informing us that "...new Japanese Snow Babies, bearing only a 'Japan' paper label are being produced this season. However, even a cursory examination of their faces alone, is again sufficient to differentiate between the old German Snow Babies and the new Japanese reproduction."

Marks Found on German Dolls and their Identification

By Luella Hart

THE following table of marks is the result of ten years of careful study and research on the part of Mrs. Hart. In addition to painstaking research in Europe, the author has had the cooperation of a member of the Borgfeldt Corporation of New York and Mr. John Paul Edwards, long time buyer in Europe for Hale's of California, now retired. The latter traveled the European market for many years and has authenticated these marks and related data as being "a very thorough and accurate listing of the doll makers of Germany, particularly those whose products were sent to America." The author gratefully acknowledges the help of these two gentlemen who, she feels, "know more about old German dolls than anyone now living."

The asterisk preceding the company name in various listings indicates that an illustration for that company's product may be found on the following pages.

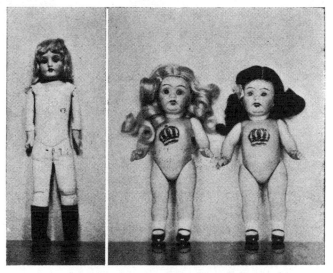

"Kestner" dolls. Doll at left is 12" tall with bisque head and lower arms, about 45 years old. Kestner trademark is stamped on middle front of body. Right, bisque twin dolls, 5" tall by Kestner. One blonde, one brunette, both with blue sleeping eyes. Note trademark on chest of each.

Company making doll	Mark on doll	Type or part made
Alt Beck & Gottschalk of Vanesdorf	....	Bisque heads. (One of three makers commissioned to make bisque Bye-lo head.)
Alfred Heller of Meiningen	"Diana" 1903	Doll heads. Diana trademark issued 1903.
Armand Marseilles of Koppelsdorf	"A & M" and sometimes a Horseshoe	Made "Queen Louise" doll for Louis Wolfe Co. of Boston and New York. Made "Floradora" doll for Borgfeldt Corp. of N. Y.
C. M. Bergman of Waltershausen. U.S.A. agent for these dolls was Louis Wolfe Co. of N. Y.	....	Jointed doll with bisque head.
* Bruno Schmidt of Waltershausen	"B.S.W." inside a heart	Dolls.
G. Benda of Coburg	....	Doll Heads. Patent taken out in 1872.
Fritz Bartenstein of Huttensteinach	....	Double faced wax doll. Patent taken out in 1881.
* Bushow & Beck of Nossen, Saxony. A Vischer & Co. of N. Y. was American agent for this firm.	"Minerva" with Goddess of Minerva helmet	Complete celluloid dolls and head. Also metal heads.
George Borgfeldt & Co. of New York Was U.S.A. agent for many German dolls	Some were marked: "Uwanta", "Floradora", "Mildred Prize Baby", "Bonnie Babe".	(Rights of "Bonnie Babe" were bought by Borgfeldt from Georgene Averill, American designer.)
Catterfelder of Thuringia	....	Jointed Dolls.
Craemer & Heron of Sonneberg	"Baby Ruth" 1893	....
Cuno & Otto Dressel of Sonneberg	"C.O.D."	Represented many makers of dolls and heads.
....	"Deutsche Geschaft" "D.G."	These words and letters mean "german made."
....	"D.R.G.M."	Term for an incorporated German company.
....	"D.R."	Signifies "Deutsches Reich."
* Gebrueder Eckhardt of Oberlind, near Sonneberg	Mark is an oval in which are words "House of Seco Service"	Maker of Strauss & Eckhardt trademark dolls. New York firm.

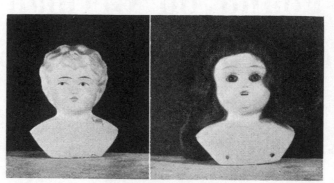

Metal head with "Minerva" mark. Trademark "Minerva" with the Goddess of Minerva helmet embossed on the bust, glass eyes.

Juno celluloid (left) and metal (right) heads. The Karl Standfuss Company of Deuben bei Dresden had made "Juno" metal and celluloid heads with the name Juno and a Crown mark since 1900. In 1914 the George Borgfeldt Company took out trademark 100,255 for "Juno" and picture of a Crown. They became the U. S. agent for the "Juno" dolls.

Name heads, made by Hertwig & Co., of Katzhutte, Germany, and Porzellan Fabric Co., of Veilsdorf, came as blondes or brunettes. Other names included Bertha, Mabel, Agnes, Pauline, Daisy, Florence, Esther and Edith.

Company making doll	Mark on doll	Type or part made
Julius & Paul Fleischmann of Sonneberg	....	Doll patented in U.S.A. 1892.
Fisher & Nauman & Co. of Illmenau	....	Made bodies of kid.
Paul Fuchs of Berlin, Germany. Assigned to Truede & Wiltz of Westphalia	....	Patented a doll with walking mechanism for dolls. 1904.
William Goebel of Bavaria	"Bavaria" and a Crown picture, "F" over "W.G."	Bisque head, papier-mache body. Arms and legs of wood.
Gebruder Heubach of Lichte, Germany	Name "Heubach" embossed on bisque	Smaller manufacturer of heads. Made pretty heads. One type of white bisque head bonnet type with flowers painted. These heads were fitted to kid, composition and cloth bodies by means of elastic.
Ernest Heubach of Koppelsdorf	....	Made bisque bust type heads.
* Hertwig & Co. of Katzhutte and Porzellan Fabric Co. of Veilsdorf	"Agnes" "Florence" "Bertha" "Helen" "Daisy" "Mabel" "Edith" "Pauline"	Both companies made china name heads 1870-1890. Very old companies. These dolls were known to the trade as "china limb dolls." (See picture.)
Heinrich Handwerck of Gotha	"Handwerck"	Made jointed doll bodies of papier-mache and composition. Purchased heads of Simon Halbig. Halbig used Handwerck's models for dolls they made. High grade dolls.
Hartman Middleman for many German factories	Hartman DRGM "Globe Baby"	....
....	"Holz Masse"	Name of wood pulp.
Kammer & Reinhardt of Waltershausen	"K & R" and a six pointed star	Maker of finest jointed dolls. Bodies of papier-mache and composition. Used heads of other firms such as Simon Halbig or celluloid head by Rheinische Co. with turtle mark. Therefore "K & R" is combined with head maker mark.
Koeniglicke Porzellan Mfr. of Berlin	"K.P.M." in under glaze	This company was an old Berlin Royal pottery. "K.P.M." mark on dolls. (1723 onward.)
* J. D. Kestner, Jr. of Waltershausen	"J.D.K." with Crown and streamers	Maker of very fine kid body and jointed dolls. Most popular of all dolls for years. Bisque heads. This trademark used since 1895. Made complete bisque Bye-lo dolls. Three other doll makers made only the Bye-lo heads to be shipped to Borgfeldt Corp. for assembly.
Frau Kathe Kruse	"Kathe Kruse" on one foot and "Germany" on other shoe sole	About 1912.
C. F. Kling & Co. of Ohrdruf	....	Made bisque heads. One of the three makers of Bisque Bye-lo heads.
Koenig & Wernicke of Waltershausen	"K & W"	Made very fine jointed doll bodies. Used Simon-Halbig heads on "K & W" bodies.
* Kley & Hahn of Ohrdurf, Thuringia	"K H" "Walkure"	Good popular priced dolls with bisque head, jointed body. Made "Walkure" marked dolls combined with initials "K H".
Albert Pulvermacker of Sonneberg	....	Low priced dolls. Patent taken out in U.S.A. 1891.
Porzellan Fabrick of Veilsdorf	....	Very old firm. Maker of so called "China limb dolls." China heads, muslin, stuffed body. Unobtainable in Germany after about 1920.

Bruno Schmidt Doll, 29", bisque head. Has the "B.S.W." trademark under the wig, letters are within a heart.

Simon and Halbig Doll with "S & H" mark on back of neck, wearing dress-up coat and bonnet of a three year old.

Kley & Hahn "Walkure" Doll, 27", bisque head, jointed body, sleeping brown blown glass eyes, about 40 years old. Marking on doll is "KH" "Walkure".

Gebrueder Eckhardt Twins, 12" dolls marked on box with trademark of Strauss Eckhardt Co., Inc., of New York City. Clothing of oilcloth. Purchased about 1934 for Annette and Joanne Jones by their grandfather the late Judge John D. Humphries of Atlanta, Ga.

Company making doll	Mark on doll	Type or part made
Rheinische Gummi Und Celluloid Fabric Co. of Mannheim, Necharau	Turtle picture	This company still makes complete celluloid dolls, and parts. Excellent dolls with world market. Other dollmakers often use these turtle marked heads.
Franz Reinhardt of Waltershausen	....	Mechanical doll with head that moves as doll walks. Patent 1903.
* Simon and Halbig of Grafenheim	"S & H"	Made only fine heads of bisque. Bodies made by other companies used with the heads.
Rudolf Steiner of Sonneberg, Saxe Meiningen	....	Patented doll 1890. (There is also a French "Steiner" doll.)
Louis Steiner of Sonneberg	....	Patent in U.S.A. in 1910 for doll.
S. M. F. Schilling of Sonneberg	....	Patent in U.S.A. 1884.
Joseph Schon of Reichenbach, Silesia, Prussia	....	Infrangible doll patented in U.S.A. 1887.
Margarette Steiff of Giengen Brenz	"Steiff"	United States Patent 1908 for stuffed dolls and figures. Heads of moulded felt. A great maker of novelty dolls. (Their Teddy Bear started the craze 1905.)
Peter Scherf George Scerf of Sonneberg	"P.Sch."	Low priced bisque head doll. Doll patent 1899. Eye mechanism patented in 1910 in U.S.A.
Hertel Schwab & Co. of Stutzham	....	Third maker of Bye-lo head of bisque.
* Karl Standfuss of Deuben bei Dresden	"Juno" with a Crown	Used on dolls since 1900. Metal and celluloid dolls, heads and parts.
Steinach of Thuringia	"Mary Jane"	Bisque head doll made for Hale's of California.
Strauss & Eckhardt of New York were agent for: Gebruder Eckhardt of Oberlind, Sonneberg	"House of Seco Service" within an oval	....
Schreyer & Co. of Nuremberg Originator of many mechanical dolls and animal novelties	"Shuco"	On character dolls of fabric, metal, wood, cardboard, 1923. Assigned doll head patent to George Borgfeldt Co., N. Y.
Ullstein Artiengesellschaft of Berlin	Picture of man and little girl	For dolls.
Wagner & Zetsche of Illmenan	....	Made kid bodies for dolls.
Witzelemus of Waltershausen. Agent for this doll maker was Hamburger & Co. of New York	"H & Co." combined with special mark such as "Viola."	....
Louis Wolfe & Co. of Boston. Agent for Armand Marseilles Co. and other German doll makers	"Cinderella" (1897) "Queen Louise" (1910) "My Companion" (1911)	....
Otto Zeh of Eisfeld	....	Process for coloring porcelain doll heads patented 1898.

Lucas Doll Costume Patterns

By Walter Schatzki

AGNES LUCAS, perhaps as well known in France as in Germany as a patternist in the art of costume some eighty or more years ago, seems to have invented the first full size patterns for doll clothes of recorded publishing. It would be unwise, perhaps, to say the first patterns for, in all truth, paper, cardboard, wood, and parchment patterns for clothes-making have a most ancient history. But Agnes Lucas' doll costume patterns were published in precisely the same form as were the paper patterns for women's clothing, most famous in America as Butterick, McCall, Vogue et cetera. Published by Otto Maier of Ravensburg and by a Paris publisher

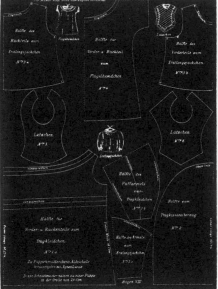

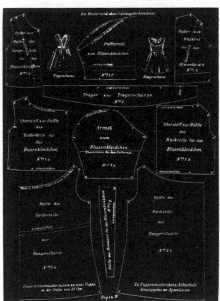

whose name escapes me, each pattern was in a folder with a full color lithographic representation of a doll dressed in the costume of the pattern. There is a book of detailed instructions in sewing, smocking, and stitchery in general, eight colored doll pictures and eight patterns, each separately compartmented.

Here pictured are two of the doll dress patterns by Agnes Lucas. The doll is dressed in the costume of the pattern to its right. These costumes are full size for a doll 29 cm. tall, or 11⅜ inches. For actual use, the pattern sheets can be enlarged to their exact size of 11¹³/₁₆ inches wide, 15⅞ inches deep.

Dolls – Rare and Unusual

In this portion of our book we introduce you to dolls with special characteristics that make them either rare or unusual — and sometimes both attributes. Among the more interesting of the rare and unusual dolls are the Peddler Dolls discussed in this chapter. "Poupée a Transformation," while not a rare doll, is certainly an unusual one. The fact that a child could transform it into three different dolls must have endeared it to a great many little girls. Dolls with two faces and walking dolls can be either rare or unusual — and sometimes grotesque. Of course, the really rare dolls are the Letitia Penn Doll, Mehetable Hodges of Salem, Anstiss Derby of Salem and others mentioned in the first part of this chapter.

Mary Merritt's Doll Museum in Douglasville, Pennsylvania, has many rare and unusual dolls. And the newly founded Margaret Woodbury Strong Museum in Rochester, New York, abounds in dolls that come into this classification.

Rare and unusual china head doll sold at a Sanitary Fair in Baltimore, Maryland, in 1861. Collection Dorothy S. Coleman. D'Aquilla photo.

LETITIA PENN DOLL

MEHETABLE HODGES OF SALEM

The Aristocracy Of Dolldom

By Ellouise D. Wilbert

W HEN we consider dolls only as playthings we do dolls, and people, an injustice. Dolls have been collectors' items for so many years that one may say, without fear of contradiction, there were doll collectors before there were collectors of American antique furniture of any kind!

It is probably no news to anyone interested in dolls that many dolls in the early days were not made as playthings for little girls, but as mannequins for the display of millinery and frocks and gowns, and as conceits and elegancies for adult ladies of the courts and of high society, which is not to disparage dolls made for young ladies of all ages.

Of all the doll collections in the United States, one of the finest in terms of truly historic and documented examples is the Imogene Anderson collection. In fact, Mrs. Anderson's dolls are so well catalogued and documented that her catalog, should it ever be published together with portraits of her delightful collection, would be a welcome addition to many libraries, and especially that

Anstiss Derby Of Salem

of the doll collector and costumer.

To attempt even the sketchiest of resumes of the Anderson collection would take more than my allotted space, so I shall confine my comments to the factual and documented story of each of the six dolls shown.

The Letitia Penn Doll. William Penn, proprietor of Pennsylvania, brought this doll to his colony in 1699 as a gift for his daughter Letitia to present to little Miss Rankin, daughter of a Friend. This is presumed to be the oldest doll in America or, more properly, the doll oldest in point of *time in America.* It is of carved wood, with gesso and enamel. Three part glass eyes, wig of flax, dress of brocade and velvet. Precise period (William & Mary) style costume. One arm missing. 20 inches tall.

The Bonaparte-Patterson Doll. Jerome Bonaparte, young brother of Napoleon, married Elizabeth Patterson, a Baltimore belle. This doll (and one other) were sent to Bonaparte for his grand-daughter, by Mlle. Huret, famed Parisian doll maker in 1855 and are marked by the maker. 18 inches tall, hair wig, hollow body of black composition, painted flesh colour. White kid covering to head. Dressed in black silk velvet, and with handmade underclothing, complete.

Mehetable Hodges of Salem. * French. Captain Gamaliel Hodges of Salem brought this doll to America for his daughter Anstiss. It was purchased in France 1715, carried on a nine year voyage and arrived 1724. Oldest French doll (of record) that has been here for so long a time. Within our schedule of dating by periods, this would fall in that of Queen Anne. Remained for seven generations in Hodges family. 21 inches tall, hand made wood head and body, features painted, three part glass eyes. Real

hair wig is dark brown. Arms of white kid. No legs. Fully dressed in pink silk court dress, with handmade underclothes. Real lace with bows and pewter pins.

Lillie Turner. Lillie comes from Paris but lived for many years with Newport people! Purchased c. 1790 in Philadelphia by Hon. Benjamin Bourne of Bristol, R. I., a member of the Congress. Given to his niece, Lillie Turner. 11 inches tall, brown glass "open and shut" eyes, operating by wire pull. Cloth body, handmade shoes, wax head, bust and arms. Marie Antoinette costume. Grey hair (the height of fashion on State occasions), thread lace cap, silk poke bonnet, sheer linen dress.

Peddler Doll. Purchased at Christie's,

Bonaparte-Patterson Doll

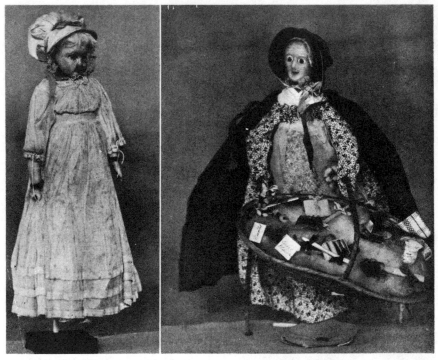

Lillie Turner   *Peddler Doll*

London, 1932. Date is early 18th century. 9¼ inches tall, wood, jointed, wax head, glass eyes. Red cape, blue silk poke bonnet, with undercap of white. Basket displays "Court Plaister," needles and finery. Such dolls are among the most desirable—and scarcest—of dolldom.

Anstiss Derby of Salem. Date is 1826. 14½ inches tall. Composition head wax covered, brown glass eyes, kid body and arms, wooden legs. Real hair in elaborate dress entwining pink roses. Costume of blue silk. Once given to Martha Prickman of Salem, grand-daughter of the famous Elias Haskett Derby. This is a "fashion doll" and was purchased not for a child but for a young lady who had the dress on the doll copied as her first ball gown. Fashion dolls have a record of ever increasing use from the 13th century. They were finally superceded by fashion plates. Note the perfect miniature Queen Anne Spanish footed side chair with this doll.

Three Interesting Doll Collectibles

By Ruth Ricker

A DOLL does not have to be a beauty to be treasured by collectors. Some choice old dolls, made for children's everyday play are comical, even downright ugly, yet they are eagerly sought, and command high prices. One such is the so-called "Bartenstein doll."

THE BARTENSTEIN DOLL HEAD

Fritz Bartenstein of Huttensteinach, Germany, patented his movable double-faced doll head in this country on July 5, 1881, under patent #243,752. Because the patent number is sometimes stamped on the doll body, collectors frequently designate the whole doll as the "Bartenstein doll;" rightfully the name should be attributed to the head only.

The head of this doll, with its two faces, one smiling, one piteously crying, is turned to hide one face in a permanently attached hood or cap by the pulling of a string at the lower left side of the body. The same string also connects with a bellows-type cry and an arm, so that by raising the arm while the doll wears its crying face, appropriate wails are emitted.

Time seldom improves the expression of these dolls, for the heads of poured beeswax are often softened and distorted with age. This added distortion does not impair the value of the Bartenstein head doll, for as unhandsome as it may be, it is considered a rare collector's item, and holds a high place in rarity and monetary value.

THE COLEMAN WALKING DOLL

Another much sought-for doll of dubious beauty is the Coleman Walking Doll, patented November 8, 1921, by Harry H. Coleman of New York, an Englishman, at that time in the process of U. S. naturalization.

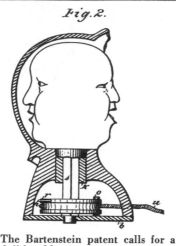

The Bartenstein patent calls for a doll head having two opposite faces of different expression and capable of turning on a vertical axis, so that either of the two faces can be turned to the front by mechanism while the head-gear remains stationary and covers the opposite face. The mechanism consists of pulley, string, and stop-pins.—*Illustration from patent papers.*

Mr. Coleman, a ventriloquist on the stage, used large life-size dummies in his act, and his walking doll was developed somewhat along the same lines.

Not only did Mr. Coleman invent his doll, but he also manufactured it, in that he had the parts turned out and assembled them himself. It is made almost entirely of turned wood, wire screening, and coiled springs. The feet, rounded at the bottom, appear to be solid wood, but are actually filled with lead to give proper weight for walking.

Head and hands are of cheap composition, poorly enameled, and the head is connected to the upper wooden body frame by ordinary large nails. The torso is made of coarse wire screening and is cone-shaped to fit the frame of the body. This also is fastened with ordinary small nails or tacks. The face is typical of dolls of its period, with none of the delicacy of the old bisque dolls or the new

A section of H. H. Coleman's patent drawings for walking doll, patented November 8, 1921. Joints of both arms and legs are held and enabled to move by ordinary hinges, those in the legs having an extra opening to snap the leg erect after bending. This patent, #1,396,321, covered improvements on his previous walking doll, (Patent #1,221,970, April, 10 1917) which were not limited to dolls but could be embodied in other figure toys such as birds, animals, etc.

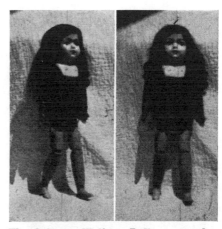

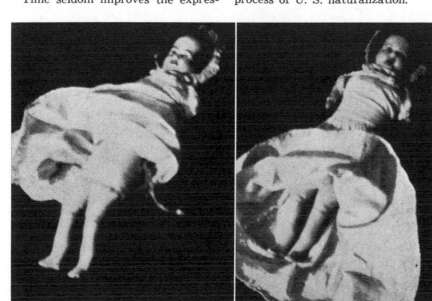

Two-faced Bartenstein head doll, with head of tinted poured beeswax, oval blue-brown eyes embedded in each face, cap or bonnet of papier-mache covered with cotton cloth and trimmed with ruffles about the face; body is a cylinder-shaped cloth-covered cardboard, made to house the mechanism; arms and legs are of composition. Note string at side of smiling face doll, raised position of right arm in crying doll.

The Coleman Walking Doll, a somewhat crude affair, too large and cumbersome for holding, with all the mechanism involved in the walking process in plain view, presents when dressed a favorable appearance, and with practice, can be made to walk very nicely.

Chase Stockinet boy doll wears high button shoes, white shirt with Peter Pan collar, and black velvet suit in child's size 1. The excellence of the condition of Chase Stockinet dolls found today is a constant amazement to collectors, and speaks of careful workmanship and sound structure.

plastic ones. The wig, however, is nicely made of real hair.

There is no trademark on the doll, but at the bottom of the torso, between the legs on a block of wood, apparently rubber stamped, appears

Each Chase Stockinet Doll bears this trademark, either under the left arm or on the left leg between the knee and the hip.

PATENTED IN U. S. A.
OTHER PATENTS PENDING
PATENTS APPLIED FOR IN ALL
OTHER COUNTRIES.

The example pictured was once erroneously classified as a "Schoenhut Mousetrap Doll" by a dealer undoubtedly influenced by the "mousetrap" effect of the wire screening, and the fact that Schoenhut turned out many wooden dolls prior to 1921.

Though far from beautiful, and certainly not very old, this doll is desirable as an example of the early attempts of manufacturers in this country to produce strictly American dolls.

THE CHASE STOCKINET DOLL

The Chase Stockinet doll, lifelike and lovable, was intended for children's play. It was designed and made by Mrs. Martha Jenks Chase, of Pawtucket, Rhode Island, as a soft, unbreakable, washable toy for her own children, in the early 1890s.

The construction was intricate and painstaking. The head, cut in two pieces—the face and the back—was jointed at the top in a stitch similar to that used on baseballs. It was stuffed, like the body for which she used tan sateen, with cotton. Head, arms, and feet were finished with flesh colored waterproof paint. The face, which was very solid, and seemed impossible to push in, was meticulously contoured and the features painted in natural tones. The ears were well defined and appear to have been applied separately. Arms and legs were stitched at elbows and knees for bending. The thumb was applied separately to the hand, with each finger individually fashioned. The feet were remarkably lifelike, each toe distinctly outlined.

This glorified "rag doll," found such favor with the Chase children and their friends, that Mrs. Chase soon found herself, somewhat to her own surprise, manufacturing the same doll commercially, and on a rather large scale. The tan sateen body early gave way to one of waterproof finished stockinet, making the doll entirely washable. Many sizes and types were made—little boys and girls, colored mammies, story book characters, even George Washington.

Eventually Mrs. Chase's "rag doll" grew up to take a part in the adult world of education. About the time of the first World War, she made up an actual-sized baby doll with internal containers that could be bathed and handled as a human baby, for use in nurses training groups. Later came the life-size adult Hospital Doll, widely in use in nurses training schools today. Mrs. Chase died in 1925, and production of the toy dolls has not been continued.

What Shall I Put in The Peddler's Pack?

IT WAS A pleasurable pastime of Victorian females to assemble these realistic little figures of the peddler women who cried their wares in London streets and through the English countryside, and outfit their baskets with all kinds of wee trinkets. Original examples are rare today, and out of reach of the average collector—some may cost as much as $400 or more. But the enjoyment long ago ladies had in outfitting them need not be confined to the past. Delight in miniatures still persists, and for those who like to collect them but are plagued with the problem of display, why not a peddler doll?

The originals were made of many materials—china, wood, or wax were usual. One in Mary Merritt's Doll Museum in Douglassville, Pennsylvania, has a bread crumb face; another is of papier-mache. The Mary Callinack, Darcy believed, was a penny wooden, carved to a portrait and stained a leathery shade.

Their hoods are traditionally black with ruffles of white, their capes red; their calico dresses may be caught up to show a black quilted petticoat. As for their stock in trade, sometimes as many as 125 fascinating objects

Miniatures, of Course!

A peddler doll is perfect to display wee trinkets and treasures. Ideas for assembling your own may be gleaned from dolls others have made—long ago, or only yesterday.

By MARCIA RAY
in collaboration with
LUELLA HART

hung from their woven baskets.

In Mary Callinack's pack, some of the objects were pinned into the cotton lining of the one-inch tall handmade basket; others were strung on black strings and pinned into the top of the pack. Ranging from one-half to two inches, these items include: 5 Frozen Charlottes; 6 penny woodens; 2 jointed bisques with hand crocheted dresses and bonnets; tiny potholders and pincushions; ivory crosses; an ivory horse; a china dog; a one-inch silver box filled with tiny beads; a one-inch card with a dried fish on it and the handwritten words "Caught at Littlehampton"; on the back is a hand painted sea scene; a tiny coronation chair of metal; a metal locomotive; strips of handmade passementerie. *(Pictured.)*

Present Day Peddlers

Carolyn Abbott's Polly Penny came from a London antiques shop. The foundation doll has a china head and feet, kid hands. A mask, representing a witchy old woman has been fastened over the original face. Among the 25 to 30 small articles in her basket are a tiny doll, kid gloves, scissors, bag, beads, thread, charms, purse, baskets, and bookmarks. Like most Peddlers, Polly Penney has always existed under a glass dome. *(Pictured.)*

All sorts of possibilities present themselves to today's peddler doll makers. Peg Steele of Harrisburg, Pennsylvania who makes them for sale, uses apple faces and padded wire bodies. The apples—she prefers Winesaps—are pared, roughly carved, and set to dry on wood—never on metal. She dresses them appropriately and fills their crocheted baskets with dried lavender flowers.

For the collector of miniatures who likes a diversified stock—and all items must be in scale — any type doll can be used. Penny woodens, either old or new are perhaps the most popular. (The gift shop in Museum of the City of New York is one place that carries new ones.)

Mary Callinack, *correctly "Kelynack,"* 1867-68. *Luella Hart Collection.*

Polly Penny, *original; owned by Carolyn Abbott, Westfield, Massachusetts.*

Notion Nanny, *assembled by Fearn Brown, Oakland, California; doll is old.*

Above, left to right: rare bread crumb face peddler holds line of hot pads, ca. 1820; papier-mache, ca. 1840; leather face peddler, label on bottom, "C&H White, Milton, New Hampshire," ca. 1830. *From Mary Merritt's Doll Museum.*

For her Notion Nanny, Fearn Brown used an old penny wooden which Luella Hart found for her in Waldo Lanchester's Puppet Center in Stratford-on-Avon. Entranced with the old Apothecary Shop in Williamsburg, Virginia, she started Nanny's pack with apothecary items. Lavender she could purchase, but rock candy, horehound, and tiny medicines she created herself. Some of her notions are present-day — the Five and Ten is a good hunting ground — but many are antiques.

Among her old pieces are a paper of small black china head veil pins from France, a small metal lantern, a one-inch square satin pillow hand painted "Bethlehem 1902", filled with sand from that ancient city, tiny doll earrings, a wee metal flatiron. For heart interest she has added a gold locket and miniature baby picture of her mother, born 1860, the tiny ½-inch wide aviator's compass her Air Force son carried on D Day as he flew across to France, and his miniature set of 1st Lieutenant's silver wings. *(Pictured.)*

Luella Hart made "Buy a Doll, Miss?" for her granddaughters. Her penny woodens, large and small, also came from Waldo Lanchester. The small 1½-inch size are more expensive and harder to obtain than the large ones. *(Pictured.)*

Ruth Russell, of Long Beach, California, who has made some fifty dolls for her own pleasure, let one of her favorites speak in verse. The recital of basket treasures is an inspiration and a goal for all miniature collectors who aspire to a "proper" peddler.

"My goods are fresh and clean and new
  Pray you, buy of me
There's cloth and lace and ribbon, too,
  And thyme and rosemary.
The little doll from Italy
  Is surely very sweet;
My remedies are made by me,

  My brushes keep things neat.
The spoon and fork and knife and bell
  Are used to get a meal
Of all their use I need not tell—
  I've yarns and good castile.
The rolling pin and amber beads
  Are surely worth their price;
There's everything to fill your needs—
  The pictures, too, are nice.
The casket holds so many things.
  I've goose-grease for your chest,
Some smelling salt is strong and
    sharp;
  My paregoric's best.
The shell was brought from far away
  Your whatnot to adorn;
My notions help you every day,
  The Bible, night to morn.
There's scissors small and buckles
    brave
  And books and candles, too,
A cushion for your pins to save;

"Buy a Doll, Miss?" *Collection Marjorie & Terry Morse, Boulder, Colorado.*

The pomander is new.
The sampler, tidies, that you see
  Are useful gifts, I trow,
So, get your pence and trade with me
  And you'll be pleased, I vow."

UNUSUAL DOLLS

by ALBERTA FULTON

THE MAKER of the beautiful French dolls with the "A.T." mark is still to be authenticated; serious doll researchers are trying diligently to identify this "unknown." In the meantime, the great beauty of the distinctive A.T. faces intrigues collectors; the dolls are not common, and the prices are high.

The eyes are wide apart and luminous in quality; stationary and paper-weight in construction. The bisque is fine, with delicate coloring and artistic sculpting. Sometimes the bodies are of wafer-jointed kid with bisque heads, shoulder-plates, and to-elbow arms. Other bodies are of jointed papier-mache with wristless forearms.

As to "when," various factors indicate they were probably produced from the 1870s through the 1890s. However, unless the maker is determined, no definite date can be assigned. Until then, experts generally accept the possibility that not all bodies on which A.T. heads are found are original.

In *The Collector's Encyclopedia of Dolls,* by Dorothy S., Elizabeth A., and Evelyn J. Coleman, the authors suggest the maker of the A.T. dolls as A. Thuillier of Paris, France, ca. 1875-1890. Thuillier made jointed dolls with wooden or kid bodies, as well as jointed composition bodies or "b⁶eb⁶es incassables." Although this has never been proven, "A.T." bisque heads have been found on wooden, kid and composition bodies which seems to support the Thuillier attribution.

Poupee a Transformations

The container for this boxed item, handsomely gold lettered in French, "Poupee a Transformations," is precisely compartmented to accommodate its contents—a complete doll, two bisque doll heads, and an extra set of bisque arms and legs. Though the box is apparently of French manufacture, the dolls are not. The bisque heads are incised on the shoulder, "English Made. D.R. Co. 59-6." The torso is ink-stamped with a square containing the words, "Exchange Dolls—Patented."

The heads are interchangeable, the same body serving them all. The first head, attached here to the body, has a smiling Heubach face; the second, a sad face; and the third is in brown bisque with matching, interchangeable brown bisque arms and legs. It may be suspected that when this item was made, the German Heubach head was long in the public domain, and that the other two were molded from whatever was handy because they were cute and appealing.

The arrangement for exchanging and securing the heads is simple. The shoulder plates have two holes in front and two in back through which long, large-headed straight pins are inserted into the hard stuffed body. The device for holding the bisque arms and legs in place is a small circular bracelet-clip, on the principle of a bicycle clip. The torso is hard stuffed, probably with sawdust, but the upper arms and legs are hollow tubes of a heavy cloth, sewn to the body. The bisque arm or leg is inserted into the hollow tube, and the bracelet-clip clamps it on.

While at first glance this triple doll appears to be a salesman's sample, it differs in that there is provision here for the heads and limbs actually to be interchanged and that is not possible in the known salesmen's samples. [*Editor's note:* Originally thought to be rare, several other identical boxes have been recently reported; one is on display at Mary Merritt's Doll Museum, Douglassville, Penna.]

"A. T." dolls, left to right: kid body, bisque head, shoulders, and arms, (dressed doll is its small counterpart); open mouth version, bisque head, papier-mache body; closed mouth version. All heads are marked.

Largest doll is 23″ jointed Jumeau, with "Bebe Jumeau" label on her original dress. In front of her, the French Huret with painted eyes, in going-sway dress, also has lovely bridal gown with French lace veil; 16″ Rohmer with lustre china face, glass eyes, original costume. Infant, of possible Church origin, has glass eyes of the late 18th or early 19th century. China head, 4″ tall, shows deep sloping shoulders of earliest china dolls.

Standing: Pair of shell dolls in mint condition; heads believed to be of wood. *Left to right below:* Parian head with glass eyes, pierced ears, ca. 1860; miniature china, with fancy hair-do, china hands and feet; china head, with so-called "spaniel puffs" over ears dating her in late 1840s.

Mary Merritt's Doll Museum
Douglassville, Pennsylvania

MARY Zerbe Merritt began collecting dolls and doll things when she was eight years old, dreaming even then of a doll museum for everyone to see. Now, a husband and grown children later, her dream's come true. Since June 19th, 1963, some 1,500 dolls from her collection of over 5,000, have been receiving daily visitors in a home of their own. Dating from about 1725 to 1900, displayed dolls are rare and quaint as well as beautiful, from an early 18th century pedlar doll with age-darkened bread crumb face to gorgeously gowned French fashion dolls and mechanicals that seem almost human.

In addition, there are over 40 miniature period rooms, exquisitely furnished, papered, and curtained, inhabited, of course, by dolls of appropriate era. There are also 59 complete dollhouses. To further delight, there's a full size replica of a Philadelphia toy shop, mid-19th century, well stocked with toys of bygone days. The Museum Doll Hospital, where broken limbs, cracked skulls, and age wrinkles are remedied, accepts out patients, too.

Foot-high schoolmaster's desk and balloon-back chair suggest the unusual furnishings found in the dollhouse collections.

After this Montanari-type wax doll's broken arm was restored in 1848, her little English owner, Heather Smith, placed her in the box shown, had a miniature on ivory painted to hang over her head, and wrote the poem which is pinned to the lid. Little Heather died; the doll remained as Heather left her.

Black Rubber Gem

by GENEVIEVE ANGIONE

OLD RUBBER dolls come to light occasionally, but most of them are the hard, painted, shoulder-head type. Often they are chipped or even broken, and many of them are almost without paint. They are cherished nevertheless. The soft, or vulcanized, type are too often left flat on their backs in attics. They come to us without backs to their heads, with heads melted out of shape by years of high summer temperatures, and cracked open from long, cold winters.

The little 8¾-inch fellow pictured here is an exception to almost all rules. It never had any paint except the white of the eyes and the red on the lips, which is almost intact. The uniform blackness of the body would indicate that the rubber was colored before molding. The coloring material probably was carbon, better known as lamp black, used in many black rubber products. Although there is some graining of the surface texture, the doll is soft to the touch and still entirely flexible.

This is an old doll. The question is: how old? Unfortunately there are no marks of any kind to help us, so we can only know what the doll itself can tell us.

The face is the old, sweetly bland kind which was typical 100 years ago. The hair is molded in a slightly curly cap such as we find on old celluloids. Although the doll is pitch black, it is not a Negro.

The torso has wide sloping shoulders and the gourd-shaped abdomen of very old bisques, both French and German. The arms and legs are molded with all the ridges of fat which were the signs of a healthy, happy baby in the 1800s.

All the limbs are easily moved on a full circle and will still hold many positions. The chunky little hands have molded palms. There is a small hole, similar to the pour hole in fine china and bisque figurines, on the inside surface of each arm and leg, probably air releases.

The ⅜-inch flat, scalloped squeaker button in the back is tin rather than the familiar rounded chrome metal buttons used for many years in dolls and toys. Careful manipulation discloses some sort of core of soft material in the head, which probably accounts for its wonderfully preserved shape.

Limb Attachment

One of the most interesting features of this doll is the manner in which the arms and legs are attached. Although they cannot be taken out for examination, the joints seem to be similar to those used in modern plastic dolls. Sturdy pointed thorns must have been molded on the flat upper ends of the limbs, and holes or soft spots centered in the flat hip and shoulder flanges. Once these thorns were thrust through the holes, the arrowheads kept them from being pulled out, but permitted the full circle movement on the thorn shaft.

On page 30 of *Dolls, Makers and Marks,* Elizabeth Coleman lists an interesting patent:

"HAMMOND, 1858. Thomas Rundle Hammond of Paris, a trader, was granted a French patent in 1858. His invention was for *invisible joints* on dolls, heretofore they had been visible. The dolls were to be made of *flesh colored vulcanized rubber to prevent harm from paints.*" (Italics are ours.)

This little black beauty qualifies on all three counts. The joints are invisible; black is certainly one flesh color; and the doll is vulcanized rubber. Because it could hardly be seriously considered as a French doll, the suspicion arises that some German manufacturer made use of this patent, with or without permission. Perhaps the fact that it is pitch black was the patent loophole.

At any rate, a similar doll, still in the hands of the widow of the original owner, dates the doll back approximately 90 years, to 1875.

No matter what its origin, this is a fine specimen of that diminishing tribe, old rubber dolls of all kinds.

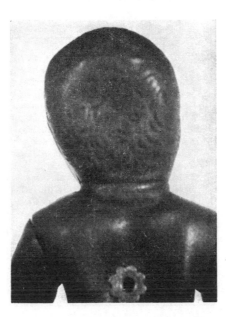

Above: *Closeup of Face and Shoulders.* Right: *Back view, showing squeaker. The doll, while black, is not Negro.*

Author's concept of invisible joints used on this old rubber doll.

CORNHUSK DOLLS

by ROGER L. WELSCH

IN THE pioneer Plains States, life centered around corn. Cornbread was a sodhouse staple; mattresses were stuffed with cornhusks; Christmas trees were decorated with strung popcorn. Foodstuffs were "stretched" with corn; toasted corn was added to coffee; cornsilk was added to tobacco.

Popcorn with sorghum molasses and milk was served for breakfast—perhaps with some fried cornmeal mush;

ILLUSTRATION No. 1

ILLUSTRATION No. 2

roast ears of corn and cornbread often graced the noon table; and corncakes, dodgers, and corn soup were supper—with popcorn pudding for dessert. On Saturday nights, there might have been a bit of whiskey—from a corn mash.

The children, too, turned to corn for their amusements. Cornstalks made knightly swords and quarterstaffs. Half of a cob with two or three pheasant feathers stuck into the pith made a good game bird, or a dart. A couple of slits between stalk joints made a primitive cornstalk fiddle.

When steamed or soaked in warm water, cornhusks become flexible; dried, they remain as they have been re-formed, so the pioneer mother fashioned cornhusk dolls for her little girls. Some of these dolls were exceedingly simple; others were no less charming—and undoubtedly as much loved—as some of today's twenty-dollar automations.

The dolls were decorated in ingenious ways, reflecting the pioneer's need for improvisation. The two ladies in *Illustration No. 1,* for example, sport curly cornsilk hair. The one on the left has a cornhusk shawl and apron, while the lady on the right carries a cornhusk purse and has a bit of calico for an apron. The faces and buttons have been drawn on with ink and colored pencil.

The pixie-ish coquettes in *Illustration No. 2* have colorful sashes and caps dyed with berry juices, walnut-husk ink, and ink; their hair is also cornsilk.

In *Toys in America,* Marshall and Inez McClintock tell us it's likely the cornhusk dolls so beloved by white settler's children were first made by the Indians. Pioneer children painted features on their dolls' faces; the Indians may not have done so for, in many tribes, the drawing of a face endowed the doll with a soul. In Puritan days when most play was frowned on, babies were allowed corncob dolls, and boys used discarded corncobs for blocks. By the 18th century, most girls had some sort of doll, occasionally an elaborate creation from Europe, more often one carved from wood, or made of stuffed rags, twigs, or *cornhusks.*

ILLUSTRATION No. 3

ILLUSTRATION No. 4

Illustration No. 3 shows, on the right, a more primitive example of the cornhusk doll—the only male member of my collection. The prissy grandmother on the left is particularly interesting because her features—eyes, nose, and mouth—and her starburst brooch are made of wheat and weed seeds glued to the husk. Her shawl and bonnet, as well as her hair, brushed severely back, are bits of cornhusk. (See close-up, *Illustration No. 4.*)

Such dolls, when played with, do not last long. Some of the examples pictured are relics of the past; others are recent products fashioned in the old tradition. Old or new, these cornhusk dolls prove again that "homemade" is not synonymous with "crude," and that the products of yesterday, revived today, are no less delightful, no less clever, than they were then.

European Creche Dolls

AS FAR back as the Middle Ages, creche dolls were used at Christmas in the churches of Europe to portray the Christ Child's birth. In the scene of the Annunciation to the Shepherds, figures were shown sleeping with their herds; in Nativity scenes, the three Kings paid homage to the Baby Jesus. Many of the great artists of Italy modeled these figures for the Church. Most often they were fashioned of terra-cotta, though wax or papier-mache were sometimes used; occasionally they were carved of wood. Naples, renowned for its creche dolls, continued to make them in the time-honored manner until the early twentieth century. Now and then, as churches are remodelled, and old figures replaced with new, early creche dolls find their way into the hands of collectors, who treasure them for their age, beauty, and significance.

In addition to Holy Figures, creche scenes often included representations of everyday people who came to worship. The creche dolls pictured here show, at top, an elderly Italian couple of terra-cotta, 12" tall, ca. 1800-50; the man has no teeth, the woman a goiter.

In the second row are dolls from France and Spain. The 14" French Madonna, ca. 1730, and all original, has head, arms and upper torso of wood; the hair appears to be natural. Her gown is brocade, embroidered with roses; her blue silk cape is edged with silver braid; and her crown is of silver and pearls. The small Spanish carved wood doll with gesso finish, possibly the Christ Child, is jointed at wrist, elbows, and shoulders. His sandals are silver. He is all original, though at some time through the years the mid-section was altered and painted blue. A Spanish creche "Christ the King", ca. 1800 or earlier, is 14" tall, with head and body of wood; the eyes are glass. The green velvet garment, trimmed in gold braid, is belted with a gold cord; the robe is chartreuse satin; crown and sandals are of washed gold. These Spanish pieces came from Spain, by way of Mexico, to Boston where the present owner found them.

The figures in the bottom row are all Italian, and of terra-cotta. From left to right: a 13" figure represents an actor, ca. 1800-20, all original; woman with blue silk jacket over cotton dress, has terra-cotta hair, glass eyes, ca. 1800-30; smaller woman, also with glass eyes, has hair of undetermined material; 14" woman wears beautifully made blue silk dress, tan silk apron, vestee of fine pleated white linen with lace trim, all original. Her legs are wrapped with hemp, as are many of the terra-cotta creche dolls. The hands of all these dolls are particularly expressive.

The "Pearly" King and Queen

By LUELLA HART

ON THE GRAVE of one Henry Croft in St. Pancras Cemetery at Finchley stands the statue of a man, oddly garbed in suit and top hat covered with buttons. The legend below reads "The Original Pearly King." This monument, provided by donations from many London hospitals, gives testimony to the gratitude of these organizations for the funds raised for them by Henry Croft and the Pearlies who followed him.

Of all strange guilds of London, the quaintest perhaps is that of the London Pearly, ruled by the Pearly King and Queen of Hempstead Heath.

In the 1880s, a venturesome Cockney dandy decided to add to the bell bottomed trousers of the Victorian mode what was termed "a flash." A "flash" was a single line of buttons, about six in number, sewn vertically on the piped seam of the bell bottom, just above the show line. At every step, the swinging bell bottom caused the pearl buttons to strike the London pavement and proclaim the wearer a smart lad.

This high style youth had to be prepared with tongue and fist for the sideline hectoring his "flash" brought forth. Navies, barge-workers, brewers, draymen—the toughest of them all—were the first to dare. The carmen or 'ostlers growing fancier used buttons with a fox head pattern or of horseshoe shape, silver plated.

From bell bottomed trousers, to jacket, to cap, and on to the velvet collar of the Edwardian period jacket, the "flash" travelled. Then one night in the late 1880s, on the eve of a horse show and carnival, a certain costermonger had a stroke of genius. He

Both doll and button collectors alike will find these London Pearly King and Queen Dolls a welcome addition to their collections. Above two, from collection of the author, are made by "Old Cottage Toys," England. *Photo courtesy Mark Farmer Company, El Cerrito, Calif.*

covered his entire rig-out with "flashes." This coup de grace was ascribed to Henry Croft and he was hailed as the one and only original Pearly King.

Before the end of the century, every Cockney district in the East End of London had its own Pearlies. In 1904, they began to organize. Membership was made up of London costermongers who worked in London street markets. Their dress was bizarre, with marvellous hats and extravagant clothing weighed down with quantities of pearl buttons — sometimes as many as 40,000 were utilized in one outfit.

Pearly Queens caught on. Each family and each district jealously guarded and upheld its crown. At the height of Pearly popularity, London had about fifty Pearly families. When the Ford motor car came to replace the donkey and barrow, there was a decline in Pearly families, though each was ready to turn out in full regalia at every festive occasion.

Events with which the Pearlies are identified are many. The Van Horse Parade of Easter Monday gives the London costermonger an opportunity to display the horses he uses in his daily work. On Bank Holidays the Pearly is much in evidence on Hampstead Heath. On Derby Day at Epsom, he acts the clown. At the Festival Garden, Battersea, he collects funds for London charities.

At all these events, the Pearly is in the van of every national effort to raise funds for charity. The Red Cross, ex-servicemen's associations, hospitals, children and animal rescue missions, the blind and poor—all have reason to thank the colorful, pushful folk who shake the collection box and never take "no" for an answer.

Once a year at St. Mary Magdelene Church on old Kent Road, East End, the brotherhood gathers for the Harvest Festival. For thirty years, food offerings from the market have been brought there for the London needy.

Recently in an American tour of London buses, sponsoring a "Come to Britain" effort, Mr. and Mrs. Bert Mathews of Hempstead, came along as Pearly passengers, to give America a hint of the picturesque possibilities any London tourist may find.

In London, a recent Pearly King and Queen television show portrayed the versatility of these folk, who have that glorious gift of making people laugh as they reach for their purses—to give to charity.

Cobo-Alice Dolls by RUTH POCHMAN

The late Mrs. George Prince of Madison, Wisconsin, recalled for me her childhood on the Isle of Guernsey, one of the Channel Islands off the coast of England and France. There, in the 1880s, she had a favorite doll, such as all the other little girls had, and all the dolls had the same name—one of two names, that is. They were called either "Cobo-Alice" or "Cobo-Judy."

The dolls originated among two families, the LeHurays and the Guilles, in the English coastal town of Cobo. The two women who owned the business were named Alice and Judy. Mrs. Prince's doll was a Cobo-Alice, and later, when she bought others for her daughters, they, too, were Cobo-Alices.

These dolls are unbreakable, being made of heavy unbleached muslin stuffed with dry hardwood sawdust. The body is easy to copy, since neither fingers nor toes are separated from the shaped hand and foot.

The head, however, has an individuality that is difficult to reproduce. Round like a ball, it is painted with ordinary household paint in flesh colors. The features are painted on in black; Mrs. Prince said a match was used for this work instead of a brush, and I am inclined to believe it, for the large oval eyes with their tiny dots for iris and pupil, the heavy brows, and the nostrils are crudely done. The mouth is outlined in red but not filled in.

Through a friend still living in Guernsey, Mrs. Price was able to get a new doll for me, but the most outstanding feature of the old primitive looking doll is missing in those made today. In the old ones the brows and nose were needle-molded before any of the painting was done—even before the head was sewed up and stuffed hard with sawdust. The new ones lack the needle-molding altogether.

To indicate hair, the heads of both the old and the new dolls have been painted a medium brown (again ordinary household paint was used); no attempt has been made to have brush marks around the hairline or comb marks in the rear. The cloth used for the heads was a wider weave than that used for the body and limbs; possibly it is part of a cotton sock. The paint used for both the face and hair extends down onto the shoulders, and there is no evidence of a seam at the joining. The hard stuffing under the dried paint makes the head heavy enough to be a lethal weapon; one wonders whether this had anything to do with the dwindling popularity of the doll in the early 20th century. No ears are sewed on or otherwise indicated. And no lashes.

The dolls were sold undressed, and clothing was made by the new owners. Mrs. Prince said people usually dressed the dolls like the women of the Islands who worked in the fields —full skirts, loose blouses, and slat bonnets. The bonnet was like those worn in our Southland by women working in cotton fields; the wide brim was stiffened by slipping reed or cardboard strips into slots sewn for this purpose, thus shading the face of the wearer from the burning sun.

Mrs. Prince's dolls are 13 and 18 inches long; the one she secured for me is 15 inches long.

Joints are at the shoulders and the hips only. The hands and forearms are painted flesh color; the feet are painted to represent flesh colored socks and black slippers.

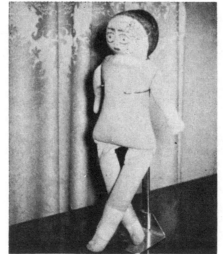

Cobo-Alice doll, 1880 period.

Cobo-Alice, 1880; left: new Cobo-Alice.

hand-carved wooden dolls
from early times

by HELEN BULLARD

HAND-CARVED WOODEN dolls may not have been the first dolls to be made, but they had survival qualities greater than cloth, wax, or any other simple material except clay. The oldest known dolls, which were probably votive objects, were clay and date around 2500 B.C.

Encountered nowadays in posh exhibitions of antique dolls, the "Queen Anne-type" woodens are the earliest type of dressed wooden doll which appears in modern collections. They are also known as "Queen Anne-Georgians" because they were made in both those English periods, from about 1690 to 1740. Each differed from all others in details.

With a knife and a few pieces of wood a creative and skillful carver can produce practically anything he has in mind; of that the distance between funny old "Aunt Thirza Cantrell," a country doll carved by a hunter for his little girl, and the earlier Queen Anne lovelies is proof enough. "Aunt Thirza" may not be elegant, but she has worlds more personality than the elegantes.

"Queen Anne" dolls were all wood, hand-carved, with human hair wigs, extra fancy court costumes, and rather vacant expressions. A surprising number of them exist. Probably because of their expensive, "worth-saving" costumes, they were cared for, passed down to heirs, and finally sold to collectors or, as with those in the photographs here, given to the Victoria and Albert Museum in London.

Another very old wooden, now preserved in the museum at Salisbury, England, is not a Queen Anne-type, but a French doll which Queen Marie Antoinette dressed while she was in prison in 1793.

Penny woodens were produced by the tens of thousands in many sizes and were very cheap. Also called "Dutch," a

Group of penny woodens celebrating May Day.

corruption of "Deutsch," they were made in cottage industries in Germany's Black Forest during the 15th to the 19th centuries, with whole families working on dolls. Of simple construction, they were jointed and fastened together with wooden pegs. Faces were flattish with sharp little carved noses protruding from the simple round faces. Hands were spoon-type; legs were usually sticks, sometimes with slippers indicated on a slightly swelled stick-end by painting. Later bodies, legs, and arms were lathe-turned. The dolls in Queen Victoria's famous collection, which she is said to have costumed when she was a very young girl, are penny woodens.

The pattern of the penny wooden varied little over the centuries. Modern copies were produced for a time in England, and good reproductions were made in this country by the House of Seven Gables in Marblehead, Mass. Few American hand-carved dolls owe anything to these penny woodens except for the jointing, which is so simple and functional that almost anyone could have figured it out.

The earliest hand-carved wooden doll in the collection of water color renderings in the Index of American Design, located in the National Gallery of Art, Washington, D.C., is a ball-jointed wooden with over-large head and hands, and fat legs, whose date of 1800 is unverifiable. The carved wooden heads of a Cree Indian pair, also from the Index, are artistically stylized, especially that of the man.

"Queen Anne" woodens. The smallest is 12", tallest, at far right, 24". 1690-1800.

Wooden doll (not Queen Anne type), dressed by Queen Marie Antoinette while in prison in Paris in 1793.

"Aunt Thirza Cantrell" ("Old Bullet Eyes"), carved by a hunter for his daughter, is a real country doll.

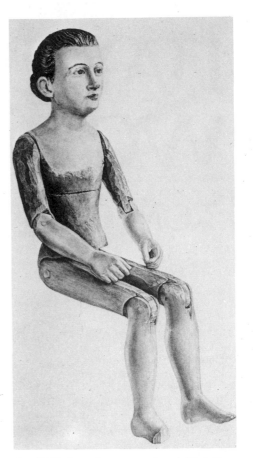

An 1800 American wooden, 16" tall; owned by the Society for the Preservation of New England Antiquities.

"School for Scandal" detail. The hair on the oversize head is human, dressed with flowers made of velvet, beadwork, pearls, shells, wax berries, etc.

Penny wooden doll, English, early 19th century, costumed as an English peddler by Mrs. Clive S. Hinckley.

Cree Indian dolls have carved heads and stuffed fabric bodies. Designed and made by Marie Rose of the Montana Cree Reservation late in the 19th century. 10" tall. Now at the Wenham (Mass.) Historical Society.

"School for Scandal" dolls, made completely of wood with jointed arms and legs; hands crudely carved where visible, with leather gloves. Tallest is 23". Late 17th and early 18th centuries.

Pincushion Dolls

While pins were known and used from ancient times, pincushion dolls probably didn't appear until the late 18th century. It is speculated that the first pincushion doll was made with a Queen Anne doll head. A pincushion doll with a painted wooden head and stuffed body dating from the early 19th century is represented in the collection of the New-York Historical Society, and a similar wooden-headed pincushion doll is in the collection of the Shelburne Museum, Shelburne, Vermont. But most of the pincushion dolls collectors find today were made in Germany and date about 1920 to 1930. The firm of *Dressel, Kister and Company* of Passau, Germany, produced some of the finest porcelain half-figures which ladies made into tea cosies, pincushions, lamps, and so on. Other manufacturers known to have made half-figures for pincushion dolls and other uses include the firms of *William Goebel* in Oeslau, Germany, and the *Royal Rudolstadt* factory, also in Germany. *Godey's Lady's Book* gave complete instructions for the making of a pincushion doll in at least two issues published in the 1860s; those illustrations and instructions have been included in this chapter.

Porcelain half-doll, nicely modeled and decorated in pastel colors with gold lustre trim; 5½ inches high. Collection Frieda Marion.

PINS WERE KNOWN and used from ancient times. However metal pins were expensive luxuries and some kind of safe depository for them was required. Covered boxes of various sorts were first used for this purpose, but pincushions also date back to the Middle Ages. Doll pincushions came into existence several centuries ago.

In Medieval times, pincushions of silver-tinseled satin often hung from the waist of figures of the Virgin Mary. These were probably the first pincushions related to dolls, although not exactly a doll pincushion. Similar pincushions were suspended from the waist of wooden dolls of the Queen Anne type made in Paris in the mid-18th century.

The first doll pincushion was probably not made until the late 18th century; these were made with a Queen Anne doll head. A doll pincushion with a painted wooden doll head and stuffed body dating from the early 19th century is represented in the collection of the New York Historical Society, and a similar type wooden-headed doll pincushion is in the collection of the Shelburne Museum, Shelburne, Vermont. These early doll pincushions are extremely rare.

Doll pincushions were also made of composition, such as papier mache, with fashion doll heads and with wax, bisque, Parian, and china heads. The china pincushion heads were made in various colors, including Negro types. At first pincushion dolls were made by breaking off the arms and legs of an ordinary doll, using just the head for this purpose. Sometimes the whole doll was stuffed down into the cushion.

The cult of the pincushion did not reach its zenith until early Victorian days when pins were machine-made and available in quantity. Bazaars became fashionable at this time and stalls selling home-made fancy work included pincushions which could be made with scraps of left-over materials. Mrs. Pullan and Mrs. Warren devoted much space to pincushions in their book, "Treasures of Needlework," but the first American doll pincushion in the form we know it today was illustrated in Mrs. Leslie's "American Girls' Book," in 1831. In the latter book, directions were given for making several doll pincushions. A doll bag or reticule held a small pincushion concealed in a muff. Another design for a "Woman Pincushion" was the model for the doll pincushion as we recognize it today.

Most doll pincushions of the 1834 period were similarly made and stuffed with bran. Also, the borders and designs of circles, diamonds, or stars made of pins were a characteristic feature of 19th century doll pincushions.

When dolls with china heads became popular, these doll heads were used instead of the earlier wooden and composition heads. Directions for making a "Miss Dinah Pen Wiper" were also given in Godey's 1861 issue. For these, it was suggested that the maker "get a black china baby." The "Bonbon Doll" illustrated in their 1870 issue called for the "head of a china doll."

"The Work Table Companion"

Left: Pincushion doll wearing a faded green silk dress with white at the neck; her shawl is natural colored linen. The tinted china head, painted blue eyes and black hair with vertical curls in the rear, is believed to be of German origin, ca. 1845. Height 4 1/3 inches. **Collection Henry Ford Museum.**

Below: "The Ladies' Friend" doll pincushion was illustrated in Godey's Lady's Book and Magazine (1864).

Doll Pincushions

by KATHERINE MORRISON McCLINTON

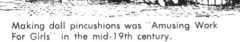

Making doll pincushions was "Amusing Work For Girls" in the mid-19th century.

illustrated in Peterson's Magazine (1860) was dressed as a Civil War nurse in a red dress with blue bands. Her pockets held scissors, thread, and other sewing necessities.

In 1865, Peterson's gave directions for making a "Little Companion." Godey's in 1864 illustrated a similar doll under the title "The Ladies Friend." This doll was dressed in a full stuffed skirt to serve as a pincushion, and the sash of her dress contained pockets for thimbles, bodkin, scissors, etc. A roll or spool of cotton thread was fastened to her back, and the basket atop her head held buttons.

In an 1876 edition of *American Agriculturist* "Aunt Sue" answered the request of "Cecilia" for directions for making a doll pincushion. She suggested a china doll head set within a ball made of sections of red and white flannel trimmed with black braid. There were no arms on this doll pincushion.

The popularity of doll pincushions lasted throughout the era of the china-headed Victorian doll, and on to the end of the 19th century. As popular as they were in Victorian times, there isn't a single one of these doll pincushions represented in the collection of Queen Victoria's dolls in the London Museum.

Although pincushions of some kind have been in continuous demand, simpler types that could be carried on the person or contained in a sewing basket gradually displaced the doll pincushion. Doll pincushions came back into popularity about 1910. At this period the doll heads or busts were made expressly for doll pincushions or other doll novelty articles.

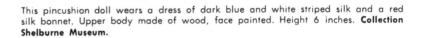

This pincushion doll wears a dress of dark blue and white striped silk and a red silk bonnet. Upper body made of wood, face painted. Height 6 inches. **Collection Shelburne Museum.**

Above and Below:

A pincushion doll dressed in Dutch costume was illustrated in Peterson's Magazine (1865). Directions were given for making this doll by Mrs. Jane Weaver:

"Get a small china doll. Break off the legs. Cut a round piece of cardboard two inches and a half across; sew securely round it a piece of calico the size of the round and three and a half inches deep. Stuff it firmly with wadding at the bottom of the round, and put less wadding as you go toward the waist, so as to make the doll a nice shape. Fasten the calico neatly round the waist. For the frock procure a piece of scarlet flannel ten inches wide and five inches in depth. Join it round, turn in the bottom and gather it, put in the doll and cushion, and draw the gathering round beneath the cardboard bottom. Fasten it firmly; gather with a strong thread round the top which needs a small turn in, and make another gathering one inch below for the waist. Tie these two gatherings round the shoulders and waist. Two holes must be made to pass the arms through, and two small, straight pieces of flannel sewn round the arms for short sleeves. The frock is then complete. The apron is a piece of white muslin three inches square, gathered at the waist and pinned on. The bib of the apron must be cut out to the diagram. The cap is of the same muslin as the apron, cut three inches and a half in depth, three inches and a quarter in width at the widest part, and two inches at the plain part which ties with a piece of cotton around the face. The whole is cut as nearly as possible in the horse-shoe form, gathered from one side of the front to the other, and drawn tightly up at the back. Then a little bit of china ribbon is tied round, with ends waving at the back. The doll is very quickly dressed."

New Information On

Pincushion Dolls *by FRIEDA MARION*

THE CHINA OR bisque half-figures, most of them with unglazed bases and sew holes, generally known as "pincushion dolls," were not always made to top pincushions. They were also found on powder boxes, clothes brushes, perfume bottles, small lamps, even umbrella handles. The bulk of them seem to have been made in Germany, and only a few bear their maker's mark.

The firm of Dressel, Kister and Co., Passau, Germany, gave us some of the finest half-figures. Dorothy Coleman, in *The Collector's Encyclopedia of Dolls*, lists this firm as having made, in 1925, porcelain doll busts for candy boxes,

tea cosies, pincushions, lamps, and so on. Their trademark is similar to a question mark in reverse and painted in blue.

Among the 72 dolls stolen in 1971 from the Yesteryears Museum in Sandwich, Massachusetts, was a beautiful half-doll described by the museum as "7-inch Elaborate Tea-cosy porcelain bust and head only, w/lazy question mark symbol, pink molded china cap w/'Dresden-type' basket of flowers and two doves on top of head. She holds a rose in her right hand; top quality."

Other manufacturers known to have marked their half-dolls were the William Goebel porcelain factory, which Coleman places in Oeslau, Thür, and Royal

Rudolstadt factory, Germany.

In the 1968 issue of the convention book published by the United Federation of Doll Clubs, Inc., a pincushion doll pictured is described as bearing a 4-petal flower impressed in blue on the base of the figure. Although the author says this indicates the piece was made before 1881, she does not tell us what company used this trademark nor how she arrives at the 1881 cut-off date. Other authors have suggested that pincushion dolls were made from the 1880s, but we can find no solid evidence to prove they were on the scene, at least in this country, before the 1900s. However, porcelain busts were quite

Left to right: Doll with beaded band in hair; unmarked; 3" high. A comb is set into the delicate blond hair of this half-figure holding a purple flower; incised "Germany 15502"; 2⅞" high. A blue fan and blue-plumed orange hat distinguish this half-figure; incised "Germany" with indistinct numerals; 3" high. Arms held away from body and a wreath of roses tied in her hair, this charming girl has rosy tinted breasts; marks indistinct: 2¼" high. Egyptian man with lips pursed and arms extended as if blowing a horn held before him; incised "14288 Germany"; 3¼" high. Egyptian woman with sloe eyes and beckoning finger; Egyptian decor became fashionable following the opening of King Tutankhamens tomb in the 1920s, which gives us a clue

as to the age of these two Egyptian half-figures; 2¾" high. Very detailed modelling with hair style of horizontal curls at sides and wide braid in back, topped with a dark blue bow; ribbon at bodice is painted a bright red-orange known as "Chinese Red—a very popular color during the 1930s; unmarked; 3" high. One of many types known to collectors as "Colonial Dames"; gray hair piled on top of head, she holds a pink fan striped with blue and green; the rose she holds is unpainted; incised with William Goebel mark; 3" high. Another grey-haired young lady, this one holding a mirror of silver lustre; incised "Germany 3673"; 2¾" high.

Photographs by WILLIAM T. LANE

Left to right: Known to collectors as "Spanish Dancer," this black-haired beauty has a blue comb in her hair; fine detail, but no flesh tones; incised "Germany"; 3" high. Blond curls piled high on her head and held with blue ribbon band; a fan to flirt with puts this lady in the "Garden Party" class; incised "Germany"; 3" high. Holding the ribbons of her close-fitting, rose-trimmed bonnet, this demure young lady has her right hand in a clenched fist behind her back; incised "Germany"; 3" high. A fine "Marie Antoinette" type with gray curls spilling on her shoulders and ruffles around her low-cut bodice; this half-figure has a Japanese counterpart of inferior quality; incised "Germany 8030"; 3¾" high. Bonneted "Garden Party Girl" with grey

eyeshadow, an unusual feature; good details and decoration; incised "Made in Germany" front and back, indistinct numerals; 4⅛" high. A true "Garden Party Girl" with black curls beneath her yellow-lined bonnet; this half-figure holds a single rose, a favorite pose for these fancy ladies; incised "6348 Germany"; 3¾" high. Roses beneath her wide hat brim and also held in her right hand, this pretty blonde half-figure has also been reproduced in Japan; incised "358 Germany"; 3" high. Another "Spanish Dancer," this one has a pink comb in her hair; delicate flesh tones distinguish her from the same model shown at the extreme left of this row, but the details are not as fine; incised "582(?) Germany"; 3" high.

probably popular in Europe and Great Britian for some time before their introduction in the United States.

An article in the *Woman's Home Companion* for April 1913, "Dolly at the Fair," by Martha Cobb Sanford, provides the earliest mention we found of pincushion dolls in an American publication. In it, directions were given for making bazaar items using dolls or dolls' heads. One of these, a "Watteau Cover for a toilet bottle," was fashioned from "one of the charming little Watteau bisque busts found in almost any fancy-work department." The illustration clearly indicated that the "Watteau bust" was a pincushion doll.

Catalog No. 28, issued by the Charles Williams Stores, Inc., Fall and Winter 1920, pictured a Dutch doll bust similar to one shown in Genevieve Angione's "Pincushion Dolls," *Spinning Wheel*, December 1963. The catalog cption reads: "Porcelain Doll Pincushion. Trimmed with satin. Pink and Blue. $1.19."

Surprisingly, the Sears Roebuck catalog of the same date yields nothing, but a reprint of the 1927 catalog, now on the market, shows a "Charming china lady, artistic dresser puff" for $1.48 and "Milady's Dresser Puff," also a "china lady" for $.98. Both are dressed in silk skirts and set in small glass compotes with, we presume, powder puffs in place of lower torso and legs. The collector is greatly indebted to the publisher who reprints old catalogs, as the originals are hard to come by, but in this case frustration was built in for the researcher. "Pincushion doll heads" were listed in the index, but the page carrying them was, alas, one of those deleted by the publisher.

The Daniel Low company, Salem, Massachusetts, offered several uses for a china half-figure in their 1927 catalog; here again is shown a child's figure with a Dutch cap. Termed a "French Powder Jar," this half-doll was described as a "Charming maiden with skirts of rose or blue silk, gold lace ruffles. 4" high, conceals glass powder jar with puff, $2.50. Or she may be a pincushion exactly the same size, $2.00. Set of the two, $4.25."

On the next page the same little girl, atop a silk-draped wire frame complete with electric socket and cord, was priced at $2.95, and her caption read, "A soft diffused light or a brighter one for reading by raising the skirt!" Nine inches high, this china half-figure was also "very specially priced" at $1.00, undressed.

Montgomery Ward and Company, in catalog No. 108, Fall and Winter 1928-29, displayed a china figure topping a powder puff, with a ribbon skirt partly covering the puff. About 4 inches high, this was priced at 23 cents! The little doll wears a fanciful hat, with ribbons and flowers, a type we category as a Garden Party Girl.

By mid-Depression days, these items had sunk to an even lower price. Sears, Roebuck's No. 106 Spring and Summer catalog 1933, advertised a hat brush with a china doll head, length about 8 inches, for 10 cents! The cut shows the doll, which forms the brush handle, with arms close to the body but bent at the elbows, raised to hold onto the brim of a floppy hat.

Collectors prefer dolls with arms away from the body since these show more workmanship. The better the

Left to right: A "Garden Party Girl" holds onto her pink bonnet; incised "Germany" and painted black numerals "19009"; 3¼" high. (Note: the next seven pincushion dolls fall into the "Flapper" category and were all probably produced during the late 1920s.) Bobbed hair with blue band, incised "5102 Germany"; 2¾" high. A feather in her blue head band sets off the short hair style of the 1920s; incised "Germany"; 3" high. Eye makeup *a la* Clara Bow, the cloche hat pulled low on her forehead, and her mannish tie all put this Flapper in the 1925-1928 period; indistinct markings; 3¼" high. Again, the dark-rimmed eye makeup and the insouciant pose depict the Flapper, but this young lady has a broad-brimmed hat and Bertha collar; incised "Made in Germany"; 4" high. Red hair with ears showing in what was known as the "boyish bob", practically covered by a close-fitting black cap; the china is thick and of a creamy tint; incised "4346 Germany"; 3½" high. Similar to another doll in this same row, this one is minus the bouquet held by her larger sister; incised "Germany"; 2" high. Delicately modeled of fine porcelain, this Flapper wears a red headband on her short black hair; it is interesting to note that the Flappers tend to have straight hair, often painted black, while the fanciful ladies usually have curls; incised "5882 Germany"; 2¼" high. A bonneted lass who fits into the loosely categorized "Garden Party Girls"; nice detail with blue ribbons and a blue-lined bonnet; back of half-figure is unpainted; incised "Germany 8039"; 3" high.

Left to right: Orange bodice trimmed in black, incised "Germany"; 2½" high. Nice quality with very good details; blue dress and pink bows; skirt held out over base to produce a peplum when the doll is made into a pincushion; stamped "Germany" on base; 2¾" high. Little girl with yellow bonnet and blue tassles; one arm held away from body; incised "Germany"; 2" high. Well modeled and delicately decorated Pierott marked "Germany 7" on bottom; 2¼" high. Little girl wearing Dutch cap, holding armful of yellow flowers; incised "Germany"; 2¼" high. Young woman with green parrot perched on her shoulder, sitting down with feet tucked under her, one slipper protruding beneath her skirt; 2¼" high. Young woman holding a mirror; this half-figure was originally a stopper for a perfume bottle with glass rod and cork inserted in the bottom; the author also has two unpainted glazed dolls of the same model but in a reverse position, with head turned to the other side and mirror held in the left hand; 2¾" high.

design and nicety of detail and the finer the decoration, the higher the value. Because so many models were made, the collector can choose from a number of categories to develop an interesting collection. Besides the Garden Party Girls, there are the amusing Flappers with their sloe eyes and shingled hair. Some wear close-fitting cloche hats drawn low over the eyes; some sport "spit curls"; and others are adorned with plumes or forehead bands.

Children and men pincushion dolls are rare. Dolls holding fans, mirrors, books, teacups, letters, or other accessories, especially if executed in good proportion and detail, have added interest and value. Animals are occasionally found, but these would make a very small collection indeed. There are also those rare *complete* figures, made with a base and sew holes that must be classed as pincushion dolls although they are not half-figures. A red-clad

bathing beauty of this type is in the Gerritt Beverwyk collection, and a lady with a parrot on her shoulder, seated with her legs curled under her, is in this author's collection.

Although trade-marked pincushion dolls are not common, most of them are incised "Germany." Many also appear marked "Japan," usually of lesser workmanship. Quite apparent reproductions, these seem to be duplicates of a larger German-made figure.

A pair of exquisite porcelain half-figures bearing the mark of Dressel, Kister & Co. painted in blue. Made from the same mold, the doll on the left wears a wreath of pink and yellow roses in her hair, while the one on the right has only a single full-blown rose and bud. Each holds a rose in her right hand. The narrow waist, minus a flange, seems to be typical of Dressel, Kister & Co. pincushion dolls. These dolls were purchased in France during the early years of this century. 3¼" high.

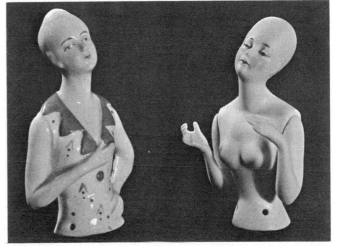

Two half-figure dolls made with bald, unglazed pates on which to glue wigs. The doll on the left is marked "Germany" inside the figure; her collar is painted orange. The doll on the right is of white bisque with delicately tinted eyes, mouth and cheeks; this doll has the added feature of having movable arms, elastic-jointed; incised "6078"; 3½" high.

An exceptionally fine porcelain half-figure bearing the incised mark of William Goebels. It was from this original that the "Mannikin Doll" was reproduced. Formerly in the collection of Genevieve Angione, it was illustrated in Mrs. Angione's article about pincushion dolls, SW dec.'63. 5" high. Author's collection.

Profile view of William Goebel's half-figure formerly in the collection of Genevieve Angione.

It is an intriguing thought that for every little one made in Japan there may be somewhere the original model from Germany.

Almost every doll collector has one or two pincushion dolls tucked on the shelves of her doll cabinet, and many books about dolls have a few paragraphs or a couple of photos devoted to them. Pincushion dolls with elastic-strung moveable arms are illustrated in *Handbook of Collectible Dolls* by Merrill and Perkins, and also in a series of advertisements by the Mary Merritt Doll Museum which appeared in the *Toy Trader* in 1967. The Merritt Museum dolls were bisque, bald, and needing wigs. The Merritt illustrations show a variety of other models, including clowns, Dutch girls, Egyptians, and plenty of Garden Party Girls. They were captioned "Old Store Stock" and, as we were informed later, were bought in France where they had been stored for years.

Among the early books for doll collectors, Janet Johl's *Still More About Dolls* reproduced a page of pincushion dolls distributed by the New York

Left: Mark used by William Goebels, Oeslau, Thuringen, Germany. **Right:** Mark used by Dressel, Kister & Co., Passau, Bavaria, Germany.

importers, Foulds and Freure, Inc. The caption tells us that the firm went out of business several years before Mrs. Johl's book was published in 1950. The dolls were called "Imported China Glazed Novelty Heads," and Mrs. Johl noted that the most expensive averaged about 67 cents apiece, wholesale.

Foulds and Freure also advertised china legs, often painted with gold slippers, at $2.40 a dozen, wholesale. These were to be sewn onto the pincushion so as to protrude beneath the fancy skirt and add a flippant touch to a dainty pincushion lady.

A group of excellent photos of very fine half-dolls is shown in the 1970 edition of the convention book put out by the United Federation of Doll Clubs, Inc., all of which are in the collection of one of the members. The author mentions four different sizes of one model.

Like many other antiques and collectibles, pincushion dolls have been reproduced. We class as contemporary those made in Japan even if they were copies of German Dolls, but within the past few years a revival of interest in the half-figures prompted the Mark Farmer Company in California to add

reproductions of two pincushion dolls to their stock of reproduced china-heads. Called "Flapper cushions," the dolls shown in the 1969-1970 catalog were described as "delicate and lovely in bisque." The kit containing the decorated torso and materials for making up the pincushion was priced at $6.50, while the completed doll was marked $12.50. Another pincushion doll, made from a copy of a china-head play doll was also advertised. Apparently the Flapper reproductions never caught on as they did not appear in the 1970-71 catalog.

A rather curious reproduction of a pincushion doll has been on the market for several years, offered as a complete doll with the lower part being made of wood in the manner of the old peg-woodens. This doll's head appears to be a copy of the model shown at the top of page 18 in Mrs. Angione's story in *Spinning Wheel*, December 1963. Only the head and shoulders have been used in reproduction, the arms being of wood like the body.

This doll has been advertised in a number of gift catalogs, priced around $3. The accompanying blurb is always the same: "Handmade Bisque Mannikin Doll with Jointed Wood Body. European Museum Replica. Lovely bisque top, hand-decorated with fully jointed arms and legs to take any position. 9 inches." The doll is made by the Shackman Company. The original

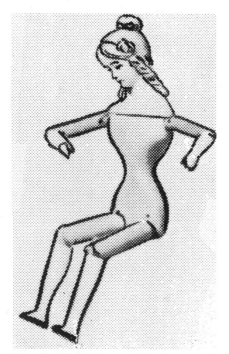

This wood and bisque Mannikin doll, advertised by the Standard Doll Co., Long Island, N. Y., was obviously copied from the finely made William Goebels' doll shown in our illustrations. The half-figure was made in Japan for the Shackman Co. of New York and appeared on the market in the late 1960s.

bears the William Goebel mark.

Although pincushion dolls are usually found minus their lace and silk furbelows, it is desirable to include at least one sample in a collection which shows how these figures were originally made up. Besides their infinite variety, an asset to any serious collector, pincushion dolls can be displayed in small space. On shelf or table, in groups or singly, they create interest but are, alas, subject to breakage. Better to put a really fine piece under a glass dome where it can be securely held on a dowel. The lovely Dressel and Kister items tend to have narrow waists and lack the broad flanges needed for firm balance and a small wooden dowel can protect them from falls.

A large collection of half-dolls can be exhibited in a glass-fronted shallow cabinet hung on a wall. Often a choice old picture frame can form the basis of such a cabinet.

Many doll pincushions were dressed in period costumes, such as the Queen Elizabeth illustrated in Godey's Lady's Book, March, 1867. The directions for making this doll pincushion were as follows:

"Procure a doll about six inches high. Cut a round piece of pasteboard for the foundation, then sew muslin around it; place the doll in center, fill with bran, and fasten around the waist. Then proceed to dress her, as follows: An underskirt of white satin, embroidered with gold thread; an overskirt of black velvet trimmed with embroidered bands of white satin; the waist and sleeves to correspond. The neck and wrists are finished by a Queen Elizabeth ruff. Three rows of beads around the neck. Handkerchief in hand. A turban, made of fine white muslin and black velvet. The pins are to be placed around the edge of bottom of skirt."

Contemporary Dolls

Most of the dolls in this section of our book were made by members of the National Institute of American Doll Artists, Inc. They range in size from Lilliputian one-inch tall dolls to full-size mannequins. Made of various materials, they represent the finest contemporary dolls available to collectors. Some, like those portrait dolls made by Dewees Cochran, have superbly modeled features and bodies. Still others are fine character dolls meant to amuse rather than portray real live people. To join the N.I.A.D.A, prospective members must submit samples of their work to a board comprised of current members of this distinguished group for their approval. If the dolls meet the high standards this organization insists upon, the prospects are enrolled and certified as members. The dolls range in price from under $50 to considerably more than that figure. Most are limited editions and once sold will never be made again. Special orders can also be placed with members of the N.I.A.D.A. Currently, a book is being compiled about the members of the N.I.A.D.A. which will report on their backgrounds and the kind of dolls they create. This should be on the market by the end of 1975.

"Thomas," a Kate Greenaway-type boy doll created by Eunice Tuttle in 1970.

DEWEES COCHRAN'S
Dolls Are People!

by R. LANE HERRON

IN 1934, DEWEES COCHRAN arrived in New York after eight years in Europe. There she had studied Art History, given lectures, and won recognition for her own work in painting. Now that she was home again, she chose to turn to the dollmaking craft rather than continue her painting.

She took some examples of the unusual dolls she had developed to exclusive shops in New York and Philadelphia. TOPSY and TURVY and some American period dolls popularizing the pantalette era were her first sellers. Adult collectors proved the best buyers; the dolls were too cleverly wrought for children. She was told that if she intended to get into the doll business seriously, which meant designing for children, the doll should be realistic. Parents did not want their children playing with anything fantastic or grotesque that might warp their impressionable minds.

At first she was stunned. Then, if adults wanted reality, Dewees reasoned, what better than a living portrait doll of their child? She took the idea to a popular upper Madison Avenue children's shop. Her new toy would be a "Portrait Doll," meticulously sculpted and dressed, made of a durable casting compound.

Portrait Dolls (1936). Cincinnati sister and brother with plastic wood heads on Eff-An-Bee doll bodies of Dewees Cochran design.

Within five days, orders literally rained upon her from the Madison Avenue shop—orders from their prominent patrons. Carved balsa wood and stuffed silk bodies were used for these first orders. So successful were they that *Harper's Bazaar* gave them space and started a chain of publicity which has lasted to this day.

Children, debutantes, brides, screen stars, even dignified school principals wanted a doll portrait of themselves. A well-known doll collector had her mother done from photographs taken in 1868 when she was 18 years old and just married.

Dewees soon realized the hard work entailed. Although she worked basically from photographs, eliminating tedious sittings, there were parts to buff, designs to be made of sturdy flexible joints, wigs to be brushed, combed, styled, shoes to be made that would not come unglued, costumes to be realistically fashioned, as well as the painting and finishing.

At first she did everything herself. But with the onslaught of mail orders, the work had to be shared among wig makers, special leather workers for shoes, dressmakers, and molders while she concentrated exclusively on portraiture.

To create a doll that looks "real" is not easy. There must be restraint to avoid a "dummy" appearance. If too much photographic realism is modelled into a head which is then painted, wigged, and lastly given the broken neckline to make the head swivel, the result can be a strange little "effigy" figure instead of a pleasant doll likeness.

Originally from Philadelphia where she had attended the

Grow-Up Doll (Belinda Bunyan) at age 5 years and 20 years.

Portrait Dolls (the daughters of Lt. Comm. Hutton) by Dewees Cochran (1963).

Academy of Fine Arts before going to Europe to live, Dewees and her husband had owned a little cottage in New Hope, Pa. On their return to American shores they rented a tiny stone house, part of an old Quaker estate, Holikong, five miles from their old home. There her doll success began.

She sold her first doll-joint patent for cloth dolls with molded faces (used on Topsy and Turvy) in 1935, and with the money obtained, moved to New York to continue doll research and develop her Portrait Dolls. A workshop and showroom was opened at 4 East 46th Street with a staff of assistants. The Silver Spoon set weren't the only ones interested in the incredible dolls. There was a considerable number of orders which definitely required financial sacrifice on the part of fond parents.

A less expensive portrait doll materialized in 1936 when Dewees, calling on her knowledge and study of physiognomy, developed six basic face shapes for American children. With these, any artist who could paint fairly well and select the correct type for a given subject could create a reasonable portrait doll.

Eff-An-Bee Doll Company contracted four of the first examples. These were manufactured briefly as "Portrait Dolls." They were an immediate success in the higher priced doll field, and were the first realistically proportioned character dolls, with the exception of baby dolls, ever mass-produced in the United States.

The *Cindy Doll* manufactured by Dewees Cochran Dolls.

In 1939, Saks Fifth Avenue featured these dolls from the angle of special order for likenesses for which they had been designed originally. *Life* gave them the April 3, 1939 cover and feature story.

All went well until that September when the war years brought doll production to a halt for Mrs. Cochran. Latex was the culprit, having been requisitioned as a strategic war material. For a while Dewees made portrait figurines in terra-cotta and unique figures and heads in plastic wood. Then she laid aside her dollmaking to go to work for the R. H. Donnelly Corp. By 1944, she was Art Director of that firm.

In 1945 she became Design Director of the School for American Craftsmen in Hanover, N.H. Two years later, when the school moved to Alfred, N.Y., Mrs. Cochran elected to remain in Norwich, Vt., across the river from Hanover, where she had been living, and established a workshop studio. Here she perfected her "Look-Alike" doll based on physiognomy types. She retained the New York studio, and formed, with an associate, a company called Dewees Cochran Dolls.

"Cindy," the modern Cinderella, was created in 1947. She was a 15-inch doll of latex made by a patented process which was owned by a New Jersey firm. This company contracted for fabrication of the dolls.

At the "Cindy" workshop at 10 East 46th Street, New York City, the doll was assembled, wigged, dressed, packed, and shipped. Dewees was gratified with the substantial first orders. However, the fabricator, with an eye to mass production, failed to keep up the first high standards. The contract was broken and Mrs. Cochran withdrew from the company. (Authentic Cindys are marked "Dewees Cochran Dolls" on the left side torso, embossed.)

Dewees Cochran's *Little Miss of 1830*. One of a series of six periods of American children (1934-1935).

In 1948 a new version of "Look-Alike" dolls was ready. Marshall Field and Co. of Chicago featured them that October, with Mrs. Cochran making a personal appearance to introduce them. The lower priced quality doll now became a reality. These were sold wholesale throughout the country as "fine handmade character dolls, no two alike."

As it was difficult to get someone to finish cast latex properly, Mrs. Cochran soon found herself doing it all in her Norwich workshop. Cast latex of top quality, she is convinced, is definitely a hand process.

In 1952 came the famous "Grow-Up" dolls. The girls grew up through ages 5, 7, 11, 16 and 20; the boys grew up through ages 5, 14, and 23. Faces, bodies and sizes developed in accordance with age. These doll children were Susan Stormalong, Angela Appleseed, Belinda Bunyan, Peter Ponsett, and Jefferson Jones.

In 1960, Dewees closed the Norwich studio and moved to California. Now at her "one-man" factory in Felton, California, she still makes dolls—portraits, Look-Alikes, and the "Grow-Up" series.

Dewees Cochran and two of her *Portrait Dolls* (1960).

Dewees Cochran with her six basic *Look-Alike* heads and two complete dolls (1960).

Dolls That Sleep In Thimbles - The Irma Park Story

"Peddler Grannie," an early Park creation, stands 11" tall.

by R. LANE HERRON

IRMA PARK'S "tinies" have won the hearts of children and doll collectors alike, have made her one of the busiest of dollmakers, and earned her membership in the prestigious National Institute of American Doll Artists. Their story—and Miss Park's—is one of try this, try that, and try again, with the happiest of storybook endings.

It began in the depression-wracked 1930s when Irma Park and her mother, Lenore, found themselves broke and alone in Los Angéles. Things looked up when Irma found a $16 a week bookkeeping job, and by 1939, they had saved enough to buy out two small gift stocks. While Mrs. Park took charge of the gift shop, Irma continued in an office. In her spare time she found numerous outlets for her vast creative energy. She modeled figurines for magazine covers, wrote newspaper articles and hobby pages, made up puzzles and pattern books, and invented such diverse gadgets as a household steak cuber, a weed digger, and a doll with movable facial expressions.

In the early 1940s she began collecting antique German bisque dolls, and in her first dollmaking venture she made up several 12-inch character dolls, using buckram pressed into molds for the heads.

In the meantime, her artistic mother,

who had been painting oils which she sold in the shop, branched out into some rose-trimmed trays made of a composition material. A salesman saw them and brought her some ceramic clay. Irma bought a kiln and set it up in the shop. Shortly she gave up her job to work with her mother making ceramics. The salesman, travelling East, took samples of their work with him. By mid-1945, the Parks had purchased a home, built a workroom in the rear, installed a 20-cubic foot kiln, and "Lenore's Ceramics" were being shipped throughout the United States. The line consisted of such items as hand-crimped and molded bowls, trays, baskets, boxes, and vases, hand-decorated with the roses, stems, and buds which were Mrs. Park's inimitable specialty.

This was Mother Park's success, for the ceramics were hugely popular, but the work proved too exhausting for the two women, and in 1950 they closed out the business. Though they opened again five years later, adding to the rose line leaf bowls and items with flowers and leaves with the original veins impressed in the ceramic copies, working conditions soon forced them out of the ceramic business permanently.

Through it all, Irma had never lost touch with dolls. Her bisque-headed doll collection now numbered over 300.

With a projected doll museum in mind, Irma began a series of 6½-inch dolls, costumed as Kings and Queens. Only 40, covering but a few centuries, had been completed when, in 1961, tragedy struck. Mrs. Parks became an invalid overnight and remained helpless until her death nine years later.

To fill her hours at home, to keep her hands and mind busy, and to help out financially, Irma turned seriously to dollmaking. She deserted the one-of-a-kind King and Queen series as too intricate with detail to be a successful money maker, and turned to 11-inch character dolls with wire base bodies and wax coating over a cornstarch formula for the heads, arms, and legs. Still dissatisfied, she went back to a Peddler Grannie which she had created earlier and which had sold well. Grannie also proved unprofitable and was soon discarded.

Recalling an advertisement in Kimport's *Doll Talk* for Dothy Hesner's 1-inch "Minnie Prue," she decided to try tiny dolls herself. Eventually her 2¾-inch Notion Grannie emerged, to be followed, in the same size, by Mary Queen of Scots, Queen Elizabeth, Joan of Arc, a group of clowns, Grannie in a rocker, and Hobo Joe. These were all sold through Kimport.

In 1966, Irma determined to try some-

Left: "Walking Dolly." **Right:** "Arms Full." Both 1⅞" tall,

Left: "Katie." **Right:** "Betsy," a two-faced doll. Both 2" tall.

The regal "Queen Elizabeth" and "Sir Walter Raleigh" dolls from the 6½" King and Queen series started some years ago.

Lenore Park's flower-studded baskets.

Left: "Fisher." **Right:** "Lost." Both 1⅞" tall.

Doll scene aptly entitled "First Love," 2" tall.

Left: "Waif." **Right:** "Help." Both 1⅝" tall.

"Doll's Dolls," ranging in size from ¼ to 1" tall.

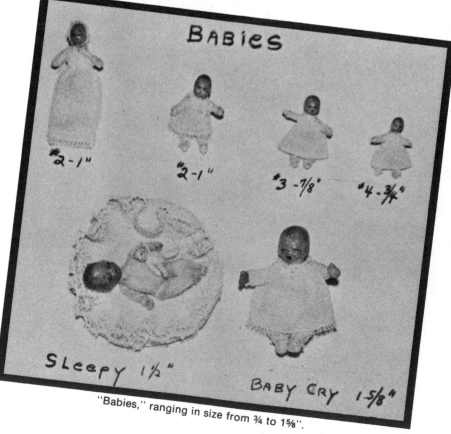

"Babies," ranging in size from ¾ to 1⅝".

thing even smaller—1⅝ and 1⅞-inch doll children with even tinier 1-inch doll children of their own. These she would market herself. Creating a dainty body on a 1-inch doll and making clothes for it that did not look bulky presented problems, but with inspired persistence she developed her own eminently successful techniques.

In September of that year, she had perfected a 1-inch Tom Thumb, and three children, 1⅝ and 1⅞-inches tall —Broken Doll, Little Mama, and Waiting—with their own 1-inch dolls. Irma's friend and encourager, Edna Atchison, took the wee dolls to doll club meetings —and to this day, Irma has never been without an order.

"Doll's Dolls"—May, Sal, and Peg, each 2" tall.

Miniature Rag Dolls, all about 1" tall.

She now has around three dozen characters in her line, the tallest 2 inches, the smallest, an infinitesmal $1/4$-inch tall. The current crop of dolls are wax over composition; most of the bodies are on a wire base. She works with the aid of a magnifying glass, a tray on her lap.

"The hard part is to get the clothes to fit properly," Miss Park confesses. "An hour can easily be spent on some unnoticeable detail to get it to look just right. If my fingers fumble and a doll or part of the clothing drops, what a search begins! Once a shirt for a fisher boy was there one moment, gone the next. I found it finally—dangling from a strand of my hair, whisked there by the breeze of the fan."

"Diamond Lil" in all her glory; 16" high.

Dewees Cochran working on one of her famous "Look-Alikes." Herbert Vanek's favorite doll; 14" high.

Vanek's son, Peter, as the eternal Little Leaguer; 14" high.

Herbert Vanek Dolls
A Viennese Sculptor Turned Dollmaker

by R. LANE HERRON

Charlie Chaplin doll in four of his most characteristic poses; 16" high.

Close-up of the Charlie Chaplin doll.

HERBERT VANEK had been doing portrait sculpture for about 16 years when he was approached to do a head for a "pouty" doll. The idea of making dolls fascinated him immediately. And why not? Weren't they, after all, miniature sculpture at its finest and most intricate?

Thus began his career as a dollmaker. He chose porcelain bisque as his medium, finding in it an almost human translucence and believability, textured and warm appearing. Porcelain also lends itself to a wide variety of treatment, from the traditional satin finish to a rugged, almost carved effect. For Herbert Vanek, porcelain is the supreme material about dolls, he began a search for information, finally stumbling upon Helen Bullard's *The American Doll Artist*. He wrote to some of the artists mentioned therein and received from them invaluable advice and encouragement, particularly from Astry Campbell, Magge Head, Wee Paulson, and the master herself, Dewees Cochran.

During his period of trial and error and much hard work prior to his acceptance to the National Institute of American Doll Artists in Omaha, in 1972, he was sustained by the loyal friendship and encouragement of Mrs. Cochran who lives near him in California's Santa Cruz mountains. During their frequent visits she consented to sit for a portrait doll sculpture which, after a year's labor, resulted in his latest and most satisfying endeavor—a likeness doll of Dewees, characteristically at work on one of her own dolls.

Mr. Vanek's first "doll" was after a bust of his young son, Peter, created 11 years ago when the child was 18 months old. The next doll was Peter as he appears today, engaged in his favorite sport, baseball—the popular "Little Leaguer" doll. A rock and roll guitar player became Herbert's third creation, christened "Modern Troubador" by the imaginative Mrs. Cochran. Other outstanding Vanek creations are his "Diamond Lil," "Charlie Chaplin," and "Tom Sawyer."

His greatest challenge as a dollmaker is the doll that combines "flexibility" with realism. "It is an intriguing problem of design and articulation," he says. "All parts of the doll must be modeled and lifelike."

"Charlie Chaplin," for instance, is designed to assume many of his characteristic poses, and his face is sculpted so that he appears droll looking up and sad looking down. "Tom Sawyer" is Mr. Vanek's most ambitious effort so far. He is completely articulated so that he can stand, sit, crouch, fish, and paint fences!

The work required to complete a single doll is considerable. The preliminary stages include modeling, "sectioning" the figure into various parts, designing joints, and firing each individual piece. Next, molds of each part are made and a cast of either porcelain slip or clay is made from the molds. The cast pieces are then reworked, given final detail and finish, and again fired. From these pieces come the working molds from which the final doll parts are cast. These are cleaned, polished, fired, polished, fired, and polished again. Lastly comes the frosting on the cupcake—the china is painted, eyes set, wigs affixed, parts assembled, and the dolls costumed.

Herbert Vanek does not come by his talent casually. His father was a painter and musician. His grandfather was a sculptor, woodcarver, and maker of musical instruments. Born in Vienna, he moved to England prior to the war in 1939. In 1945 he was apprenticed to a commercial art studio in London, at the same time attending evening classes at the Slade School and Croyden School of Fine Arts. In 1948 he came to America as an exchange student, studying art and literature at Friends University, Wichita, Kansas, and then at the University of Nebraska, Lincoln.

Mr. Vanek felt at home in America. He stayed, married, and had two children. He has returned to Europe only to visit his father from time to time. His son, now 13, provided the inspiration for "Baby Peter" and "Little Leaguer." His daughter, now 19, will eventually be the model for a companion to the "Modern Troubador."

After graduation from the University of Lincoln, Herbert worked for several studios and companies as a commercial artist and editor, at the same time developing his true interest—portrait sculpture. He moved to California in 1960.

The Modern Troubador doll, so named by Mrs. Cochran; 14" high.

Close-up of Tom Sawyer doll.

Tom Sawyer "Just a fishin'." 16" high.

SATIRE DOLLS in the GRAND MANNER

by R. LANE HERRON

"Lady in fur cape," 14" tall.

Left: Little feathered friend," 11" tall.

"Hypochondriac," 11" tall.

THE SATIRE DOLLS which Herta Forster, born Herta Horst in Darmstadt, Germany, now makes in California were not evolved overnight, nor without travail. Their faces reflect a lifetime's observation, understanding, and rueful acceptance of mankind's frailities and foibles.

Both Herta's grandfather, Prof. Wilhelm Horst, and her father were painters, sculptors, and restorers of museum paintings, numbering among their clients the Hesse Landes Museum in Darmstadt. Both men enjoyed making toys and miniatures, and Herta was introduced early to the joys of artistic creation.

Her childhood was pleasant enough, but the years under Hitler, through the World War II—she avoided military draft by studying to become a kindergarten teacher—and the early years of the Allied occupation were difficult indeed. The Horst home in Darmstadt was completely destroyed by Allied bombs in 1944, and the family was given haven by friends in a nearby village. With banks and their records destroyed and no work to be had, Herta helped out as best she could by making stuffed dolls and Teddy Bears from rags and drapery material provided by more fortunate friends. In 1946 when times had stabilized, she entered art school and for two years studied anatomy, sculpture, and painting.

In 1948 she met and married Rudolph Forster, an investigator for the U. S. military intelligence, and as a war bride, came with him to California. There her husband joined the Immigration Service, and for four years Herta worked for the telephone company. From then on, she has devoted herself to her home and dollmaking.

She has made felt children, puppets—a 12 character Punch and Judy theatre complete with stage, marionettes for local

"Soothsayer," 14" tall.

"Centaur," 17" tall.

puppeteers, and stuffed animals galore, some of which have been used in local Los Angeles TV commercials. Ruth Buzzi of *Laugh-In* fame bought her "Gladys and Thyrone" dolls.

Her boy and girl dolls stand 14 inches high. Their plastic wood heads are made from a mold, and felt covered. Hair may be fake fur, mohair, or synthetic. Black button eyes are enhanced with lids. Body, arms, and legs are of felt, stuffed with firm kapok. Fingers are individually hand-stitched; legs and head are swivel-jointed; arms move freely. A 13-inch Baby doll wears jacket, diaper, and booties.

About 1960 she began her satires, inspired by the powerful impressions made on her as a child by the photo album of Wilhelm Busch, German satirist and humorist, a book she

"Empire lady," 11" tall.

"Baroque man," 16" tall.   "Biedermeir lady," 20" tall.

had clung to through all her travels. To date she has made 97 satires.

The satire characters are one-of-a-kind. Their wood composition heads, modelled separately for each character, are hand-painted. Various materials are used for the hair—vicuna wood, human or synthetic hair, fake fur, and crepe-hair. Arms and legs are of felt, stretched over a wire frame and

"My goodness what a beak!"; 14" tall.

"Peddler woman," 11" tall.

kapok stuffed. Fingers and arms are carefully hand-stitched.

With few exceptions, Mrs. Forster has made all their clothing, accessories, and accompanying furniture. Sizes range from 12 to 22 inches, the 14-inch size being her favorite. She prefers not to work on order, but remains open to suggestions and ideas. The satires vary in price from $75 upwards.

Felt Dolls With A French-Canadian Accent

by R. LANE HERRON

ALTHOUGH MADELINE SAUCIER of Montreal, Quebec, has created dolls in every conceivable medium, it is for her felt dolls she has won international recognition.

When the collector of dolls thinks "felt," the mind conjures visions of two other women whose dolls delighted the world in the 1920s—Nora Wellings of England, and Elena Konig di Scavini who, as "Lenci," became famous for her large-eyed children dolls and elaborate portrait dolls.

Madeline Saucier's dolls are less flamboyant than Lenci's and more realistic. Since 1966, she has specialized in felt portraiture of living children and adults. Presently she is completing a new series of portrait and one-of-a-kind originals in various sizes, commissioned by museums and private collectors.

Most of her dolls are registered in Canada as works of art, copyrighted, and of limited edition. Her more recent creations are dated and initialed on the body. Her dolls, with pressed felt (hardened) faces, are fully wired for articulation at neck, hips, and fingers. The features are hand-painted; inserted eyelashes and wigs are of Saran.

Madeline's dollmaking dates to her childhood. She was eight years old when, during a long convalescence after an illness, she was given an assortment of small dolls in need of repairs and additions. Intrigued with the repair work, she was soon making her own dolls, using wired cloth bodies and wax, and giving each a costume.

At convent school, her interests gravitated toward the Fine Arts—drawing, painting, modeling, and sculpture—and she became the youngest member ever to win the *Ecole des Beaux Arts* Award. Despite her natural artistic leanings in the broad arena of art, her mind continued to stray toward dollmaking, and she began experimentation in the various media, trying to find the one that would please her most.

After convent, Madeline attended the Pedagogique in Montreal and later the Art School of the Montreal Museum of Fine Arts, studying anatomy, portraiture, painting, and drawing. At Sir George Williams University she studied sculpture and modeling. Later she took further portrait work under Adam Sherriff Scott of the Royal Academy of Arts.

With this impressive background, Madeline opened her

Portrait of John as Canadian Snow Baby, 17"; red-haired Fanchon in 1860 style dress, 14½".

Portrait of Suzanne in red pants suit, 14½"; Canadian girl in Sunday best, 1890 style, 12"; Farm boy, 12".

"La Cantiniere," (canteen girl of New France), 14"; portrait of 6-year-old dressed as Canadian Beaver, 16½".

own studio where she taught drawing and portraiture. Continuing her study of dollmaking, she produced dolls of wood, wax, needle modeling, composition, cloth, papier-mâché, and finally felt. During this busy period she worked as a designer for Raphael Tuck & Sons and also via mail, for the Wilkinson Company, both of New York.

In 1938, her bronze bust, "Grape Woman" was exhibited by Marcus and Company, New York. That same year she was offered a bursary to take medical drawing and sculpture at Johns Hopkins Medical School in Baltimore, Maryland, but World War II intervened to prevent her acceptance. During the war years she headed a Red Cross group, but war or no war, she never slighted her dolls.

In 1947, she married Maj. André Morin a military attaché in Paris; six years later their son, André, Jr., was born. Major Morin died in January 1961 after a lengthy illness.

Madeline continued with her art work. Setting her goals toward dollmaking where her real interest lay, she took a special course in applied arts. She was commissioned to make a series of 17 dolls, dressed in the national costumes of various countries, for a show entitled, "Fashion International," put on by the Fashion Group of America. (Three years later,

Madeline Saucier holding Fanchon and Snow Baby.

Royal Canadian Mounted Police, 19"; Drummer boy, Les Compagnies Franches de la Marine, 1730 period, 14"; Samuel de Champlain, first Governor of New France, founder of Quebec City.

Jordan Marsh, a department store in Boston, Massachusetts, reproduced this series with other special dolls.)

In 1965, Madeline presented some 30 dolls in a one-man show in a Fine Arts Centre at Stewart Hall, Point Claire on the Island of Montreal. At Expo '67 in Montreal, she showed 35 other unusual dolls, many of them life portraits of Canadian children. Also in 1967, she showed these dolls at the Convention of the United Federation of Dolls' Clubs, held in Boston, where they won the Patrons Award given by the National Institute of American Doll Artists. The following year she became a member of that prestigious organization. In 1969, she gave an important doll exhibition at the Montreal Museum of Fine Arts.

Her masterful creations reached even higher levels in the educational field when the University of Ottawa's Dept. of

Madeleine de Vercheres, 14-year-old historical heroine, 14"; Canadian girl in Red River outfit, 14" (also made in larger size); "Habitent" woman of 1806, 14".

Lili with doll purse, 16½"; Pierrette in Red River outfit with snowshoes, 16½"; Suzanne in blue, holding lilies, 14½".

DOLLMAKER AT WORK

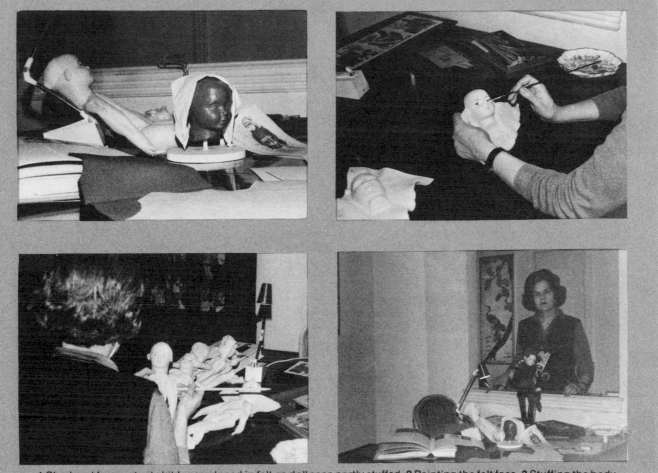

1 Clay head from actual child reproduced in felt on doll seen partly stuffed. **2** Painting the felt face. **3** Stuffing the body after wiring. **4** Madeline Saucier with the finished doll.

Psychology and Education, asked her for a monograph on "Doll Art," and the University of Montreal's Dept. of Anthropology asked for another on "Doll Creation."

In 1964, the Montreal Historical Society donated some of her dolls to the New York Military Museum for permanent display; Walt Disney commissioned a group for Disneyland; McGill University in Montreal followed suit. She has appeared on Canadian television eight times, three of them on coast-to-coast network; she has also lectured on educational television and taped, in French, a radio broadcast for use over Belgian stations.

Madeline Saucier's work in the doll field is living testimony to the durability, importance, and educational value of dolls in relation to human environment and growth, and exemplifies that the making of them is an important branch of the Fine Arts. She has paved a wide road for dollmakers of the future.

Fig. 1: Children dancing the Horra. Dolls, 7 and 8 inches tall, by Edith Samuel.

Fig. 2: Edith Samuel's workroom. Dolls and models sit on and about her sewing machine and on shelves.

Two German Doll Makers

by MARY HILLIER

— A Study In Contrast —

THE SOFT TOYS of Kathe Kruse and of Margarethe Steiff are familiar to all collectors and the history of these two famous German dollmakers is well known. Now two German dollmakers in our own time have continued the best tradition of making dolls by hand, and their work, too, will be collected.

Edith Samuel (1907-1964) and Helma Gotz were both born in Germany, and both, as children, dreamt of an ideal doll. Both had professional art training and set about making dolls for a livelihood. There the parallel ends. In output their work could not be more different nor their destinies more opposed.

EDITH SAMUEL

Edith Samuel was not born under a lucky star. In person she was small and fragile, curious in appearance with a tragi-comic face and huge expressive eyes. She depicted herself in models and portrait dolls which seemed to recall her childhood.

She was born in Essen in 1907, the youngest child of the head Rabbi of the Jewish Community there. Her father and brothers were musical, but from their mother she and her sister inherited artistic talent. They were brought up in an atmosphere of culture, surrounded by books and educated to an interest in art and literature by visits to museums and galleries.

From travels abroad, her father brought back foreign dolls. Inevitably among her toys was a Kathe Kruse model dressed like a toddler. Like any other little girl she acted out the small injustices of her life with dolls and to her they seemed to possess living souls. As she grew older she excused her love of doll-play by making models from cloth material or paper. Always her theme was children and she liked to write and illustrate fairy stories with little characters. Her first stuffed doll was a *"wandervogel"* the German outdoor child, with sturdy limbs, flaxen hair, and sun-tanned face. From this evolved less idealistic types.

She received the title of Master Student at Art School in Dusseldorf and the making of portrait dolls remained her favorite creative work. She made 200 dolls a year—not always exact portraits, but often based on some child she had watched during her work as a teacher in Essen. Her figures often depicted poor children in faded clothes with pale faces and unkept hair. Some stood open-mouthed, some with their lips tightly pursed as though under tension. Part of her art lay in discovering suitable materials and she would wash and artificially fade fabric on purpose. Great care was taken in matching the leather and cloth for uniforms, shoes, belts, etc.

From 1933 to 1938, she worked in Berlin as a sculptor and graphic artist, illustrating children's books and making puppets. In other circumstances she might have become famous in this capacity since she had the singular gifts of inventiveness, practical dollmaking, and the living out of fantasy which marks the master puppeteer. But it was neither the moment nor the place for a young girl of Jewish faith to make a success. With thousands of others, talented and successful in every walk of life, but not possessing true Aryan blood, she was forced eventually to flee from Nazi Germany. Edith's sisters and brothers already lived in Palestine and in the summer of 1939 she followed them. Her mother and father remained in Essen; she never saw them again.

Fig. 3: Edith Samuel's Newspaper Boy, 14'' tall.

Fig. 4: A group of sad-faced children dolls by Edith Samuel, 12 to 14'' tall.

Fig. 5: Sleeping Baby by Helma Gotz.

Fig. 6: Eric and Astric ''Schlumpel'' dolls, 12½'' tall, made by Helma Gotz.

Fig. 7: The children that inspired Helma Gotz' dolls.

In a strange land she set up home at Rischon le Zion. The scene, she wrote later, reminded her of Bocklin's ''Island of the Dead'': barren sand wastes and cactus plants. She set to work to make a new start in dollmaking though they barely had the necessities of life. It seemed like a miracle when some old friends who were running a workshop for making advertising tableaux got in touch. Edith joined them and made models, often working all through the night.

She found no lack of subjects in this new world: small Arab goatherds, girls with bright baskets of oranges (used for marketing advertisement), and groups almost Biblical in their picturesqueness.

Soon she was back to her original media of composing dolls of fabric and at one time attempted to produce commercial play dolls. The amount of time she spent in the construction made her output unprofitable. She was a perfectionist but she did not lack imitators. In fact a newspaper article called her ''the most plagarized artist in the land.''

She was happiest in composing characters to re-enact the little scenes of life around her: children on their way to school, or playing instruments in an impromptu orchestra. Inevitably when ''Israel'' was formed, her help was enlisted to provide groups for public exhibition demonstrating the achievement of these people: a childrens' village; a "kibbutz"; a ring of young people dancing the "Horra" dance. (*Fig. 1*)

Though her work never brought her great financial return she was recognized as a master craftsman and won prizes in International Exhibitions at places as far apart as Tokyo, Milan, Munich and Istanbul.

When she died in 1964, she had completed a few moving pages of autobiography and left behind many examples of her work scattered about the world. Many people will judge them to be beautiful, others may feel them disturbing for they show not merely the work of a distinguished dollmaker but an entry in the world's history, a protest against man's inhumanity to man.

Thin-legged, narrow shouldered, and often with a pathetic vulnerability, the Samuel dolls appeal more to the adult than to the child. One is apt to question them like a foundling—"What is the matter? Who are you? What has happened?" Their expressions often show uncertainty, truculence, even tragedy. Certainly they lack the gay self-confidence of the Gotz children.

HELMA GOTZ

In a recent visit to Frankfurt I was delighted to meet with Helma Gotz, one of Germany's foremost modern dollmakers. She told me that as a child (born just before World War II) she had few toys; her favorite plaything was a penknife with which she could fashion figures and animals to her own design. The dolls of the period she found ugly and unsympathetic. She carried in her mind's eye an ideal doll: pretty and cuddlesome, a type that later she was to bring to life.

In 1956, after conventional Art School training, when the teacher of sculpture declared that in dollmaking she could teach her no more, she started to make dolls on her own. Good fortune introduced her, in 1959, to an Americn family stationed in Frankfurt who bought a few of her dolls. She discovered in their flaxen-haired children the perfection of features she had always sought and began modelling dolls based on sketches made when she visited them. The father was a Lt. Colonel in the Victory Corps, and as he had nine children she did not lack for models!

Inspired by the latest baby, Eric, she designed first "sleeping baby (*Fig. 5*) and then "wide-awake baby." The dolls grew as the children grew. Presently three-year old Eric and his five-year old sister Astric appeared as *"schlumpel"* (*Fig. 6*). This is a colloquial term applied to any sort of rag baby a mother might make for her child, an inseparable, clutched-all-the-time in sleeping and waking, constant comforter and dearly-loved toy.

The Christmas 1961 issue of *The Guardian* (a Victory Corps newspaper) carried the story of Helma Gotz: "This Christmas hundreds of German and American children will cuddle dolls modelled after the nine children of a V-corps officer stationed in Frankfurt," with engaging photos of the children. (*Fig. 7*). The same models have been made ever since and the quality has never deteriorated.

"A good doll should be *handmade*. It should be soft and it should look like a little child," says Helma Gotz with an echo of those famous earlier toddlers of Kathe Kruse. She works at home in a cheerful room with two buggerigars for company. A devoted mother and father assist her. Outworkers help a little with the assembling of bodies and clothes, but every head is personally made by the artist. A master mould is used to shape the head's foundation which is covered with soft fabric. Touches of paint and deft stitches complete the features with a flair of artistic genius. Some eyes are painted and some stitched. All dolls are washable. Like so many fluffy nestling chicks, the little heads with brown or flaxen hair await on a workbench for a final shaping trim.

Among the most sophisticated products of modern doll factories, these little characters stand out as exceptional. Founded on real children, they are a personification rather than a realistic copy. The baby displays a soft helplessness which is irresistible, and the features, like the artist's autograph, are essentially Gotz design. Despite their American inspiration they remain truly Germanic in type.

Les Belles De Parisiennes

CONTEMPORARY

by JUDITH WHORTON

LES BELLES DE PARISIENNES, the historical fashion dolls designed by Jacques and France Rommel of Paris, France, and referred to as documentary dolls, appear to have stepped out of paintings or from the pages of style magazines. Their fashions not only follow but are duplicates of specific costumes, recreated with exquisite detail.

The Rommels find their inspiration in rare books, engravings, etchings, and paintings. As much as possible they use authentic antique materials, including jewels, such as opals and garnets, for the costumes and appropriate accoutrements. Mme. Rommel says the quest for the old materials is one of the hardest tasks.

She became interested in making dolls because she wanted to create examples as lovely as her mother's antique dolls which were kept in a sealed glass cabinet. However, her first attempt to create a doll was so unsatisfactory that she threw it away. It took months to perfect a body with the correct proportions. While she spends from 40 to 200 hours in making a doll, the research for a costume or character can take months.

M. Rommel, a graduate of the Academy of Fine Arts of Brussels currently teaching art at Central Connecticut State College, does the research and selects the materials appropriate for the costumes.

Their dolls are now in collections in five countries, and many have been displayed in museums and at art festivals.

The dolls, between 13 to 14 inches tall, are made of papier mache, cotton, wire, and rubber. The figures and postures vary with each period and fashion. Each creation, one of a kind, is sealed in a transparent dome with a velvet covered base. The name of the doll, year, style of the dress, and the number is engraved on a brass plate. Unless a doll is made by special request, all the styles are French, representing periods from 1542 to a bridal gown of 1972. Mme. Rommel left the faces featureless because the dolls depict fashions, not facial characteristics.

Fig. 1. Mme. Rommel models a recreation of a costume of 1898, a duplicate of the miniature version worn by a doll. The taffeta blouse has pleats, three inserts, and mutton leg sleeves. The skirt is midnight blue; the hat is decorated with ostrich plumes.

Fig. 2. The 1542 court dress of Diane de Poitiers is recreated by a combination of white satin, purple velvet, lace made of real gold, and a rare brocade

Fig. 1

Fig. 7

Fig. 8

Fig. 2

Fig. 3

of pleated silk with an intricate trim of gold thread. Velvet bows with pearls dot the back of the dress. A very tight undergarmet creates an erect posture. (Because the real duchess wore such a garmet, she was forced to walk as stiffly as a statue.) The black beauty spot on her face is called a fly. Her fan is of pink feathers.

Figs. 4 and 5. Marie Josephine, a lady-in-waiting to Marie Antoinette, wore this dress two years before the French Revolution. (The jeweled ceremonial court dresses cost thousands of dollars and were no doubt a factor in the discontent of the people.) This yellow silk dress is covered with 800 pearls and rhinestones, and 13 yards of trim, including three varieties of handmade lace. The dresses were so wide that metal armatures supporting the skirt were designed with hinges to facilitate entering doorways. Long gloves of silk are embroidered with jewels.

from Italy. Decorations on the gown include 700 gold beads sewed to the purple and gold brocade and a girdle of antique jewels. The doll wears two rings on one hand; a jeweled French hood has a velvet train to cover the dark hair. Diane de Poitiers defied tradition by refusing to marry the man selected by her family. The doll's posture is designed to illustrate her stubborn personality.

Fig. 3. The Duchess of Bourgogne wears a court dress of 1700 of ultramarine velvet decorated with genuine pearls, gold thread, and mink. The dress has elaborate sleeves covered with jewels and four rows of lace; five rows

Fig. 8. Claude has a more natural looking figure, illustrating the freedom found in the clothes of 1913 and the absence of restricting undergarments. The loosely fitted afternoon dress of yellow silk with a black design has a low-cut neck and a beige silk muslin insert. The shape of the skirt resembles a fish with the opening at the hem creating the effect of a tail, revealing the black high heels. Decorations include a long neckline of black wooden beads, pearls on the sash and in the hair. Claude is the first Rommel doll with short hair, for in 1913 a few brave French women dared to cut their long tresses.

Fig. 6

Fig. 4

Fig. 6. Adele, a young girl of 1838, is dressed in a promenade dress made of 120-year-old gray and pink silk. The three-piece sleeves are trimmed with flowers and lace; the Bertha collar has two rows of Belgium lace; the skirt has ruffles of silk; the bonnet is trimmed with ribbon. The handmade shawl matches the pink color in the skirt. She carries a little dog.

Fig. 7. Elvire of 1878 is costumed in a ball gown made of silk and silver white moire with pleated tulle and ruffles of silk ribbon. The low-neck dress has short sleeves and is covered with multicolored flowers. The accessories include double strands of pearls, aquamarine earrings, and leather gloves. The doll has a tiny waist described as "strangulated."

Fig. 5

EUNICE TUTTLE'S DOLL CHILDREN

by JUDITH WHORTON

Pepito

Thomas

AS A LITTLE girl in Brooklyn, N.Y., Eunice Tuttle played with chubby all bisque dolls from Germany that cost 25 cents at a neighborhood store. She loved her small dolls, but often wished they looked more like her American playmates. Retired now, after 30 years of schoolteaching, Eunice Tuttle is again "playing dolls," though nowadays she is making them herself to her own designs and desires.

She still favors little dolls and most of those she has made are no more than 4 3/4 inches tall and represent American children under the age of eight. "As of now," she says, "all my dolls are dollhouse-size children, scaled at 1 inch to a foot, and represent either modern little girls and boys, black or white, or children from famous paintings."

One of her first efforts was the creation of twin girls made of ceramic clay. She soon discovered this material was too fragile for practical use. In porcelain clay she found the material that was right for her. The dolls still resembled American children with slender arms and legs, but did not break so easily.

Through the years, the little dolls have undergone some changes, but the same method is used in every creation. Miss Tuttle had given demonstrations of the various processes used in her doll-making at doll clubs, conventions, schools, and churches. "I have no trade secrets," she says.

The artist starts with plastilene clay. After modeling all the parts, a plaster cast is made. Then porcelain slip is poured into the molds. After setting and removal from the cast, all parts are trimmed with a sharp tool to eliminate any evidence of seams. The porcelain figures are fired in the kiln. Afterwards they are polished with a nylon cloth; then refired at 2400 degrees.

Lively eyes are a characteristic of Miss Tuttle's dolls. She explains: "I paint the eyes with water color and then use three coats of fingernail polish. Even my early dolls' eyes still have that bright alert look. I use the engine colors intended for model trains for the rest of the features. The dolls are of pink or

Angel Baby

Rennie

Collette

brown porcelain bisque, jointed at the shoulders and hips, with swivel necks so the heads move from side to side.''

Some of the early examples had molded hair. Others had a combination molded hair with holes behind the ears to allow for wool braids or a ponytail. Now all have wigs. ''Human hair,'' Miss Tuttle says, ''is too coarse for such small dolls.'' The brunette wigs are made from strands of raveled rayon shoelaces; the blonde wigs, from raveled soutache braid. The minute strands are sewn to silk tape before styling. The hair can be freshened by dampening and recurling.

Dressing tiny figures is a challenge, but Miss Tuttle feels all outfits must be realistically made. No part of a costume is sewed to the doll; all clothes can be removed. A pattern is first designed out of craft paper. Then the clothes are made of an inexpensive material, such as muslin. ''I once had to make a dress five times before I was satisfied. Small pleats are especially difficult to achieve.'' Most are finally dressed in Swiss tissue taffeta.

As regular size thread is too large for small dolls' clothes, she buys china silk, dyes it to match the material that the child will wear, then ravels the amount needed for thread. ''Taking out stitches is difficult because they are so hard to see,'' she says. She orders her tiny size number 12 needles from England.

''I prefer that customers do not order the color of clothing. Each doll has her own personality,'' she explains. ''I choose the material after the doll is finished. Each doll has his or her name, number and date of firing, as well as my name incised in the porcelain on the back.'' Each comes complete with a stands, except the babies which lie on

Katie

tiny quilts. The one-of-a-kind dolls all have plexiglass cases. Prices range from $50 to $250.

Her dolls have won Miss Tuttle national recognition. In 1968, she was elected to the National Institute of American Doll Artists. One of her girls, inspired by a historical painting, is featured in Genevieve Angione's *All-Bisque and Half-Bisque Dolls*.

Photography is another of Miss Tuttle's hobbies, and at the beginning of her dollmaking, she issued delightful catalogs with color photographs of her tiny creations. When more and more of her dolls were limited to one-of-a-kind,

the catalogs became impractical and were discontinued; now they are collector's items in themselves.

Dollmaking and photography combined again for Miss Tuttle's holiday greeting cards. ''For fifty years I have been designing my own Christmas cards. Since 1966, I have been making each year a new doll which I have photographed and used for that season's Christmas card.'' On the 1974 card (illustrated) she used a photograph of three dolls dressed in costumes of 1879, inspired by a tintype of her mother at age seven and two brothers, aged eight and four.

Don Manuel Orsorio

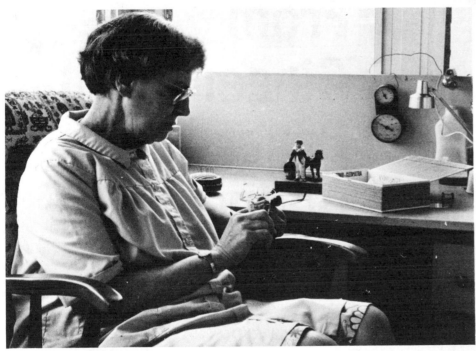

Eunice Tuttle in her patio workshop. She is holding "Collette," a 4-inch 5-year old child doll made in 1974.

Miss Tuttle's Comments.

ANGEL BABY started a new trend in this artist's dollmaking — a swivel neck. "Up to then, the doll head and body had been in one piece, but the baby seemed much too stiff when made that way. The result of my efforts to make it look more nautral is a baby with a head that bobbles, just like a real baby. Since then I have made 88 copies of this doll. And from that time on all my other dolls have had swivel heads, too." Angel Baby is 2 1/2 inches long, and represents a four-months-old baby.

RENNIE, one-of-a-kind, was the Christmas card doll for 1966. "She is shown decorating her espalier tree for Christmas. Her nightgown is white,

trimmed with red, and she wears a tiny red bow in her hair."

DON MANUEL ORSORIO, the Christmas doll for 1968, was inspired by the painting by Goya (1798) how in the Metropolitan Museum of Art in New York. A toy horse is used in place of the pet magpie shown in the painting. The doll is dressed in a red suit with an ivory sash and lace collar. He is posed with a 35 mm. camera to show his comparative size. Nine of the Don Manuel dolls have been made and the edition is now closed.

THOMAS, one of the two Greenaway children used for the 1970 Christmas card, was designed from an illustra-

tion in one of Kate Greenaway's children's books. "He is dressed in a fashion made popular by Miss Greenaway in the late 19th century. His suit is dark blue, his straw hat brown, and he is pulling a mechanical toy of that era."

"KATIE was one of the three different Greenaway children made for a regional meeting of the United Federation of Doll Clubs. Dressed in white batiste with aqua sash, and an aqua bow on her mop cap, she is posed with her penny-wooden doll, Jensina (in cart), before a page from a Kate Greenaway book."

JENSINA is a 1 5/8" tall wooden doll modeled after the penny wooden dolls of the Victorian era, and is jointed at shoulders, elbows, hips, and knees. "Her head and body were turned on my handmade miniature lathe. Her legs and arms are of round toothpicks. She is posed here with her removable wardrobe."

PEPITO was the subject for the 1973 Christmas card. "Taken from the portrait by Goya (painted 30 years after he painted little Don Manuel), Pepito is shown in his child's military outfit with his horse and drum. He is dressed in a dark green jacket trimmed with gold colored braid; his pantaloons are white satin and his black beaver hat has a red plume. He is a one-of-a-kind doll." The horse was also made by the artist.

"COLLETTE, another one-of-a-kind, is a modern little girl, dressed in a party dress copied from a 1973 Sears Roebuck catalog." Lacking print material of the type shown, Miss Tuttle used lace and embroidery floss to approximate the print in the catalog offering.

This 9½" composition doll is a portrait of a woman who has passed the Nordell house every day for years with her German Shepherd dog. Straw hat, print dress, and navy sneakers are typical of her attire. Shopping bag and glasses with lenses are made by hand.

From Gingerbread Baker to Dollhouse Dollmaker

by JUDITH WHORTON

MANY A DOLLHOUSE enthusiast has sighed at tiny empty chiars in an unlived-in dollhouse, regretting so few quality dolls are available in the one-inch to one-foot (1" to 12") scale. Now to their delight comes Carol Nordell, elected member of the National Institute of Doll Artists in 1974, who for several years has been increasing the population of such miniature homes, filling orders for dolls from minute 1/4-inch to 2 inches to the foot scale. Adult dolls in the one-inch to one-foot scale are five to six inches tall. Dolls in other scales range from one inch to twelve.

Mrs. Nordell's background for doll-making is unique. "It began," she says,

"with my baking gingerbread boys and girls of my own designs which were boxed individually and sold as gifts. Business expanded to include many kinds of decorated foods including candy eggs, molded flowers, and cakes. Later, while playing around with making miniature furniture and accessories, I became intrigued with making three-dimensional dolls."

She experimented with all kinds of materials—papier-mâché, clay, latex, even apples—before she developed her own composition formula which satisfied her requirements of being both durable and natural looking. Now she makes wax dolls as well as continuing

her experiments with different formulas.

Her first dolls were tiny ones for miniature dolls to carry. She called them Pretty Pennies because she sometimes used pennies for stands. Now she regards these discontinued dolls as novelties. Their faces were smooth oval with the features only painted. From there she moved on to somewhat larger dolls with modeled features, the first of this size being the 12 characters from the *Nutcracker Suite* ballet. Though she has now graduated to larger scale dolls, her tools still include magnifying glasses and tweezers.

All her dolls from the one-inch to

Plump "Little Buttercup," 12" tall, of wax, steps out of Gilbert and Sullivan's *H.M.S. Pinafore*. According to the opera, she should carry snuff, tobacco, and peppermints, but here Mrs. Nordell has added a loaf of bread, ribbon, laces, and a Bible with a bookmark; in her left hand Little Buttercup holds a pocket knife.

Carol Nordall holds two of her 3½" composition dolls. To the left, a child of 1800; to the right, a little girl of 1910 holding a tiny doll of her own.

Inspired by an 1690 American folk painting by an unknown artist, this 10" "Mrs. Freake and Baby Mary" (6 months old) is of wax. Baby Mary has a completely jointed body that can be posed in many positions.

one-foot scale and larger are one of a kind, with individually molded faces. She does not like to do the same doll subject over and over, and feels customers are happier with a doll that has been made for nobody else. She prefers working in the one-inch to one-foot scale or even larger, since she feels she can get a more alive expression in the larger dolls. The prices for the 1" to 12" scale range from $30 to $60; for the 2-inch scale, from $75 to $150.

Not all her creations are designed to live in dollhouses. Among the diverse characters she has produced are President Teddy Roosevelt, Lady Greensleeves, Isolda, and the Fairy Queen from *Iolanthe*. Her inspiration comes from people she sees, characters from history, novels, folklore, operas, and paintings—American folk art portraits are her special love.

To make a doll, Mrs. Nordell starts with a wire skeleton and builds out from it. The posture of a doll is important; joints are made in the wires so that the dolls will bend where they are supposed to bend. The wires are taped together with floral tape. The skeleton is covered with strips of nylon hose, then quilt batting, then more nylon. The outer cover depends on the subject.

The color for the complexions is added to the wax or composition before the heads and arms are fashioned. The features of the face are painted with acrylics. No molds are used. The wigs are of mohair—a soft texture excellent for small dolls.

She solved the problem of doll stands, which she feels create an awkward, unnatural appearance, by modeling the feet around magnets which are attached directly to the metal bases. On the bottom of one foot are her initials, "C.N."; on the other, the last two digits of the year of production. Top and sides of feet are covered with leather to form the shoes.

Material for the clothes is chosen carefully. Sometimes, when she has trouble finding the small prints she wants, Mrs. Nordell paints little patterns on plain material. After the clothes are sewed on the dolls, the outfits are sprayed with Scotchgard to keep them looking fresh.

As a special touch, many of the dolls carry such objects as smaller dolls or pets; one old-fashioned girl holds a miniature hornbook.

"I don't like to think of how long I take to complete my dolls; I work at least six hours a day, sometimes longer," says Mrs. Nordell. "The longer I make dolls, the longer it seems to take me. I keep developing new ways to make them better; there is always a new challenge to be tried, but the more time spent in perfecting is always rewarding."

"Elizabeth Copley" is based on a 1776 painting by John Singleton Copley of his daughter. The 7½" composition doll has caught a piece of her long silk sash in her hand; stripes on her dress were painted by Mrs. Nordell.

"The Girl in Red," a 6½" composition doll, is a recreation of the 1834 painting by Ammi Phillips, American folk painter. To effect fur on the cat, the wax form was covered with nylon, coated with glue, and dipped in flock.

Judith Condon - All Bisque Doll Specialist

by JUDITH WHORTON

FEW DOLL ARTISTS would go to such extremes in research as taking karate lessons to create an authentic shihan (master). Yet when Judith Condon decided recently to make a karate doll, she did just that. She wanted not only the costume to be accurate, but the stance of the figure as well. Her ''Zeke, the karate freak,'' has upturned toes to prevent broken bones when kicking an opponent; the fingers of his hands are held in a typical karate position. Although most of Judith's creations do not require such strenuous preparation, all require careful planning and engineering.

In 1971 Judith's desire to make a Gibson Girl for her mother's collection led her to a meteoric career as a doll maker. Choosing Wehrly, her maiden name as her trademark, she experimented with several materials including wood, plastic wood, and papier-mâché before

Zeke, the Karate Freak, is made with a combination of humor and accuracy in depicting a master of the art of self defense.

Photographs by Gene Sprouse.

Kathy, Charles, Hilda and Laura are dressed as typical teenagers in slack outfits complete with open toed sandals.

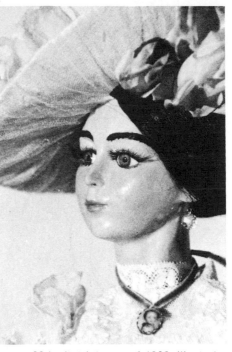

Ann, a 28-inch aristocrat of 1900, illustrates the results of the wax finish over porcelain. Her mutton leg sleeve dress was inspired by the antique costumes in the collection of Judith's mother. Her accessories — including parasol, flowered hat and high heeled shoes — are handmade. The best sources of the cloth flowers used on the hats are old millinery creations found in flea markets and thrift shops. Ann will be discontinued shortly.

specializing in all porcelain dolls. "For me", she finds, "working with one medium is more satisfying in creating a life-like appearance than using a combination of materials." The following year, 1972, she became one of the youngest to be voted into the National Institute of American Doll Artists.

Unconsciously, Judith began preparation for her career as a doll artist when she was a child. Living across the street from the Museum of Fine Arts in Boston, Mass., she started studying art at the museum when she was eight years old. Although she won awards for her paintings, sculpturing fascinated her more.

Even with training in sculpturing, she discovered that large all-porcelain dolls created unique problems. Her early dolls were designed with joints only at the shoulders and hips. Dissatisfied with the results, feeling that the dolls were

This group of ballet dancers consists of 10- to 13-year-olds, and Sanford, the dance choreographer, who is 18½ inches tall.

Louisa and Lelia, wax over porcelain dolls, 18½ inches tall, are dressed in luxurious styles and materials of the early 20th century. Kid gloves and molded shoes with applied lace bows add a final touch of elegance.

Judith Condon – All Bisque Doll Specialist cont'd.

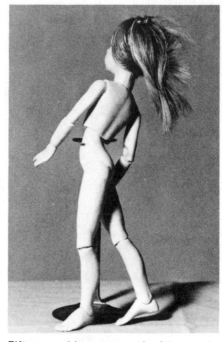

Fifteen molds were required to create the multi-jointed 12-inch Hilda. The joints are designed so that a doll will hold its position. As with all the Wehrly dolls, Hilda is incised with her name on the back of her head. On the shoulder are the initials JLW in the design that the artist has used to sign her work for years. Hilda comes dressed as a ballerina or a modern teenager.

Paul, 15 inches, Lena 10½ inches, and Leroy 8½ inches, have Afro style wigs made from Afro adult wigs, molded eyebrows, and glass eyes with pupils. Lena and Leroy are designed to hold hands. Details on Leroy's clothing include pockets, top stitching, and plaid bow tie.

unnaturally stiff and far too fragile, she added joints to the waist, elbows, wrist, hips, knees, and ankles in such a way as to make even fragile porcelain a more durable product. Later dolls are also swivel necked. Each body is individually designed to fit the personality of the doll.

The dolls range from 8 1/2 inches to a surprising 28 inches in height, and are currently limited to no more than 25 dolls in a series, in some cases as few as 10. Each one is numbered as it comes out of the mold and a record is kept of the purchaser. For the protection of the collectors, when Judith finishes a series she retains the mold in case a part is damaged and needs replacing.

A Wehrly doll is first sculptured in ceramic clay, with each hollowed part molded separately and then fired in the kiln. Before assembling this creation for her private collection, Judith casts plaster molds from this model. The molds must dry several weeks before the porcelain slip can be poured. Because of the great shrinkage in porcelain, the original clay dolls are considerably larger than the finished dolls.

After the first firing, the entire doll is china-painted. Following a second firing, oil base rouges are applied to create a skin-like finish. At this stage painting errors cannot be corrected. (One head had to be discarded when even boiling in turpentine would not remove the mistake.) After three weeks drying time the faces are coated with a sealer.

The human hair and synthetic wigs are applied to the heads with rubber glue especially developed by Judith to allow the wigs to be washed and combed without harm.

Wax over porcelain is used in the lady dolls depicting the early 1900s to recreate the beauty of protected complexions of that era. The features are painted with brighter colors than the majority of the dolls; wax is then applied by paint brush, carved, and sanded with a synthetic fiber normally used to clean greenware. After the wax is sealed with a sealer, eyebrows of human hair are applied strand by strand. Although Judith creates the Wehrly dolls at her home on the edge of the Everglades in Florida, the tropical climate has no effect on the wax finishes.

Judith likes to make dolls on subjects which will challenge her imagination. Court jesters, witches, and clowns are among her favorite subjects. Fond memories of a dancing school inspired a series of mobile ballet dancers. "Pretty dolls are not as interesting to make as dolls with character faces," she explained. Always seeking to improve her creations, she has begun to make characters with painted as well as glass eyes.

The price range of the Wehrly dolls is from $85 to $275.

Hugo, the court jester, is always dressed in bright colors with bells from his head to the toes of his upturned boots.

A Negro lad, Frankie, is an example of Judith's early work. Unlike most of her creations, his hair is molded. He has full lips, slightly parted in a whimsical smile. His unjointed arms and legs seem long and thin, resembling a child which is growing rapidly. His clothes, sewed to his body, are simpler than Judith's later works. He wears a shaggy pink sweater with a black stripe, and white cotton shorts, his green stocking hat is glued to his head. Frankie is now in the collection of Emily Brett.

Avant-Garde Doll Artist : Beverly Cerepak

by YOLANDA M. SIMONELLI

Lynn: A classic beauty created in 1973. Fully jointed, Lynn has sculptured eyelids accentuating her dark glass eyes. Standing 14" tall and reproduced in ceramic, she may be cast to portray storyland characters like Sleeping Beauty, Rose Red, or a child of today.

Patches & Puddin: This impish 8" tall brother-sister set, created in 1973, captures the dash of yesterday's nostalgia often found in contemporary novelty art. Reproduced in ceramic-bisque, each grin is individually sculpured to bare four tiny teeth. Ceramic molded shoes and wee button noses effectively tie in the nostalgia mood.

CONSTANT EXPERIMENTATION with plastics, glues, fabrics, clay, wax wood, rubber, papier-mâché, and ceramics distinguish Beverly Cerepak as an outstanding, free-thinking, free-spirited modern artist, one of the bright stars of the National Institute of American Doll Artists, Inc.

Her career in design began ten years ago with participation in a daughter's school project. Beverly fondly recalls her starting point: "My first dolls were portrayals of Humpty Dumpty, Little Miss Muffet, Captain Hook, Robin Hood, and many other nursery rhyme and storybook characters. These were widely displayed at schools, museums, and institutions and led to an appearance on N.J. Television Channel 13. I remember how nervous I was just knowing that my family and friends were watching."

By 1966, Beverly was designing fantasy figures scaled large enough for commercial use. She tried many new materials and methods and added such detailed extras as luxurious fur eyelashes and beautifully styled hairdos of soft Dynel. Her figures were soon appearing in New York City department

Kim: Sculptured in 1971; named for the artist's daughter, Kim is ceramic bisque, 14'' tall, fully jointed, with glass eyes and long blonde hair of kanekalon layered into a rubber base cap. Each tooth is finely sculptured in the greenware stage of ceramic art. (Kim is sometimes cast in character roles such as Little Bo-Peep, Tommy Tucker, or as an Indian maiden or contemporary child.

stores, on national television for Tabby Cat Food commercials, and on a Johnny Carson New Year's Eve special.

Her interest in creative doll design led to participation in club activities. A 21-inch wood carved likeness of Jacqueline Kennedy in her inaugural gown won Beverly first place at the 1967 meeting of the National Doll & Toy Collectors Club in New York City; a felt miniature likeness of Barbra Streisand earned her the same award at the Womens' Club Convention at Atlantic City. Club activities also introduced her to the National Institute of American Doll Artists. Dolls made by NIADA members are usually one-of-a-kind (often commissioned), or of small limited editions which are registered, signed and certified. NIADA allows each member artist the freedom to work independently, utilizing his own points of view and choices of material.

Election to membership in this prestigious group was a highlight of Beverly Cerepak's dollmaking career. Further confidence in her ability was evidenced when her fellow artists elected her Standards Chairman for 1973-75. Her interest in NIADA is exemplified by her willingness to talk about its high standards of admission and its high expectation of performance.

"Each year the Standards Committee reviews many applications. Much correspondence is necessary and original dolls must be judged for basic elements such as form, movement, anatomy, construction, technique and craftsmanship. Whether an artist has succeeded in

Sugar Sugar and Honey-Honey: Inspired by the popular tune of 1969, these dolls are fashioned of styro-foam balls sculptured and layered with water putty. They have swivel heads and wired jointing. Wigs are dynel and acrylic plush set into grooves on their heads.

Elfin Babies — Patty Cake, Pixie, & Peaches: These fully jointed little elves, created in 1971 and 1972, are reproduced in ceramic bisque. Pixie's soft mohair wig, brown glass eyes, and impish face reinforce the reality of fantasy-land. The tiny features of Patty Cake and Peaches are hand-painted and air brushed in fine detail.

Nancy: Inspired and created in 1972 as the portrait image of her real self, Nancy captures one of the memorable faces of childhood expression. Golden pigtails are of kanekalon; doe eyes are of blown glass. Of ceramic bisque, fully jointed. 15'' tall.

conveying any message and if he has been able to contribute anything new and vital adds to the overall success of his artistic efforts. Because of its high ideals and standards, NIADA grows slowly. Notable talent is welcomed and admired and NIADA stands alert and ready to advise and direct artists of merit.''

As current head of the Standards Committee, Beverly Cerepak relishes the never-ending challenge to explore the work of aspiring doll artists. ''Creative artists have golden hands and must be guided with loving kindness to their highest capabilities.''

Regarding her own artistic efforts, Beverly regards sculpture as a prime

Jahn: Reflecting childish awe in his large brown glass eyes and opened mouth, Jahn was originally sculptured for Russ Berri & Co., Inc. in 1973, and reproduced in plastic as a bank for commercial trade. (Other designs for the same use include a football child and a Kewpie type.) Jahn was re-sculptured into an art doll and is now reproduced in ceramic; fully jointed, wearing sculptured ceramic shoes.

interest and dollmaking remains a first love. ''Ceramics has become the medium with which to design my specialties — babies and elfin children. Eventually, I plan to master porcelain which will add new dimensions to my work.''

What does Beverly Cerepak do when she is not involved with dolls? We find she is a resident of Saddle Brook, N.J., wife of a Fairleigh Dickinson University professor, and mother of three teens. Slim, attractive, with long free-flowing blonde hair, she could pass as their big sister. Employed as a full-time designer for Russ Berrie & Co., Inc., she has traveled around the country to various branches supervising production of novelty designs including plush toys, sculptures, plastic banks, and planters. Assignments have sent her to Tokyo and Hong Kong for study and production of velveteen animals, papier-mâché banks, and rag dolls. Her ingenuity is often taxed by manufacturing processes which limit size and restrict colors, yet she succeeds in designing many eye-stopping items. Some free-lance work for television commercials and designing for Bell Ceramics of Florida have provided her with other channels of creative expression.

The Cerepak complete catalog of dolls includes an extravaganza of nursery rhyme and storybook characters; a completely unrelated category, U. S. Presidents and many VIPs; and her specialty, babies and elfin children. All dolls are completely hand-crafted and costumes are designed and executed by the artist.

Beverly Cerepak with two of her creations.

The Suzanne Gibson Doll Story

by R. LANE HERRON

Kalico Kid Girls, all 18" tall.

DOLLMAKER Suzanne Gibson's winsome Kalico Kids, with their scrubbed and wholesome look of childhood, are having a tremendous success and have brought their creator to national attention. Conceived in 1972, they are now being sold through exclusive showrooms in Los Angeles, Denver, San Francisco, Dallas, and at the World Trade Center in Houston.

The Kalico Kids — four girls in printed cotton dresses and sprigged pinafores, a boy in denim jeans and striped shirt, carrying a fish pole and a worm can — also appear on Suzanne's note cards, posters, and advertising. Though they are the latest of Gibson creations, they are by no means the first, for Suzanne has been enamoured of making dolls for years.

As a small child, impossibly wanting every doll in every shop window, Suzanne decided the only way to have all the dolls she craved was to make her own. She began carving dolls from

wood, using a razor blade; she gave them all away. When her parents presented her with an "Exacto" carving tool, she made a dozen or more dolls of soft pine, frocked them elaborately — and gave them to her little nieces.

Next, over the years, came cloth sculptured dolls; then puppets with carefully sculpted faces. From puppets she graduated to pretty ceramic dolls with kid bodies. Porcelain, in which she now works, followed the ceramic. Her first porcelain dolls were little girls, inspired by a doll her mother had owned as a child.

Luck was with her. The exclusive I. Magnin store in San Francisco agreed to purchase all the dolls she could make for two years, even decorating their display windows with her elaborate Gibson Girls. When that contract expired, Suzanne turned to mail order, with even greater success. Orders came from all over the world.

Marquerite Ostrander, first president

Gibson Girl, 18" to 20" tall.

of the Santa Cruz Doll Club, sought her out and introduced her to the Doll Club world. By 1967, her dolls had reached such high degree of perfection she was elected to the National Institute of American Doll Artists.

In 1969, she opened a small doll shop in Capitola, Calif. One of her first visitors to the shop was Marcello Storti, who had recently come from the Royal Academy of Art in Naples prepared to teach art in California. Instead, they were married and he found himself a partner in a doll business. He is now working on several doll creations of his own.

Nanny with baby, 23" tall.

Gibson Girl, 18" to 20" tall.

Fashion lady, 15" to 23" tall.

Gibson Girl, 18" to 20" tall.

Fashion lady, 15" to 23" tall.

A grouping of Suzanne Gibson's "little girl" dolls. These have Dynel wigs, glass eyes, cloth bodies, head and limbs of porcelain.

Though dolls have always fascinated Suzanne, she has another love — ballet. Brought up in Minneapolis where her father was choreographer, Ballet Master and Director of the Twin City Opera Company ballet, Suzanne spent her childhood watching rehearsals, dancing, playing piano for classes, designing and making costumes for the ever-constant performances.

Later, with two of her sisters, she toured the country, performing musical comedy in theatres and at fairs. She wrote, produced, and staged shows in Kansas City, Minneapolis, Buffalo, and Toronto. In 1956, she opened the *Ecole de Ballet* in San Leandro, Calif. She wrote a three-act children's ballet, "Pinocchio," which so impressed the Italian State Tourist Office and officials of the City of Pistoria, home of the legendary Pinocchio, that she was asked to perform it at one of their annual festivals.

In 1966, she felt compelled to close the ballet school and seek other avenues of creativity. Some years before, she had designed little girls' party frocks for Marshall, Field Company and Saks Fifth Avenue, and she felt certain she could find profitable markets in California. To help finance the designing project, she turned again to dolls. This led to teaching classes in dollmaking design at Cabrillo College in Aptos, Calif.; she also taught a class in ballet there. The "party frock" idea was laid aside.

After her marriage in 1970, her husband's help in the doll department

Kalico Kid Girl, 18" tall.

Suzanne Gibson gives "Twiggy" some final touches.

Kalico Kid Boy, 18" tall.

Kendra, 18''. Black porcelain with cloth body, glass eyes, Dynel styled wig.

Godey Ballerina, portrait of Taglioni. Porcelain with cloth body. 19'' tall.

Little girl with large bows, 10'' to 16''

was immeasurable. Soon her ballet classes grew into the Storti Ballet Center in Santa Cruz, and recently a Santa Cruz Civic Ballet Association has been formed.

Knowing ballet has been an important factor in Suzanne's understanding of anatomy and positioning for the Ballerina dolls she has made in abundance. In her latest catalog, she shows an exquisite porcelain portrait Ballerina, depicting the great Marie Taglioni, and an unexcelled group of four different Ballerinas, the *Pas de Quatre*. Besides the popular Kalico Kids and the Ballerinas, she offers adorable little girls and boys, a baby, High Fashion Ladies, Gibson Girls, "Kendra," a Negro girl in Afro wig, and her more stylized "name dolls" — Harriet, Peter, and Twiggy.

Behind any success story are years of struggle and hard work, but Suzanne Gibson has finally reached a level of personal satisfaction, for she has successfully combined her two diverse loves — dolls and dancing — and done outstandingly well in both.

Baby Peter, dressed in red, black, or brown velvet suit; all porcelain.

THE VARIED ARTS
of TONY SARG

by JUDITH WHORTON

A PERFORMER was changed into a doorknocker. Another shrank before the audience's eyes. A beautiful young girl was transformed into an old hag without trick photography or makeup.

These performers were marionettes which cost up to $500 to make. The magic spells were created by Tony Sarg, the most prominent American puppeteer in the 1920s and 1930s.

Tony Sarg was a 20th century version of a Renaissance man, having many interests and talents. He was a doll and toy maker, author, illustrator, and one of the pioneers in animated cartoons.

A naturalized American citizen, Sarg was born in Guatemala. His German father was owner of a plantation, and his English mother was an artist.

When asked how he first started working with marionettes, Tony Sarg gave a humorous reply in *Literary Digest* of 1927. When he was six years old his father ordered him to feed the chickens at 6:30 every morning. "We did not see eye to eye about the hour. I set out to get around it without starving the chickens. I rigged a system of pulleys

Axel, Victoria and Bertie, were created in 1936-1937.

Tony Sarg's Marionette has "Gretel, Madame Alexander, N. Y." printed on a tag attached to her original costume. The 12" marionette is marked on the body "Tony Sarg, Alexander," *Collection Shirley Buchholz.*

"Dopey," a 9" tall marionette, has a tag with only Madame Alexander's name on it. The majority of the marionettes in the Snow White Series had sarg's name included. *Collection Shirley Buchholz.*

The puppet on the left was created in the likeness of Tony Sarg by Eunice Tuttle. Miss Tuttle says: "He never set eyes on it until the night of the show — the grand finale of the course. He took over as the emce of the show — all completely impromptu." The other puppet called Axel did a tap dance during the show. *Photo by Silas B. Tuttle.*

running from the chicken yard to my bedside. Well after dusk I placed grain in the outer chicken yard. Promptly at 6:30, if I couldn't get up, my pulleys squeaked, little doors opened, the chickens responded appropriately . . . and that, I suppose, was the beginning of my becoming a Marionette Man, because it was my first serious mechanical adventure. . . .''

Instead of an art school Tony Sarg was educated at Lichterfeld, a German military school. At 17 he was a lieutenant in the horse artillery.

Dissatisfied with military life, he went to England and became a naturalized citizen.

There he saw a performance of Holden, one of England's finest puppeteers. He was so intrigued that he attended 60 performances, studying Holden's techniques with the use of binoculars. Then he started his own show at Dickens' Old Curiosity Shop which he had earlier rented as a tourist attraction. In his early shows he used some of his grandmother's antique Chinese marionettes.

He was becoming quite successful until World War I generated so much hostility against any one of German heritage that he left for the United States.

When Sarg came to America he found in contrast to England there was little interest in puppet shows. However, his creations made a strong impact. *Newsweek* declared his name was a "household word" for almost 20 years. Not only were his shows successful but there was a great clamor for marionettes for children. This demand for mass produced marionettes also led to the making of toys and other products for children.

Most of the marionettes for commercial shows were about two feet high, but some were as tall as a man. They were elaborate creations made out of plastic wood and sponge rubber. Over 200 cities were toured in a single year. The marionettes also performed at two World Fairs.

One of the reasons for Sarg's popularity was that his performers could accomplish magical feats that would be

impossible for human actors in a live show. Sarg explained in the *Literary Digest:* "I like plays which make people believe in fairies."

Some of the devices were simple, others quite complicated. In the case of the shrinking marionette a rubber ball was placed inside the hollow body which could be deflated and inflated. Changing a character into a doorknocker involved 36 strings and a small hole in the backdrop through which the figure's arms and legs could be pulled, leaving the face to form the doorknocker on the castle door.

Unlike many showmen who keep secrets hidden, Sarg always seemed willing to share his ideas with the public. Sometimes he even attended performances of marionettes produced by children and gave them helpful advice.

Although he produced marionettes for sale, Tony Sarg wrote a detailed article for *Ladies Home Journal* describing how children could make a toy marionette theater. He included a three act play about Jack and the Bean Stalk. He also taught a marionette

Jewelry was another one of Sarg's interests. These charms were found in their original envelopes printed with the words "Tony Sarg Marionette Charms." Only one and one-eighth inch tall, all are jointed at the shoulders and hips. The tiny faces have molded features. All have gold finish and bright enamel colors.

course for New York University in which the students were given college credit.

In 1927 the first children's marionettes were made in Italy and sold with a book of six plays.

Ten years later Madame Alexander advertised eleven sets of marionettes designed by Tony Sarg. Most had three or more characters. There was a wide variety among the sets including Rip Van Winkle, Tingling Circus, Dixieland Minstrels, and Alice in Wonderland. All had composition heads and at present are the most desired of the Sarg marionettes.

In 1940 Selchow & Righter, famous as the makers of Parcheesi, produced cardboard marionettes designed by Tony Sarg. The buyer assembled the pieces to make them three dimensional. They retailed at $1.00 and $2.00. Some of the characters were the Dipsey Doodles, Willie Wiggle, Jitter Jack and Jitter Jill.

His craft toys included Tony Sarg Living Picture Studio. After the child finished the picture—depicting, for example a dog—he could stick his head through a cutout. Each picture had a basic outline drawing and four stencils. This sold for 50 to $1.00. He also made toys called Rubbernecks which the child decorated.

The circus seemed to be Sarg's favorite subject. His toy circuses were so well liked that they even received mention in national magazines. One of his creations was a lithograph cardboard circus wagon with bells resembling an animal head. Each had a different tone. He even made dress fabrics with a circus motif. Also, he designed a chain of barber shops with a circus atmosphere so children wouldn't hate to get haircuts.

Animated figures in many forms appealed to Sarg. For years he made a moving holiday window display for Macy's, the electrical equipment for this display costing $50,000 to install. A Sarg cartoon film was hailed as one of the ten best movies of the year.

His huge balloon marionettes were described by the *New York Times* as a "mainstay" of Macy's Thanksgiving Day Parade.

The Tony Sarg Band Boxes decorated with colorful peasants originally designed for his wife's Nantucket Shop quickly became collectors' items.

However, the Depression was not a time for imaginative ventures. Sarg went bankrupt in 1939. In 1942 he died of a ruptured appendix, but he has left a legacy. He once commented that "a children's book has eternal life . . . It does not die out. . . ." Some libraries still have his charming books available. Many of his creations have been preserved by collectors. Students of his marionette courses are still making important contributions. One of his most famous pupils is Eunice Tuttle, N.I.A.D.A artist, whose own story appeared in this book.

This plump 18 inch composition doll wears all original clothing. Printed on a gold tag are the words "Tony Sarg's Mammy Doll, sole distributor, Geo. Borgfeldt Corp., N.Y., N.Y.

Dolls' Houses

Many dolls' houses are actually miniatures of houses built in the late 19th century. Most of the houses duplicated in miniature have been destroyed and their sites covered over and built upon in the name of progress. But collectors like Flora Gill Jacobs and others, have preserved the miniatures for future generations to enjoy. The furnishings for dolls' houses are as skillfully made as their full-size counterparts. Old furnishings are not too easily found now, but there are a few craftsmen throughout the United States that carry on the old traditional way of producing these Lilliputian replicas. Commercially made furnishings are also available to collectors. The dolls that occupy these miniature houses are as carefully costumed and scaled to size as the furnishings they live with.

The most extensive collection of dolls' houses and furnishings can be viewed at Flora Gill Jacobs' *Washington Dolls' House & Toy Museum* in Washington, D.C. In the Rochester, New York area, *The Margaret Woodbury Strong Museum* also has a rather comprehensive collection of dolls' houses and furniture.

Dolls' house of lithographed paper on wood construction. Continental (possibly German), circa 1900. Opens at each side and contains four rooms and a staircase. Height 32 inches. Collection Flora Gill Jacobs.

Dolls' Houses

The World of Antiques in Miniature

By Flora Gill Jacobs

All photographs by Harry Goodwin, Washington Post photographer and shown here by courtesy of Scribners.

ANYONE in the market for a small, select way to collect a little of everything, might consider the doll house.

Those of us who cannot bear to draw the line at a cupboardful of goblets or buttons or spoons, but feel impelled to surround ourselves with everything antique that engages our fancy, can do no better than to invade the doll house realm. There is almost nothing to be found in full-size in an antiques shop which, granted a pleasant amount of prowling, is not also to be found in miniature.

Besides, the contents of an eight-room (doll) house can be stored in a bureau drawer. This alone is probably some sort of advantage!

Since the process of miniature household reproduction has been going on for at least four hundred years, the most elderly examples are to be found in museums where elegant specimens represent customs as well as the furnishings of various countries and eras.

For moderate collectors (if there are any moderate collectors), doll housing items of the last century or so are still to be found in the antiques market. They are not in plentiful supply, for even yesterday's children, who reportedly were not as hard on their toys as today's, tended to smash their little treasures. But doll house items appear often enough to keep the dili-

ABOUT THE AUTHOR: Mrs. Jacobs, the author of *A History of Doll Houses* published in 1953 by Scribners, was born in Washington, D. C. and attended George Washington University there. She is a former reporter for the Washington Post and wife of an attorney with the Department of Justice. She has researched the subject of doll houses both here and abroad and so recognized was her recently published book it is being re-published in Britain in the early spring of 1954.

gent searcher from becoming cranky, and seldom enough to prevent said searcher from going broke.

Those who seek out the houses as well as their contents add architectural awareness to their collecting scheme. In this writer's collection are four doll houses, the most impressive of which is a grand affair believed to be a model of a South Jersey house of about 1850. (see illus.) One of the fanciest American examples we have seen, this one is practically a study in windows. There are bays and hinged casements, stained glass windows and peaked dormers, the latter perched upon a convex mansard roof. Friezes and cornices embellish the "sandstone" exterior. Inside there are such wonders as hand-carved "panelled" doors, and ceilings with designs painted on them.

Bliss Manufacturing Company's "gay nineties" doll house; author's collection.

A considerably more modest house is the one manufactured by R. Bliss Manufacturing Co. in 1895. (see illus.) This is a mere three-room affair, but the lithographed gingerbread in combination with porches and gables and eaves is a highly-detailed indication of the sort of residences which lined Main Street in the just as highly-detailed year.

The interiors can do no less in terms of verisimilitude, and they don't fail us. In addition to furniture with marble tops and chandeliers with blown bristol globes, there are wall telephones which ring when cranked and lamps which may be lighted if one is brave with (miniature) kerosene. Furniture styles are similarly faithful to actuality. One French Empire drawing-room set (see illus.) not only preserves every contour of its

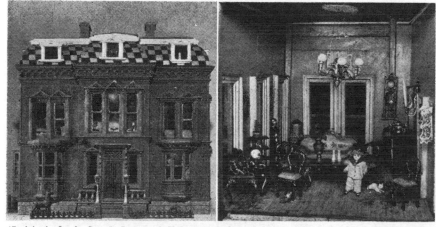

(Left) Author's South Jersey doll house, believed to be the model of a South Jersey house of about 1850. (Right) Drawing room of author's South Jersey doll house. Note gilded chandelier with six Bristol globes, wag-on-the-wall clock, German bisque boy in sailor suit, pot bellied stove, lead filigree hanging wall shelf and a terrestrial globe (on desk to left) found in Paris.

A workable kerosene chandelier from the author's collection.

curvaceous period, but the upholstery is suitably embellished with birds and flowers, and the wood adorned with actual ormolu trim.

A sampling of collector's items in miniature is more striking than even these practical notions. Every house must have a sofa (though not necessarily French Empire!), but it may be lacking a blue pottery mold equipped to turn out half a dozen puddings the size of thumb tacks. One of our doll kitchens contains this little gem, as well as a tea-set of a delicate thistle pattern with octagonal cups. We have seen (but, alas, do not own) such collector's items as framed miniature lithophanes and a set of Blue Onion Meissen kitchen utensils and canisters. The most improbable miniatures have a way of turning up. An unlikely item we recently acquired is, of all things, that late-Victorian fancy, a landscape carved in cork, in an ornate metal frame.

But perhaps the final word on what might be expected to appear in miniature came to us not long ago, the gift of an elderly English-woman who said that it was dug up in Surrey. This, if you please, is a small, plain, Victorian, wooden coffin.

These are just a few highlights of a personal and relatively modest collection, most of it scaled one inch to the foot. Multiplied by the numerous collectors who have turned to this wonderfully diversified field, the total, as one might suppose, encompasses, as much as any area of antiques collecting can, a thorough study of domestic history.

Kyoto Palace In Miniature

by FLORA GILL JACOBS

THE exquisite doll palace pictured here is a diminutive version of the palace in the old capital of Kyoto, Japan, complete with Emperor, Empress, and Court. A number of dolls personifying the Japanese Court, varying in age and magnificence, have found their way to this country since the war, but a doll palace, particularly one of such beauty and detail, is exceedingly rare. Its fortunate owners are Mr. and Mrs. Walter Nichols of Washington, D. C.

With its carefully thatched roof, two staircases, central balcony, and Ceremonial Hall, this impressive palace belies its substantial appearance by packing intricately — 150 or so sections—into a single box. Thirty-four other wooden boxes, with sliding lids and decorative labels, contain the dolls and the paraphernalia.

In Japan, such dolls and their furnishings, handed down from generation to generation, are brought out each March 3rd for the Hina Matsui, or Doll's Festival, when Japanese parents pray for the protection and happiness of their young daughters, and a traditional tea ceremony features very small refreshments. Markets offer tiny vegetables grown by specialists, along with miniature fish and a variety of Lilliputian cakes.

Shelves below the Nichols' palace hold the handsomely lacquered furnishings, their gold leaf decorations individual works of art. The crest of the family to which this set belonged is emblazoned upon every piece. Small drawers contain infinitesimal accessories—bronze mirrors, ivory combs, bamboo brushes, an abundance of wigs and garments. There are even articles for the outmoded cosmetic custom of blackening the teeth!

Although in traditional display, court ladies, musicians, dignitaries, and servants are arranged on rigidly prescribed shelves below the Emperor and Empress, the Imperial Family here is situated within the palace itself. On the lowest tier stands the Emperor's ox-drawn carriage—horns and fur are specific. Washington Evening Star Photo

Victorian Pre-Fab Doll House

by GENEVIEVE ANGIONE

Printed wooden box which held the Combination Doll House, patented 1881. Box became the foundation, and sliding lid, the roof.

IN THIS day of apartments and compact houses, we are inclined to think of all toys from the "good old days" as gigantic creations. All of us have seen dolls, carriages, hobby horses, mechanical trains, fire engines, table and chair sets, and doll houses so large they would require the addition of a children's wing to a modern dwelling. It is encouraging occasionally to find a toy from the past which conforms to that most important modern consideration—size.

The "Combination Doll House" pictured here is such a toy, and a delightful one! The varnished paper on the containing box is flaking badly, but in the right hand corner this much can be read without difficulty: "Patented 1881 by Stirn and Ly---, New Yo--." The sturdy wooden box is only 18 inches long, 9½ inches wide, and 3¼ inches deep.

As *Figure 1* shows, the box becomes the foundation of the doll house. Six holes, one in each corner and one centered on each side, hold the 15-inch corner and center posts which have dowel stick studs at each end. The sliding lid of the box becomes

the roof and it has the same six holes. All the posts are grooved lengthwise on two sides so that the sidewall pieces can be slipped into place. The second floor is supported by little wooden bars glued to the inside of the wall pieces.

Two holes on one side of the foundation box hold the uprights of the steps and the treads fit into slots cut into the uprights. The little parlor porch, as well as the full length porch on the second floor, are held by pegs inserted into extra holes in the front uprights (*Figure 2*). The decorative pieces also fit onto the same pegs.

The fancy cut-out top rests on the roof, securely held in place by two little slotted and pegged post-like pieces which fit into the super-imposed trim pieces which are slotted to fit onto the roof's front edge.

The brownstone appearance was pressure-printed in blue-gray on the soft, ⅛-inch-thick untreated wood stock which has aged, very appropriately, to a light beaver brown color.

Figure 3 shows the holes bored into the bottoms of all the windows in order to make an entry for the jigsaw

blade which then circled the printed shutters. Once cut out, the windows and doors were sawed down the center and hinged to the inside walls with adhesive tape.

Only the back walls are without windows and they could be left out entirely for play purposes without imparing the sturdiness of this mansion.

When the house is assembled, it will hold quite a few pieces of the lightweight wooden furniture which was in vogue in the 1880s, either divided into four 9x9 inch rooms or two 8x18 inch rooms. There is no dividing wall provided to make four rooms, but the center posts clearly define each area because the floor has cut-out sections to fit around the center uprights.

What modern household couldn't find use for such an interesting compact as this? The battered box indicates that it was played with aplenty; yet it must have been the responsibility of the little owners to see that all the parts were carefully replaced. They were faithful to their trust because it has popped up 84 years later, all ready to be erected again!

Left to right: Fig. 1—Foundation showing steps in place; uprights with porch, roof and trim. Fig. 2—Backs, one side and one front panel in place. Fig. 3—Completed house.

The Miniature Merchant

Lilliputian Shops Reflect the Mercantile World

by FLORA GILL JACOBS

THE charming milliner's shop pictured nearby (Fig. 1) is twenty-seven inches wide and about twelve inches deep. Its clerk has evidently stepped out for a moment, and its smartly-bonneted customer looks vague, but this quaint rectangle, all blue and gold and mirrored, offers us more than a smattering of information about milliner's shops, circa 1900.

When this piece was recently added to the author's collection, it was welcomed for its historic interest as well as its charm, being plainly the addition to mercantile history that all miniature shops inevitably become. But this beautiful plaything proved to have an extra feature, of use to all toy historians—the seller's original label intact on the bottom, that of F.A.O. Schwarz when the famous New York toy seller was on West 23rd Street. Fortunately for toy collectors, the firm has had five different addresses, and these addresses with their dates are offered in the box below, a guide to the age of all toys still bearing the Schwarz label.

Since Schwarz was on West 23rd Street between 1890 and 1911, our milliner's shop was given an approximate era, further pinpointed to 1900 by the style of the tiny felt and straw hats on its shelves, as well as the style of the shop itself. Not all the miniature shops to be found in museums and private collections today are as specifically dateable, but like all items in the toy microcosmos—the small houses and kitchens and vehicles—they reflect their full-size counterparts so realistically that they virtually date themselves.

The very earliest miniature shops of which we have seen mention belonged to the little Dauphin of France. The Inventory of the Crown in 1696 lists "Nine shops of the market place filled with little figures of enamel."

Within half a century of that date, some of the earliest miniature shops still extant were made in a small duchy of the Thuringian Forest. Duchess Augusta Dorothea of Schwarzburg-Arnstadt spent much of her long widowhood, with the help of the nuns and friars of her court, recreating in miniature her early eighteenth century world. There are numerous shops among the small houses, theaters, fairs and other wonders, fully populated by dolls. One is a delightful apothecary shop (Fig. 2) in which the chemist stands behind a small canopied counter weighing some medicinal wonder for a waiting courier while his apprentice works with brass mortar and pestle at a handsomely carved wooden stand nearby. Glass retorts, rows of blue and white numbered porcelain jars, and a profusion of copper and brass inspire confidence; this chemist will never put arsenic in a prescription by mistake.

There is also a charming mercer's shop, its bolts of silk and brocade neatly arranged on shelves, and its early eighteenth century bonnets on long necked hatstands. A white-wigged customer and clerk occupy the premises of one who must be the earliest miniature purveyor of millinery on record.

Halfway between this eighteenth century fashion salon and the relatively modern turn-of-the-century affair from Schwarz, there may be seen, in the museum at Nuremberg, a lovely example from the Biedermeier period (Fig. 3). The bonnets on the shelves are displayed literally upon

SCHWARZ LOCATIONS

"As far as we can ascertain," says the present management of F.A.O. Schwarz, the famous New York toy store, "the various dates on our location are as follows:

1862 — 1870
765 Broadway
1870 — 1890
14th St. and Broadway
1890 — 1911
23rd Street
1911 — 1931
Fifth Ave. and 31st Street
1931 — 1937
Fifth Ave. and 58th Street"

doll heads, miniature versions of the be-rouged, be-coiffed busts which served as display stands at that time. Quaint accessory for a milliner, false curls, both blonde and brunette, may be seen tumbling from boxes on the counter. It is tantalizing that in the photograph various box labels are just this side of legible.

Actually, the heyday of the miniature shop *is* the nineteenth century, and the British, logically, as the nation of shopkeepers, are staunch rivals of Germany in this field. It seems further in character that this land of the beefeater should boast especially charming examples of the miniature butcher shop. And, lest anyone question the "charm" of a butcher shop, it seems necessary to add that even gore can be attractive in miniature—the tiny hams and roasts and even the explicit haunches, have a curious innocence.

Such a butcher shop (Fig. 4), at Cooper Union in New York, dated "about 1800," is very similar to the one in the Victoria & Albert Museum, labelled "mid-century," and it is plain that the two are from the same atelier. Except that Cooper Union's butcher has a grander establishment with far more numerous cuts of meat suspended from the little hooks, most details are identical—from the butchers and their apprentices to the charming little potted plants—a pleasant vegetarian touch—which look down along with the windows upon the pink and white proceedings. The apprentices are identically garbed —but Cooper Union's butcher, unlike Victoria & Albert's, is wearing his hat.

There has been every variety of miniature shop—grocer, confectioner, fish monger, draper. Of the latter, the Museum of the City of New York has a beauty (Fig. 5), circa 1880, its origin proclaimed by the "Moden-Haus" sign which crowns the premises, and a supplementary one which exclaims, "Heute Reste-Tag!" below.

That museum's fine toy collection also has a grocery store (Fig. 6), circa 1875, in which the drawers are labelled in English, but this is quite outdone by a fine specimen owned by Mrs. James B. Childs of Washington, D.C. This interesting toy, plainly made for a world market, has labels in four languages—French, German, English, and Dutch! Tobacco, cough drops, even green sealing wax, are among the items so multilingually identified.

For the collector, unearthing miniature shops is a challenge, for, as with all fragile toys, the degree of breakage was high, and the rate of survival low. Often the shop frame survives and the important accessories are dispersed. But many shops were made, especially inexpensive ones in the late nineteenth and early twentieth centuries. A series imported from Britain in 1909 featured real foods in miniature packages. These were known as "Pets' Stores" and ranged from the U.S. equivalent (retail) of one penny to thirty shillings. Since the manufacturer boasted that in six years nine million were sold, there must be a few intact somewhere. John Wanamaker's Christmas catalogue in 1899 advertised a quaint butcher shop (the illustration suggests poultry) for a dollar, complete with butcher.

Just as the doll house taught its young owner a thing or two about housekeeping, the toy shop must have taught her young brother a thing or two about shopkeeping. These were the earliest of educational toys, and now they are educational to us; with the charm that all things miniature possess, they are informative about mercantile customs of the past, and as all these toys must be, about social history in general.

FIG. 1

FIG. 2

FIG. 3

FIG. 4

FIG. 5

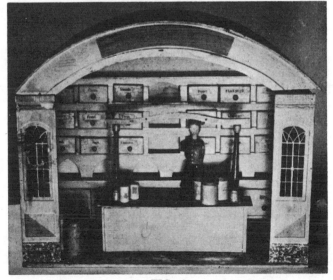

FIG. 6

The Old Curiosity Shop, right, not mentioned in the text, is a general favorite in the collection of miniature antique rooms owned by Madame Helena Rubinstein, and one of her most prized examples. The collection, in Madame Rubinstein's New York home, is occasionally open to view when she loans her house for fund-raising or charity purposes. In this Dickensian shop are jumbled realistically some 500 pieces of miniatura from the 17th, 18th, and 19th centuries—furniture, ornaments, and enchanting miscellany.

In the model house of 1864 the front walls open like doors for a complete view of the interior. A photograph of Nellie McComb, last owner, is hanging on the third floor, right wall.

A Model House Of 1864

By Ruthanna Hindes

FROM June 7 to June 28, 1864, The Great Central Fair for the U. S. Sanitary Commission was held in Philadelphia. For splendor and magnificence this fair was the epitome of its period. Financially speaking it was a great success, realizing over $1,000,-000 for the relief of sick and wounded soldiers who fought in the Civil War. Its influence extends to our time because out of the embryonic ideas of the Commission evolved the Red Cross of today.

The main building of the fair was appropriately named Union Avenue. Running along each wall and down the center of this building were arranged the various exhibits of books, sewing, silver and jewelry, wallpapers, clothing, and the numerous other depart-

ments. One section consisted of Model Houses, and it is with one house in this section that we are concerned.

This particular house of the 1860 period is over 5½ feet high from the floor to the top of the rail of the captain's or widow's walk on the roof. The house and all its furnishings were made by first class workmen of the period who lived in Philadelphia. It consists of three floors and nine rooms; one room on each side of the center hall on each of the three floors, making six rooms to the front of the house and one room on each floor at the rear of the house. The rest of the space is taken up with a magnificent stairway going from the ground floor to the top floor. Completely furnished and equipped are a kitchen, dining

room, parlor, art gallery, library, game room, two bedrooms and a maid's bedroom. The house has doll sized inhabitants (6-8 inches high) presumably by the name of Grant, for the silver name plate on the front door proclaims that U. S. Grant resides here.

Each room has a different color scheme — blue, green, turkey red, white and gold predominating. Lace curtains and taffeta draperies hang at the windows, blending perfectly with the wallpaper and carpets. Some of the carpets closely resemble Aubusson. The books in the book case are meant to be read and contain advice to young minds. The gold luster tea service on the dining room table and the food are being arranged for expected guests by two maids, while the lady of the house sits at her piano in the parlor and gives instructions to the man servant. Upstairs another lady is looking at the oil and water color paintings in the art gallery which are marvels. The largest of these measures 5 by 3 inches, the others are much smaller. All were painted by well known artists of the period, including James Hamilton, landscape painter, E. D. Lewis, and Peter F. Rothermel, all of Philadelphia. The kitchen is complete with a range, wash tubs, and all the cooking implements necessary to a well run household. The game room furniture includes a small table with an inlaid surface suitable for a game of checkers or chess. The master bedrooms are handsomely furnished with lace bed draperies and taffeta up-holstered furniture, while that of the maid is much simpler. Marble top tables are real marble as are three of the fireplace mantels. One of these required three day's work of an expert marble cutter to complete. Magnificent gold leaf framed mirrors hang over three of the fireplaces.

At the time of the exhibition, this model house was valued at $1,000 and was contributed to the Fair by Miss Biddle. Subscriptions at $10 were received and brought in $2,300 to the Treasury. After the close of the Fair, the subscribers had the privilege of deciding what disposition to make of the model house. Whether there was a drawing, auction or a lottery is not known, but whatever happened, Col. Henry S. McComb of Wilmington, Delaware, emerged as the proud possessor of the house.

At the time, he had a daughter, Nellie, who was 7 years old. One can only imagine her ecstatic delight at becoming the "mistress" of such a fabulous doll house. Her parents placed the house in a large room on the third floor of their residence on 11th Street between Market and King Streets and the neighboring children were permitted to come in and look at it. From its present state of preservation it is obvious that little hands were not allowed to touch the delicate fabrics or the finely turned wooden furniture. Twelve years ago, Nellie's descendants presented the doll house to the Historical Society of Delaware in Wilmington, where it can be seen today, the delight of all, young and old alike.

Washington Dolls' House & Toy Museum

Reed's "U. S. Capitol at Washington, D.C." patented in 1884. When the hinged section beneath the dome is lowered, a movable paper strip unreels showing interior views of the Capitol and the White House, and the likeness of every President up to Chester A. Arthur. "Thousands who have never seen this magnificent structure," a label advised, "have here an opportunity without the expense of a visit."

At long last, Flora Gill Jacobs' dream of a museum to house her fantastic collection of dolls' houses and old toys has come true. On February 20th, 1975, the Washington Dolls' House & Toy Museum was opened with a champagne preview for the benefit of D.C. Citizens for Better Public Education, a private non-profit organization dedicated to improving public education in the District of Columbia. Patrons for the benefit preview included the First Lady, Mrs. Gerald K. Ford, Alice Roosevelt Longworth, Dr. S. Dillon Ripley, Secretary of the Smithsonian Institution, and Mr. James Biddle, President of the National Trust for Historic Preservation.

The museum will feature rotating exhibits from the collection of Mrs. Jacobs, the author of books about dolls' houses and the leading authority in America on miniature antiques of all kinds. Most of the miniature houses, shops, schools and churches date from the early 19th century and include the Tiffany-Platt house (illustrated) and "U. S. Capitol at Washington D.C." toy (also shown here).

Featured at the opening, in honor of George Washington's birthday, was a miniature replica of Mount Vernon and its outbuildings, complete with figures of George and Martha Washington. This rare toy was patented in 1867.

The Washington Dolls' House & Toy Museum will be open to the public Tuesdays through Sundays from 12 noon to 5 P.M. The admission charge is $2 for adults, $1 for children under age fourteen. It is located at 5236 - 44th Street, N.W., Washington, D.C.

The interior of the big mid-19th century Tiffany-Platt dolls' house, a New York City brownstone with typical Italianate details on the exterior. Some of the original furniture remain, such as the tester bed with its original pink silk curtains, but there are later additions, such as the turn-of-the-century electric sconces with pointed bulbs in the large drawing room. A full account of this early dolls' house, with pictures of the exterior and interior, is included in Flora Gill Jacobs' new book, "Dolls' Houses in America—Historic Preservation in Miniature."

Paper Dolls & Toys

Except for rarities, paper dolls are the least expensive dolls to collect. Children have been playing with paper dolls and toys for just about as long as they have conventional dolls. Commercial producers of paper dolls and toys, like the well-known firm of *Raphael Tuck & Sons,* have supplied collectors with literally hundreds of things to seek and find. And not too long ago, nationally circulated magazines often included paper dolls for children to cut out and enjoy. Collectible paper dolls range from simple ones drawn on scrap paper to the more elaborate kinds mentioned in Marcia Ray's *Paper Castaways* (included here). Among the more colorful and animated paper dolls and toys are those produced by *Raphael Tuck & Sons* of London, England. Tuck's paper playthings were circulated all over the globe, but more especially in England and the North American Continent — the United States and Canada. They were produced for both boys and girls to enjoy.

Paper dolls and toys made by Raphael Tuck & Sons, about 1900. This one is entitled "A Matinee." Extra heads are of Judy (Punch and Judy) and Red Riding Hood. Collection Barbara Whitton Jendrick.

Fanny Elssler and four of the six costumes for the dancer, here pictured in her undergarments, ready for dressing. Note that the costumes carry the changes in pose, while the feet remain static in the first passe of the ballet.—Paper Doll of 1845 from Herbert Hosmer Jr., Collection.

EARLY PAPER DOLLS

WHEN the official program of the 1951 convention of the United Federation of Doll Clubs, Incorporated, published Clara Fawcett's essay "Value in Old Paper Dolls", it was fairly evident that the paper doll, as an item of antiquity and collectibility, had arrived. The comment of one collector, "I have all the real dolls my house will accommodate; now I am collecting paper dolls . . ." is perhaps a clue to the direction many three dimensional doll collectors will take, not to mention the fact that for quite some years collectors of children's books have been quietly, yet purposefully, collecting paper dolls. Men and women who do not own a single "real doll" have scores and hundreds of paper dolls, some of them being unbelievably fine ones.

That paper dolls may, conceivably, be as old as paper, it is not ours to deny. But this much we do know: the vogue, as we understand it, began during the reign of Louis XVI and Marie Antoinette of France, while our own Benjamin Franklin was at that court. In fact, there was a paper doll made of our great philosopher. The ladies and gentlemen of the court called these dolls "pantins" and quite frequently they wore them as a part of their costume. The dolls were articulated, often handmade, and had action when a silken thread was pulled. That these dolls were quite sophisticated in subject and action cannot be denied. But whether they were "decadent" or not, England took hold of the idea, and converted the doll into a playtoy of educational and moral significance, for children. And then, in the 1790's, **that** kind of paper doll was introduced to France from England.

From the 1790's the paper doll enjoyed almost mass production. By the early 1800's if not earlier, they were a featured part of the publications of one Philadelphia art dealer. Because the arts of the engraver and later the lithographer, were called into service, a paper doll could be produced rapidly, to reflect a vogue, a style, fashion, sensation, new stage or dance star, and new social or political figure. Here pictured, from the great Hosmer collection, is the French made "Dancer of Paris" paper doll, reproducing the immortal Fanny Elssler, famed ballerina of the 1840's.

Paper as a material for toy making came into its own in the 18th century and from that day to this almost everything conceivable in paper form or reproduction has been produced in endless variety and quantity for cutting out. In this medium one of the most beloved types is the doll with costumes and hats designed and published in paper or produced to be cut and made from paper.

Cover of the Box holding the Paper Doll of Ballerina Elssler. Gilt paper border, full color cover. — Herbert Hosmer Jr., Collection.

Paper dolls by John Greene Chandler, to whom the author's Museum is dedicated. Issued in 1857, these are from original proofs in the Museum. Included are the dolls "Charley," "Betty the Milkmaid," "Little Fairy Lightfoot," costumes, and pets. Shown also are original packages, and some of the dolls as printed, before cutting out. Chandler was a Boston lithographer, (Samuel W. and John Greene) from the mid 1840's.

From the late 18th century to the present day, book publishers, newspaper syndicates, magazine producers, toy manufacturers, companies specializing in paper production, have introduced variation upon variation of countless sets and series of paper dolls. Prevailing fashions have been beautifully illustrated by paper dolls for nearly two hundred years; famous personages and celebrated people have been depicted in paper doll form with changes of costume. Great companies have used the paper doll as an advertising medium for generations; and generations of grandmothers, aunts, mothers, sisters, and little girls have made home-made and hand-drawn paper dolls from bits of scrap paper, wall paper, drawing paper—any kind of paper, down the years. Artists have spent long hours skillfully designing and coloring paper dolls to be sold at benefits or for reproduction in quantity.

Though she be six feet tall like the paper doll we are told toured France to illustrate Court costumes in the 18th century or an inch high with tiny dresses made by hand; though she be cut from a published cut-out book, or a newspaper supplement, or a sheet from a magazine; though she be found in a box on Christmas morning, or bought with a spool of thread or discovered in a box of cereal ready to be colored—the paper doll is one universally loved and played with, and never forgotten out of long ago childhood.

PAPER DOLLS
The PRINCESS CINDERELLA

In 1894, Raphael Tuck & Sons of London, publishers to Her Majesty, The Queen, issued this package of Cinderella paper doll and complete wardrobe of transformations from hearth slavey to Princess, and to double in brass also as the Fairy Godmother. The costume shown immediately to the right of Cinderella is not for her, but for another doll, "Goody Two Shoes" a character as famed in her own right as the girl who wore the glass slipper.

This Cinderella doll was by no means limited in distribution to England and her possessions. Raphael Tuck had a New York office, salesroom and warehouse. The doll was sold everywhere, in the box pictured. It is now however, a rare item.

Paper dolls did not last so well as three dimensional dolls of kid, wood, wax or even papier-mache. They were often worn out within a year or two of use. That is why they're so scarce today. Yet the almost limitless production (Cinderella was the ninth doll of the Fairy Tale series of Dressing Dolls called "Artistic" which Tuck continued into the 1900's) gives us, the collectors of today, the break we want. We may not be able to locate precisely the paper dolls we want by just asking for them, but we can be sure we will find paper dolls if we go about it with a right good will.

Ada Rehan, Fanny Davenport and Rose Coughlin
Paper Dolls

By DAPHNE CARROLL

ABOVE, in the order named are the three sirens of the American stage who thrilled our grandfathers. Here they are as paper mannequins, with articulated arms and legs, ready to be dressed, but not in paper finery. No, indeed! These paper dolls are 14 inches tall and no matter how daringly strip-teasy they may look, they were made with the idea of costuming in silks, satins, and laces and to be stood against a dressing table, or a bachelor's chest mirror; perhaps for the same reason that prompts today's collectors to clip pictures of their favorite movie celebrities and tuck in the corner of their dressing table mirror.

The name of the maker is not given on these examples. It may be suspected though that he was an assembler of the die-cut, color lithographed parts, and that he had a patent on the assembly method. At any rate, each doll is stamped "Patented 1880". Of course, Ada Rehan is the most daring of the dolls and, according to theatrical lore, was the most daring of the damsels. Here she is in opera hose and gloves, ballet slippers and baby blue unmentionables. Each of the figures has an actual, perfect, hourglass torso. This is the only plain cardboard piece of the doll.

These dolls, perhaps the most ambitious paper dolls issued in the last half of the 19th century, are not so rare as to be unprocurable. We have heard that one shop on Sixth Avenue,

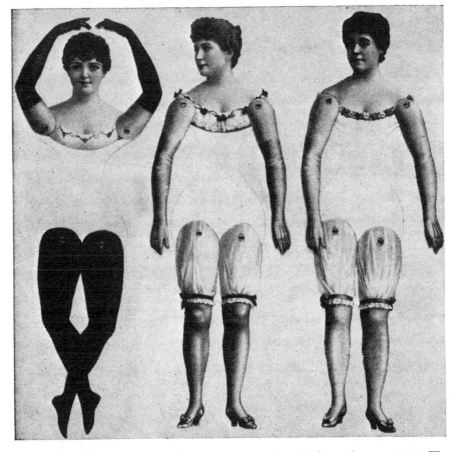

New York, sold out a remainder of several thousand of them within the past decade at $1 each. These, then, would seem to be the main source of currently available examples. Paper dolls, however, are not generally items of antiques shop merchandise. Rather, one must go to the antiquarian bookshops which specialize in childrens' books and paper toys. The history of the stage stars who inspired these dolls, plus the patent marking, dates them beyond question. But who shall say they will not again shine in bright lights? Here is a possible inspiration for a Disney Hollywood production in these high spots of our paper doll parade.

FIGURE 2

The Case of the
PAPER CASTAWAYS

by Marcia Ray

THERE'S a bit of Sherlock Holmes in everyone who takes his antiques seriously. Whats, whys, whens, and wheres are part of his stock in pleasure. The answers, when he finds them, or somebody finds them for him—he's always hailing others to join the fun—are counted personal triumphs over time and tide.

The mystery *Spinning Wheel* is privileged to present here has everything—a unique treasure, missing dates, undetermined motives, uncertain initials—and clues enough to make solution possible. Everyone with paper dolls, old scrapbooks, 19th century magazines, and all those blessed with serendipity, are invited to help solve it. Here, then, is the tale so far.

THE ENVELOPE

There it lay, a large age-yellow envelope, on a pile of trash set out for

collection on a mid-Manhattan sidewalk. An advertising gentleman, whose curiosity was no respecter of wastebins, stopped to examine it. Fancy lettering in the corner, redolent of turn-of-the-century "art in advertising" techniques, proclaimed "Photo Engraving Co., 67–71 Park Place, New York." He picked it up, peeked inside. "How much?" he asked the janitor in the doorway. "Just junk," was the answer. "Take it along and welcome." The gentleman, whose curiosity had just paid another dividend, whistled off happily, the envelope under his arm. Through him, some years later, its contents were acquired by an equally intrigued *Spinning Wheel*.

THE CONTENTS

The contents of the envelope proved to be original drawings for paper dolls

from which others were made—a rare and unusual thing to find anywhere. The styles seem to date from the 1880s; apparently they represented a long term of paper doll plate making. Quite possibly these paper dolls were published in some magazine, perhaps one for children.

Take, for example, the sheet marked "A Lesson in Doll Making," shown in *Fig. 1*. Though the "steps" necessary to make the doll pictured are readily apparent, some text must have accompanied the publication of the picture. However, the possibility that they were intended for "giveaway" cards with advertising on the back should not be overlooked, once their finished size, indicated as 6 by 8½ inches, is considered.

Four of the drawing sheets, in 8 by 10-inch size, bore notations to the engraver to reduce them to a 6-inch

No 1.

No 2.

No 3.

No 4.

Rim.

No 7.

Crown.

Hat.

No 6.

No 5.

No 8.

A Lesson in Doll Making

FIGURE 1

FIGURE 3

FIGURE 5

FIGURE 4

width, indicating the finished size of the printed paper doll page or sheet. On some were noted dates by which the plates were to be delivered to the printer; unfortunately only day and month were given. Two larger sheets, measuring 12 by 17 inches, were also marked for the same 6-inch width reduction. These were signed SB or SJB, which may be presumed to be the signature of the artist.

THE DOLLS

The six original drawings, as found, are shown on the cover and on the opposite page. The bridal doll *(Fig. 2)*, with back and front costumes, displays styles comparable to those shown in fashion journals of the late 1880s. The sheet containing housemaid, costumes, and little girl *(see Cover)* would seem to lack the basic figure for the maid until it is realized that the maid with broom can be covered completely by the costume with bucket. Obviously tabs of some sort were to be added by the child who played with them. The nursemaid and baby sheet shows costumes, cap, rattle, toy, pillow, and doll for the wee one *(Fig. 3)*. The two initialed sheets portray children with a wealth of toys *(Figs. 4 and 5)*.

Fig. 1: French boy with the Dancing Dolls described in *Memoirs of a Doll;* the second doll from the right is Manon, the doll he appropriated.

Dancing Dolls

by EVELYN JANE COLEMAN

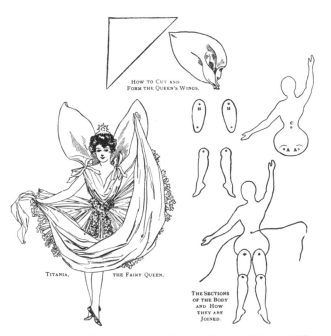

Fig. 4: Dancing Fairy shown in "The Delineator," May 1905.

AMONG THE oldest recorded toys are versions of dancing dolls. Around 1200 A. D. a picture of two people holding strings and making figures move on a table appeared in Herrad von Landsperg's *Hortus deliciarum*. The figures were knights in armor and the movement gave the illusion of combat. In 1557 a book, *De Varietate Rerum*, by Hieronymus Cardanus appeared in Nurnberg and stated:

"I have seen two Sicilians who did real wonders with two wooden figures which they made to move. A single string was carried through both. It was attached on one side to a fixed post and on the other to the leg which the showman moved . . . . They made the most astonishing movements with their feet, legs, arms and heads."

This seems to have been an early version of the *Marionettes a la planchette* (puppets on a board) which were popular in France and Italy during the 18th and early 19th centuries. The English translation of *Memoirs of a Doll* (preface dated 1853) tells of these Marionettes a la planchette:

"The boy with the Dancing Dolls (**Fig. 1**). . .on the banks of the river Meuse . . . had some puppets, which danced merrily to the sound of his drum and flageolet. He soon began to sing and amiably tried to amuse me (a little girl of years ago), and at length asked me if he should make my doll dance too.

"How could I refuse? He soon tied my poor innocent Manon to the puppets, and then she began to dance about like the others. . .

"'Now,' said this little villain, 'it would be a pity to leave a young lady, who has such a talent for dancing, buried in the country, so I shall take her with me to Paris."

Another type of dancing doll, the "Pantin", was also widespread for a long period of time. Prior to the 19th century, the dancing dolls appear to have been made either for professional performances or commercially manufactured.

Around the mid-19th century, instructions for making adaptations of these traditionally popular playthings began to appear in books and periodicals. Among these were *The Girls' Own Toy Maker*, published in London during the 1860s, *Godey's Lady's Book* in 1861, and *The American Home Book* by Mrs. Caroline L. Smith, published by Lee and Shephard of Boston in 1873. The last named contained a section entitled "To Make Dancing Dolls" under "Amusements for Little Girls." Identical information was given in a partial version of this book titled *Home Games for Old and Young.* **Fig. 2** shows the patterns and method of stringing these dolls which appear to represent Columbine.

The section read in part: "The dolls, when well printed and prettily dressed, are welcome gifts to little dwellers in the nursery, as well as nice contributions to a fair.

"To make them you must have a large sheet of thick cardboard, some fine twine, paints, etc. . . .

"She must be dressed in full light, ballet-dancer's costume . . . not much lower than the knee, just covering the joint in the cardboard. A wreath of flowers can be fastened on to the head. The clothes are sewed on to the cardboard body . . . The shoes should be painted on the feet.

"If you prefer, you can make a boy (dressed as a Turk) in the same manner . . . The arms and legs are fastened to the body by loose strings passing through eyelet-holes made in

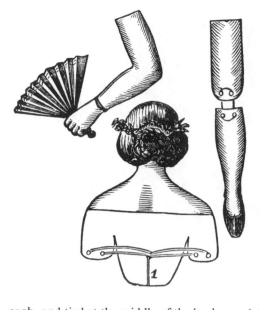

Fig. 2: Ballet Dancer from "American Home Book" 1873.

each, and tied at the middle of the back . . . A long string or narrow ribbon fastened to the horizontal strings will, when pulled, move all the limbs at once. A Highlander makes a good dancing doll. His legs should have the cross gaiters painted on them, and his kilt must be stiffened a little, so that it may not impede the free movements of his limbs.

"The common paper Harlequin is far inferior to these dressed dolls. . .

"If the little manufacturer is not able to draw, and cannot persuade any older person to paint the dolls' faces, you can take a head from some fashion plate . . . and paste it onto the body. But of course the head must correspond with the body."

"The common paper Harlequin," spoken of disparagingly, was, no doubt, the commercially printed "Arlequin" pantins. The "Polichinelle and Arelequin" pantins printed in color on a sheet of paper have recently been reproduced by the Merrimack Publishing Company from the original French Imagerie D'Epinal Pellerin. The reproductions are properly labeled as such at the bottom of the paper and also contain instructions for assembling the jointed dolls, not found on the originals.

Another book probably published in the 1870s, *The Happy Nursery* by Ellis A. Davidson, London, provided detailed instructions for making a Dancing sailor. "The boys will soon learn to make these . . . and they can try to paint them too."

The clothes on the sailor (**Fig. 3-A**) were to be painted rather than sewed and therefore presumably more attractive to boys. The back view (**Fig. 3-B**) shows how the sailor is made to dance.

The directions are to trace the separate parts, cut them out, and place them on cardboard, then "carefully draw your pencil around the edges . . . mark in the eyes, mouth, hair, etc. Then pierce the holes . . . with the stiletto out of your workbox or with a large darning needle . . .

"The pieces should be painted separately before they are put together, and the colour should be laid on the back as well as the front, as this keeps the card from twisting . . .

"In this (**Fig. 3-C**) *a a a a a* show the knots by which the legs and arms are attached. Run a piece of thread through *b* in the one arm, and tie it. Carry it across to *b* in the other arm, and tie it there. When you move the arms so that the elbows are against the sailor's sides, there would then be a straight line of thread running from one arm to the other.

"Draw the legs down quite straight, and fasten a piece of thread from *b* to *b* at the top of the thighs.

"Now whilst the elbows are against the hips, and the legs are straight, tie a piece of thread at *c* in the middle of the thread which joins the arms. Carry this thread downwards, and tie it at *d* to the piece which joins *bb* of the thighs . . .

"Make a thread loop in the hat, by which you can hang Jack

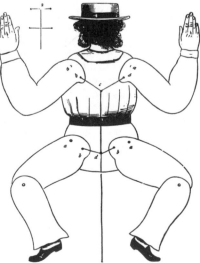

Figs 3-A & 3-B: Dancing Sailor of the 1870s, front view and piece patterns.

Fig. 3-C: Dancing Sailor, back view, showing method of stringing.

Tar to a nail in the wall, and as you pull the thread you will find he will dance a hornpipe . . .

". . . let the children *learn* to make the toys. They will then understand the labour required, and if they. . .buy the materials with their own pocket-money, they will be taught the money value as well."

Thus early lessons in thrift and industry were provided. Apparently boys of this period were presumed to have a workbox, though it seems more likely that the "stiletto," a tool used in doing punch work embroidery would be found in his mother's workbox.

As late as May 1905, *The Delineator* published an article on making a dancing doll. This one represented Titania, Queen of the Fairies. Like the *Marionettes a la planchette,* this doll had a string through the middle of its torso by which it was manipulated on a stage (**Fig. 4**). The directions are simple:

"The Queen . . . made of light-weight cardboard . . . should measure 10 inches in height . . . Join the two parts of each leg together, according to the dots with a strong thread and needle, and fasten with a knot on front and back, so that the two pieces will be strung upon the same thread and sandwiched between two knots of the thread. Attach the legs to the body in the same manner . . .

"Find a pretty head in some old paper or advertisement, cut it out and gum it on the pasteboard head. Remember, though, that the printed head must not be of very heavy paper, as the upper part of the doll should be lighter in weight than the lower, otherwise the figure will not balance . . . paste slippers of gilt paper on the feet.

"Puncture a hole with a coarse needle through the centre of the belt-line . . . Make a skirt of plain white tissue paper. Cut it 16 inches wide and 3 inches long . . . Gather the top of the skirt with thread and needle, and fasten it on the doll, then slit up each side from the lower edge to allow of the free motion of the doll's limbs.

"Make the dress of pink chiffon. Cut the dress skirt 3 inches long and 1 yard wide, press it in knife-blade plaits (pleats) running up and down, then gather and tie it on the doll over the white tissue-paper skirt. Do not . . . hem any portion of the clothing . . . Fashion the waist of a smooth strip of pink chiffon tied with narrow pink ribbons at the shoulders . . . Form a silver girdle of the tinsel ruching used on Christmas trees. . .Glue a little of the same tinsel around the front of her dark hair . . .

"Queen Titania's wings must be of the pink chiffon cut common shawl shape . . .

" . . . practice moving the Queen by means of the thread until you can make her glide, post and dance."

These are some of the principal types of antique Dancing Dolls but there are other variations which the fortunate collector may find. If anyone wishes to reproduce these dolls, the reproduction *must* be properly labeled as such.

DOLLY'S DRESSMAKER

258

by BARBARA WHITTON JENDRICK

A RARE FIND today for both doll and paper doll collectors is *Dolly's Dressmaker,* a combination paper doll and real doll pattern book, published in 1896 by Raphael Tuck and Sons, Ltd., London, Paris, and New York, proud "Publishers to the Queen."

The introduction to this 7 by 10 inch book with its gaily lithographed cover reads: "This book will show you how to make new dresses for your dear Dolly, so you will have something to do on a rainy day and Dolly will always look lovely."

It contains three sheets of colored paper dolls, printed on white paper, each followed by a double page of patterns to fit a 9-inch doll, printed on a light tan stock. The patterns embrace the paper dolls' clothes, and include an apron, mantle (long cloak), skirt for blouse, blouse, cape, frock with yoke, and mantle with yoke. The colored paper dolls, like a fashion sheet, indicate variations in trimming and materials.

Because many of the patterns are printed across the centerfold of the book, the little dressmaker was supposed to trace them on a tissue paper for use. And because the directions for cutting and sewing were printed on the back of the paper doll sheets, the cutting of the paper dolls was supposed to be left until after the doll clothes were cut and sewed. Such restrictions were hard on impatient little girls who preferred paper dolls to sewing or couldn't quickly find the proper tracing paper for the patterns. Undoubtedly few books, even in their own time, remained intact. We are fortunate to have a complete book from which to show the paper doll illustrations.

Figure 1 shows a blonde doll in white underclothes with blue trim. Her brown coat and hat are trimmed with ermine; her blouse and skirt are blue with white trim, and her apron, or pinafore, is pink.

Figure 2 shows a doll with light brown hair. She wears a white chemise with a pink petticoat. Her cape is tan with a pink and blue checkered collar; her double-breasted jacket is brown; her pink dress is trimmed with white lace. The "middy" dress is blue with a white collar and dark blue trim.

Figure 3 shows a brunette in white underclothes. Her pinafore is white with pink ribbon trim; her jacket is brown; her blue dress is trimmed with white and gold lace; and her cloak is yellow with matching lining.

Figure 4 shows the cover for "Dolly's Dressmaker," published by Raphael Tuck and Sons, Ltd., in 1896.

Fig. 1   Fig. 2   Fig. 3   Fig. 4

In 1892, Mr. F. Cairo Copyrighted this

Paper Doll Furniture

For Sale at the Chicago World's Fair!

WE seldom realize how close we are to antiquity when we deal with toys. Our parents played with many of the toys collected today and nobly designated, or accepted, as antiques. As a matter of fact, many of the men who collect model trains, the old ones, that is, played with trains of the very same kind, as boys; or wanted to! We have not, up to now traced Mr. F. Cairo. But we have located what purports to be the story of the discovery, and distribution, some five years ago, of over 100 sets of Dining Room, Parlor and Bedroom paper doll furniture sheets, measuring 18x20 inches, and lithographed in full colors. This is the story: Made especially for sale during, and at, the World's fair, which was postponed from 1892 to 1893, many items of souvenir nature were thus given opportunity for distribution everywhere in America before the fair opened. These sets of paper doll furniture came from the forgotten stock of an old Connecticut store, in Hartford. In 1946 they were proffered —100 sets—to a dealer for $25. From thence onward the price has advanced considerably. The paper, or cardboard, has become very brittle and, somehow, the ink of the printing becomes tacky in damp weather and acts like glue, adhering to anything touching it. This defect was not known until a considerable number of sets were spoiled.

Dining Room of the Paper Doll Furniture sets copyright 1892 by F. Cairo.

Paper Dolls & Paper Toys of Raphael Tuck & Sons

by BARBARA WHITTON JENDRICK

ON THE OCCASION of its Centenary in October 1966, Raphael Tuck & Sons Ltd. published a quite detailed history of their company —and a romantic story it was.

Raphael Tuck left Breslau, Germany, in 1865, at the height of the Prusso-Danish and Austrian War, to seek a more secure future in London. His wife and seven children followed soon after. In October 1866, he opened a small shop in what is now Brushfield St., Bishopgate, for the sale of pictures and picture framing. His wife, Ernestine, was a capable businesswoman, a natural organizer and administrator; Raphael was creative, technical, and a perfectionist—a good combination for success.

Within three years the Tucks had moved to larger quarters and had entered the publishing field, producing chromolithographs, oleographs, and black and white lithographs with special attention to color reproductions. Sons Herman, Adolph, and Gustave joined in the enterprise. The business prospered.

In 1871, Raphael Tuck published his first Christmas cards. By 1880 he was exporting his artwares worldwide; and as of January 1, 1881, the firm became Raphael Tuck & Sons.

The brochure continued to list in detail the family's fortunes and the company's achievements. During World War II their plant, Raphael House, built in 1899, was bombed and destroyed, and in 1962 Raphael Tuck & Sons, Ltd. became a member firm of the British Printing Corporation.

But in all this great array of accomplishments and productions, the Tuck paper dolls and toys, as fascinating to today's collectors as they were to yesterday's children, were never mentioned. Unless, perhaps, they were hidden under some other classification in the list of "expansions" introduced by Adolph in the 1890s and early 1900s. Enumerated there, besides the greeting cards which had been in production earlier, were calendars, books and children's publications, wall texts and scripture mottoes, educational productions, reproductions of fine engravings and paintings of leading artists, relief and art novelties, pictorial postcards, and "many other projects."

The present Tuck company can furnish no information on their paper doll and toy production; all their records were lost in the bombing. Only through the efforts of caring—and sharing—collectors to locate, list, and photograph the various Tuck paper dolls and toys as they are found can an approximation be made

of Tuck's complete production in this line.

TUCK'S MARIONETTES

About 1906, as indicated by design patent dates on some examples, Raphael Tuck & Son began to produce mechanical Marionettes whose arms and legs could be made to move by the pulling of a string. Some were put out in boxed sets; others like valentines, seem to have been sold individually.

The three valentine marionettes pictured are about 12 inches tall. The young lady, "Fluffy Ruffles," is marked "Original design copyrighted 1907 by The New York Herald Co. All rights reserved." "Buster Brown" is marked "Design Copy 1906 by Raphael Tuck & Sons." The Irish gentleman is unmarked, but the mechanics of the toy and its workmanship proclaim it definitely a Tuck.

The box cover of *Father Tuck's Marionettes,* informs that the box holds "10 Groups of Humorous Figures with Mechanical Movement. Descriptive Verses to Each by Clifton Bingham," and promises "Endless Fun and Enjoyment." It dates after 1906. Because the edges of the box are missing, on which the names of the 10 figures in the set were printed, it cannot be definitely stated just which of the 12 puppets pictured belonged in the original set; at least two have come from other sets, so far unidentified, and perhaps more. Only the finding of complete box tops for this and for other sets can put them in their proper series.

Shown from left to right are: box top, with "Dolly from Japan." "Three Little Kittens"; "Our Friends, the Bears"; "Jolly Jack";

"Clown Doll"; "Scout Doll"; "Dolly from Chinaland"; "Bonnie Scotland"; "Red Riding Hood"; "Dear Dolly"; "Dolly Daisy Dimple"; and "Puss in Boots."

Belonging to this same classifica-

tion of mechanicals worked by a string are Tuck's "Climbers," which can be made to actually climb a string. Two of them, the "Scout" and the "Eskimo," both copyrighted 1907, are pictured.

The Heavenly Twins. U. S. patent June 9, 1893.

Dating

To precisely date the paper dolls and toys Raphael Tuck & Sons produced is almost impossible without company records, and those were lost in a World War II London bombing. Even some items which carry a United States patent date—"The Heavenly Twins," patented June 9, 1893, was the first for their paper dolls—may have been produced in England before that date.

Fortunately for collectors, Tuck was both meticulous and generous in their imprints, and the printed matter on dolls, toys, and box tops will establish a solid time frame for their production, if not the exact year.

In 1880, Raphael Tuck adopted the "easel and palette" trademark with the slogan "The World's Art Service"; it is still in use. In 1881, the firm became Raphael Tuck & Sons, and in 1895, Raphael Tuck & Sons, Ltd.

In 1893, in recognition of its publication of the Queen's letter to the nation on the death of the Duke of Clarence, the company was granted

Winsome Winnie; Artistic
Series 103; 5¾'' doll.

the Royal Warrant of Appointment by Queen Victoria. In each succeeding reign, the House of Tuck has been similarly honored by the reigning sovereign. These warrants became an integral part of the Tuck imprint.

Thus, from 1893 until 1901 when Queen Victoria died, the imprint read, "Publishers by appointment to Her Majesty, the Queen." Sometimes the introductory phrase may be "Publishers by Royal Warrant to . . . ," "Publishers by Special Appointment to . . . ," or similar wording. Only the sovereign's identification is important to the time frame.

From 1901 to 1910, during Edward

VII's reign with Alexandra as his Queen, the line read, " . . . their Majesties the King and Queen." A great many paper dolls and toys were produced in this period.

From 1910 to 1936, George V was King and Mary was his Queen. Until Queen Alexandra died in 1925, the line read, " . . . to Their Majesties the King and Queen and H. M. Queen Alexandra." After 1925, it became " . . . the King and Queen and the Prince and Princess of Wales."

These are the imprints in use during the period Tuck paper dolls and toys were enjoying their greatest popularity. Production slowed with World War I, and children of the 1920s and 1930s found livelier interests. The few dolls and toys which appeared during the reign of George VI (1936-1952) bore the special appointment line " . . . the King and Queen and H. M. Queen Mary."

In addition to the Royal Appointment and the patent date, if any, the imprint named the cities in which Raphael Tuck & Sons, Ltd., had branches—usually London, Paris, New York, though some will list London, Paris, Berlin, New York, Montreal. According to the Public Archives of Canada, those items on which "Montreal" appears were produced between 1907 and 1913.

While it does not help much in dating, the imprint will also inform if the item was printed elsewhere than in London. Many dolls and toys are found marked "Designed at the Studios in England. Printed at the Fine Art Works in Bavaria," "Designed at the Studios in New York and Printed at the Fine Art Works in Bavaria," "Printed at the Fine Arts Works in Saxony," or simply "Printed in Germany," or "Printed in Holland."

Rosy Ruth, Dolls of All Seasons. 9'' size. Box top missing.

Victorian Paper Dolls
(1893-1901)

The dolls pictured here are all from Queen Victoria's period—1893 to 1901. The Fairy Tale dolls and "Darling Hilda" were pictured in *Paper Dolls and Paper Toys of Raphael Tuck & Sons,* but without the box tops which identified them by name.

The sets in Artistic Series 101, 105, and 106 are complete, but until their box tops are located, the dolls can only be known by their Series number. Happily, each doll and her clothes are numbered, so correct sets may be assembled even though their names are still unknown. The two "Winsome Winnies" in Artistic Series 103 and 104 and the nameless Nos. 105 and 106 illustrate Tuck's habit of producing the same doll under different numbers with different outfits.

Sweet Alice,
Dolls for All Seasons,
same as Artistic Series 503, but in
9'' size. U. S. patent Feb. 20, 1894.

Artistic Series VIII, The Fairy Tale Series of
Dressing Dolls; Red Riding Hood, Mother
Goose, Miss Muffet, Bo-Peep. 9'' doll.
U. S. Patent, Feb. 20, 1894.

Sweet Abigail, Artistic
Series VI. Among others in this
series were Royal Regie, Lordly Lionel.

265

PAPER

Artistic Series 101; 5¾'' doll.

Artistic Series 105; 5¾'' doll.

''Darling Hilda''
and Her Wardrobe,
New Series of Dressing
Dolls, Artistic Series 21; 9'' doll.

Winsome Winnie; Artistic Series 104; 5¾'' doll.

Artistic Series 106; 5¾'' doll.

A Riding Lesson

Out for a Run

VICTORIAN TOYS

While little boys of the 1890s may have scorned the paper dolls Raphael Tuck & Sons were producing, they were not above playing with paper toys, and the House of Tuck catered to their interests.

War subjects were left almost entirely to the makers of lead soldiers of which boys were then intensely fond, though one rare 13-inch paper soldier, a mounted officer with five changes of uniform is shown in *Paper Dolls and Paper Toys of Raphael Tuck & Son*. Tuck de-

Christmas Cheer;
Mouse Quadrille;
A Jolly Romp

Romp with Fido;
A Good Innings;
Little Dickey

A Morning Canter

Evening Prayer; The Young Artist

signfor preferred to portray such familiar pastimes as romping with dogs, riding horseback, or building sand castles
at the beach. If girls had dollhouses,
boys had farms, stand-up comic figures,
animals, and Fairy Tale characters-
—there were then no Sesame Street
monsters nor TV Flintstones to distract
from the Brothers Grimm.

The toys pictured here were made between 1893 and 1901, marked with the
Tuck name and trademark and the
proud "Publishers to Her Majesty The
Queen." Later toys were more elaborate, with greater mechanical
abilities—rocking, walking, waving
arms and legs, climbing strings, and act-
ing in theatres, but they would never
have been produced if these early

A Ride on
the Sands

Meadowsweet Farm set up.

stand-up toys had not proved popular.

Healthy Pastimes is No. 121 of the Artistic Toy Novelty Series; 4 toys in the set. Each toy is in two parts, held together by a strip of paper that folds out to allow it to stand. Shown are the box cover; "Out for a Run"; "A Morning Canter"; "A Riding Lesson"; and "A Ride on the Sands." Another set in this series, *Fun on the Sands,* was pictured in *Spinning Wheel,* June 1972.

In the *Royal Art Novelty Series 143,* the front pieces fold out to form stands; the toys are lettered as well as numbered. Part of the set is shown; "A Romp with Fido," 143A; "A Good Innings," 143D; "Little Dickey," 143E; "Christmas Cheer," 143F; Programme

Part I "The Mouse Quadrille," 143H; and "A Jolly Romp," 143E.

The set from which "Evening Prayer" and "The Young Artist" are taken is not numbered. The bottoms and back legs of the chairs fold out to make stands.

Meadowsweet Farm, No. 2173, affords the construction of a busy farm scene. The box measures 15 by 12 inches. Its bottom is the base of the scene; the shell for the back and sides folds up from the base, and the back and side are then placed into the shell along with the stand up-animals and children.

Rocking horses were made in this early period, too; they were always standard fare; more about them later.

Right: Meadowsweet Farm cover.

Below: Box top.

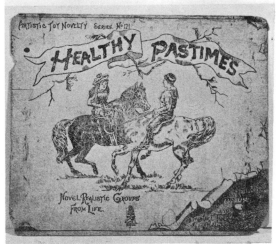

Serene Sybil

side was devoted to the address, the other to the message. Any pictorial decoration had to be shared with the message and was necessarily of small size.

Adolf Tuck negotiated with the Postmaster General for four years before a larger size card was made legal, allowing address and message on the same side, and leaving the other free for the picture. Thus a new industry was born; Raphael Tuck & Sons, Ltd, pursued it with enthusiam. At the turn of the century, Tuck was producing nearly 40,000 different pictorial postcards.

It is small wonder that in such concentration on postcards—still a staple Tuck production—the company's concern with paper playthings was minor. Search of Tuck listings in Montreal City Directories from 1901 to 1907 when Tuck maintained a branch there reveals no mention of paper dolls and toys though other of Tuck's art productions were named.

Playful Polly

The first Tuck pictorial postcard was published in 1894 as an experiment. It featured in the top left corner a small picture of Mt. Snowdon in Wales and was first offered for sale by mountain guides on Snowdon itself.

At that time English postcards were limited to a length of 3½ inches; one

Lovely Lily

This seeming neglect strengthens the feeling among collectors that the playthings were a sideline, sold along with Tuck's other art productions but never featured. It does not mean that the company skimped in any way on the artistry, workmanship, or ingenuity of these playthings.

Gentle Gladys

Sweet Sybel

Bonnie Babbie

Edwardian Paper Dolls—1901-1910

The paper dolls pictured here were all produced between 1901 and 1910 while Raphael Tuck & Sons Ltd. were "Publishers to Their Majesties The King and Queen" (Edward VII and Alexandria). In this time span a conspicuous change in children's fashions took place, and it is reflected in the paper doll outfits.

"Serene Sybil" (No. 42), "Playful Polly" (No. 43) are 13-inch dolls belonging to *Little Maids New Series of Dressing Dolls*. The series number appears
(Please turn the page.)

only on the box cover; the clothes are not numbered.

"Lovely Lily," No. 5 (without box top), "Gentle Gladys," No. 6, and "Sweet Sybel," No. 7, are 9-inch dolls from the *Dainty Dollies Series of Dressing Dolls;* their dresses are marked like the dolls, but without the name.

"Bonnie Bessie," "Bonnie Billy," and "Bonnie Babbie" are 9-inch dolls from *Our Bonnie Series of Dressing Dolls.* They were designed at the Studios in New York, printed in England. Their clothes, marked with the Tuck trademark, numbered and lettered, are up-to-date American styles for the 1907 to 1910 period.

Bonnie Bessie

Bonnie Billy

The Merry Clowns.

Jumbo and His Babies; Puppy Dogs.

Lovely Louise; From China Town.

A Proud Parent; Bright Darkies.

Raphael Tuck & Sons Ltd. brought out their first rocking toys between 1893 and 1901 when Victoria was Queen. Rocking horses of all sizes and materials were favorite playthings in the Victorian nursery, and Tuck made some of cardboard.

The set of six "Rocking Horses," Artistic Toy Novelty Series No. 120, pictured with the box top, fold out in back to form actual rockers. They are not individually marked. Children must have delighted in the unusual riders—a monkey, dogs and puppies, cat and kittens, Negro children, Punch and Judy, and clowns, one of whom takes the place of Horsie.

The rockers published between 1901 and 1910 are larger, more sophisticated in movement, sturdier in construction, but equally brilliant in coloring and filled with as many Happy Children and Comic Animals. *Father Tuck's Toy Rockers,* No. 52, pictured, rock with a front to back movement. Appropriate verses by Norman Gale are printed on each. In this set often are "An Accomplished Bird," shown on the box cover; "A Proud Parent"; "Bright Darkie"; "Joy, Joy"; "A Well Known Friend" (Red Riding Hood); "The Merry Clowns"; "Jumbo and his Babies"; "Puppy Dogs"; "Lovely Louise"; and "From China Town."

Advancing from the fun and enjoyment to the amusing and instructive,

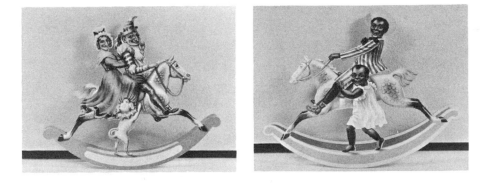

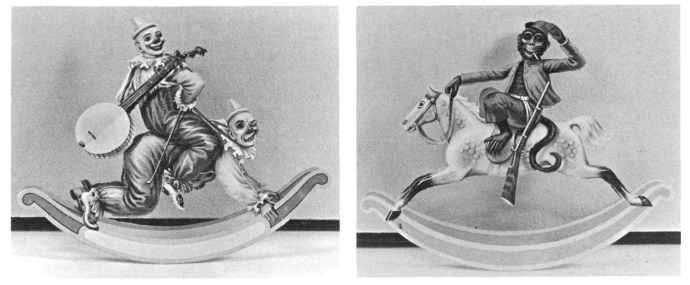

"Rocking Horses" (1893-1901) and contents.

Left: ''Father Tuck's Toy Rockers,''
(1901-1910); box top shows
An Accomplished Bird.

Father Tuck's Rocking Animals, was
produced in the 1920s when the Tuck
Warrant read, ''Publishers to The King
and Queen and Their Royal Highnesses
The Prince and Princess of Wales.'' It
contained ''Realistic Models of Domestic and Wild Animals with an interesting
description of each.'' This is definitely a
nursery set for younger children.
Shown from this set are the cat, pictured
on the box cover, a donkey, a cow, and
a St. Bernard.

Joy, Joy;
A Well Known Friend.

St. Bernard.

Cow.

''Rocking Animals'' (from the 1920s); box top shows Cat.

Donkey.

Panoramas

Raphael Tuck & Sons Ltd. met the continuing Victorian concept that toys should teach as well as entertain with a series of Panoramas. Tots were introduced to their immediate world in these colorful fold-outs as Father Tuck took them to the zoo, the circus, the seaside, the farm, the forest, or repeated familiar fairy tales.

Tuck's Panoramas came in varying sizes. Some were as large as 10¾ × 12 inches when closed, extending when

open to a miraculous 4 feet. Some were as small as $9\frac{1}{2} \times 6$ inches closed, opening to 21 inches in length. The children themselves contrived the pictures by arranging numbered cut-out figures in matching numbered slots in the scenery. Thus the Panoramas became also "number-teaching" books. A "pocket" on the last section held the numbered cut-outs.

Pictured here, in the large size, are "Father Tuck's Zoo Panorama," No. 8593; "With Father Tuck at the Circus," No. 7891; and "With Father Tuck at the Seaside," No. 789. Shown in a smaller size are "A Day in the Forest—To Myrtle Grove," No. 1506, (Painting copyright 1895); and "The Way to the Farm," of which the back page carrying the number is missing.

General Index

Index of Dolls by Name

❖❖❖❖❖❖❖❖❖❖❖❖❖❖❖❖❖❖❖❖❖❖❖❖❖ (See also General Index) ❖❖❖❖❖❖❖❖❖❖❖❖❖❖❖❖❖❖❖❖❖❖❖❖❖